# SIR PHILIP SIDNEY

1586 AND THE CREATION OF A LEGEND

PUBLICATIONS OF
THE SIR THOMAS BROWNE INSTITUTE
LEIDEN
(WERKGROEP ENGELS-NEDERLANDSE BETREKKINGEN)


NEW SERIES, No. 9

# SIR PHILIP SIDNEY

## 1586 AND THE CREATION OF A LEGEND

EDITED BY

JAN VAN DORSTEN · DOMINIC BAKER-SMITH
ARTHUR F. KINNEY

PUBLISHED FOR THE SIR THOMAS BROWNE INSTITUTE

E. J. BRILL / LEIDEN UNIVERSITY PRESS
LEIDEN 1986

Published with financial support from the Netherlands Organization for the Advancement of Pure Research (Z.W.O.)

PR
2343
.S57
1986

ISBN   90 04 07923 8

PRINTED IN THE NETHERLANDS BY E. J. BRILL

In memoriam Jan Adrianus van Dorsten
1933-1985

# CONTENTS

List of Illustrations ........................................................ VIII
Preface ....................................................................... IX
Abbreviations ............................................................... XII

Retrospect .................................................................. 1
   R. W. Zandvoort

The Myth and the Man ...................................................... 3
   W. A. Ringler

The Final Year ............................................................. 16
   Jan van Dorsten

'The Desired and Destined Successor' ..................................... 25
   Marjon Poort

Sidney's Funeral Portrayed ................................................ 38
   Sander Bos, Marianne Lange-Meijers, Jeanine Six

Fact and Anecdote in Fulke Greville's Account of Sidney's Last
days ....................................................................... 62
   John Gouws

Great Expectation: Sidney's Death and the Poets ......................... 83
   Dominic Baker-Smith

Shakespeare's *Venus and Adonis* and Sidney ............................ 104
   John Buxton

Building Sidney's Reputation: Texts and Editions of the *Arcadia*    111
   Victor Skretkowicz

Intimations of Mortality: Sidney's Journey to Flushing and
Zutphen ................................................................... 125
   Arthur F. Kinney

Sidney, Leicester, and *The Faerie Queene* ............................. 149
   Jan Karel Kouwenhoven

Sidney, Stella and Lady Rich ............................................ 170
   Katherine Duncan-Jones

The Quantitative Poems and the Psalm Translations: the Place
of Sidney's Experimental Verse in the Legend ........................... 193
   Seth Weiner

Some Unfamiliar Sidney Allusions.......................................  221
  Jackson Boswell, H. R. Woudhuysen

Note on Contributors ....................................................  238

Index....................................................................  240

## LIST OF ILLUSTRATIONS

1. Map of Holland from: J. J. Orlers, *Nassauschen Laurenscrans*, Leiden, 1610. (University Library Leiden, Collectie Bodel Nijenhuis)
2. Engraving of Maurice of Nassau and Sir Philip Sidney before Axel from: Wilh. Baudartius, *Afbeeldinghe ende beschrijvinghe van alle de veldslagen ... in de Nederlanden, geduerende d'oorloghe teghens den Coninck van Spaengien*, Amsterdam, 1616. (University Library Leiden, Collectie Bodel Nijenhuis)
3. Map of Zutphen from: Baudartius, *Afbeeldinghe ende beschrijvinghe*. (University Library Leiden, Collectie Bodel Nijenhuis)
4. Lant engraving, plate 1. (British Library)
5. Lant engraving, plate 15. (British Library)
6. Lant engraving, plate 16. (British Library)
7. Lant engraving, plate 18. (British Library)
8. Lant engraving, plate 19. (British Library)
9. Letter, Greville to Walsingham, November 1586 (PRO SP12/195), page 1.
10. Letter, Greville to Walsingham, November 1586 (PRO SP12/195), page 2.

# PREFACE

The distinguished Dutch historian Johan Huizinga once described Sir Philip Sidney as 'a spiritual treasure for the world', as 'almost a Grecian embodiment of the beautiful man'. To him Sidney was the epitome of self-cultivation, that 'impulse to the highest individual development' which he derived from Jacob Burckhardt's interpretation of the Renaissance, and throughout his life he continued to refer to Sidney as the great exemplar. It is clear that Huizinga, who had read *Astrophil and Stella* during his wife's fatal illness in 1913, responded unreservedly to the Sidney legend which the nineteenth century had cultivated and to which he himself contributed in our own age.[1] The legend is as haunting as it is persistent, surfacing in Yeats' lament for Major Robert Gregory, 'Our Sidney and our perfect man'. Like other legends it has its foundation in fact, but in the closing decades of the twentieth century we respond with greater reserve than our predecessors did. Now we wish to know not only how 'true' it is, but also how it came about, and why.

This, then, is the theme of our book. It does not claim to answer all these questions. Yet every article contributes somehow to a better understanding of how a young man who had 'slipped into the title of a poet', a soldier-politician without one notable success to his name, came to be regarded immediately after his early death as the embodiment of every virtue which early-modern Europeans (and, apparently, modern Europeans too) have cherished. The legend is so powerful that even objective scholars can find it difficult to detach themselves from its implications. We are grateful, therefore, that a number of scholars who, as editors of the works of Sidney and his friend Greville, have devoted so much time to the literary heritage agreed to make this special effort for our book. To these articles we have been able to add several essays which, we believe, contribute substantially to the subject of this volume. Occasional contradictions only emphasize the complexities of our theme.

Jean Robertson, the editor of the Oxford *'old' Arcadia*, was the first to suggest to the Sir Thomas Browne Institute that a quatercentenary volume was called for. We are indebted to her for this, and for her advice. We also wish to thank R. W. Zandvoort and A. C. Hamilton for their comments, and Adriaan van der Weel and Jeanette Schoondebeek-Willemsen for their help in preparing this volume. For permission to reproduce materials in their possession we are grateful to the British Library and the Public Record Office in London, and to the University Library of Leiden. Publication in this series was made possible by a sub-

sidy from the Netherlands Organization for the Advancement of Pure
Research (Z.W.O.).

> Jan van Dorsten, Leiden
> Dominic Baker-Smith, Amsterdam
> Arthur F. Kinney, Amherst

*Postscript*

Jan van Dorsten died suddenly at Leiden on 29 July 1985. He was
fifty-two. The materials for this book had already been checked and he
was due to begin the final process of copy-editing when he died. His enthusiasm made it imperative that we, his fellow editors, should see the
work carried through to completion. We feel privileged to share in this,
his last contribution to Sidney scholarship, and we dedicate the volume
to his memory.

Given the difficult circumstances which have attended the final
preparation of the book for press, we wish to express our special gratitude
to Conny Elderhorst, Marjon Poort, Ernestine van der Wall and Paul
Hoftijzer of the staff of the Sir Thomas Browne Institute and to its
Secretary, Cootje van Doorn-Beersma, for their invaluable assistance.

D. B.-S.

A. F. K.

---

1   Quotations from *Address Delivered by J. Huizinga ... on the Occasion of Uncovering a
    Memorial to Sir Philip Sidney at Zutphen on July 2nd 1913*, n.p., n.d.. Sidney's example
    is stressed, for instance, in Huizinga's *Nederland's beschaving in de zeventiende eeuw*,
    Haarlem, 1941, 79. Additional information on Huizinga's interest in Sidney was
    communicated to us by W. E. Krul, Groningen.

# ABBREVIATIONS

CSPFor/Dom      *Calendar of State Papers, Foreign/Domestic.*
*EETS*      *Early English Text Society.*
*ELH*      *English Literary History.*
*ELR*      *English Literary Renaissance.*
*HLQ*      *Huntington Library Quarterly.*
*JEGP*      *Journal of English and Germanic Philology.*
*MLN*      *Modern Language Notes.*
*MLR*      *Modern Language Review.*
*MP*      *Miscellaneous Prose of Sir Philip Sidney*, ed. Katherine Duncan-Jones and Jan van Dorsten, Oxford, 1973.
*OA*      Sir Philip Sidney, *The Countess of Pembroke's Arcadia (The Old Arcadia)*, ed. Jean Robertson, Oxford, 1973.
*OED*      *Oxford English Dictionary.*
*Poems*      *The Poems of Sir Philip Sidney*, ed. William A. Ringler, Jr., Oxford, 1962.
*Ren. Q.*      *Renaissance Quarterly.*
*RES*      *Review of English Studies.*
*Works*      *The Works of Sir Philip Sidney*, ed. A. Feuillerat, 4 vols, Cambridge, 1912-26; rpt. 1962.
Zouch      Thomas Zouch, *Memoirs of the Life and Writings of Sir Philip Sidney*, York, 1808.

Note on Dates: throughout the volume these have been standarized to 'Old Style', i.e. ten days earlier than 'New Style'. Thus Sidney is wounded on 23 September ( = 2 October 'New Style') and dies on 17 October ( = 27 October 'New Style').

# RETROSPECT

On 2 July 1913, a few days after I had passed the school-leaving examination (equals matriculation) of the Zutphen 'Gymnasium' (on my 19th birthday, as a matter of fact), the Groningen historian Johan Huizinga pronounced an address on the occasion of the unveiling of a statue of Sir Philip Sidney on what were formerly the ramparts of the city of Zutphen. I remember being vaguely aware of the event, but only just. I certainly had no presentiment of my future connection with Sidney as an author.

Ten years later, when I was in search of a subject for a doctoral dissertation, I came across Albert Feuillerat's edition of *The Complete Works* of Sir Philip Sidney. In the Preface to Volume III (1923) (originally planned as the concluding volume of the series) he announced the addition of a fourth volume containing the text of one of the recently discovered manuscripts of the original version of *Arcadia*. I wrote to Professor Feuillerat (then of the University of Rennes) to ask whether, in his opinion, anything of importance could be added to what had already been said on the relation between the two versions. In reply, he not only assured me that the subject deserved a more thorough treatment than had hitherto been accorded to it, but offered to resign to me a project he himself had formed of undertaking such an investigation. My natural scruples to avail myself of this unparalleled generosity Professor Feuillerat allayed in the most amiable manner.

Volume IV appeared in 1926. In May 1929 I presented my *Sidney's* Arcadia: *A Comparison Between The Two Versions* to the Literary Faculty of the University of Leiden. It was accepted (Professor J. H. Kern acting as my 'promotor'), and the doctor's degree conferred on May 24.

This is not the place for a survey of *Arcadia* criticism between then and now. What comes to mind as I write this are two lines from Lucretius' *De Rerum Natura*:

> inque brevi spatio mutantur saecla animantum
> et quasi cursores vitai lampada tradunt. (DRN II, ll. 78-79)

If I may substitute *the torch of learning* for *the torch of life*, they express the satisfaction I feel over the fact that the University that placed the stamp of its approval on my dissertation more than half a century ago continues to cherish the memory of Sir Philip Sidney—fame and after-fame.

Amersfoort, March 1985.                                          R. W. ZANDVOORT

W. A. RINGLER, Jr.

## SIR PHILIP SIDNEY: THE MYTH AND THE MAN

There is something unbelievable about Sir Philip Sidney. When we see how his contemporaries and successors described him, we perceive an image of almost impossible perfection. Though at different times he was admired for different qualities, he was always described by superlatives. In his early manhood he was looked up to as the model of perfect courtesy and piety, and in the latter part of his life he was hailed as the perfect soldier-statesman. Immediately after his death he was looked upon as the perfect pattern of heroic virtue, and after his writings were printed and had become generally known he was regarded as the supreme literary artist of his time.

In 1579, when Sidney was only twenty-five, Edmund Spenser addressed him as the 'president', that is the perfect pattern, 'of nobless and of chivalry'.[1] Somewhat later Charles FitzGeffrey referred to him as 'nectar-tongued Sidney, England's Mars and Muse'.[2] His friend, Sir Walter Ralegh, in a famous epitaph called him the 'Scipio, Cicero, and Petrarch of our time'[3]—Scipio who in the Renaissance was looked upon as the ideal military leader, Cicero the model orator-statesman, and Petrarch the perfect poet. Fulke Greville, whose *Life of the Renowned Sir Philip Sidney* was until little more than a century ago our main source of knowledge concerning him, said: 'Indeed he was a true model of worth; a man fit for conquest, plantation, reformation, or what action soever is greatest and hardest among men'.[4]

Greville's biography is the source, and the only source, of the one anecdote about Sidney that everyone knows. At an engagement with the Spanish forces before Zutphen, Sidney, according to Greville, came to the field completely armed; but on the way he met the Marshal of the Camp (Sir William Pelham) only lightly armed, and 'the unspotted emulation of his heart, to venture without any inequality, made him cast off' his own cuisses, or thigh guards. In the ensuing skirmish, his unprotected thigh was shattered by a musket shot. According to Greville, though Sidney suffered excruciating pain, he managed to stay on his horse:

> The horse...forced him to forsake the field, but not his back, as the noblest and fittest bier to carry a martial commander to his grave. In which sad progress, passing along by the rest of the army, ...and being thirsty with excess of bleeding, he called for drink, which was presently brought him;

but as he was putting the bottle to his mouth, he saw a poor soldier carried along, who had eaten his last at the same feast, ghastly casting up his eyes at the bottle. Which Sir Philip perceiving, took it from his head before he drank, and delivered it to the poor man with these words, 'Thy necessity is yet greater than mine'.[5]

Some two hundred years later Shelley gave poetic expression to the idealised picture of Sidney that had been built up by adoring friends and admiring later generations:

...Sidney, as he fought
And as he fell and as he lived and loved,
Sublimely mild, a spirit without spot.[6]

Such absolute perfection is hardly believable, and such sentimentalized hero worship even becomes distasteful. Horace Walpole expressed the scepticism of a more rational age when he looked at what he could find of the facts, and came to the conclusion that no man has been 'so astonishing an object of temporary admiration. When we at this distance of time inquire what prodigious merits excited such admiration, what do we find?' A few poor verses, 'a tedious, lamentable, pedantic, pastoral romance, which the patience of a young virgin in love cannot now wade through', and nothing more. 'He died with the rashness of a volunteer, after having lived to write with the *sang froid* and prolixity of Mademoiselle Scuderi.' Sidney, Walpole concluded, has been ridiculously overvalued.[7]

In a way, Walpole was right. No man as great and perfect as Sidney has been described could exist. He has become a myth, 'England's Mars and Muse'; admiration has exaggerated his virtues and given his faults to silence. But because his portrait had been over-idealized does not mean that the man himself had no merit at all. We today find it hard to evaluate the Elizabethans, because their modes of expression are different from our own. For emphasis we use understatement, they used hyperbole. When they admired anyone, they made their pens 'walk in the superlative degree'. Their exaggeration of Sidney's good qualities has distorted the picture of the man himself. When we try to get behind the words to the man, we find a person quite different from the one described by the panegyrists; different, but none the less admirable.

Let us look at the facts, so far as they are recoverable after four hundred years. In the first place, when we survey the events of Sidney's life,[8] we must admit that he never acted in any event of great consequence. He studied at Oxford, and then spent three years travelling on the continent. He returned to England in 1575, wise in the ways of European politics, and with a wide acquaintance among statesmen and men of learning. For the next ten years he was one of the most socially brilliant, and felt himself to be one of the most ineffectual members of Queen Elizabeth's court. He dreamed dreams and made grandiose plans for great deeds, but the Queen did not allow him to act. The 'great cause' to which he wished to devote his life was the formation of a Protestant League in Europe that could check the power of Spain. In 1577 he was sent on an embassy to the German Emperor, in the course of which he discussed the formation of a league with various Protestant leaders on the continent; but Queen Elizabeth would not act—perhaps Sidney was too sanguine—and he did not receive another government appointment for eight years.

Sidney was one of the few Englishmen of his time who had some notion of the importance and promise of the New World. He contributed financially to some of the voyages of exploration, and once he tried to sail to the Indies with Sir Francis Drake, but the Queen peremptorily called him back. Instead of a life of heroic action, with opportunity to sway the decisions of the world's statesmen, he was forced to dance attendance at court and to dissipate his energies on what he considered pastimes rather than work. He rode on progress with the Queen; he devised and participated in tournaments—those elaborate entertainments, half athletic contest and half symbolic spectacle, which were the chief amusement of the court; he acted as greeter and entertainer of distinguished foreign visitors—a Lasko, Casimir, Don Antonio, even the Duke of Anjou whom he hated. At length he was given an opportunity to do something. An English expedition under the Earl of Leicester was sent to oppose the Spanish forces in the Netherlands, and Sidney received his first military command. After a year of indecisive campaigning, he died from a wound received in an unsuccessful minor engagement. He was not yet thirty-two.

The deeds are not a measure of the man, and do not explain the greatness of his reputation. Neither Leicester nor Burghley, Ralegh nor Drake, among the statesmen and soldiers; neither Spenser nor Shakespeare among the poets, received as much or as high praise from their contemporaries as did Sidney. His attraction and greatness were personal, a matter of character, immediately perceptible to those who came in contact with him, but in these later ages apprehensible only dimly and indirectly. He had so persuasive a charm of manner, as one who knew him personally said,

That all men's hearts with secret ravishment
He stole away and weetingly beguiled.[9]

Evidence of how completely he captured the minds and hearts of his countrymen is found, not so much in the deliberately-composed essays

of praise, as in informal asides and remarks by the way. Two years after
Sidney's death, the Lord Admiral Howard, in the midst of the great sea
fight against the Spanish Armada, wrote in an official dispatch about the
wounding of one of his men: 'He was hurt, even like Sir Philip Sidney,
above the knee, and the bone all broken; a very great hurt'.[10] There is
no need for comparisons in a military dispatch, but the image of Sidney
came irresistibly to mind. Early in the seventeenth century a former
courtier, writing to obtain a small position, could think of no better
testimony to his desert than that he had served 'under the colours of that
worthy Sir Philip Sidney for many years' and had been 'respected by
him'.[11] And forty years after Sidney's death, Fulke Greville, looking
back on his lifetime of distinguished public service that had culminated
with his appointment as Chancellor of the Exchequer, composed this
epitaph to memorialise his own achievements: 'Fulke Greville, Servant
to Queen Elizabeth, Councilor to King James, and Friend to Sir Philip
Sidney'.[12]

But this man was not loved and admired by the Elizabethans because
he was the epitome of impossible perfections, because he was, as Shelley
would have us believe, 'sublimely mild, a spirit without spot.' Mild is
probably the least appropriate adjective to apply to him. His charge at
Zutphen through the entire array of Spanish foot soldiers shows his fiery
courage. On another occasion, when he suspected a servant of revealing
the secrets of his private correspondence, he wrote sharply:

> Mr. Molyneux: Few words are best. My letters to my father have come to
> the eyes of some. Neither can I condemn any but you for it...if ever I know
> you do so much as read any letter I write to my father, without his com-
> mandment or my consent, I will thrust my dagger into you. And trust to
> it, for I speak it in earnest...By me. Philip Sidney.[13]

Nor was he entirely without spot, at least in words. His sister and some
of his friends appear to have been disturbed by his passionate sonnets to
Stella; they at first tried to prevent their circulation, and failing that,
countenanced the evidently false interpretation of them given in
Spenser's *Astrophel*.[14] His eye was easily attracted by feminine beauty, as
is amply shown by many of the descriptions in his *Arcadia*. Pyrocles
watched Philoclea bathing in the river Ladon: she disrobed 'like the sun
getting from under a cloud'; and when she entered the river, 'the touch
of the cold water made a pretty kind of shrugging come over her body,
like the twinkling of the fairest among the fixed stars'.[15] Thomas Moffet,
who seems to have known more about Sidney than any of his other contemporary biographers, reported that in his youth 'he was somewhat
wanton...but observed a measure and felt shame'.[16] Sidney was no Sir

Galahad with blood of very snow broth, but a normal Elizabethan with normal physical interests and desires.

His panegyrists have made him out to be inhumanly perfect, and have praised him for the wrong things. They have represented him as one of the last representatives of a dying chivalry; but instead of being an unworldly visionary and the follower of a romantic but outworn code, in practical affairs he was actually one of the supremely competent men of his age. To illustrate this needs only a careful examination of his military campaigns and his career as a courtier. His good sense and diplomacy in threading his way among the warring factions of court and camp are nowhere better exemplified than in his relations with his uncle the Earl of Leicester. He managed, without compromising his principles, to keep the good will of the Earl, and at the same time to maintain the respect even of those who were bitterly opposed to him. Another illustration of his ability to cope with political realities is his letter addressed to Queen Elizabeth on the question of her proposed marriage with the Duke of Anjou. This is such a rational and pragmatic analysis of the political situation that its affinities with the harshly realistic doctrines of Machiavelli have been commented upon.[17]

The impractical story-book hero into which Sidney has been turned is in part the result of a misunderstanding of Elizabethan hyperbole, and in part the result of the well-intentioned misstatements of his friend Fulke Greville. Greville, and Greville alone, is responsible for the story of his quixotically casting off his cuisses in order to expose himself to as great a risk as a less-well armed companion, and for the incident of the bottle of water. Both are not facts, but fabrications.

If Sidney cast away his cuisses for the reason Greville said he did, Walpole is justified in his criticism that he died 'with the rashness of a volunteer'. But everything we know about his conduct in the Netherlands campaign shows that, though he was a gallant leader ready to take a risk when a risk was justified, he was careful not to expose his men or himself when there was nothing to be gained. His discretion was exemplified in his earlier attempt on Gravelines, where his wariness and caution prevented the entrapment of all but a small part of his company. He was a highly competent soldier, who had no respect for merely theatrical heroics.

Several eyewitness accounts of the skirmish at Zutphen testify that Sidney did not wear cuisses. But he did not put them on, and then cast them off for the sake of a theatrical gesture. He rode into battle without cuisses deliberately, because he thought that not wearing them was the most efficient way to fight. His reasons are indicated by another Elizabethan soldier, Sir John Smythe, who wrote:

> These our new fantasied men of war do despise and scorn our ancient arming of ourselves...saying that we armed ourselves in times past with too much armor, or pieces of iron as they term it.... Their horsemen...they think very well armed with some kind of headpiece, a collar, a deformed high and long bellied breast, and a back at the proof; but as for pouldrons, vambraces, gauntlets, tasses, cuisses, and greves, they hold all for superfluous. The imitating of which their unsoldierlike and fond arming, cost that noble and worthy gentleman Sir Philip Sidney his life, by not wearing his cuisses.[18]

Smythe was writing a work of controversy; in the age of the arquebus and caliver, he wishes to revive the use of the outmoded longbow. Smythe was the impractical traditionalist, Sidney the 'new fantasied' man of war, the modernist. Clearly Sidney believed, with the more advanced military tacticians of his day, that if he went into battle lightly armed, he would achieve both greater safety and greater striking power through his increased mobility. It was the misfortune of war that he was wounded; but the history of warfare in his own day and ours shows that his principles were sound. He went into battle without cuisses, not for the sake of a chivalric gesture, but for the calculated and practical purpose of more efficient fighting. And so legends grow, from misunderstanding.

But what of the bottle of water? I am afraid that we shall have to discard that anecdote as a fabrication also. Fulke Greville, although he was Sidney's close friend, was not in the Netherlands at the time of the engagement at Zutphen and did not write his account of it until some twenty-five years after the event. There are more than a dozen accounts of the skirmish, written by or derived from the descriptions of eyewitnesses, whose authors are just as eager as Greville to praise Sidney, and who magnify every incident to enhance his glory. They tell in minute detail of his gallantry, his wound, and his riding from the field; but none of them mentions the bottle of water, an incident they all would have been delighted to report if they had known or thought of it.[19] The action would have been characteristic of Sidney, but not the words of unctuous self-approval.

Greville's account of the action at Zutphen, which is the only one to mention the quixotic casting away of the cuisses and the incident of the bottle of water, is wrong in most of its factual details. Greville says the purpose of the action was 'to stop the issuing out of the Spanish army', when actually it was undertaken to prevent a supply train from getting into the town. He says the skirmish took place 'near to the very walls of Zutphen' so that the troops were 'engaged within the level of the great shot, that played from the rampiers', when actually it took place a mile and a half from the town walls, well beyond artillery range. He says the English gentlemen 'go on, every man in the head of his own troop'; but

Sidney took part as an unattached individual—he had no troops to lead, because his cornet of horse had been left at Deventer. Since Greville is wrong in so many other details, we cannot accept as authoritative his unsupported statements concerning the cuisses and the bottle of water. They must take their place with the other properties of the mythology of hero-worship, like Parson Weems's story of George Washington and the cherry tree.

The myth that has become attached to Sidney's name is one thing, the man himself is something quite different. Sidney as he fought and fell and lived and loved was neither an impractical follower of a vanished chivalry, nor 'sublimely mild, a spirit without spot'. But he was a true hero, a man of exceptional courage and integrity, who held and lived by the finest ideals of his day; his qualities of mind and character aroused the admiration of everyone he met, and his personal charm stole men's hearts away. In addition, he was one of the supremely competent men of his age in practical affairs. Sidney has been unintentionally maligned by his admireres. He is a different, and at the same time a far greater man, than his praisers have made him out to be.

It is not what Sidney accomplished, but what he was, that made him the idol of his own generation and of many generations to come. For he tried to be, and succeeded in becoming, the living embodiment of what his age thought the best men ought to be—the complete gentleman. One of the many differences between the Middle Ages and the Renaissance is that the social ideal of the former came to full flower in the knight, of the latter in the gentleman. Both the knight and the gentleman had many things in common: gentle birth, faithful service to the prince, proper regard for ceremonial observance (what we today call good manners), excellence in arms, and respect for religion and the cardinal virtues. But there were several significant differences. Chaucer's very perfect gentle knight was a specialist, primarily a soldier and a general; the Renaissance gentleman was an all-round man, of diversified interests and capacities. This ideal of the universal man, this striving to develop what Plato and Ascham and Lyly called the 'euphues', the naturally apt, finely tempered, and harmoniously developed nature, is one of the important contributions of the Renaissance to modern times. It gives us the concept that underlies our own ideas of a *liberal* education—the education that aims at producing the completely developed and well-rounded nature and character that is appropriate to the free man.

Another important aspect of the Renaissance ideal of the gentleman is the notion that he should be an artist in human relations, that all his actions should be carried out with apparent ease and grace. The gentleman should use effort, but should never give the appearance of effort; he should have the graceful negligence of the talented amateur, rather than the awkward seriousness of the plodding professional. Castiglione, in his *Book of the Courtier*, illustrates the necessity for social graces and diversified accomplishments by an anecdote of a guest at a noble house who refused to dance or to listen to music or to take part in other entertainments on the ground that such silly trifles were not his business. One of the ladies asked, 'What is your business'? And he replied with a sour look, 'To fight'. Whereupon the lady said, 'Now that you are in no war and out of fighting trim, I should think it were a good thing to have youself well oiled, and to stow yourself with all your battle harness in a closet until you be needed, lest you grow more rusty than you are'.[20]

In Sidney we see the actual embodiment of this ideal of the gentleman. He was born with exceptional mental and adequate physical capacities, and improved them by rigorous training. He became an excellent horseman and skilful in handling weapons, so that he could perform creditably as a soldier. He studied politics, government and international affairs, so that he could act as an adviser to his sovereign in the conduct of national policies. He was sincerely and truly religious; and though steadfast in his Protestantism, he was to an extent unusual for his time tolerant of individuals, as is shown by his many Catholic friends. He was well read in history and philosophy, and was interested in all the arts, especially painting, music, and literature.

Among the many social accomplishments required by the code of the Elizabethan gentleman was that he be able to turn a verse for a lady and write a graceful letter or well-argued political memorial for his prince. It was therefore expected that Sidney should become a writer; but that he should become one of the major writers of his time was partly because he was a greater artist than most of his fellows, and partly because of his frustrations as a courtier. If he had had the opportunity to live the life of heroic action that he desired, if he had been allowed to take a more important part in the government of his country, he probably would have written less. But Queen Elizabeth, for reasons of her own, did not give him the opportunities he craved. So, instead of doing, he spent long periods of time in enforced idleness. It was then that he turned, for relaxation and as an outlet for his energies, to literature. His writings were in part play, in part a projection of the ideals he had not been able to realize in action. In his revised *Arcadia* he presented his ideals as a man of action, in his *Defence of Poetry* he expressed his ideals as an artist, and in his *Astrophil and Stella* he revealed his ordinary humanity.

Also, because he was a gentleman, Sidney carried over his principles of personal conduct into his writing. Everything he produced has an air of ease and effortless grace, shows a light touch and a playful wit—a wit that sometimes has a barb to it for all its playfulness. In a personal letter, explaining his absence from court because of his poverty, which the Queen would do nothing to allay, he remarked, bitterly yet wittily: 'So long as she sees a silk doublet upon me, her Highness will think me in good case'.[21] In the *Defence of Poetry*, arguing seriously that the improper use to which some poetry has been put is no proper charge against the excellence of the art, he said: 'Truly, a needle cannot do much hurt, and as truly (with leave of ladies be it spoken) it cannot do much good: with a sword thou mayst kill thy father, and with a sword thou mayst defend thy prince and country'.[22] By 1584 Queen Elizabeth had passed her prime, but her courtiers were still unblushingly praising her maiden beauty. In his revised *Arcadia*, describing the Queen of Laconia, a lady rather plain in appearance, Sidney remarked acidly: 'But she was a Queen, and therefore beautiful'.[23]

Sidney wrote for his own amusement and that of his family and friends, and made no attempt to reach a larger public. Except for two anonymous sonnets, possibly of his making, printed by Henry Goldwel in 1581,[24] none of his writings was printed during his lifetime and only his intimate friends knew that he was an author. Only six allusions to Sidney as a writer appeared in print before his death.[25] Of the 270 poems by 143 authors in the Oxford and Cambridge memorial volumes, only a handful knew or guessed that he had anything to do with literature;[26] and of the numerous other panegyrics and printed allusions to Sidney during the four years after his decease, only twenty-one indicated that he was an author, and only six of these quoted his writings.[27] Sidney was at first known and praised primarily as a learned soldier and an accomplished courtier; but before the end of the century, by which time his major writings had been given to the press and had been gathered in a collected edition, the terms by which he was regarded had changed fundamentally.

Sidney first legitimately[28] appeared in print as an author in the early part of 1590, when Ponsonby published *The Countess of Pembrokes Arcadia, Written by Sir Philippe Sidnei*. This was the incomplete revised version, or *'new' Arcadia*, which ended abruptly in the middle of a sentence in the Third Book when the story was less than half told. It was edited by Fulke Greville, with the assistance of Dr Matthew Gwinne, from the unfinished manuscript that Sidney had left with him before departing for the Netherlands. Three years later Sidney's sister, the Countess of Pembroke, with the assistance of her secretary Hugh Sanford, completed the story by reprinting the 1590 text and adding to it *en bloc* Books III-V of the original version, or *'old' Arcadia*, from the manuscript Sidney had presented to her in 1580. In the 1593 printing of these last three books the personal names were altered to conform to the revised narrative, there was some reordering of the eclogues, and there were a few other changes, evidently dictated by Sidney himself. The main changes were the deletion of all references to Musidorus' attempted rape of Pamela, and the change of Pyrocles' motive in visiting Philoclea's bedroom from attempting to seduce her to persuading her to elope with him so they could be married.[29] But no attempt was made to alter the conclusion of the narrative to conform to the new plot elements introduced in the incomplete revision, especially the change which the revised oracle demanded of the charges in the trial before Euarchus, the completion of the new story of Amphialus (he evidently revives), and the transfer from the eclogues to the main narrative of the story of Erona which obliges Musidorus and Pyrocles to rescue her in a tournament with the champions of Artaxia at the end. This strange hermaphrodite, a revised beginning with an unrevised conclusion and a hiatus in the middle, remained the most admired work of English fiction for more than a century.

Meanwhile, in the summer of 1591, Thomas Newman published, from an exceedingly corrupt manuscript, *Syr P. S. His Astrophel and Stella*. This edition was suppressed and later the same year Newman issued a second edition with only a slightly improved text. Early in 1595 Henry Olney published *An Apologie for Poetrie. Written by...Sir Phillip Sidney, Knight*, which he had entered on 12 April; but William Ponsonby had earlier entered the same work on 29 November 1594; he published it in 1595 as *The Defence of Poesie* and Olney's entry was cancelled. Then in 1598 Ponsonby published the first collected edition of Sidney's works under the title, *The Countesse of Pembrokes Arcadia. Written by Sir Philip Sidney Knight. Now the Third Time published, with sundry new additions of the same Author*. This reprinted the combined texts of the 'new' and 'old' *Arcadia* from Ponsonby's edition of 1593, *The Defence of Poesie* from Ponsonby's edition of 1595, and added from excellent manuscripts *Certaine Sonets*, an improved text of *Astrophel and Stella* (but with Astrophil's name still misspelled as in Newman's edition), and the untitled *Lady of May*.

With all of his major writings before the public, allusions to Sidney changed from praising him primarily as a hero to praising him primarily as a man of letters, and he was hailed as the foremost literary artist of his century. For example, Richard Carew in 1614, after naming the chief English writers from Chaucer and More to his own time, concluded: 'Will you have all in all for prose and verse, take the miracle of our age, Sir Philip Sidney'.[30] Michael Drayton in 1627 called him 'that hero for numbers, and for prose'.[31] And the biography appended to the 1655-edition of the *Arcadia*, after noting that no monument had been erected above his grave, concluded: 'But he is his own monument, whose memory is eternised in his writings'.[32]

Strange as it may seem to us, Sidney's reputation as a man of letters among his immediate followers even exceeded the reputations of Spenser and Shakespeare. Through the year 1625 we find 72 printed allusions to Shakespeare and 130 to Spenser,[33] but 207 to Sidney for his writings alone.[34] He was not only referred to, he was also read, and lived to after ages primarily through his written works. A measure of their impact on English readers before the eighteenth century can be determined by the number of collected editions that were called for in comparison with the other most admired writers of the time: two of Beaumont and Fletcher, three of Spenser, three of Jonson, four of Shakespeare, and eleven of Sir Philip Sidney. It was not the fame he would have preferred.

## NOTES

1 *The Shepheardes Calender*, 1579, 'To his Booke', lines 3-4. The lines were originally intended for the Earl of Leicester, see *Renaissance News*, 14 (1961), 159-61.

2 *Sir Francis Drake*, 1596, sig. B4ᵛ.

3 'An Epitaph upon...sir Philip Sidney knight', line 58; first printed in *The Phoenix Nest*, 1593, sig Clv (ed. H. Rollins, Cambridge, 1931, 18).

4 Written c. 1610, first printed 1652, sig. D3ᵛ (ed. Nowell Smith, Oxford, 1907, 33).

5 Sig. L2ᵛ-3 (ed. Smith, 129-30).

6 *Adonais*. 1821, lines 401-04.

7 *A Catalogue of the Royal and Noble Authors of England*, 1 (1758), 163-64.

8 The best factual biography of Sidney is by M. W. Wallace, Cambridge, 1915, which should be supplemented by James M. Osborn, *Young Philip Sidney 1572-1577*, New Haven, 1972.

9 Spenser, *Astrophel*, 1595, lines 21-22.

10 CSPDom, 1581-90, CCIX, 9; printed by J. K. Laughton, *State Papers Relating to the Defeat of the Spanish Armada*, 1 (1894), 101.

11 Folger Shakespeare Library MS V.a. 321, f. 63ᵛ, Peter Feryman to the Governors of King James Hospital.

12 Inscription on his tomb in the Chapter House of the Collegiate Church of St. Mary, Warwick.

13 Viscount de L'Isle and Dudley MS B.16, a transcript; printed in *Works*, III, 124.

14 H. H. Hudson, 'Penelope Devereux as Sidney's Stella', *Huntington Library Bulletin*, 7 (1935), 120.

15 *Arcadia* in *Works*, I, 217.

16 *Nobilis and Lessus Lugubris*, 1593 (ed. and trans. V. B. Heltsel and H. H. Hudson, San Marino, 1940, 74).

17 Irving Ribner, 'Machiavelli and Sidney's Discourse to the Queen', *Italica*, 26 (1949), 177-89.

18 *Discourses...Concerning the Formes and Effects of Divers Sorts of Weapons*, 1590, sig. B3; first noted by Philip Bliss in Wood's *Athenae Oxonienses*, I (Oxford, 1813), 522, n. 6.

19 There are at least five eye-witness accounts of the unfortunate skirmish near Zutphen: (1) three letters by the Earl of Leicester, in his *Correspondence*, ed. John Bruce, Camden Society, 1844, 414-17; (2) an anonymous note, 'The maner of the latt scrimeshe', *HMC Salisbury*, 3.189-90; (3) George Whetstone, *Sir Philip Sidney* [1587], sigs. B4-C1, from information supplied by his brother Bernard; (4) T[homas] D[an-

nett], *A Briefe Report*, 1587, sig. D1; and (5) Henry Archer in John Stow's *Annales*, 1592, 1251-53. Other accounts, by contemporaries who drew upon eye-witness reports, are: (6) Edmund Molyneux in Holinshed's *Chronicles*, 1587 uncensored issue, 1554-55; (7) George Carleton in the Oxford *Exequiae*, 1587, sigs. L2-3ᵛ (reprinted in his *Heroici Characteres*, 1603, sigs. G2ᵛ-3ᵛ); (8) Thomas Lant, Funeral Roll, 1588, f. 1; (9) Thomas Moffett, *Nobilis*, 1593 (ed. Heltzel and Hudson, 89-102); (10) John Stow, *A Summarie of Englyshe Chronicles*, 1590, 735; (11) Emmanuel van Meteren, *Historia Belgica*, 1598, 407-08 (translated in Edward Grimeston's *Generall Historie of the Netherlands*, 1608, 926-27); (12) Thomas Churchyard, *A True Discourse of the Governours in the Netherlands*, 1602, sigs. N4-O1; and (13) William Camden, *Annales...regnante Elizabetha*, 1615, p. 394. In addition many of the 270 poems in the Oxford *Peplus* and *Exequiae* and the Cambridge *Lachrymae* of 1587, and of the English commemorative poems written between 1586 and 1595 (by an anonymous writer in the *Phoenix Nest*—'Silence augmenteth grief', Nicholas Breton, Lodowyck Brysket, Thomas Churchyard, A[ngel] D[ay], John Philip, Ralegh, Matthew Roydon, Spenser, and Thomas Watson in *Amintae Gaudia*), mention circumstances connected with Sidney's wound, but say nothing of the discarded cuisses and the bottle of water. Moffet, p. 102, says his thigh was not armed because he was in a hurry, all the rest say he did not wear cuisses, without comment.

20  Translated by L. E. Opdycke, New York, 1902, 26.
21  *Works*, III, 129.
22  *MP*, 105.
23  *Works*, I, 103.
24  See E. G. Fogel, *MLN*, 75 (1960), 389-94.
25  See *Poems*, lxi-lxii.
26  In STC 4473 John Boyle D3ᵛ and William Temple M1; in 22551 Matthew Gwinne D3, Edward Saunders D4, Richard Latewar E2, Francis Cook F2ᵛ, and Charles Sonibanke I1.
27  STC *4253, *4256, 4285, 4473, 5228, 6409, 11097, *11338, *11343, 13099, 13569, *18149, 19534, 19546, 19871, *20519, 23080, 25119, 25120, 25121, and 25349 (asterisks indicate quotations of specific passages).
28  In 1587 appeared *A Worke concerning the Trewness of the Christian Religion...Begunne to be translated into English by Sir Philip Sidney Knight, and at his request finished by Arthur Golding*; but this appears to be all the work of Golding, and whatever once may have existed of Sidney's version has been lost (see *MP*, 155-57).
29  The changes are discussed by Jean Robertson in *OA*, lix-lxii, and listed in her apparatus, 168-417—see especially 201-02, 217, 236-37, 314, 355-57, and 405.
30  'The Excellencie of the English tongue', first printed in Camden's *Remaines*, 1614, sig. G2ᵛ.
31  'To Henery Reynolds Esquire of Poets and Poesie', line 96, in *The battaile of Agincourt*, 1627, sig. Dd1ᵛ.
32  By Philophilippos, sig. c1.
33  *The Shakespere Allusion Book*, re-ed. John Munro and Sir Edmund Chambers, 1 (1932), 1-332; *Spenser Allusions Part I, 1580-1625*, ed. William Wells, *Studies in Philology*, 68 (Dec. 1971), 1-172.
34  There are over 400 printed allusions to Sidney through 1625, but for purposes of comparison with Spenser and Shakespeare I am counting only 207 that refer to him as a man of letters or draw upon his writings. Berta Siebeck, *Das Bild Sir Philip Sidneys in der Englischen Renaissance*, Weimar 1939, 184-91, lists 38 printed literary allusions to Sidney from 1591 through 1625. Later in this volume, pp. 221-37, H. R. Woudhuysen gives an account of 31 hitherto unnoted allusions during the same period. In addition to the 34 allusions in notes 25, 26, and 27 above, the 38 noted by Siebeck and the 31 by Woudhuysen, the following 104 should be added: STC 378, 768, 1480, 1488, 1559, 1598, 1667, 1676, 3189, 3191, 3631, 4159, 4253, 4256, 4493, 4521, 4522, 4541, 4636, 5077, 5567, 5638, 6151, 6238, 6261, 6373, 6412, 6500, 6820, 7095, 7193, 7217, 7226, 7229, 7255, 7525, 7574, 11055, 11097, 11340, 11497,

12503, 12504, 12774, 12775, 12776, 12779, 12781a, 12783, 12784, 12903, 13276, 13582, 13617, 13800, 14763, 15685, 16885, 17352, 17450.5, 17385, 17386, 17669, 17894, 18041, 18115.5, 18230, 18369, 18370, 18376, 18514, 18611, 18904, 18984.5, 18993, 19503, 19886, 20167, 20637, 20905, 21649, 21658, 21661, 21662, 21853, 22294, 22299, 22634, 23338, 23341, 23788, 23779, 23800, 24610, 25112, 25117, 25173, 25174, 25175, 25176, 25178, 25224, 25905, and 26051. This makes a grand total of 207 from printed sources alone, and many more are to be found in manuscript works composed throughout the first quarter of the seventeenth century. William H. Bond, *The Reputation and Influence of Sir Philip Sidney*, Harvard Ph. D. dissertation 1941 (typescript), doubtless has many more allusions than those listed here. A cooperative Sidney Allusion Book is much to be desired.

JAN VAN DORSTEN

# THE FINAL YEAR

Quite a number of people who have never read a Sidney poem are
familiar with the anecdotes that surround the young poet's death in the
Netherlands, but very few Sidney scholars have paid attention to the facts
that preceded them. This is particularly surprising because 1585/86 is
such a crucial year in the biography, and not simply because it was his
last. It was a year of great expectations. At long last Sidney could play
the political role for which he had been cast in the past decade. He would
become the prominent English leader in a Protestant league about which
he had spoken so often. More specifically, he could begin to act his part
in the Dutch Revolt against Spain, as first discussed with William of
Orange in 1577 when Sidney had stood as godfather (for Leicester) to one
of the Prince's daughters, Elisabeth, named after the English Queen. At
the time it was rumoured that the Dutch leader had suggested marriage
between young Philip Sidney and one of his elder daughters. The prospect of a Stadtholdership (of Zeeland, a key Province in the Revolt) had
also been indicated, and the idea was still very much alive in 1586 when
at least 'a number of persons present at the States' meetings' implied that
this post should go to Sidney. And there was more to come; for one year
later, in 1587, a Dutch diplomat declared that the States General had
looked upon the late Sir Philip Sidney as their future Governor General.
Without any doubt Sidney's political prestige was always greater abroad
than it was in England; and the only important position he ever held was
in the Low Countries, as Governor of the cautionary town of Flushing
in Zeeland (which controlled the sea trade with the Spanish Netherlands)
and as General of the Horse. The final year was in many ways a year
of promises fulfilled. It turned out to be a year also of disillusion,
disaster, and finally death.

It is appropriate to begin this essay with those weeks in October 1586,
400 years ago, when Sidney was being given medical treatment in Arnhem after he had received a bullet wound during a skirmish in the fields
near the town of Zutphen in the eastern part of the Dutch Republic. The
story has been told before, but some of the dates have often been
confused. Sidney was wounded on 23 September. His uncle, the Earl of
Leicester, Governor General of the United Provinces, was on the spot
leading the last campaign of the season against the Spanish troops. He
described his nephew's wound as 'very dangerous, the [thigh] bone being

broken in pieces', but said that the surgeons were in good hope. Shortly after, the army physician John James (who incidentally had been the first English student at the new university of Leiden) wrote that he was not yet sure that Sidney would recover. Sidney was transported to Arnhem, some 20 miles south of Zutphen. On 27 September Leicester received word from the surgeons that, although Sidney had had a bad fever on the 26th, after a good night's rest he 'found himself very well, and free from any ague at all, and was dressed, and did find much more ease than at any time since he was hurt, and his wound very fair'. On the following day, 28 September, Leicester wrote that he had 'received great comfort and hope, ... specially this day, ... from his surgeons and physicians'. On 29 September Leicester paid a visit to Arnhem. He was probably present when Sidney had his will drawn up on the 30th, naming his uncle as one of its supervisors. Leicester returned to Zutphen and two days later, on 2 October, wrote that 'all the worst days be past, as both surgeons and physicians have informed me, and he amends as well as is possible in this time, and himself finds it (for he sleeps and rests well and hath a good stomach to eat) without fear, or any distemper at all'. Clearly, Sidney recovered with miraculous speed; and on the following Thursday (6 October) Leicester wrote to Walsingham that his son-in-law was 'well amending as ever any man hath done for so short time. He feeleth no grief now but his long lying, which he must suffer'. The next day Leicester again went to Arnhem to visit Sidney and Sidney's wife, who had also come to Arnhem. Leicester then returned to the camp at Deventer, near Zutphen. We do not know exactly when, but very suddenly, by the end of the following week, Sidney's condition deteriorated. On Sunday 16 October a Dutch visitor reported that Sidney was too ill to read a letter, or even to sign one—although he was still willing to give instructions on behalf of various persons. That Sunday, too, Leicester returned to Arnhem. On that same day Sidney did actually manage to write one short note (in a very spidery hand) to the ageing German physician Johan Wyer. The following morning he had a codicil added to his testament. That same day, 17 October, he died.

What needs to be emphasized is that after the first few days no one, including Sidney himself, thought that he would die. Everyone expected that he would recover completely until only a few days, possibly even hours, before his death. Of course, most people, especially young people (Sidney was only 31), do not actually believe that death is upon them. Sidney had mentioned the possibility that he might die several times in the preceding weeks, even before he got wounded—but after all, it was war time, and one recognizes at least the possibility of death, even if one does not actually expect it to happen. The fact, therefore, that after a

period of optimism, the certainty of death came with alarming sudden-
ness must be borne in mind when we read the various descriptions of the
death scene: especially Thomas Moffett in *Nobilis*, the text of Sidney's
own will, George Gifford's 'The Manner of Sidney's Death', and
Greville's *Life*. In a British Academy lecture entitled 'Philip Sidney's
Toys' Katherine Duncan-Jones has commented upon Sidney's final rejection of his *Arcadia*, his 'Anacreontics', his 'Lady Rich', and all his
other vanities. She says:

> Even allowing for strong elements of convention, both in Sidney's actual
> behaviour and in later accounts of it, I think there may be a kernel of truth
> in all this. Sidney's desperate last letter to Dr Wier shows him as a young
> man in agony and terrified of death. ... Very little time was left him for
> repentance and preparation, and his remorse may have been all the more
> violent. An element in Sidney's terror, when it became apparent that he
> really was going to die, may have been the realization that he would never
> now be able to move on to the more serious forms of writing on which he
> had so eloquently based his *Defence of Poetry*. Like Keats, he may have felt
> that his name was writ in water: all that he had managed to create were
> glass and feathers, fit, according to his own criteria, to be swept away.
>    When Sidney referred to his poems as ink-wasting toys, he was to some
> extent being modest, since he must have known that even the slightest of
> his lyrics were technically superior to most of the English poetry written
> since Chaucer. But he knew also that virtually everything he had written
> was secular, much of it lascivious or trifling.

I agree almost entirely with this, although a neo-stoic convention may
also underlie the poet's rejection of his 'trifles', but I should like to add
that Sidney's thoughts during those last few weeks developed along a
slightly different pattern.

He was wounded on 23 September. The first days were filled with
shock and a lot of pain. He was taken to his tent first, then to a house
in Arnhem. He was feverish—no time for profound thoughts, just survival: doctors, the dressing of his wounds, pain-killers perhaps. Then the
initial shock began to wear off. The last recorded feverish night was on
26 September. He began to recover. And it was then, and only then, that
he began to realize, consciously, that he might have died—unprepared,
in every way. He called for his preacher Gifford, who arrived not later
than 30 September. On that same day Sidney drew up his will. Gifford
describes his first visit to Sidney in some detail. He records how Sidney
had come to realize, to his own joy, that the anguish of the first few days
(now past) had been a God-sent 'loving and fatherly correction, and to
his singular profit, whether he should live or die'. And, Sidney added,
because of this realization 'I have with unfeigned purpose of heart vow-
ed, if God give life, to addict myself wholly to his service, and not to live

as I have done. For I have walked in a vain course'. With this resolution in mind he 'continued', according to Gifford, 'certain days'—that is, the fortnight during which they all expected him to recover. Therefore it is, I think, important to remember not only those last few days in which 'a young man in agony' tried to face the fact that there was nothing he could do to make up for opportunities missed and vanities indulged, except pray. We should consider, rather, that crucial phase of awareness, remorse, and new resolutions: the days, that is, in which his doctors told him that he would live. And we will find, curiously enough, that his rejection of his past life and his determination to change that life strike us as particularly convincing because we know that he was *not* anticipating death, but believed that he would have the time to act out these recent resolutions.

It is probably futile to speculate about what he would have done, and written, if he *had* lived longer. But it is reasonable to believe that he did look back on his life and writings with genuine dissatisfaction. What was there to be so dissatisfied about, as a writer? The poet may have remembered that in *A Defence of Poetry* he had defined the scope of true, responsible, useful poetry, but that in October 1586 he had not (yet) written any such poetry. All his writings were essentially *juvenilia*, written during brief spells of inactivity. They had been preparations for something more serious which he would write 'one day', and never did. (It is not surprising, therefore, that in his correspondence he never mentions his literary exercises). Even his longest piece, the *Arcadia*, before or after the revision, did not come anywhere near the Christian, heroic poem, which he had outlined in the *Defence*—singing the praise of God, and encouraging men to virtuous action through inspiring, unforgettable images of public virtue. Now, in October 1586, according to Greville, 'when ... his piercing inward powers were lifted up to a purer Horizon, he then discovered, not only the imperfection, but vanity of these shadows, how daintly soever limned'. Of course he had embarked on a number of translations of 'serious works': the *Psalms*, Aristotle's *Rhetoric*, Du Bartas' *La Sepmaine*, and Du Plessis Mornay's *De la Verité de la Religion Chrétienne*; but none of the translations had been completed.

In fact, even the *Defence* itself, the only other literary piece that shows a direct concern with public morality and the responsibilities of a poet, is not an essay or a treatise on poetry in which the author actually says what he believes. The maddening thing about the *Defence* is that Sidney chose to write a *defence* of poetry, which observes the rules of rhetorical persuasion before the dictates of one's own personal opinion. This is why Sidney sometimes contradicts himself; and it is also the reason why Sidney scholars continue to make the mistake of assuming that if Sidney says something in the *Defence*, this is what he himself believed to be true. Of course, in judicial rhetoric a speaker need not subscribe to everything he says, as long as he influences a jury in favour of his case; and of course he is allowed to contradict himself as long as it does not weaken the impact of his presentation of the case. In the opening pages of the *Defence*, for instance, Sidney establishes the dignity and importance of poetry by emphasizing (like everybody else in the sixteenth century) that the ancient moral and natural philosophers were all poets and that, from time immemorial, science and poetry have always been companions. But only a few pages later, having proposed another point of departure, he declares quite happily that of course that kind of poetry is not really poetry. Thus we can never be quite certain which point of view Sidney himself would have supported although one likes to think that the second view was really his. Even his most general, detached theoretical statements were dictated by the occasion: How to Make a Persuasive Case in Favour of Poetry? But we can never say with any certainty that this is what Sidney believed because he said it. *A Defence of Poetry*, like so much else, is brilliant and persuasive but in the end not entirely conclusive. If he thought of such things in mid-October 1586, perhaps what he regretted most was precisely this slippery quality in his writings, a certain lack of commitment—the fact, in short, that he had never set a clear, memorable example of virtue in any of them. Of course he could not then anticipate the Sidney legend which was to create this very image of virtue, but of the man himself, after his death—a legend which would encourage posterity, quite wrongly, to find the thoughts of that kind of writer in the writings.

It is likely, however, that in his weeks of repentance and resolution Sidney was less preoccupied with his literary past than with his private life and his recent military and political achievements. After all, the past ten months had been the only period in his life in which he had had real power and real responsibility. What had he done with it, and what should he do after his recovery? Though he was a mere knight of small means, not a great aristocrat like his uncle, his prestige in Holland was considerable. There Master Philip was generally referred to as 'Mylord Sidney', 'Baron Sidney' (that curious Parisian title which he never paraded at home but which was remembered at the time of his funeral), or even mistakenly as 'Comes Sidneius'. He was singled out for much praise and appears to have been the person to whom many turned for help, support, or patronage. Primarily, of course, he was Governor of the important port of Flushing, and, as General of the Horse, second-in-command of the English expeditionary forces in the Netherlands—in spite of the fact that he had no military experience other than in the

Queen's tiltyard. Some of the military facts are mentioned in every Sidney biography. One is his last battle, at Warnsveld near Zutphen—a futile skirmish, even if Sidney had not died, because the enemy convoy which he had attempted to stop just trundled on to the city of Zutphen after the victorious English gentlemen had retired to their camp. (According to one Dutch source, the convoy had in fact completed its victualling mission and was on its way home, away from the city.) The other military event was Sidney's attack on the town of Axel a few months earlier, made memorable by John Stow's description of Sidney's neo-classical oration to his soldiers the evening before the attack. This military engagement, though succesful, did not change the war in any way, and nobody thanked him for his victory—on the contrary, the States of Zeeland were cross because they were now forced to put a garrison in Axel. As a military commander, Sidney's contribution was very modest indeed.

He probably did play a significant part—which may have been an additional cause for regret during his last days—in the involved diplomatic negotiations before and during his uncle's expedition to the Netherlands. His exact role—if it can be traced—has never been fully analysed; but it would seem that, especially during the last year of his life, Sidney's public role was chiefly that of helping to 'master-mind' the English involvement in the Low Countries. Various sources tell us that, had he lived, Sidney was destined to become (if Queen Elizabeth would allow it) a leading, possibly the leading, politician of the Protestant Netherlands. It is perhaps significant that his uncle decided to go home, to England, immediately after the death of his rather more charismatic nephew. If we knew more about Sidney's own expectations, and about what other people expected of him in 1586, it would help us to understand more accurately what he meant when, in October 1586, he promised that he would change his life.

Some conclusions can be drawn from Sidney's relations with Dutch humanist scholars in 1586. Abroad, one remembers, he was regarded as the coming man, likely inheritor to great titles and great fortunes, already a Baron, already the son of the Viceroy of Ireland. Politicians and scholars of a humanist disposition were agreeably impressed by his literary and humanistic curiosity, and looked upon him as a future, tolerant leader of a Protestant United Nations. Also, without exception, they appear to have genuinely liked him. Sidney tried to live up to an image of himself that was so much more real abroad than it was in England. In the Netherlands his reputation became even higher when he arrived in 1585 with his troops and the choicest young men of England's aristocracy leading the Protestant crusade as a man of action, the 'learned soldier' soldiering at last. All the classical parallels came to mind. It is difficult to believe that he himself was not conscious of his image. He rose to the occasion, as he did before the attack on Axel when he addressed his soldiers like a reincarnation of Alexander the Great, or Pompey, or Julius Caesar. The Dutch humanists who met him indicated that they knew he was a practising poet, and they responded to his presence with great enthusiasm. His prestige was never greater.

One of the irenical Dutch humanists who looked upon Sidney as a patron was the greatest northern classicist of the late sixteenth century, Justus Lipsius, a professor at the young university of Leiden (founded in 1575). Lipsius and Sidney had met before, at Louvain, on 25 February 1577, and they had been in touch ever since. Sidney came to Leiden on 2 January 1586 when Leicester made his first triumphant entry into that city. Lipsius was there. Leicester returned to Leiden eight days later, without Sidney this time, because Sidney was in The Hague negotiating the terms of Leicester's Governor-Generalship. Leicester and his train were given a full academic welcome, and attended one of the lectures: a lecture by Lipsius, obviously, who held forth on his favourite subject, Tacitus. The lecture topic was Tacitus' short biography of Agricola, the Roman Governor of Britain who in the first century A.D. subdued most of the Earl's native country—an interesting choice. After the lecture Lipsius was entertained by the Earl of Leicester, and in return he presented his noble visitor with an inscribed copy of his most famous treatise, *De Constantia*—another interesting choice. Sidney joined them a few days later, and returned for a third visit on 28 February. During these three visits, Lipsius and Sidney met more than once. They did not have far to walk. Lipsius lived in the main street, almost directly opposite the printing house of Christopher Plantin which was now run by Franciscus Raphelengius. Sidney was lodged in the same street, in the house of the town secretary, Jan van Hout, who was a good friend of Lipsius', and who also happened to be a leading neo-Latin poet of the Northern Netherlands—and who, incidentally, had been taking English lessons shortly before Sidney's arrival. In their conversations literary subjects appear to have been secondary to topical, political issues. This is the way sixteenth-century humanism works. Lipsius frequently mentions Sidney's love of literature and learning (and in fact during these weeks he wrote a little treatise, written for and dedicated to Sidney). But, as the surviving letters of these months show, they met as men of learning but talked politics: that is, the moral, social, and political well-being of the state.

The social code of the age dictated which roles Sidney and Lipsius played. The great scholar addressed Sidney as his noble, learned, and illustrious patron; the young Englishman signed his correspondence with great informality, 'certe tuus Philippus Sidneius', but took a lot of trouble to write learned Latin when he wrote to Professor Justus Lipsius. The two letters to Sidney by Lipsius that we have show that Lipsius made use of his familiarity with Sidney to involve him in the opposition against his uncle's all-Puritan policy, because that policy ran counter to the rather less orthodox, anti-Spanish league which Sidney and many of Lipsius' friends had been promoting for so many years. 'That you will have free and firm use of the reins of government', Lipsius wrote, 'that I approve of and do recommend; but only if it is done with moderation'. Lipsius of course was a curious ally. He has often been described, probably unfairly, as a turn-coat because after he had left Louvain for the Protestant university of Leiden, he left Leiden again several years later and was 're-converted' to Roman Catholicism. It is perhaps more accurate to describe him as a man who abhorred religious fanaticism and who avoided theological controversy as much as he could. At Leiden, where the neo-Stoic professor and some of his friends even became associated with a particularly liberal branch of the spiritualist sect known as 'The Family of Love', he enjoyed the company of scholars whom he trusted and whose attitude towards religion he shared. There he was happy, until 1586, when even Leiden was affected by a new wave of intolerance, to which Leicester's interpretation of Governor-Generalship certainly contributed. It is remarkable that Lipsius' conversations with Sidney led him to believe that Sidney would defend a moderate religious position, even against his own uncle. In fact, as late as 20 August 1586 Lipsius travelled to Utrecht in order to discuss these matters with his patron. He missed him by a few hours, because Sidney had just left for the eastern provinces, for the last campaign. Two weeks later, not long before the fatal battle, Sidney wrote to Lipsius from the camp at Deventer. In his letter he begged him not to leave his friends because of his disgust with the régime; he indicated that he could make Lipsius a most welcome visitor to England, and that he would do something about it soon so that Lipsius could take advantage of this offer even if his patron should die; and he promised that he would help one of Lipsius' friends, a prominent Dutch politician who had been imprisoned by Leicester in spite of his many services to their cause. This letter, which repeatedly mentions long days of negotiation to which Sidney devoted nearly all his time, reveals to us a Philip Sidney who has suddenly risen to a position of power and responsibility, who remains a loyal patron, and who is willing to advocate religious moderation. Sidney was wounded a fortnight later; and Lipsius never went to England.

This example enables us to see more clearly why, only a few weeks later, Sidney realized that he had not yet been able to achieve anything significant, and that he hoped that God would give him time to make up for it. Only recently had he actually experienced 'power' and the problems of loyalty which power involves, as in the current conflicts between the Dutch Puritans and his uncle on the one hand and his Dutch friends on the other. I believe that it adds considerably to the intensity of his remark to Gifford that God had sent him this wound as 'a loving and fatherly correction' to make him aware of the 'vain course' in which he had 'walked'. Of course he was thinking primarily of his private life and of his public life as a politician, not as a writer. But even as a writer, his 'Dutch year' must have made a great difference to him. If he had lived to write an heroic poem about the virtues and duties and about the weaknesses and insufficiencies of princes, he would have remembered his own months of firsthand experience of actual war, actual power, real friends, real enemies. In *Arcadia* he had written about such themes. But when we look at the new, hard-won, Dutch experience of 1586, we begin to understand that when in October 1586 he described his *Arcadia* as (in Greville's words) an 'unpolished embryo', the poet for once said what he really thought.

MARJON POORT

## 'THE DESIRED AND DESTINED SUCCESSOR'

*A Chronology of Sir Philip Sidney's Activities 1585-1586*

In the early months of 1587 an embassy of some six Dutch delegates was in England to negotiate increased English assistance in the war against Spain. They wrote a detailed report of their visit, which lasted from 13 January until 13 March. Besides the lengthy negotiations themselves, two events which took place in London during those two months found their way into the report. The first of these was the execution of Mary, Queen of Scots, summarily dealt with in a single matter-of-fact sentence: 'Wednesday 18 February s.n. which was the day on which the Queen of Scotland was executed by the axe ...'.[1] The second, though a far less conspicuous event in the course of English history, aroused a great deal more emotion among the Dutch delegates:

> On Thursday was held the solemnity of the funeral of the ... lord Sidney which was very magnificent. His body was brought into St. Paul's Church. From there the most important gentlemen present at the funeral and the delegates from the States General rode with his Excellency [i.e. Leicester] to his house and stayed with him during the afternoon.[2]

The report tells us that the delegates had been invited to the funeral by Sir Francis Walsingham (who also provided the necessary horses), and that the Earl of Leicester had not been aware of this invitation.[3] That the Dutch were present at the funeral is not in itself surprising. The real interest of the report lies in the verbatim account of the speech delivered by the Dutch spokesman at the funeral banquet which includes the following two revealing sentences:

> ...his death... is most sad for us, because we had hoped that through his help and advice our country would be rescued from this long and miserable war, and that the true Christian religion (of which he has been a most ardent champion) would be safely preserved in the Netherlands. Through the outstanding and incomparable talents of his character he was, in the opinion of all, the desired and destined successor to that illustrious and magnanimous prince, Robert Dudley, Earl of Leicester, the deputy of her Majesty and Governor General of the United Provinces ...[4]

In reply, Robert Sidney thanked the delegates for their presence and declared that he had the same sympathy for their cause as his brother had had, and that he hoped that they would find use for his services.[5]

From this important document it appears that Sir Philip Sidney had been regarded by the Dutch, and probably also by Leicester, as the logical successor to his uncle. In this light his appointment as governor of the strategically important town of Flushing can be looked upon as a period of preparation for his future role as Governor General of the United Provinces.

The treaty of Nonsuch which arranged the nature and the extent of the assistance offered by the English and the guarantees the Dutch had to give in exchange for that help was concluded on 10 August 1585, just a few days after the fall of Antwerp. The English were given three 'cautionary towns' in the sea provinces of Holland and Zeeland: The Brill in Holland, Flushing and Rammekens, a fortification just a few miles east from Flushing, in Zeeland. Of these, Flushing and Rammekens undoubtedly were the most important, situated as they were in the mouth of the river Scheldt, the only entry to the port of Antwerp.

The first mention of Sir Philip Sidney's possible posting at Flushing is in a letter from a Captain Roger Williams (a professional soldier who had been in the Netherlands for a long time) who wrote the following cryptic remark in a letter to Sir Francis Walsingham, Secretary of State and Sidney's father-in-law: 'If your honour would place Sir Philip in Flushing, that will be a road all ways worth the best duiche [duchy] in England ...'.[6] As can be seen from a letter by William Davison, the English representative in the Netherlands, the Dutch delegation negotiating the treaty in England had been in touch with Sidney and had sounded him about the governorship of Flushing:

> The deputies returned have given some hope of Sir Philip Sidney, whom they have greatly recommended, and if her Majesty send him, I think the town will without any difficulty be delivered into her hands.[7]

On 22 September those deputies of the United Provinces who had remained in England to await the official ratification of the treaty wrote to the Earl of Leicester that they had received letters from the States of Zeeland

> from which it is clear that these States are resolved on the negotiations with her Majesty and have agreed with the town of Flushing in the sense that they agree to receive the garrison of her Majesty as it was said and negotiated, only wishing to have there as their governor Sir Philip Sidney.[8]

Meanwhile, Sidney himself seemed to despair of his being posted to Flushing, as may be seen in a letter from Walsingham to Davison:

> Sir Philip Sydney hath taken a very hard resolution to accompany Sir Francis Drake in this voyage, moved hereunto for that he saw her Majesty disposed to commit the charge of Flushing unto some other,[9] which he

1. Map of Holland from: J. J. Orlers, *Nassauschen Laurencrans*, Leiden, 1610. (University Library Leiden, Collectie Bodel Nijenhuis)

> reputed would fall out greatly to his disgrace to see another preferred before
> him, both for birth and judgment inferior unto him. This resolution is
> greatly to the grief of Sir Philip's friends, but to none more than to myself.
> I know her Majesty would easily have been induced to have placed him in
> Flushing, but he despaired hereof and the disgrace that he doubted he
> should receive hath carried him into a desperate course. There is some
> order taken for his stay, but I fear it will not take place ...[10]

How serious were Sidney's plans to join Drake in his expedition? It is
possible that all this was just a scheme to try to force Queen Elizabeth's
hand,[11] and if this was the case, the plan was successful. It was decided,
finally, that Sir Philip would have the governorship of Flushing, though
not before Leicester had given him the strongest possible support in a
note to Burghley, Lord Treasurer and Secretary of State: 'I will never
agree to Flushing to any but to my nephew'.[12]

On 18 November Philip Sidney arrived in Zeeland. Foul weather
prevented the English from landing at Flushing as planned. Instead they
had to switch their course to the fortification of Rammekens, which was
also under Sidney's jurisdiction. After their landing, the English had to
walk some distance to Flushing wading through mud so that, when they
finally arrived, but little of their dignity remained and the welcome
prepared for them had to be cut short.[13] On 22 November Sidney took
the oath at the States of Zeeland's House at Middelburg,[14] and he was
there again on the following day to receive in return the States' oath to
Queen Elizabeth and to himself as the new governor of Flushing.[15] He
took up residence in a house rented from a local magistrate, one Jacques
Gelée,[16] and he stayed in Flushing to muster the garrison and inspect the
fortifications, having sent his brother Robert to Ostend for the same purpose.[17] These musters proved that the garrisons were too weak in almost
every respect, and made it clear that there were many more men on the
pay list than were actually present.[18] The two Sidneys immediately set
to work to put things right.

On 10 December the Earl of Leicester arrived in Flushing where he
was met by Count Maurice, together with deputies of the States General,
and of course his nephew.[19] On the following day Leicester and Sidney
went to Middelburg where they planned to stay five or six days before
going to Holland.[20] On Friday 17 December the English party boarded
ships which were to bring them to Dordrecht, the first town of Holland
and the first they were to visit. During their journey they were held up
by fog until Monday morning, an unexpected delay which caused serious
shortage of food.[21] Not until Tuesday did the eventful trip come to an end
when they arrived in Dordrecht.[22] There they were welcomed with the
same enthusiasm which was to mark their whole journey through the

Netherlands. On 28 December 1585 they arrived in The Hague,[23] where the States General at the time held their assemblies. Here, Leicester was officially welcomed by the States General and the States of Holland:[24] negotiations about the nature and extent of Leicester's authority could now begin.

The States General presented their ideas about the arrangement to Leicester[25] who had decided to take up residence for the time at the near-by town of Leiden where his nephew kept him company.[26] On 7 January six deputies of the States General met Leicester, Davison, and Sir Philip Sidney.[27] To open the negotiations proper the first day was spent on questions from the English about formulations, and clarifications by the Dutch,[28] which continued on Sunday 9 January.[29] At the end of that meeting Leicester announced that he had chosen deputies, Sidney among them, to continue the negotiations that same evening. The convened meeting, however, was not held, for 'the ambassador communicated to them [i.e. the Dutch deputies] that it was not convenient for Sir Philip Sidney, because of the muster of the cavalry'.[30] The next day the deputies met and began considering the exact authority Leicester would have and from whom he would have it.[31] At this meeting Sidney clearly functioned as Leicester's spokesman, especially on the subject of the Councils the Dutch wanted to place close to Leicester, both to advise him and to limit his power. On this occasion, Sidney made an illuminating speech, saying that

> he had learnt from history that when the state of the Republic of Rome had been in utter peril or danger, as the Netherlands nowadays are, which we [i.e. the Dutch] fully acknowledge, it had been necessary to create a dictatorship, with absolute power and disposition over everything concerning the prosperity of the country, without any instruction, limitation or restriction...[32]

This amounts to a plea for absolute power for his uncle. Here, the poet, 'companion of camps',[33] voices an ideology of power. The plea was probably inspired by what Sidney had seen of the state of the country and its defences, but the States General naturally were none too keen to give in to this excessive demand. They pointed to the treaty with England and said that for an appointment on such terms they would need the approval of Queen Elizabeth and of all the provinces. Given Queen Elizabeth's reluctance to enter the treaty in the first place, and the difficulties the Dutch had already had with governors from abroad, such an appointment was not likely.

In the end, after some changes had been made giving him a few more responsibilities, Leicester accepted the offer of the States General, and a commission and a proposal for an oath were drawn up, which were

agreed upon on 16 January. The oath on the commission was taken by
Leicester on 25 January,[34] and administered by Count Maurice of
Nassau.[35]

The negotiations thus concluded, Sidney planned to go back to
Flushing, but Leicester did not want him to go yet.[36] In fact, he stayed
with his uncle until at least 9 February. On that day, Leicester wrote a
letter to the States of Zeeland saying that he was sending back his nephew
to them so that he might set up his government.[37]

In England, meantime, unrest about Leicester's appointment had
begun to show itself. In a letter dated 17 January, probably to Leicester
himself, Walsingham wrote that

> her Majesty is offended with the title of Excellency given to his Lordship,
> and therefore it is likely that she will mislike of the authority that the States
> have given him over them.[38]

The official letter expressing the royal anger was sent to Leicester by the
Lords of the Council on 26 January. The Queen wanted Leicester to give
back his commission to the States General and to be content with his being her Lieutenant-General.[39] In answer to this, Leicester sent Davison
to England to explain the way things had turned out and to plead his and
the Dutch cause.[40]

On 18 February Sir Philip Sidney was back in Flushing,[41] but he did
not stay there long, for we find him back in Leiden on 28 February,[42]
again with Leicester. Leicester must have asked him to go and plead his
cause with Sir Thomas Heneage, sent by Queen Elizabeth from
England, who was expected to arrive shortly, so that on 3 March Sidney
was back in Middelburg to welcome Heneage there,[43] and to travel with
him to Haarlem, where they arrived on 8 March,[44] four days after
Leicester's arrival.[45] What Sir Philip thought about Queen Elizabeth's
attempted intervention can be read in a letter from him to the Lord
Treasurer, Lord Burghley, of 8 March:

> The news here I leave to Sir Thomas Heneage, who hath with as much
> honesty in my opinion done as much hurt as any man this twelve-month
> hath done with naughtiness; but I hope in God when her Majesty finds the
> truth of things her graciousness will not utterly overthrow a cause so
> behoveful and costly unto her, but that is beyond my office. I only cry for
> Flushing and crave your favour, which I will deserve with my service.[46]

Queen Elizabeth was appeased in the end,[47] but great harm had been
done to Leicester's position in the Netherlands. It had become clear that
English assistance had its strict limits and that Leicester himself was no
more than a puppet on the Queen's strings. The euphoria of the first
months was over, and complaints about Leicester's administration began

to be heard. Leicester made matters even worse when on 25 March he published a new edict on trade with the enemy, which was much too strict. Its effects were disastrous for the financing of the war, which had always depended largely on that trade, and also for the harmony within the Union of the Provinces, which became disrupted through the differences between the trading provinces and those that could do very little trading because of their geographical situation. The tension caused by his autocratic action forced Leicester to moderate the prohibitions of the edict less than four months after he had issued it.[48]

In this period of troubles over the edict Leicester sought and found allies on the side of the staunchest Calvinists, which was probably one of the reasons why he had taken up residence in the town of Utrecht where Orthodox Calvinism had a strong presence. In his letters Leicester wrote about 'his popularity with the people and the hatred they felt against the States, who were not orthodox as they were, and were unwilling to suppress as they wished not only the Catholics, but all Protestants with a non-Calvinist belief'.[49] To please these Calvinists Leicester called for a general synod which started on 10 June in The Hague.[50] This synod decided upon a very orthodox Church ordinance, which was never ratified by the States General, however. Needless to say, Leicester's attitude did not heighten his popularity with the States General.

At first, Leicester's military activities seemed to offer him a good chance to improve his standing in the country. When he came to the Netherlands the war situation had cut the eastern provinces in half, the southern front being the river Meuse, with only the province of Zeeland further to the south. But Leicester's optimism suffered a severe setback when on 28 May 1586 the Duke of Parma took the town of Grave, the easternmost stronghold of the States on the river Meuse. The general opinion was that Leicester had been too optimistic about Grave's ability to defend itself, and so the surrender of the town was blamed on him. After only a month of campaigning Parma had control of the entire river Meuse—the provinces of Gelderland and Utrecht being threatened as well. Leicester desperately needed military success to brighten up his tarnished reputation. On 6 July, on the Zeeland front, he was given his chance. The plan for an attack had come from Count Maurice of Nassau, who sent Leicester a letter containing information about the defence of the town of Axel. Secrecy was called for, and only Sidney was notified of the forthcoming attack, as his presence was needed and asked for by Count Maurice.[51] Sidney went on a reconnoitring trip and found that the plan did have possibilities of success, so a force was sent to the town. According to some reports Sidney was the first to enter Axel after it had fallen,[52] others only give him third place.[53] The States of Zeeland are said

2. Engraving of Maurice of Nassau and Sir Philip Sidney before Axel from: Wilh. Baudartius, *Afbeeldinghe ende beschrijvinghe van alle de veldslagen ... in de Nederlanden, geduerende d'oorloghe teghens den Coninck van Spaengien*, Amsterdam, 1616. (University Library Leiden, Collectie Bodel Nijenhuis)

to have been less than enthusiastic over the success, as they now had to put a garrison in the town to defend it.[54] On 17 July Sidney attempted to take Gravelines, a Spanish stronghold in the south of Flanders. This attempt failed, because intelligence about the willingness of the garrison to surrender had not been correct, and what appeared a sound military proposition became a dangerous trap when Gravelines turned out to be occupied by a much larger force than the reports had said. When this became clear, Sidney left for Flushing with his troops.[55]

At the end of August war activities were transferred to the much more endangered areas of Gelderland and Overijssel, and Sidney joined Leicester again. They set up camp near Amerongen, moving on from there to lay siege before the town of Doesburg on 30 August. After a few days Doesburg surrendered,[56] and the army proceeded to the nearby town of Zutphen. Here, on 23 September they engaged in the futile skirmish which became famous, because it was to prove fatal for Sir Philip

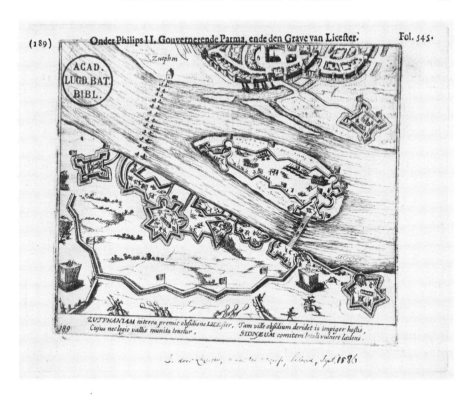

3. Map of Zutphen from: Baudartius, *Afbeeldinghe ende beschrijvinghe*. (University Library Leiden, Collectie Bodel Nijenhuis)

Sidney. The story of his courage on the field as well as on his deathbed is too well known to relate again.[57] Wounded, Sidney was taken to the town of Arnhem, the safest city in the neighbourhood. The trip was probably made by boat since that was the most convenient means of transport. On 17 October Sidney died, and shortly afterwards his body was embalmed. When the Earl of Leicester withdrew his troops to Utrecht, he took the body of his nephew with him.[58] They arrived at Utrecht on 20 October.[59] Sidney's body was sent to England by way of Flushing and arrived in London on 5 November.[60] The funeral was held in magnificent splendour in St. Paul's Cathedral on 17 February 1587. What were the reasons for this delay we do not know, but the considerable costs may have been a very important one.

Conclusions about the impact of Sir Philip Sidney's presence in the United Provinces cannot easily be drawn. From what can be gathered about his whereabouts during his ten months' stay in the Netherlands he cannot have spent more than about three months at Flushing, and probably even less. Most of his time was taken up by the installation of his uncle as Governor General and by the summer campaign. From more than one source, however, we get the image of a man generally liked and even loved. The States of Zeeland and the town of Flushing complained several times about his prolonged absence, saying that they needed and loved him very much.[61] The letters of condolence from the States General, the States of Zeeland and the town of Flushing express the same sentiments, as does the funeral oration by the Dutch delegation in London: 'This country [has lost] a lord and a friend, of whom we were expecting—knowing his virtues, experience, and sympathy for our cause—more benefit and service; ... we knew how many merits he had and that he was worthy of a much greater charge'.[62] We need little imagination to think of the 'much greater charge' as that of Governor General. That Sidney did not think much of his uncle's tactics, either politically or militarily, may be inferred from a rather cryptic remark in a letter to Walsingham: 'To complain of my lord of Lester you know I may not, but this is the case'.[63] In the Netherlands, Sidney had always been at the heart of power, whether the decisions that had to be taken were political or military. The reservations he had about the felicity of some of these decisions must have brought him much closer to the Dutch than Leicester ever was. If to no one else, to the Dutch at least Sidney's future role was quite clear. And as the funeral speech and the various other sources indicate, there was nothing secret about that. Sir Philip Sidney to them was indeed the 'desired and destined successor'.

## NOTES

1  Gemeente Archief Arnhem, inv. nr OA 5515.
2  Gemeente Archief Arnhem, inv. nr OA 5515. The Dutch text is as follows: 'Donderdaeghs heeft men gehouden de solemniteyt vande begravinge des voorseiden heeren van Sidney die zeer magnificq is geweest ende tlichaem gebracht in sinte pauwels kerke van waer de principaelste heeren die te groeve geweest hadden mitsgaders de gedeputeerden vanden heeren Staten Generael met zijne Excellentie gereden zijn naar sijn huys ende zijn smiddaeghs bij hem gebleven'.
3  Gemeente Archief Arnhem, inv. nr OA 5515. Dutch text: 'Sdyncxdaeghs hebben wij verwacht nade compste van zijne Excellentie te hove die eerst swoensdaeghs daer gecommen is. Na den welcken gereijst zijn de heeren Menin, Sille ende Valcke maer en hebben zijne Excellentie daer nyet gevonden deurdyen hij van daer gereyst was naer Londen om hem te bereyden totte begravinge vanden lichame des heeren Gouverneurs van Vlissingen Philips Sidney alwaer de voorseiden gedeputeerden hem gevolcht ende gevonden hebben in sijn huys ... [the Earl of Leicester] seggende voorts dat hij sanderen daeghs moest wesen op te begravinge vanden voorseiden heeren Philips Sidney daer wij zijne Excellentie souden accompagneren alse wij des versocht waren van wegen den heere van Walsingam die ons tot dyen eynde peerden bestelt hadde...'
4  Gemeente Archief Arnhem, inv. nr OA 5515. The complete text: 'Opt bancquet naden middach hebben wij oirloff genomen van zijn Excellentie mitsgaders van Sir

Robert Sidney broeder des voorseiden heeren van Sidney wesende de principaelste vanden rouwe aenden welcken den heeren Menin van weghen die geunieerde provintien het geclagh in deser vougen gedaen heeft: Quod omnium virtutum exemplar absolutum totiusque anglicanei nobilitatis decus atque ornamentum fortissimus vir D. Philipus Sidneius Gubernator oppidi flissinges ac portus celeberrimi in Zelandia cum arce Rammekens serenissime Majestati fidellissime magistratui populoge totius provincie carissimus sane nature concessit nos in circulo parentum propinquorum amicorum merore ac luctu publico provinciarum unitarum Belgi perpetuo testatum volumus mortem illius tanti viri ali quidem merito dolendam ac lacrimabilem nobis vero longe luctuosissimum extitisse quod ipsius ope concilio patriam hoc diuturno ac funesto bello liberatam et veram religionem christianam (cuius ille semper fuit acerrimus propugnator) in Belgio stabilitam ac conservatam sperabamus quodque ob excellentes atque incomparabiles ipsius animi dotes illustrissimo ac magnanimo principi Roberto Dudleio Comiti Leycestrie vicario Majestatis serenissime et Gubernatori generali unitarum provinciarum prudentissimo vigilantissimoque omnium animis ac vocis successor exoptatius atque destinatus esse videbatur verum hoc magna ex parte nos consolatur quod pro bona causa hoc est pro protectione veri religionis christiani proque servitio serenissime Majestatis in acie fortiter pugnantem ac cadentem in eternam per gloriam vivere et cum omnibus fortibus ac puris viris de patria etque religione christiana bene meritis in Christo conquiescere credamus'.

5  Gemeente Archief Arnhem, inv. nr OA 5515. Dutch text: 'ten welcken den voorseiden heere Robert Sidney antwoorde met cortte woorden in franchoische tale dat die doot van zijne broeder voerwaer zeer beclaegelyck ende hem voeral bedroefflyck was. Bedanckende den heeren Staten Generael van de eere hem ende de familie van Sidney gedaen int compareren inden rouwe opde begravinge deur heurluyder gedeputeerden verclarende tzelve hart ende affectie te hebben sulcx als zijnen overleden broeder ten dienste vanden lande daermen hem soude willen employeren ofte gebruycken'.

6  CSPFor, XIX, 687.

7  CSPFor, XX, 7.

8  W. van Everdingen, *Het leven van M. Paulus Buys, Advocaat van den lande van Holland*, Leiden, 1895, 179. The French text: '... par lesquelles il appert, que les dits Estaz sont entièrement resoluz sur la négotiation avec Sa Majesté, aussy accordé avec ceulx de Vlissinghen tellement, quilz sont contents de rescevoir le garnison de Sa Majesté comme il fust dict et convenu, requerant seulement d'havoir là pour leur chief le seigneur de Sidney ...'

9  CSPFor, XIX, 677; CSPFor, XX, 33. From these letters it may be concluded that Sir Henry Norris of Rycotes had been suggested for this post. How serious a candidate he was cannot be judged.

10  CSPFor, XX, 23-24.

11  A. H. Bill, *Astrophel or the life and death of the renowned Sir Philip Sidney*, London, 1938, 279.

12  CSPFor, XX, 53.

13  CSPFor, XX, 176-77.

14  CSPFor, XX, 177.

15  CSPFor, XX, 177.

16  Resolutions of the States of Zeeland, 1585, 13 December 1585; Resolutions of the States of Zeeland, 1586, 4 May 1586; CSPFor, XX, 213.

17  CSPFor, XX, 191.

18  CSPFor, XX, 177, 184, 192, 285.

19  CSPFor, XX, 209, 212.

20  CSPFor, XX, 212.

21  CSPFor, XX, 243.

22  CSPFor, XX, 243, 245.

23  CSPFor, XX, 249.

24 CSPFor, XX, 249.
25 CSPFor, XX, 177.
26 CSPFor, XX, 277; R. C. Strong and J. A. van Dorsten, *Leicester's Triumph*, Leiden, 1964, 60, App. 2.
27 H. Brugmans, *Correspondentie van Robert Dudley, Graaf van Leicester, en andere documenten betreffende zijn gouvernement generaal in de Nederlanden, 1585-1588*, Utrecht, 1931, 31.
28 Brugmans, 31-41.
29 Brugmans, 41-44.
30 Brugmans, 44.
31 Brugmans, 45.
32 Brugmans, 46. Dutch text: '...dat hij hem oeck wat geoeffent hadde in de historien ende daeruut verstaen, dat soe wanneer den staet van den republicque van Romen int uyterste perickel ofte dangier gecomen was, sulcx die Nederlanden jegenwoordelijck zijn naer ons eygen seggen ende bekentenisse, nootshalven moste worden geprocedeert tot creatie van een dictateur, dat deselve volcomen macht ende dispositie heeft gehadt over al tgene twelvaeren van den landen was concernerende, zonder eenige instructie, limitatie ofte restrinctie ...'
33 *MP*, 105.
34 Pieter Bor, *De Nederlandse Historien, Oorsprongh, begin en vervolgh der Nederlandsche oorlogen, beroerten en burgerlijke oneenigheden, 1555-1600*, Amsterdam, 1679-84, 690.
35 Dr. N. Japikse, *Resolutiën der Staten Generaal van 1576-1809*, V. 406.
36 CSPFor, XX, 303.
37 Brugmans, 77.
38 CSPFor, XX, 303.
39 CSPFor, XX, 322-24.
40 Bor, 697; CSPFor, XX, 303.
41 Brugmans, 85.
42 Strong/Van Dorsten, App. 2; J. A. van Dorsten, *Poets, Patrons and Professors: Sir Philip Sidney, Daniel Rogers, and the Leiden Humanists*, Leiden, 1962, 115.
43 CSPFor, XX, 409.
44 CSPFor, XX, 556.
45 CSPFor, XX, 413, 556.
46 CSPFor, XX, 458-59.
47 CSPFor, XX, 510-11.
48 F. G. Oosterhoff, *The Earl of Leicester's Governorship of the Netherlands, 1586-1587*, Ph. D. Thesis, University of London, 1967, 140-44.
49 J. Reitsma and J. Lindeboom, *Geschiedenis van de Hervorming en de Hervormde Kerk der Nederlanden*, 's Gravenhage, 1949, 156.
50 Bor, 718; F. L. Rutgers, *Acta van de Nederlandsche Synoden der zestiende eeuw*, Utrecht, 1889, 514-15.
51 Bor, 738; CSPFor, XXI, Part 2, 75, 77, 81.
52 CSPFor, XXI, Part 2, 75.
53 CSPFor, XXI, Part 2, 77.
54 J. A. Dop, *Eliza's Knights*, Alblasserdam, 1981, 175.
55 Bor, 738; CSPFor, XXI, Part 2, 99-100.
56 Bor, 750.
57 Fulke Greville, *Life of Sir Philip Sidney*, Nowell Smith ed., Oxford, 1907, 128 ff; M. W. Wallace, *The Life of Sir Philip Sidney*, Cambridge, 1936, 377 ff.
58 Bor, 751.
59 Brugmans, 246-47; Bor, 753.
60 *MP*, 144-45.
61 Brugmans, 104; Provinciaal Rijksarchief Zeeland, Staten, inv. nr 6.
62 Brugmans, 248. Complete French text: 'Nous avons hier sur le soir receu la lettre, qu'il a pleu à Vostre Exc. nous escrire, et par icelle entendu avecq ung marissement extrême la confirmation du mauvais bruict, qui avoit couru icy du trespas de feu de bonne mémoire le sr. de Sidney, lequel regrettons aultant que chose que nous eult

peu advenir, pour avoir Sa Majesté perdu ung fidel, sage, advisé et trèsvaillant vassal, Vostre Exc. son trèscher nepveu, lequel elle aimoit et duquel elle espéroit choses trèsgrandes, et ces pays ung seigneur et amis personnaige, duquel cognoissans les vertus, experience et trèssinguliere affection, ilz attendoient plus de bien et service; ce que nous avoit esmeuz à requéris Sa Majesté de vouloir envoyer ledict seigneur pardeça et l'employer au gouvernement de la ville de Flissingue, auquel il s'est trèsbien acquité avecq grand contentement d'un chascun et de toute la bourgeoisie; combien qu'il méritoit et estoit digne de plus grande charge et honneur, ayant si valeureusement monstré son bon coeur au rencontre des ennemis devant Zutphen, auquel ce désastre luy est advenu, dont il luy en demeurera une mémoire et gloire éternelle'.

63  CSPFor, XXI, Part. 2, 162.

SANDER BOS, MARIANNE LANGE-MEYERS, JEANINE SIX

# SIDNEY'S FUNERAL PORTRAYED

i

Although we are now commemorating the fourth centennial of Sidney's death, we are, even at this far remove, still able to gain a vivid sense of the elevated scene through engravings and records which have come down to us and for which we are, in chief, indebted to the efforts of three men: Thomas Lant, Richard Lea, and John Stow.

Lant's[1] rendering of the funeral proceedings, known as *The Funeral Procession of Sir Philip Sidney* or, more concisely, as *Lant's Roll*,[2] is the most familiar of the three, and would almost seem entitled to this fame by virtue of its size alone. The series of engravings which constitutes *Lant's Roll* comes to a total length of ten metres, and it is space well-used. Detailed pictorial illustration is supplemented by letterpress text which provides the names of many of those attending and their rank or function, thus enabling us to achieve a fairly precise conception of the internal structure and over-all appearance of Sidney's funeral cortège.

Closely related to Lant's description of Sidney's funeral is that rendered by John Stow in the *Annals or a generall Chronicle of England*.[3] The resemblance between the two is so great, in fact, that we must assume that the writer of the *Annals* actually based his representation of the event on Lant's engravings, leaving out only some minor details.

A rather more intriguing set of similarities and differences is established by comparing Lant's account of the funeral to Lea's.[4] Lea, like Lant present at Sidney's burial, was a member of the Herald's College or College of Arms, and his presence should be seen in the light of his capacity as assistant to Robert Cooke, Clarencieux King of Arms, whose duty it was to arrange and marshal the funerals of all baronets, knights, and esquires south of the Trent. Lea's list, drawn up for the College of Arms, corresponds in many respects with Lant's account, but Lea is even more precise in his description of the front ranks of the procession.[5] He names more of those present and includes two groups of which Lant makes no mention: the two conductors and the gentlemen of the Inns of Court. Yet, in spite of this preliminary precision, Lea's description of the latter part of the procession becomes rather vague. He leaves out names or whole groups of those attending, the most striking omission being that of Sidney's noble relatives Leicester, North, Pembroke, Essex, and Hun-

tingdon. From other sources we know that Leicester was definitely present at Sidney's funeral,[6] and there is every reason to assume that
Pembroke, North, Essex, and Huntingdon were too; none of them was
abroad and, after all, there was a family tie. Lea's omission is all the
more surprising when we realize that they are also included by Stow. If
these people appear in Lant's engravings and are important enough for
Stow to single them out, why does Lea ignore them? Bearing in mind
Lea's position as assistant to the chief dignitary in charge of arranging
funeral, the most plausible explanation might well be that Lea's list was
intended only as a draft, as a list of people who were expected to be present. This would account for most differences between Lant's and Lea's
versions. Some groups listed by Lea, like 'the Arts' and the gentlemen
of the Inns of Court, were not represented in *Lant's Roll*, and it may be
that although they had been counted on they were simply absent. Conversely, other groups not listed by Lea might have turned up at the last
minute.[7] This could certainly have been the case with the Dutch
delegates present at the funeral who had received their invitations only
a few days before the event.[8] The omission of the names of Sidney's
relatives and friends can be as easily accounted for. Thus, if we regard
Lea's list as only a first draft, we can imagine how difficult it would have
been to anticipate whether or not people like Walsingham would risk ap-
pearing at the funeral. Only a week had passed since Mary, Queen of
Scots, had been beheaded and the atmosphere was so tense that Walsingham, who was already avoiding the Court, might well have had to
refrain from going to his son-in-law's funeral as well.

If we base ourselves on these hypotheses, *Lant's Roll* would seem to be
the most reliable record of the funeral proceedings. Add to that the fact
that this impressive and, for England, unique series of engravings contributed greatly to the mythicizing of Sidney, and the urgency of a more
detailed discussion becomes clear.

ii

Thomas Lant (c.1554-1600), the creator of *Lant's Roll*, joined the Sidney
household in c.1582 and accompanied Sidney to the Low Countries in
1585.[9] In the Lant-engravings he refers to himself as a 'gentleman-
servant' of Sidney's, which implies that he must have been one of the
more important members of the household staff, and his position was ensured after Sidney's death through his being taken on by Walsingham.[10]
The latter intervened along with Leicester, to bring about Lant's appointment as Portcullis Pursuivant in the College of Arms in 1588, which
was followed by promotion to Windsor Herald in 1597. It is especially
interesting to know something of Lant's whereabouts and occupations

A later engraving, plate 1 (British Library)

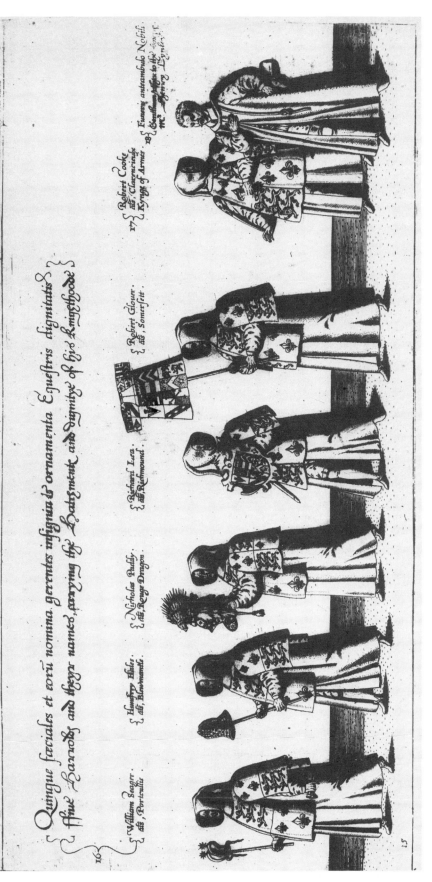

during this time for the light which it throws on our present concern, his series of engravings. As the latter are dated 1587-1588, the period in which they were created coincides with that in which Lant was a member of the Walsingham household, and it would seem far from improbable that the latter would have taken special interest in Lant's work.

Walsingham may have played a yet more important part with respect to *Lant's Roll* in bringing together its designer and the engraver of the series, Theodoor de Brij.[11] De Brij, also known for a large number of engravings grouped under the French heading *Grandes et Petites Voyages*,[12] must have been the engraver of *Lant's Roll* as he is designated as such on the second plate of the work. Born in the Low Countries and working in the German provinces, De Brij made his first trip to London in 1586, where he became acquainted with Thomas White and other members of Sir Walter Raleigh's circle. Sidney, many of his family, and a number of friends such as Sir Christopher Hatton also frequented this group, and it must have been through these channels that De Brij first met with the person or persons who commissioned the series. A second visit to London took place in 1588, during which his work on the Lant-engravings was completed.[13]

Though the engravings are of high quality, it cannot be denied that from a stylistic point of view the series seems somewhat passé when compared with the work of such contemporaries as Goltzius or other Dutch mannerists. The ornamental elements which De Brij used in the borders of the cartouches were no longer current, and notwithstanding his attempt to enliven the engravings through variations in his characters' poses and dress, *Lant's Roll* lacks that element of dashing vitality conveyed by Goltzius' figures. In many ways, De Brij's work is still a part of the early- and mid-century tradition,[14] which would have appealed to the English taste.

*Lant's Roll* totals thirty plates, numbered one to twenty-nine with an unnumbered plate closing the series.[15] Colvin tells us that it was customary to mount such sequential series of engravings on calico in imitation of a frieze,[16] and the Lant engravings were printed in a manner that would easily have allowed consecutive prints to be joined into a frieze-like representation. That this was, in fact, done is illustrated by Aubrey's following anecdote:

> When I was a boy 9 yeares old, I was with my father at one Mr. Singleton's an Alderman & Wollen Draper in Glocester, who had in his parlour over the Chimney, the whole description of the Funerall engraved and printed on papers pasted together, which at length was, I beleeve, the length of the room at least; but he had contrived it to be turned upon two Pinnes, that turning one of them made the figures march all in order...[17]

The subject of the first engraving is the conveyance of Sidney's body from Flushing to London with, above this initial scene, the portrait of Thomas Lant himself. The second offers a view of the interior of St. Paul's Cathedral with the catafalque, and in addition we find here, as well as on the first and last prints of the *Roll*, those famous cartouches with the English and Latin texts which have, since their creation, been so often quoted and given rise to so much speculation.

Next to the text on the second print the first members of the actual funeral cortège are depicted. Twenty-seven numbered groups follow, with the bier and those encircling the coffin at their centre.[18] The procession travels across an imaginary stage with only the low horizon as a backdrop; the attention is focused on the sequence and dress of the consecutive groups, both of which were prescribed by so-called 'orderings'. Even if we were to lack the textual information on the engravings, a knowledge of these 'orderings' would enable us to determine the function and rank of the majority of those presented.[19]

The procession is headed by thirty-two of the poor, a number equalling the year of his life in which Sidney died. Then come the soldiers and following them, preceded by the family colours, the members of the Sidney household, Thomas Lant included. Next appear Sidney's friends in their order of importance; as far as can be established, all have ties with either the Sidney, Walsingham, Dudley, or Devereux families. Behind the ceremonial part of the procession, consisting of two horses[20] symbolizing the deceased's valour, and members of the College of Arms carrying the attributes of knighthood,[21] follows the bier. It is carried by four close friends: Thomas Dudley, Edward Dyer, Fulke Greville, and Edmund Wotton; the four bannerol-carrying relatives also included in this central group are Edmund Packenham, Henry Sidney, William Sidney, and Edmund Walsingham, Sir Francis' second cousin. Behind the bier group we find the chief mourner, Sir Robert Sidney, and his six assistant mourners. The accompanying text informs us that these are members of the family, though the nature of Sir Henry Goodyear's connection with the Sidneys remains unknown.[22] The high nobility follows on horseback: the Earls of Leicester and Huntingdon (uncles of Sidney), the Earl of Pembroke (a brother-in-law), the Earl of Essex (Leicester's stepson), Lord Willoughby (one of Sidney's comrades-in-arms) and Lord North, who was married to Leicester's former sister-in-law. Behind them come the deputies of the Dutch States-General in the company of Daniel de Burggrave, one of Leicester's Dutch secretaries,[23] and they, in turn, are followed by the Lord Mayor, Aldermen, and Sheriffs of the City of London. The procession is closed by the 'Company of Grocers' and the London Civic Guard.

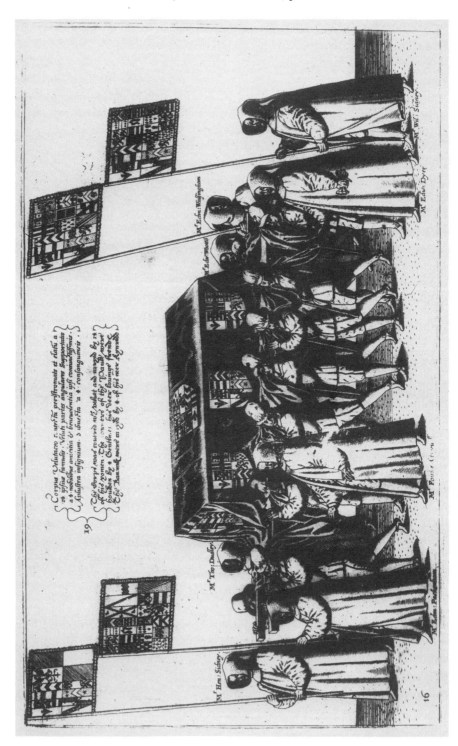

Comites & Barones e confanguinitate & Amicis.
Earles and Barons of his Kindred and Frendes.

23

Comes Huntingdoniæ.
Comes Leicestriæ.

Comes Pembrochiæ
Comes Essexiæ.

Baro: de Willowby:
Baro: de North.

81

7. Lant engraving, plate 18. (British Library)

iii

Little has, as yet, been written on those groups of engravings which have funeral processions as their subjects. Although Walpole in his *Anecdotes of Painting* noted that the Lant-engravings were the first of a long row of similar funeral series in England,[24] the validity of his statement seems doubtful. On consulting surveys of English engraving such as those of Colvin and Hind, we find that not a single example of any other self-contained series of engravings on this topic can be given for the period 1550-1700.[25] Drugulin's survey, which has more of a continental focus, is, for England, only able to point to the depiction of the burial of George Monck, Duke of Albemarle, which took place on 30 April 1670.[26] This does not concern a series of engravings, however, but refers only to a solitary print accompanied by three pages of descriptive and explanatory text.

Yet, although English contributions to this genre would seem to have been extremely few, the British Museum does possess a series of drawings, now bound into a book, which depicts such a funeral cortège.[27] It is by no means unlikely that Lant's original sketches would have borne considerable resemblance to the British Museum drawings, done by various officers of the College of Arms. However, even if some claim could be made to a certain amount of continuity in the presentation of such topics in drawings, as to engravings *Lant's Roll* is, in its English context, virtually unique.

It is important to distinguish between England and the continent here, as engraved reproductions of funeral processions were much more common in the Low Countries and the (northern) German provinces.[28] Between 1550 and 1800 forty-three such series were produced in the Dutch provinces alone, all falling into one of two main categories:[29]

a. the cortège is portrayed in a winding, ribbon-like movement or in a series of layered rows usually confined to one print, but sometimes spread over several which must then be seen in succession;

b. the procession is depicted in a frieze-like fashion over several, sequential prints.

The earliest known Dutch example of this genre reflects the ceremonies accompanying the interment of the Catholic king, Ferdinand of Aragon, at Brussels in 1519.[30] A second, much more important, series depicts the funeral ceremonies held for Charles V, again at Brussels, in 1558, while the third sixteenth-century example is Goltzius' representation of William the Silent's funeral, which took place in Delft in 1584.[31] There is also an illustration of the latter event by Hogenberg, which can be found in Baudartius' *Polemographia auriaco-belgica*.[32]

Of these three series of engravings, both the second and third are of the frieze-type. In general, these are far scarcer than the ribbon-type; of the approximately forty referred to earlier, only twelve belong to the 'frieze' category. Some explanation for this may be found in positing a relationship between form and subject matter: whereas the ribbon-like depictions are also used to render the processions of non-royal personages, the frieze-like depictions, to which group Lant's Roll also belongs, seem to be reserved only for the funeral processions of royalty. The one continental exception to this is in the portrayal of the funeral train attending Walraven van Brederode, a high-ranking Dutch nobleman, in 1613.[33]

Whether in the Low Countries or in England, Lant must have seen the Goltzius engravings made to commemorate that most important occasion of William the Silent's burial.[34] On comparing their respective works, while not ignoring stylistic differences, we find a number of striking resemblances:

a. both Goltzius' and Lant's series are of the 'frieze' type;

b. the Orange-engravings open with a view of the interior of the New Church (Nieuwe Kerk), complete with catafalque, a scene to which there is an undeniable correspondence in the second plate of the Sidney-sequence which shows the interior of St. Paul's;

c. the general lay-out of the Orange-series with its focus on the central part of the funeral cortège with the bier and its entourage is reflected in Lant's Roll.[35] The exhibition catalogue Festivities calls attention to the extraordinary degree of likeness between the two bier scenes, on the basis of which it points to the date of the Lant-engravings as the 'terminus ante quem' in establishing the date of Goltzius' work.[36]

All things considered, it would seem justifiable to look upon the Goltzius engravings as the direct source of inspiration for Lant's Roll. In any case their degree of affinity can leave little doubt that Lant's Roll should be placed within the context of the existing Dutch or continental tradition, rather than at the beginning of an English one.

iv

Looking at Lant's funeral representation it is impossible not to be impressed both by the ambitious scale of his undertaking and the conveyed splendour of the actual event. In view of this imposing account of the occasion (which affirms, among other things, the presence of the representatives of Holland and Zeeland and the impressive number of noblemen and persons of high rank), it is hardly surprising that the idea that Sidney's funeral was a state funeral has become widespread, the less so

since this view would seem to be corroborated by various passages referring to Sidney's burial. Zouch, in his *Memoirs of the Life and Writings of Sidney*, quotes from a letter of Don Bernardine de Mendoza to Philip of Spain that 'the States of Holland earnestly petitioned to have the honour of burying [Sidney's] body at the national expense',[37] a request which had already been referred to in a 1587 poem by Whetstone,[38] and in Fulke Greville's *The Life of the Renowned Sir Philip Sidney* we read that 'after his death the States of Zealand became suitors to her Majesty, & his noble friends, that they might have the honour of burying his body at the public expence of their Government.[39] That Greville continues with 'which request had it been granted' implies that it was not, but no explanatory note is offered, and no further mention of the subject is known of until Wood's *Athenae Oxonienses* (1691), in which we find that the Dutch request 'was not permitted, the Queen, in Regard to his great Worth and Accomplishments, giving Order for his Burial at her own Expense'.[40] This information was repeated and enlarged upon by Zouch approximately a hundred years later: 'This petition was rejected, the Queen having determined to manifest her veneration for his memory by directing his obsequy at her own cost, and with all the magnificence and solemnities due to a noble soldier'.[41]

To the modern reader, Zouch's and Wood's assertions can only add to the impression that Sidney received what we would now refer to as a state funeral. Yet, in spite of all the seeming evidence, in actual fact there is little to support this view. It is a question of speculation whether anything comparable to state funerals existed in Elizabethan England, but even assuming they did, there are matters which argue against Sidney's being included among them. For a state funeral to be called such it would seem only fair to demand that it fulfil two basic requirements: all costs would have to be met by the state, and there would have to be state representatives present. As to the first, the explanations given by Zouch and Wood would indeed seem to carry the issue, were it not that there is almost irrefutable evidence that Sir Francis Walsingham, Sidney's father-in-law, personally organized and paid for the funeral. Lant says that Sidney was 'interred by the appointment of the right honourable Sir Francis Walsingham Knight... Who spared not any coste'.[42] Then, we know there was a letter in which Walsingham asked Leicester to share in the financial burden of the funeral, a burden too high to be borne alone and prompting Walsingham even to approach Burghley, the Lord Treasurer, who promised to commend his suit to the Queen.[43] There is no evidence, however, that Elizabeth made any contribution, and it is unlikely that she did. It is, after all, common knowledge that she found it difficult to part with her money, and that she often forgot even to remunerate living noblemen for their services.[44] As to the supposed offer of the States of Zeeland, we can only say that there is nothing in the official documents of either Zeeland or Holland to support the claim that such an offer to bury Sidney was ever made, nor is there any evidence of money ever having been made available for that purpose.

No more can concrete evidence be put forward to show that our second requirement for a state funeral was met; had any representatives of the state been present Lea and Lant could not have failed to mention them. Leicester, who might have been eligible for such a position, does not occupy the prominent place in the procession which would certainly have been bestowed upon a state dignitary, and there is nothing to indicate that he was attending the funeral in anything other than a private capacity. Leicester was a close relative of Sidney's and it is among that group that he is listed, and then by Lant only.

Equally absent are high-ranking members of the clergy or delegates from foreign countries, with the exception of the Dutch delegates already mentioned. The latter are constantly referred to in their official capacities of 'the Stattes of Holland and Zeeland' by Lea and 'the States of Holland' by Lant, but there is no real proof that they were official emissaries to Sidney's funeral.[45] All that can be found in the Resolutions of the States-General of Holland and in the Resolutions of the States of Holland or Zeeland is that these gentlemen were in London to negotiate with Elizabeth about increased assistance in the Dutch war against Spain. Their presence at the funeral, requested by Walsingham not the Queen, may, ultimately, not have been much more than incidental.

Lastly, it should perhaps be mentioned that although Sidney's funeral was held under the auspices of the College of Arms this in no way implies that the burial was a state affair, since it was customary for the College to supervise the funerals of all members of armorial families in England.[46]

v

Having been at some pains to show that Sidney most probably was not given a state funeral, we must now hasten to add that his burial most probably was an affair of great political importance. Central to this aspect would have been the war being fought by the Dutch against the Spanish king and, more particularly, against Catholicism. Leicester had left for the Low Countries at the end of 1585 in command of the 6000 troops which Elizabeth had finally sent to assist the Dutch in their revolt against Spain, taking Sidney with him as his adviser and second-in-command. Though Leicester was ensured of support from Walsingham, the Queen was extremely reluctant to commit herself to any degree, an observation confirmed by what, in the eyes of the war party, could only be called the disappointing outcome of her talks with the Dutch delegates held at the very time of Sidney's burial.[47] It would not be so strange, then, to suppose that Sidney's funeral may not have been entirely free of propagandistic purposes. Those in Leicester's circle would certainly have been impressed with the necessity of ensuring Elizabeth's continued, and preferably increased, support for the Dutch cause, and they were surely conscious of the fact that the death of the popular Sidney and the magnificent funeral ensuing could only serve to focus attention on the cause for which he had given his life, and add weight to their plea.

Any way we look at it, the funeral, in its grandeur, would seem to have been raised from a private to a national affair. Walsingham had spent enough time abroad to be familiar with continental customs surrounding funerals on a grand scale, and if we credit him with organizing Sidney's funeral, we must acknowledge that he was not slow to put into practice what he had observed. The records of the ceremony point to many distinguishing characteristics, not the least of which is that, in spite of his being only a knight, Sidney was buried with all the pomp customarily reserved for a baron.[48] It is true that the French king had raised Sidney to a baron in 1572 and that the Dutch often called him 'Baron Sidney', but this title was never bestowed upon him in England. Yet, there were seven 'mourners' at the Sidney funeral, the number prescribed for baronial processions, instead of the 'knightly' five, and *Lant's Roll* clearly indicates that the Great Banner was carried, though normally the honour of carrying a banner was reserved for the rank of 'knight banneret' upwards.[49]

Those attending the funeral also serve to strengthen our impression of a unique occurrence. Foremost among those who catch the attention are the noblemen. Though, as has been pointed out, they were either friends or family of Sidney's, they lend the whole a dignified stateliness. The attendance of the Dutch officials, too, adds to the aura of importance surrounding the funeral, while simultaneously calling to mind the special tie between Sidney and the Dutch Provinces.

A notable, if not less surprising, group is formed also by the representatives from London: its municipality, the 'Company of Grocers', and the Civic Guard. The Lord Mayor and Aldermen are present in full official splendour though it is not completely clear why they should have joined in Sidney's funeral procession, and the mystery surrounding their presence clings to that of the other Londoners as well. The interest shown by the 'Company of Grocers' in paying their last respects to

Sidney can only be reasonably explained if we assume that he had been a member of the guild. It is known that guild members were bound to attend the funeral of a fellow member in their 'livery', and *Lant's Roll* refers to 'the Company of grocers of which [Sidney] was free', though, again, no proof has ever been found in guild records to support this hypothetical membership.[50]

A final interesting group is that composed of the cavalry and infantry. The presence of these soldiers, representatives of the troops over whom Sidney had held command on the continent, could hint at the funeral's having been accompanied by military honours.[51] The information that 'some of her Mai[es] Gaard' formed a guard of honour at 'the great west doore of St. Paules, where [the] mourners entered' would serve to support this view.[52]

Perhaps the most convincing evidence that Sir Philip Sidney's funeral was regarded as a unique event is, finally, to be found in the very creation of that work which records it: *Lant's Roll*. No such series of engravings depicting a funeral procession had ever been made in England, and aside from that, the scope of the work would, in itself, give *Lant's Roll* a claim to distinction. When we remember that on the continent a work of such size, type, and splendour would only have been executed in commemoration of royalty, it is not hard to see how *Lant's Roll*, the impressive record of a most impressive occasion, contributed toward 'the creation of a legend'.

APPENDIX 1
A comparison of the texts of Lant and Lea.

| | LANT | LEA (as in: *Notes and Queries*, CLXXX (1935), see above n. 4) |
|---|---|---|
| pl. 1 | *Brief biography; see app. II* | The account starts with the funeral. |
| pl. 2 | The Hearse | Two Conducters  John Davies |
| | *a cartouche with inscription* | John Cuffe |
| | *in Latin and English; see app. II* | Gentlemen of the Ines of Court |
| | Two Conductors to the Poore | Two Conducters  Tho. Pecoke |
| | | Thomas Purvey |
| pl. 3 | here followed so many poore men as he was years oulde, viz. 32 | Poure men xxxij |
| pl. 4 | These represent the officers of his foote in the lowe Countreys | Two seriauntes of the footemen |
| | | John Thomas |
| | Two sergents of the band | Hughe Powder |
| | Two ffyffs and two Drommes playing softly | Dromes and fyffes 4 |
| pl. 5 | Ensigne trayled by Hen: Whitten Gent. | Thensigne berrer Henry Whitton |
| | Lieutenant of foote Tho: Shotboult Gent. | The Leivetennaunt of the footeman Mr Shortbolt |

| LANT | LEA (as in: *Notes and Queries*, CLXXX (1935), see above n. 4) |
|---|---|
| Officers of his horse | |
| two Corporalis | Two Corporales for the horsmen Allexander Willney Roger Bowes |
| Trompetts | Trompettes 4 |
| Guidon trayled by Will. Boulstred Gent. | The Guydon        Will' Bulstrode |
| pl. 6 Lieutenant of hys Horse: Edw: Cryppe Gent. | The Lyvetenant of the horsmen Mr Crispe |
| Conductors to his servannts | Two yeomen Conductors Robert Snowe Tho. Jenkynson |
| The Standard caryed by Rich: Gwyn Gent. | The standrd Mr Rych Gwyne |
| pl. 7 His gentlemen and yemen servannts | S<sup>r</sup>vauntes to the defunct in Longe bl. |
| pl. 8 to the number of 60 | Clokes |
| pl. 9 Dor: James, Phisition | The Phizicio' Docter James |
| Will. Kelle, Chirurgion | The Chyrgeon Wyllm Kelley |
| Gryffin Maddox Gent. Steward of his house | The Steward Griffith Madocke |
| pl. 10 Esquiers of his kindred and | Then Esquiers in gownes |
| pl. 11 frends to the number of 60 | |
| pl. 12 Knights of his kyndred and frends in number 12 | Then Knyghtes in gownes |
| Sr George Farmer | |
| Sr George Bowser | |
| Sr Wil: Hatton | |
| Sr Hen: Unton | |
| Sr Wil. Knowles | |
| Sr Tho: Wingfield | |
| pl. 13 Knights of his kyndred and frends | |
| Sr Rob: Staplton | |
| Sr Edw: Waterhouse | |
| Sr Th: Parrot | |
| Sr Frances Drake | |
| Sr Valentine Browne | |
| Sr Wil: Harbert | |
| The Preacher & Chapleines | Two Chapleyns Mr Payne Mr Strylle      ? |
| The Penon of his Armes caryed by James Skidmore Gent. | The pennon of armes James Skydmore |
| The horse for the field (with imbrodred furniture) was led by a footman, a Page rydinge, treyling a broken lance, Henry Davers | The horse for the feld Henruye Danveres |
| pl. 14 The Barbed horse (whose Caparazin was clothe of goulde) was ledd by a footman, a page rydinge carying a Batlax the head downwarde, Daniell Batchiler | The barbd horse Danyell Bacheler |

| LANT | LEA (as in: *Notes and Queries*, CLXXX (1935), see above n. 4) |
|---|---|

| | |
|---|---|
| Yoman Ushers to the harrolds | two yeomen ushers Wyll Joanes |
| | Robt Joanes |
| The great Baner caryed by | The great Banner Captayne Whytt |
| Hen: Whyte Gent. | |

pl. 15

| | |
|---|---|
| ffive Harrolds and theyr names, carying the Hatchments and dignitye of his knighthoode, | |
| William Seager, alias Portcullis | The spurres Portculleys |
| Humfrey Hales, alias Blewmantle | The gauntletes Blewmantell |
| Nicholas Paddy, alias Rouge | The healme and |
| Dragon | Creast Rouge Dragone |
| Richard Lea, alias Richmund | The Sworde and |
| | Targe Rychmonde |
| Robert Glover, alias Somersett | The Cotte of Arms Somersett |
| Robert Cooke, alias Clarencieux | Clarencieux |
| Kynge of Armes | |
| Gentleman Usher to the Corps | Lynley the usher |
| Mr Henry Lynley | |

pl. 16

| | |
|---|---|
| The corps was covered with velvet and caryed by 14 of his yomen. The corners of the Paule were houlden by 4 Gent. his deer lovinge frends. | The Corpes. The 4 assistants: |
| | Mr Thomas Dudley |
| | Mr Fulke Grevell |
| | Mr Edw. Wotton |
| | Mr Edw. Dyer |
| The Banrols were caryed by 4 of his neer kynredd. | The 4 Banerrolles: |
| Mr Hen: Sidney | Mr Henrye Sydney |
| Mr Tho: Dudley | Mr Pagenham |
| Mr Edw: Wootto | Mr Wyllm Sydney |
| Mr Edm: Walsingham | Mr Walsingham |
| Mr Edm: Packenham | |
| Mr Foulke Gryuell | |
| Mr Ed: Dyer | |
| Mr Wil: Sidney | |

pl. 17

| | |
|---|---|
| These mourners assistants were fower knights of his kinred, and two gentlmen, the one his kinsman the other his younger brother, | |
| Sir Rob. Sidney, Chief mourner | Chyfe morner Sir Robt Sydney |
| | The other 6 morners: |
| Mr Tho: West | Mr Tho. West |
| Sir Wil: Fitzwilliams | Mr Wyllm Fitzwyllmes |
| Sir Tho: Harrington | Sir Johne Harryngton |
| Sir Hen: Harrington | Sr Henrye Harrington |
| Sir Hen: Goodyear | Sr Henrye Goodere |
| Mr. Tho: Sidney | Mr Tho. Sydney |
| Gent Ushers to the | Two Gentilmen Ushers |
| to the Noblmen | Thartes |

| LANT | LEA (as in: *Notes and Queries*, CLXXX (1935), see above n. 4) |
|---|---|
| | |

pl. 18  Earles and Barons of his
        kindred and frendes,
        Comes Huntingdoniae
        Comes Leicestriae
        Comes Penbrochiae
        Comes Essexiae
        Baro: de Willowby                The Lordes Wyllughbye
        Baro: de North

pl. 19  The States of Holland wch     The Stattes of Holland and Zeland
        were then in England
        Mr Menyn
        Mr Valke
        Mr Neuelt
        Doctour Sylla
        Mr Caminga
        Mr Ortell
        Mr Burgrave

pl. 20  The Lord Mayor, Aldermen,
        Recorder, and Shirifs of
        the Citye of London, riding
        in Purple,
        Sword Bearer                  The Sworde berrer
        Sr Geo: Barnes Lo: Maior    The Lord maiore

pl. 21  Aldermen Knights
pl. 22  Other Aldermen            The aldermen

pl. 23  Other Cittizins called the     The Companye of groscers
        Company of Grocers in theyr
        livery to the number of 120

pl. 24  Cyttizins of London practised
        in Armes about 300 who
        marched by 3 and 3 in mannor
        as followed viz In the
        foreward the Capt,
        lieutenant and three Targiters.
        Muskiters 4 rancks
        drums and ffyfe
        small shott 20 rancks       The Shotte
        Pykes 20 rancks            The pykes
        Halberts 4 rancks
        Chief officers of the field
        Drumes, ffyfe and Ensigne
        In the rereward,
        Halberts 3 rancks
        Pykes 15: ran:
        Drums and ffyfe
        Small shott 15 ran:
        and Muskiters 3 rancks
        The Capts boy

LANT

LEA (as in: *Notes and Queries*, CLXXX (1935), see above n. 4)

Capitaneus, Mr Tho: Smyth.
Locumtenens, Mr Allin Lewis
Scutati, Targiters.

pl. 25   Muskaters. Drumes and ffyffe.
pl. 26   hargebusires.
pl. 27   Pyke trayling.
pl. 28   Halberdires
pl. 29   Drumes and ffyfe. Ensigne.
pl. 30   Three Sergeants of the bande
*on the left, and on the right a Cartouche*
*with an inscription; see App. II*

List of names:

| | |
|---|---|
| Davye floyd | Johne Alex |
| Allexander Wyllmes | Roger Bowes |
| Edw. Grifftyhe | Henrye Marshe |
| Charles Cooke | Johne Roper |
| Tho: Tryll | Henrye Pettingall |
| Tho: Lant | Wyllm Page |
| Gorge Faice | Johne Evans |
| Mr Arckenwell | Mr Croche |
| Mr Dyckensone | oulde Mr Britton |
| Mr Desecourte | Mr Parry |
| Mr Watsone | Mr Cox |
| Mr Gibbes | Mr Strange |
| Mr Cleyton | Mr Bacon |
| Mr Mollyners | Mr Fraunce |
| Mr Pratt | Mr Probye |
| Mr Mollyners | Mr Turner |
| Mr Wroughton | Mr Wrothe |
| Mr Temple | Mr Uvedall |
| Mr Whytton | Mr Langesford |
| The Chergion and physicion | |
| | The steward |
| | Mr Mackered |

Mr Mantell
Mr Blunt
Mr Huninges[?]
Mr James Wrought
Mr Tho. Jobsone
Mr Edw. Hungate
Mr Edw. Jobsone
Mr Jaques Wynckfield
Mr Covert
Mr fitz Wyllmes
Mr morrysone
Sr Johne Wyngfeld
Sr Wyll Hatton
Sr Henrye Umpton
Sr Thomas Perrott
Sr Wyllm Poudrelles

| LANT | LEA (as in: *Notes and Queries,* CLXXX (1935), see above n. 4) |
|---|---|

*Endorsed* The prosedenge and Charge of the funerall of the right noble knight Sr Phyllipe Sydney at powles the daye before mensconed.

## APPENDIX 2

*The Lant-engraving: texts*

The Lant-engraving also has three longer texts explaining the plates. These texts are written in both Latin and English. The English texts read as follows:

*Plate 1*
The most honorable and thrice renowned Knight Sir Phillip Sydney (of whose singuler vertue and witt all ages will speak) being sente by hir Majesti into the lowe countries, was made Lord Governour of Vlishing he arived there the 18. of November 1585 wher he was most honorablye receaved. He was Colonell of all the Dutche regiments in Zealande and Capitayne of 200 foote & 100 horse Englishe. In ffebruary he attempted the surprising of Steenbergen in Brabant, wherin he had prevailed but for a suddeyne thawe. In Julye following 1586 throughe his wisdome and pollicie a Towne in fflanders called Axell was won. In September at the relieving of Zutphen he charged the enemye thrice in one skirmish, and in the last charge he was wounded with a muskett shott, whereoff he died at Arnhame the 17 of October, from whence he was broughte by water to Vlishing, where he was kept eighte dayes for his convenient passage. On the 1 of November 1586 he was broughte from his house in Vlishing to the Sea syde by the English Garnison which were 1200 marching by three the shott hanging downe their peeces, the Halberts, Pykes and Ensignes trayling along the grounde, drums and ffyfes playing very softely; The Bodye was couerde with a Paule of velvet; the Burgers of the towne followed mourning, and so soone as he was imbarcked, the small shott gave him a triple volley, then all the greate Ordynance about the walles were discharged twise, and so tooke their leave of their welbeloved Governoure. Ffrom thence he was transported in a Pynnis of his owne which is here portrayde, all her sayles, tacklinge and other furniture were coulored black and black Clothe hanged rounde aboute her with Escouchions of his Armes, and was accompanyed withe dyvers other shippe. He was lande at Tower Hill, Londen the 5 of the foresaide moneth and caried to the Minorites, where he was kepte until the 16. of ffebruary following on which daye he was solempnelye caried thorowe London to St Paules churche (which is expressed in the next leafe, with the Modell of the Hearse) and there interred. The church was hanged about with black clothe, the hearse was covered with velvett and most beautifully adorned with Escouchions of his Armes. The picture which you see here expressed is the true counterfayt of T.L. who was the Author and inventor of this woorke.

*Plate 2*
Here followeth the manner of the whole proceeding of his ffunerall which was celebrated in St Paules on the 16 of ffebruary 1586 with the self same state and order as the Mourners were marshalled by Robert Cooke alias Clarencieulx Kinge of Armes; withe the diversitye of eache man's apparell and action after their severall degrees. And to sollempnize the same there followed nexte unto the mourners the Lorde Maior, Aldermen and Sheriffs of the Cittye of London, ryding in purple. After them the Com-

pany of Grocers of which he was free. And lastlye certayne younge men of the Cittye marching by three and three, in blac Cassokins with their Shott, Pikes, Halberds, and Ensigne trayling on the grounde, to the number of 300. Who so soone as hee was interred honored the obsequy withe a double volley. This worke was first drawne and invented by Tho. Lant Gent, servant to the saide Honorable Knight and graven in Copper by Derick Theodor de Brij in the Cittye of London 1587.

*Last plate (not numbered)*
This worthy knight Sir Phillip Sidney, in the cause of his god and true religion, and for the honor of his Prince and countrey, spared not to spende his blud as you have harde. For his will, learninge and knowledge in divers languages he was muche admired, for his courtasie and affability towards all men no less beloved and for all other his singuler parts of bounty, courage and libiraliti (bothe to strangers and his owne countrymen) as greatly honored of all that harde his fame (which was spred about the worlde) as of those that knew him hear at home. And as he thus lived being of all beloved, so moste honorably he dyed and lamentably interred by appointment of the right honorable Sir Francis Walsingham knight, principall Secretary, and one of her Maiesties most honorable previe Councell (his father in lawe) who spared not any coste to have this funerall well performed. He was caried from the Minorites (which is without Aldgate) along the cheefe streets of the Cytye unto the Cathedrall church of St Paules ye which streets all along were so thronged with people, that ye mourners had scarcely rome to pass. the houses likewise weare as full as they might be of which great multitude ther wear few or none that shed not some tears as the corps passed by them. Of the mourners every Gent had a man, every knight 2, some Noblemen 12, some more, some less as also sundry Englishe Captaynes of the low Countrie with divers other Gent. that came voluntary and are not in this woorke expressed, so that the whole number were about 700 persons. The Great west doore of St Paules (where ye mourners entred) was kept by some of her Majesties Gaard, ye Quier and hearse by 2 Harolds of Armes. viz Nico: Dethicke alias Windsor and Edm: Knight alias Chester, who placed ye nobles and others according to their degrees. So when the sermon was ended ye offerringe and other sermons finished and his body interred ye soldiers in ye churchyard did by a double volye give unto his famous life and death a Marcial Vale. 1588 Tho: Lant Inventor.

## NOTES

1  For biographical data, see *DNB*. In some cases additional information will be given.
2  Thomas Lant, *Sequitur & pompa funebris quemadmodū a Clarencio Armorum et Insignium rege institute est, etc.,* London, 1587. The *Lant's Roll* of this article should be distinguished from the armorial book of the same title started by Thomas Lant. This last work was continued until 1660 and is kept by the College of Arms. Several copies of the *Lant-engraving* are known. See A. M. Hind, *Engraving in England in the Sixteenth and Seventeenth Centuries: A Descriptive Catalogue with Introductions*, I, Cambridge, 1952, 316-17. For a facsimile edition of *Lant's Roll* we refer to A. J. Colaianne and W. L. Godshalk eds, *Elegies for Sir Philip Sidney (1587)*, New York, 1980.
3  John Stow, *Annales or a General Chronicle of England. Continued and Augmented with Matters Foraigne and Domestique, Ancient and Moderne unto the End of the Present Yeare 1631*, London, 1631, 739-40.
4  British Library, MS Ashm. 818, 9, ff. 40-41. Published by B. H. Newdigate, 'Mourners at Sir Philip Sidney's funeral', *Notes and Queries*, CLXXX (1935), 398-401, 444-45 and 463-64.
5  See App. 1.
6  Gemeente Archief Arnhem, inv. nr OA 5515.
7  This might explain why the friends wore two different kinds of mourning clothes. All mourning clothes were supplied by the estate of the deceased. The gowns had to fit

and had to be custom made; the capes had a looser fit and could be made in advance, so they were better suited for last minute guests. On mourning clothes, see Phillis Cunnington and Catherine Lucas, *Costumes for Births, Marriages & Deaths*, London, 1972.

8 See n. 6.

9 *DNB*, XXXII, 139-40; U. Thieme and F. Becker, *Allgemeines Lexicon der bildenden Künstler von der Antike bis zur Gegenwart*, XXII, Leipzig, n.d., 360; Horace Walpole, *Anecdotes of Painting with some Account of the Principal Artists*, I, London, 1888, 192-94; Hind, *Engraving in England*, I, 128.

10 Up to the seventeenth century gentleman-servants formed the upper level of large households, those of the king and the high nobility excepted. See M. Girouard, *Life in the English Country House: A Social and Architectural History*, London, 1980, 27 and 139-40; A. Wagner, *The Heralds of England*, London, 1967, 217.

11 De Brij was born in Liège in 1528 and died in Frankfurt in 1598. Because of his Lutheranism he had to leave the Netherlands either in the period 1557-1560, or around 1570. He then probably settled in Frankfurt. He worked as an engraver, publisher, and goldsmith. In addition to prints with the New World as their subject, a large part of his work consists of portraits and emblematic engravings. Processions are a recurrent theme in his work. For general information on De Brij, see Thieme and Becker, *Allgemeines Lexicon*, V, 162-63; Walpole, *Anecdotes of Painting*, I, 138-39; S. A. Colvin, *Early Engraving and Engravers in England (1545-1695): A Critical and Historical Essay*, London, 1905, 37-41; Hind, *Engraving in England*, I, 124-26.

12 After De Brij's death in 1598 this work was continued by his two sons, Johan Theodoor and Johan Israel, and by his son-in-law Mattheas Merian. The *Grandes et petites voyages*, also known as *Perigrinationes*, appeared in Frankfurt between 1590 and 1634.

13 *Lant-engraving*, plate 2 and the last, unnumbered plate. See also App. 2; Colvin, *Early Engraving*, 6; Walpole, *Anecdotes*, I, 138; Hind, *Engraving in England*, I, 125.

14 See J. G. von Quandt, *Entwurf zu einer Geschichte der Kupferstechkunst*, Leipzig, 1826, 134; G. K. Napler, *Neues Allgemeine Künstler Lexicon*, II, Munich, 1835, 180; J. P. Passavant, *Le peintre-graveur*, I, Leipzig, 1860, 223.

15 Walpole, and others after him, counted 34 plates. He arrived at this figure, because he was not aware of the fact that the series in the possession of the Marquess of Bute included double or even triple plates. Walpole mentions that he has seen this series. See Walpole, *Anecdotes*, I, 192; Hind, *Engraving in England*, I, 132 and 136-37.

16 Colvin, *Early Engraving*, 39.

17 John Aubrey, *Brief Lives*, London, 1975, 280. Also quoted in a letter of R. Brown to his employer, Sir Joseph Banks (1743-1820). This letter is bound with Banks' copy of the *Lant-engraving* which is now in the British Library.

18 For a complete survey, see App. 1.

19 'The ordering of a Funerall for a Noble Person in Hen. 7. time (MS Cott. Julius B. xii. leaf 7, back-leaf 8)', *EETS Extra Ser.*, VIII (1863), 29-31; 'A Funeral in Popish times. (Ashmole MS. 873, art. vi. leaf 133-39. Written in the time of Charles I. or II.)', *EETS Extra Ser.*, VIII (1863), 32-37; John Nichols ed., *Illustrations of the Manners and Expenses of Antient Times in the 15th, 16th, and 17th Centuries*, 1797, 65,76. Cunnington and Lucas describe not only the costumes for funerals but also funeral customs, and quote a great number of orderings, mostly in MSS. In his introductory 'note upon funerals', John Gough Nichols, editor of *The Diary of Henry Machyn, Citizen and Merchant-taylor of London, from A.D. 1550 to A.D. 1563*, Camden Society, London, 1848, xx-xxxii, also quotes some orderings and gives further information on funeral customs.

20 On the custom of leading horses in funeral processions, see Wolfgang Brückner, 'Ross und Reiter in Leichenzeremoniel. Deutungsversuch eines historischen Rechtbrauches', *Rheinisches Jahrbuch für Volkskunde*, XV-XVI (1964-1965), 144-209.

21 The members of the College of Arms carry the Hatchments: spurs, gloves, helmet and crest, targe and sword, and the coat of arms. These, the symbols of knighthood, were left suspended in the church after the funeral.

22  Newdigate, 'Mourners', 399-401. New research did not yield more information.
23  Daniel de Burggrave, named on the engraving as one of the deputies of the United Provinces, came from Ghent. He accompanied Leicester to England in 1586. See A. J. van der Aa, *Biographisch Woordenboek der Nederlanden*, I, Haarlem, 1852, 484; H. Brugmans ed., *Correspondentie van Robert Dudley, Graaf van Leicester*, II, Utrecht, 1931, 178-80, 193-94, 336-37.
24  Walpole, *Anecdotes*, I, 192.
25  Colvin, *Early Engraving*, Appendix I; Hind, *Engraving in England*, I, 125.
26  W. Drugulin, *Historical Atlas*, Leipzig, 1867, 242; 'The solemn interment of George Monk, Duke of Albemarle', *The London Illustrated News*, 13 October 1852, 419-20.
27  British Museum MS. Add. 35324.
28  See F. Muller, *Beredeneerde beschrijving van Nederlandsche historieplaten, zinneprenten en historische kaarten*, Amsterdam, 1970; *Atlas van Stolk*, The Hague, 1895-1902; J. Landwehr, *Splendid Ceremonies: State Entries and Royal Funerals in the Low Countries 1515-1791: A Bibliography*, Leiden, 1975.
29  *Atlas van Stolk*, I-VI. Pictures of funeral processions of members of the Orange family are also to be found in A. Montanus, *'t Leven en bedrijf der Princen van Oranje*, Amsterdam, 1664.
30  Ferdinand of Aragon's funeral did not actually take place in Brussels. The ceremonies depicted were meant as a tribute to the deceased. Muller, *Beredeneerde beschrijving*, I, 356A; Landwehr, *Splendid Ceremonies*, 1.
31  The funeral of Charles V was held in the same way as that of his grandfather, Ferdinand of Aragon (see above n. 29). Muller, *Beredeneerde beschrijving*, I, 412, 412A; *Atlas van Stolk*, I, 265; Landwehr, *Splendid Ceremonies*, 27. For Goltzius' engraving of William of Orange's funeral, see Muller, *Beredeneerde beschrijving*, III, S894; *Atlas van Stolk*, I, 821; Landwehr, *Splendid Ceremonies*, 27.
32  *Atlas van Stolk*, I, 267, 822, 823; Muller, *Beredeneerde beschrijving*, I, 895. The complete title of Baudartius' work is *Polemographia auriaco-belgica. Scriptore Wilhelmo Baudartio*, Amsterdam, 1622.
33  Muller, *Beredeneerde beschrijving*, I, 1305. These prints were re-used in 1623 for the series of the funeral procession of Count Johan Albrecht of Solms. See Muller, *Beredeneerde beschrijving*, I, 1499A.
34  See O. Hirschmann, *Hendrick Goltzius*, Leipzig, 1919, 44-46; O. Hirschmann, *Verzeichnis des Graphischen Werkes von Hendrick Goltzius*, Brunswick, 1976, 265-67, W. Strauss, *Hendrik Goltzius: the Complete Engravings and Woodcuts*, New York, 1977, 192-203; *Festivities: Ceremonies and Celebrations in Western Europe 1500-1790*, Exhibition catalogue, Department of Art, Bell Gallery, List Art Building, Brown University, Providence (R.I.), 2-25 March 1979.
35  Goltzius depicted only part of the procession of William of Orange's funeral. This part is comparable to plates 13-19 of the *Lant-engraving*.
36  *Festivities*, Brown University, 101-02.
37  T. Zouch, *Memoirs of the Life and Writings of Sir Philip Sidney*, York, 1808, 284.
38  G. Whetstone, *Sir Philip Sidney, his Honorable Life, his Valiant Death, and True Vertues*, London, 1587; repr. as *Frondes Caducae*. A. Boswell ed., n.p., 1816, I.
39  Fulke Greville, *The Life of the Renowned Sir Philip Sidney*, London, 1652; repr. Nowell Smith, Oxford, 1907, 144.
40  A. Wood, *Athenae Oxonienses*, London, 1691, I, 184.
41  T. Zouch, *Memoirs*, 285.
42  *Lant-engraving*, pl. 30. See also App. 2.
43  C. Read, *Mr Secretary Walsingham and the Policy of Queen Elizabeth*, III, Oxford, 1925, 167-70.
44  Mona Wilson, *Sir Philip Sidney*, London, 1931, 64-68. *DNB*: Lord Willoughby de Eresby. Read, *Walsingham*, III, 173, 418-20, 424-25.
45  *Lant-engraving*, pl. 19, and App. 1; Newdigate, 'Mourners', 399; n. 8 above.
46  Wagner, *Heralds of England*, 217.
47  Brugmans ed., *Correspondentie van Robert Dudley*, passim.

48 Wagner, *Heralds of England, passim.*
49 For a description of the different 'flags' and their uses, see *The Diary of Henry Machyn*, xxvi-xxviii. The number of mourners was prescribed in the orderings.
50 *Lant-engraving*, last plate; App. 2.
51 The only other instance we have found of troops attending a funeral is the funeral of Sir Peter Carew who also died on the battlefield. See 'The Lyffe of Sir Peter Carewe', *Archaeologia*, XXVIII (1840), 144-45.
52 *Lant-engraving*, last plate; App. 2.

JOHN GOUWS

# FACT AND ANECDOTE IN FULKE GREVILLE'S ACCOUNT OF SIDNEY'S LAST DAYS

There are two frequently recounted anecdotes concerning Sidney: the one is of his quarrel in the tennis-court with a noble courtier (the Earl of Oxford), the other of his magnanimity on the battlefield of Zutphen when, after having been mortally wounded, and being thirsty as a consequence of losing blood, he handed the water he had called for to a dying common soldier with the words 'thy necessity is yet greater than mine'.[1] The source for both these anecdotes is Fulke Greville, and it would appear that they did not achieve general circulation until the publication, in 1652, of a volume entitled *The Life of the Renowned Sir Philip Sidney*.[2] As Sidney's friend, Greville could possibly have been a witness to the famous quarrel, and there is corroborating evidence that some kind of confrontation did take place.[3] The second story is another matter. None of the eyewitnesses refers to it, while Greville himself could not have been a witness, since he had been prevented from leaving England by express command of the Queen.[4] In addition, the anecdote bears some resemblance to a passage in Plutarch's *Life of Alexander*.[5] Under these circumstances one might be tempted to consider Greville guilty of fabulation.

Although the work containing these narratives is commonly known as the 'life' of Sidney, strictly speaking it is not a biography. The selection and presentation of the material relating to Sidney may have been influenced by the Christian hagiographic or the classical encomiastic traditions of biographical writing, but the overall strategy of the work is that of a dedication of a series of works concerned with the roles of subjects and sovereigns.[6] As such, the dedicatee (Sidney) is presented as the ideal, though perhaps somewhat neglected, subject of an unquestionably great monarch (Elizabeth I). This scheme by itself would not compel Greville to manipulate his material in any untoward way, but when the subject matter excites his anti-Catholic and anti-Spanish prejudices his narrative is demonstrably misleading.[7] Fortunately, these politico-religious preoccupations are not brought to bear on the material dealing with Sidney's last days. Instead, both the events and the narrative appear to have been shaped in terms of conventions and expectations concerning a 'good death' or noble and honourable demeanour.[8]

Apart from Greville's, the only other extended account of Sidney's death is one now tentatively ascribed to George Gifford, the 'minister' mentioned in the codicil of Sidney's will.[9] It is known from only two manuscript copies, one of which was noticed in print for the first time at the beginning of the last century by Thomas Zouch.[10] Whether or not it is Gifford's work, 'The Manner of Sir Philip Sidney's Death' (as it is now known) appears to have one advantage over Greville's narrative: it purports to be an account prepared by someone who witnessed Sidney's last seventeen or eighteen days. Careful examination reveals, however, that it contains none of the kinds of detail that would now be regarded as interesting from a biographical point of view,[11] but conforms with the conventional notion of a 'good death'. The significant features of the convention are: firstly, patient submission to suffering, which is seen as God's chastisement or as the occasion for a demonstration of faith; secondly, a confession of sins and a willingness to lead an amended life; thirdly, a confession of faith, frequently following the form of the Apostles' Creed; fourthly, an equanimous leavetaking characterised by a forgiveness of, and reconciliation with, enemies, a concern for the welfare of loved ones, and a commendation of all to God; and fifthly, a willing acceptance of death, frequently marked by the use of the *in manus tuas* formula.

The conventional nature of Gifford's supposed account is not surprising, since the author is writing 'for the comfort of those who did dearly love [Sir Philip]' concerning 'the most special things whereby he declared his unfeigned faith, and special work of grace, which gave proof that his end was undoubtedly happy'.[12] In other words, the purpose of the account is to assure the survivors that Sidney, as a good Protestant, died in the sure knowledge of his election. For this reason it would have been irrelevant to introduce material that was either too particular and personal, or not obviously consonant with the conventional ideas concerning a pious death. In consequence the account fails to distinguish Sidney's death from that of any other worthy man.[13] It would be wrong, however, to assume that the account has no connection whatsoever with the events of Sidney's last days. The convention of a 'good death' is not necessarily a literary one. Knowledge of the quasi-liturgical features of the convention was widespread. In England they had been embodied in print as early as 1490 in *A little treatise...of the art and craft to know to well to die*, and could be found in any one of a number of works in the *ars moriendi* tradition (Thomas Becon's *The sick man's salve* probably being the one most frequently reprinted before 1600), as well as in *The Book of Common Prayer's* 'Order for the visitation of the sick'.[14] Had Sidney's deathbed behaviour departed significantly from the ordinary expectations, it would

be very unlikely that a consolation such as the one attributed to Gifford
could have been written. We can therefore assume that Sidney did act
out the religious conventions, but not that this particular account
presents us with an adequate notion of Sidney's last days.

   Greville's account is both fuller and more problematic. The elements
of an exemplary Christian death are present, but in disguised form.
Before he has intimations of his death, Sidney tells his surgeons

> that while his strength was yet entire, his body free from fever, and his mind
> able to endure, they might freely use their art, cut and search to the bottom,
> for besides his hope of health he would make this further profit of the pains
> which he must suffer, that they should bear witness they had indeed a
> sensible-natured man under their hands, yet one to whom a stronger spirit
> had given power above himself either to do or suffer...[15]

Even when he acknowledges the futility of the subsequent treatment,
'he continued a patient beyond exception'.[16] He makes 'such a confession of Christian faith as no book but the heart can truly and feelingly
deliver'.[17] Being a Protestant, he does not believe in private auricular
confession, but desires those about him 'to accompany him in prayer
wherein he sought leave to lead the assembly, in respect (as he said) that
the secret sins of his own heart were best known to himself, and, out of
that true sense, he more properly instructed to apply the eternal sacrifice
of our Saviour's passion and merits to them'.[18] In making his will Sidney
demonstrates the same generosity in death as he did in life, while his
solicitude for his brother is introduced as a further instance of uncon-
taminated affection. Greville's account does not end with a final
demonstration of faith, since Sidney's salvation is implicit throughout.
Greville ends with a simple understatement that commits the reader to
confirming his claims: 'Here this noble gentleman ended the too short
line of his life, in which path whosoever is not confident that he walked
the next way to eternal rest will be found to judge uncharitably'.[19]

   Greville's account is so noticeably free from formulaic conventionality
that one is invited to speculate as to whether this artlessness proceeds
from calculation on Greville's part, or whether it is the outcome of an irreducible substratum of fact to which the visible landscape is obliged to
conform. Similar thoughts arise when elements of the narrative bearing
no relation to received religious ideas are examined: the dispensing with
thigh-armour, the relinquishing of the water-bottle, the debate on the
nature of the soul, and the singing of 'La cuisse rompue'. Strictly speaking, only the last two are part of the deathbed material, a fact which
Greville marks by starting a new chapter (Chapter XIII) after the point
where Sidney acknowledges that he is soon to die.[20]

The debate on the nature of the soul and the deathbed song are related *topoi*. The *Phaedo*, Plato's account of Socrates' last days, is dominated by a debate on the nature of the soul, but the informal preliminaries are concerned with the fact that Socrates appears to have taken up poetic composition while awaiting his execution.[21] Socrates explains:

> you seem to think I am inferior in prophetic power to the swans who sing at other times also, but when they feel that they are to die, sing most and best in their joy that they are to go to the god whose servants they are. But men, because of their own fear of death, misrepresent the swans and say that they sing for sorrow, in mourning for their own death. They do not consider that no bird sings when it is hungry or cold or has any other trouble... I do not believe that they sing for grief, nor do the swans; but since they are Apollo's birds, I believe they have prophetic vision, and because they have foreknowledge of the blessings in the other world they sing and rejoice on that day more than ever before.[22]

It was not necessary for anyone in the sixteenth century to have read Plato to be aware of these ideas.[23] Cicero refers to the passage, and specifically connects the idea of the swan-song with the notion of the death of a virtuous man:

> And so [Socrates] relates that just as the swans—who have been consecrated to Apollo, not undesignedly, but because from Apollo they seem to have the gift of prophecy, and thus have a foretaste of the blessing death brings—die with a song of rapture, so must all good and learned men do likewise.[24]

In order to show that these ideas are not merely of historical interest, Cicero cites the exemplary death of Cato the Younger as a contemporary Roman instance. It is therefore not surprising that in Plutarch's account of Cato's death we discover that Cato read the *Phaedo* just before his end.[25]

That Sidney himself was well aware of these ideas is apparent from the behaviour of the heroes of the *'old' Arcadia*, Pyrocles and Musidorus, on the eve of their anticipated execution: the princes debate whether the departed soul retains memories of its earthly existence,[26] then Musidorus,

> looking with a heavenly joy upon [Pyrocles], sang this song unto him he had made before love turned his muse to another subject.
>> Since nature's works be good, and death doth serve
>> As nature's work, why should we fear to die?
>> Since fear is vain but when it may preserve,
>> Why should we fear that which we cannot fly?
>>
>> Fear is more pain than is the pain it fears,
>> Disarming human minds of native might;
>> While each conceit an ugly figure bears,
>> Which were not ill, well viewed in reason's light.

Our owly eyes, which dimmed with passions be,
And scarce discern the dawn of coming day,
Let them be cleared, and now begin to see
Our life is but a step in dusty way,
        Then let us hold the bliss of peaceful mind,
        Since this we feel, great loss we cannot find.

The narrator then comments: 'Thus did they, like quiet swans, sing their
own obsequies, and virtuously enable their minds against all extremities
which they did think would fall upon them...'[27]

The convention of the *moriturus* lyric is not purely literary. In an account, usually attributed to Edmund Waterhouse, of Walter Devereux,
Earl of Essex's death in September 1576, we are told that on his deathbed
the Earl sang a song:

> the friday night w^ch was the night before he died, he willed Hewes his musi-
> cian to play on the Virginals, and to sing. Play, the my song (Will. Hewes)
> and I will sing it my self: so he did most joyfully, not as the howling swanne,
> w^ch still looking downe, bewaileth her ende; but as a sweet larke lifting vp
> his handes, and casting his eies vp to his god, w^t his spirit mownting the
> christall skies, and reached w^t his unweeried winges the top of the highest
> heauens...[28]

The poem which Waterhouse ascribes to Essex ('O heavenly god, O
Father dear, cast down thy tender eye') first appeared in print in *A
Paradise of dainty devices* in 1576, some months before Essex's death, attributed to F.K. (Francis Kinwelmarsh).[29] Whether or not the poem is
indeed by Essex, it is ascribed to him in the 1585-edition of *A Paradise
of dainty devices*, so that a year before Sidney's death it was commonly accepted that a prominent public figure closely associated with Sidney in
various ways had acted out part of the Socratic deathbed convention.[30]

Greville's allusion to the convention is at once precise and uninfor-
mative: 'this restless soul of his...calls for music, especially that song
which himself had entitled *La cuisse rompue*; partly (as I conceive by the
name) to show that the glory of mortal flesh was shaken in him, and, by
the music itself, to fashion and enfranchise his heavenly soul into that
everlasting harmony of angels whereof these concords were a kind of ter-
restrial echo'.[31] There is no mention of swans, either because Greville
tactfully assumes that his reader would be aware of the convention, or
because he himself was unaware that he was dealing with an incident informed by convention. We are not told that Sidney sang a song, nor that
the song was written by him, merely that he asked for a song which he
for some reason had entitled 'the broken thigh', so alluding to his condition. But Greville appears to be confident enough to be precise, indicating that he and his early readers had a specific song in mind.

Although the allusion is lost on us, it is tempting to speculate that the song in question might be Sidney's translation of Psalm 6.

Domine ne in furore

Lord, let not me a worme by thee be shent,
  While Thou art in the heat of thy displeasure:
  Ne let thy rage, of my due punishment
    Become the measure.                     (5)
But mercy, lord, let Mercy thyne descend
  For I am weake, and in my weakness languish;
  Lord help, for ev'en my bones their marrow spend
    With cruel anguish.
Nay ev'n my soul fell troubles do appall;           (10)
  Alas, how long, my God, wilt Thou delay me?
  Turne Thee, sweet lord, and from this Ougly fall
    My Deare God stay me.
Mercy, O Mercy lord, for Mercy's sake,
  For death doth kill the Witness of thy glory;     (15)
  Can of thy prayse the tongues entombed make
    A heavnly story?
Lo, I am tir'd, while still I sigh and groane:
  My moystned bed proofes of my sorrow showeth:
  My bed, while I with black night mourn alone,    (20)
    With my tears floweth.
Woe, lyke a moth, my face's beauty eates
  And age pull'd on with paines all freshness fretteth:
  The while a swarm of foes with vexing feates
    My life besetteth.                    (25)
Get hence you ev'ill, who in my ev'ill rejoyce,
  In all whose workes vainess is ever raigning:
  For God hath heard the weeping sobbing voice
    Of my complaining.
The lord my suite did heare, and gently heare,   (30)
  They shall be sham'd and vext, that breed my crying,
  And turn their backs, and strait on backs appeare
    Their shameful flying.[32]

Not only is this, one of the Penitential Psalms, appropriate to Sidney's situation and mood (as described by both Greville and Gifford), but lines 7 to 17 uncannily invite one to think of his condition at that time.[33]

The self-conscious conventionality in terms of which Renaissance gentlemen conducted their own, and perceived each other's, public behaviour is particularly notable in their deathbed activities. The conventions appear to have been so dominant that the more intimate and private moments were either disregarded or not perceived at all. In consequence it is often difficult to decide whether the actor or the reporter was responsible for the shaping of the incidents recorded in a narrative. This is certainly true of Greville's account of Sidney's deathbed, but given that there is no evidence to refute Greville's statements, and given Sidney's awareness of the conventions, we can be fairly sure that something very like the incidents presented in the account actually took place. There can be less confidence in the congruence of actor's and reporter's intentions when we turn to those parts of Greville's work dealing with incidents that appear not to be so obviously subject to recognised conventions.

There is no doubt Sidney dispensed with wearing thigh-armour on the day he was wounded. What is uncertain is his motive for doing so. Greville attributes it to a spontaneous gallantry.

> When that unfortunate stand was to be made before Zutphen to stop the issuing out of the Spanish army from a strait, with what alacrity soever he went to actions of honour, yet, remembering that upon just grounds the ancient sages describe the worthiest persons to be ever best armed, he had completely put on his; but, meeting the marshall of the camp lightly armed (whose honour in that art would not suffer this unenvious Themistocles to sleep), the unspotted emulation of his heart to venture without any inequality made him cast off his cuisses, and so, by the secret influence of destiny, to disarm that part where God, it seems, resolved to strike him.[34]

What seems on the surface a more mundane explanation is provided by Thomas Moffet, the tutor of the young William Herbert. According to him, Sidney, hastening to the rescue of the embattled Peregrine Bertie, Lord Willoughby, had neglected to put on the armour for his left thigh.[35] Moffet's editors comment:

> Moffet's relation that the suddeness of the alarm of battle did not allow Sidney time to put on his left cuisse, seems on the face of it to be more plausible than Greville's somewhat strange explanation that a chivalrous impulse prompted Sidney to remove both the cuisses with which he had just armed himself. If, at any time he was writing, there had been any choice in the matter, Moffet would undoubtedly have recorded the latter explanation as an additional illustration of Sidney's ideal character.[36]

The credibility of Moffet's version of the incident depends largely on his assumptions concerning the nature of the engagement. He seems to imply that it was a rather haphazard, unforeseen affair. In fact, the English, having been forewarned, were hoping to frustrate an attempt to revictual the town of Zutphen. They fared rather badly because they had failed to reconnoitre the enemy's position properly.[37] The idea of Moffet being stuck with the fact that Sidney was rather scatter-brained will not bear examination. If Moffet had considered his explanation unworthy of his subject he would have suppressed it. In fact, his explanation is no less flattering then Greville's, since it is designed to show Sidney, gallantly careless of his own safety, rushing off to succour an endangered comrade.

More plausible is the suggestion by Sir John Smythe that Sidney may have been following the continental fashion of abandoning heavy armour.

> The imitating of which...unsoldierlike and fond arming cost that noble and worthy gentleman Sir Philip Sidney his life, by not wearing his cuisses. For in the opinion of divers gentleman that saw him hurt with a musket shot, if he had that day worn his cuisses the bullet had not broken his thighbone, by reason that the chief force of the bullet (before the blow) was in manner past.[38]

Smythe's conservative argument against the abandonment of heavy armour certainly gains from a consideration of Sidney's fate, but it is far from clear that Smythe wishes to claim that Sidney had abandoned the customary use of cuisses. The passage considered as a whole makes no unequivocal assertions about Sidney's motives. What can be claimed without prejudice on the basis of it is that Sidney, in not wearing his cuisses on that particular day, had laid himself open to the kind of injury to which the followers of the new style would be susceptible. For a more positive interpretation to be acceptable we would need evidence either that Smythe was in a position to ascertain Sidney's motives (the passage indicates that Smythe was not an eyewitness), or that Sidney himself had displayed an active interest in the continental military fashions decried by Smythe.

Greville's interpretation of the incident need not be incompatible with Smythe's. It is possible that the marshall of the camp, Sir William Pelham, whose light armour Sidney wished to emulate, was the one who had taken up the new style. But a more likely explanation for Pelham's accoutrement is his physical condition as a consequence of having been wounded in the stomach some three weeks earlier at Doesburg.[39] As a member of the Leicester circle Pelham could well have been the one who told Greville of Sidney's action when he returned to England between April and November 1587.[40]

Greville's account is also consistent with other information we have concerning Sidney's preoccupations. We are told that Sidney was normally careful to equip himself properly, in imitation of heroic classical warriors. The reference to the 'ancient sages' is illuminated by a passage in Plutarch, *Polipidas*, I.5:

> For neither is a man to be blamed for shunning death, if he does not cling to life disgracefully, nor to be praised for boldly meeting death, if he does this with contempt of life. For this reason Homer always brings his boldest heroes into battle well armed and equipped.[41]

The same idea is alluded to in the *'old' Arcadia* when Pyrocles is trapped in Philoclea's bedchamber.

> But being up, the first ill handsel he had of the ill case wherein he was was the seeing himself deprived of his sword, from which he had never separated himself in any occasion, and even that night, first by the duke's bed, and then there, had laid it as he thought safe, putting great part of the trust of his well doing in his own courage, so armed. For, indeed, the confidence in oneself is the chief nurse of true magnanimity; which confidence notwithstanding doth not leave the care of necessary furnitures for it, and therefore of all the Grecians Homer doth ever make Achilles the best armed.[42]

Once again we are made aware that it is quite as likely that Sidney's actions were influenced by precedents and conventions as that Greville subsequently shaped his narrative in terms of them.[43] These passages also place Greville's account in its proper perspective. Greville takes it for granted that both the scrupulous arming as well as the magnanimous disarming stem from a self-confidence, a presence of mind that is neither fastidiously self-regarding, nor cowardly, nor rash. To Greville's contemporaries an action such as the one he attributes to Sidney would not seem quite so quixotic as it might to us. This is especially true if we acknowledge that Greville's providential view of history tempts us to judge Sidney's action in the light of subsequent events. If we accept that Sidney abandoned his cuisses for the reason Greville provides, we can see that at the time there was nothing inherently misguided about his decision. That a retrospective view allows us to be aware of the unfortunate outcome does not mean that the action itself was futile. Had Sidney, like so many of his contemporaries, survived the war unscathed, his gesture would have been unremarkable and unremembered.

According to Plutarch, Themistocles was so envious of the renown won by Miltiades at Marathon that it caused him sleepless nights, and brought about changes in his everyday habits.[44] Disclaiming any such envy on Sidney's part, Greville suggests that his friend had deliberately forgone his usual preparations rather than compromise his honour by means of some adventitious material advantage. Given the contemporary conception of honour, an action of this kind, rather than being considered misguided, would have been expected of any military man who knew what he was about. Several times in the 'new' Arcadia, for example, the virtuous and heroic characters live up to this standard of behaviour. Thus Pyrocles, in recounting his exploits to Philoclea, tells her how in one battle with Anaxius his opponent's horse had been killed under him. 'He (Anaxius), driven to dismount, threatened if I did not do the like to do as much for my horse as fortune had done for his. But whether for that, or because I would not be beholding to fortune for any part of the victory, I descended.'[45] In his refusing to take advantage of an opponent's mishap, Pyrocles' circumstances are not equivalent to those of

Sidney in the Greville anecdote, but the principle at issue is still the same.

At the beginning of the last century, Thomas Zouch pointed out what he took to be one biblical and two classical parallels to the famous water-bottle story.[46] Parallels can be very misleading, as can be seen from Fluellen's comparison of Macedon and Monmouth because there is a river in both. On examination these earlier anecdotes appear to have more in common with the story of the abandoned cuisses than with the superficially similar narrative of the event most frequently associated with Sidney, since each of the anecdotes is concerned with a military leader determined both to endure the same hardships as his fellow-soldiers, as well as to avoid all occasions that would compromise his honour. The biblical anecdote concerns David.

> David was then in an hold, and the garrison of the Philistines was then in Bethlehem. And David longed, and said, Oh that one would give me drink of the water of the well of Bethlehem, which is by the gate! And the three mighty men brake through the host of the Philistines, and drew water out of the well of Bethlehem, that was by the gate, and took it and brought it to David: nevertheless he would not drink thereof, but poured it out unto the Lord. And he said, Be it far from me, O Lord, that I should do this: is not this the blood of the men that went in jeopardy of their lives? therefore he would not drink it.[47]

The anecdote concerning Cato the Younger shares with the Biblical passage the idea of pouring the water on the ground, but with very different implications.

> Then, when heat expanded the air which had been contracted by the gale, and the day grew burning hot, sweat poured from their limbs and their mouths were parched with thirst. A rivulet with scanty flow was sighted at a distance; and a soldier, snatching the water with difficulty from the dust, poured it into the hollow of his helmet and offered it to the general. Every throat was furred with sand, and the general himself, holding in his hands a mere drop of water, was an object of envy. 'Degenerate soldier,' he said; 'did you consider me the one man without fortitude in this army? Did I seem so effeminate, so unable to endure the first onset of heat? How much more you yourself deserve this punishment—that you should drink while all around thirst!' So in wrath he emptied out the helmet, and there was water enough for all [i.e. they were content to do without it].[48]

Zouch's third analogy is the one most frequently referred to in connection with Sidney.

> In consequence of the pursuit of Dareius, which was long and arduous, ...most of his [Alexander's] horsemen gave out, and chiefly for lack of water. At this point some Macedonians met him who were carrying water from the river in skins upon their mules. And when they beheld Alexander, it being now midday, in a wretched plight from thirst, they quickly filled a helmet and brought it to him. To his enquiry for whom they were carry-

ing the water, they replied: 'For our own sons; but if thou livest, we can get other sons, even if we lose these.' On hearing this he took the helmet into his hands, but when he looked around and saw the horsemen about him all stretching out their heads and gazing at the water, he handed it back without drinking any, but with praises for the men who had brought it; 'For,' said he 'if I should drink of it alone, these horsemen of mine will be out of heart.' But when they beheld his self-control and loftiness of spirit, they shouted out to him to lead them forward boldly, and began to goad their horses on, declaring that they would not regard themselves as weary, or thirsty, or as mortals at all, so long as they had such a king.[49]

By comparison with these anecdotes, Sidney is not presented as a military leader honour-bound to encourage his men by his stoical behaviour. In all three the central figure declines to assuage his thirst, but it is left to the subsidiary figures to make what is generally thought of as the Sidneian gesture of offering the water to someone else, at no small cost to themselves. The point of Greville's story does not depend on there being a shortage of water which would make it unseemly for any one person to drink, but rather that Sidney, seeing another human being's needs, generously deferred to them. More importantly, Greville points out that after the thirst of the soldier had been quenched Sidney himself drank from the bottle. There is no suggestion of heroic self-sacrifice. The implicit values are perhaps those of the Good Samaritan, while a possible analogy is that of St. Martin dividing his cloak with the beggar. An alert Christian might feel prompted to recall the parable of Dives and Lazarus,[50] or, as Dame Helen Gardner has suggested, Matt 10: 42: 'And whosoever shall give to drink unto one of these little ones a cup of cold water only in the name of a disciple, verily I say unto you, he shall in no wise lose his reward'; or Mark 9: 41: 'For whosoever shall give you a cup of water to drink in my name, because ye belong to Christ, verily I say unto you, he shall not lose his reward'.[51]

> Howsoever, by this stand [at Zutphen] an unfortunate hand out of those fore-spoken trenches brake the bone of Sir Philip's thigh with a musket-shot. The horse he rode upon was rather furiously choleric than bravely proud, and so forced him to forsake the field, but not his back, as the noblest and fittest bier to carry a martial commander to his grave. In which sad progress, passing along by the rest of the army where his uncle—the general—was, and being thirsty with excess of bleeding, he called for drink, which was presently brought him; but as he was putting the bottle to his mouth he saw a poor soldier carried along, who had eaten his last at the same feast, ghastly casting up his eyes at the bottle; which Sir Philip perceiving, took it from his head before he drank, and delivered it to the poor man with these words: 'Thy necessity is yet greater than mine.'
> And when he had pledged this poor soldier, he was presently carried to Arnhem where the principal chirurgeons of the camp attended for him...[52]

It is worth noting that Greville makes no mention of the contents of the bottle. It is possible that for later generations the suggestive power of the various analogues and precedents, and especially of the Biblical passages, is so great that we have all assumed that Sidney could only have been offered water. Greville's uncharacteristic reticence in drawing attention to any of the precedents inclines me to believe that he may have been less aware of the conventions than either Sidney or subsequent readers. We should therefore be wary of imputing significances to recounted incidents where the teller appears unaware of the significance, and especially where such interpretations require the assumption of facts for which there is no warrant. It should be borne in mind that it would perhaps have been unthinkable for nineteenth-century idealizers of Sidney that their hero would partake of anything other than water. As a corrective to such earlier assumptions, it is worth considering that in late summer and early autumn water may well not have been regarded as wholesome.

The three analogues proposed by Zouch should put us on our guard against reacting sentimentally to Greville's anecdote, though Greville, in part, encourages this reaction by presenting the incident in the framework of retrospective experience. Thus Sidney's horse is seen as a bier fit to bear him to his grave. Certainly, Sidney resolutely refused to dismount, or be helped from the field. According to Whetstone

> Udal then lite, softly to leade his Horse,
> *Let goe quoth he, till I fall to the grounde:*
> *The foe shall misse the glory of my wounde*[53]

Greville then describes the soldier to whom Sidney offered the drink as one 'who had eaten his last at the same feast'. Such colouring of the narrative should not, however, be allowed to influence one's attitude to the essential material. It may be, of course, that Sidney was pessimistic immediately after being wounded, but all indications are that Sidney's life was not initially despaired of.[54] Once the retrospective accretions of Greville and his later readers have been been removed, the purported incident is hardly as glamourous as some would like it to be, but it is more plausible.

We should also be careful of giving the anecdote a specifically Christian interpretation, since it is this tendency that has encouraged the distorting prominence given to the story in the nineteenth century, and so given rise to the more recent scepticism. Instead of relying for our understanding of the Greville narrative on conjectured parallels with specific received anecdotes or texts, it would be more helpful to consider a significantly apposite passage on the irascible Count Hollock that

follows almost immediately after the narrative of the events at Zutphen.
Having spent two paragraphs on Sidney's admonition to his physicians,
and the general optimism for his recovery, Greville continues:

> Only there was one owl among all the birds, which, though looking with
> no less zealous eyes than the rest, yet saw and presaged more despair—I
> mean an excellent chirurgeon of the Count Hollock's, who, although the
> Count himself lay at the same instant hurt in the throat with a musket-shot,
> yet did he neglect his own extremity to save his friend, and to that end had
> sent him to Sir Philip. This chirurgeon notwithstanding (out of love to his
> master) returning one day to dress his wound, the Count cheerfully asked
> him how Sir Philip did; but being answered with a heavy countenance that
> he was not well, at these words the worthy prince—as having more sense
> of his friend's wounds than his own—cries out: 'Away villain, never see my
> face again till thou bring better news of that man's recovery, for whose
> redemption many such as I were happily lost.'
>
> This honourable act I relate to give the world one modern example, first,
> that greatness of heart is not dead everywhere; and, then, that war is both
> a fitter mould to fashion it, and stage to act it on, than peace can be; and,
> lastly, that the reconciliation of enemies may prove safe and honourable
> where the cement on either side is worth—so as this Florentine precept con-
> cerning reconciled enemies ['Reconciled friendship is a wound not well
> salved up'] deserves worthily to be buried with unworthiness the author of
> it, or at least the practice of it cried down and banished to reign among bar-
> barous heathen spirits who, while they find life the uttermost of all things,
> hold it safe in nobody that their own errors make doubtful to them; and
> such seems every man that moves any passion but pleasure in those in-
> tricate natures.[55]

Greville's extended comment on the incident characteristically assumes
that the reader cannot but agree with his assessment. At first sight it is
odd that he should assert that Hollock's behaviour is a single example of
contemporary great-heartedness when his earlier account of Sidney's actions is clearly meant to demonstrate the existence of that virtue. The
reason for this seems to be that Greville somehow regards Sidney as one
of those exceptional men from whom one expects nothing but a revelation of the ancient virtues, and as such he cannot be regarded as a
representative man of his time; ordinary men like Hollock nevertheless
show that some of his virtues are not unattainable. Greville's comment
as a whole depends, then, on a classical, and not necessarily Christian,
scheme of values which puts a premium on generous self-forgetfulness.
This form of nobility is neither the invention nor the prerogative of any
one person, and it is accepted that it cannot be attained by mere imitation. For this reason, it seems to me, Greville had no particular
precedents in mind when writing the narrative of Sidney's response to his
wounded companion-in-arms, though there is no doubt that many
analogues could be produced.

Other considerations aside, the Hollock anecdote is important because it increases one's confidence in the reliability of Greville's account. The relative chronology of the narrative is confirmed by other witnesses. On 4 October—eleven days after the skirmish at Zutphen, and three days before Sidney is said by Greville to have given up hope of recovery—Hollock has been 'shot into his mouth and out by his ear, so that it smote away the jewel hanging at his ear'.[56] The surgeon sent to Sidney by Hollock has been identified as Adrian van den Spiegel,[57] and is almost certainly the surgeon named Adrian mentioned in the codicil to Sidney's will.[58] It should also be borne in mind that the anecdote is consistent with so much else we know of Sidney: his impulsiveness, as seen, for example, in his irascible letter to Edmund Molyneux,[59] or the rashly benevolent terms of his will;[60] and his concern for those around him, as seen in the series of letters between November 1585 and May 1586 to Sir Francis Walsingham on behalf of various individuals.[62]

While Zouch may have regarded possible analogues to the Greville anecdote as enhancements, the modern, more sceptical, mind predisposed to recast the world in terms of its own disenchantments finds it difficult to concede that at times human beings can behave generously; the detection of analogies and precedents therefore becomes a way of undermining either the sincerity of indisputably verified actions, or the veracity of accounts for which confirmatory evidence is not blatantly apparent. In part, this is a reaction against the nineteenth-century tendency to romanticize historical events. Before Zouch, for example, the incident at Zutphen does not seem to have attracted much attention. When the story is referred to, Greville's words are quoted verbatim.[63] Zouch, the first of many nineteenth-century biographers, starts the process of emotional embellishment.

> As he was returning from the field of battle, pale, languid, and thirsty with excess of bleeding, he asked for water to quench his thirst. The water was brought; and had no sooner approached his lips, than he instantly resigned it to a dying soldier, whose ghastly countenance attracted his notice— speaking these evermemorable words; 'This man's necessity is still greater than mine.' Few incidents can afford a more animating and affecting subject to the historical painter.[64]

The relative lack of early interest in the story seems to be confirmed by the paucity of illustrations. The painting at Wilton House is thought to date from the late seventeenth century. It is significant, however, that nothing is known of the provenance of the picture before it was acquired for the Pembroke family some time between 1840 and 1863, at a time when the Romantic cult of the poet-as-hero was well under way.[65] Zouch

also provides a description of a now unlocated painting attributed to Benjamin West (1738-1820).[66]

Of the nineteenth-century versions of the anecdote, the most revealing
is found in J. Radford Thomson's twice printed biography.

> It was whilst he was quitting the field for the entrenchments, that the
> memorable incident occurred, with which Sidney's name will never cease
> to be associated. Thirsty with excess of bleeding, he called for water. This
> was brought to him, but just as he was putting the bottle to his mouth, he
> saw a poor wounded soldier carried by, who cast his dying eyes towards the
> precious draught. Perceiving this, Sir Philip withdrew his lips from the bot-
> tle, and handed it to the soldier, with the words: 'Thy necessity is yet
> greater than mine!'
> In these words spake conqueror of self, the true Christian knight.[67]

There can be no straightforward, principled response that will satisfy
doubts concerning the authenticity of Greville's claims, but in addition
to providing some kind of explanation for the general temper of in-
credulity, one needs to examine the particulars of the case against
Greville. The substance of the implied allegation is this: Greville's account is the only source of the anecdote, and given that Greville was not
an eyewitness to the event, given that none of the eyewitnesses reports
anything that would confirm his assertions, given that Greville—writing
some twenty-six years after the event, and wishing to present Sidney to
the decadent Jacobeans as the ideal subject of the ideal sovereign—had
sufficient motive for falsifying his material, it must be assumed that the
anecdote can have no factual basis.

Much of the force of a charge such as this depends upon the assumption that Greville is in general not a reliable witness. Despite appearances
to the contrary, there is no ground for such an assumption. Because
Greville's purpose is to produce a favourable impression of Sidney, he
is naturally selective in the material he uses. Thus there is no mention
of the letter Sidney wrote on the eve of his death to Johan Wyer, begging
the aged physician to attend him.[68] While a modern sensibility rejoices
in such detail, it must be recognised that Sidney's action was that of a
man, possibly delirious with pain, momentarily, and very humanly, laps-
ing in his resolve to endure his fate with equanimity. There is no
evidence that this lapse was a prolonged one, and any mention of it in
a narrative such as Greville's would have introduced an unnecessary
complexity into the design. In narratives that are fully within the *ars
moriendi* tradition such momentary waverings are not unusual. The account of Sidney's death attributed to Gifford provides a good example of
this,[69] and at least part of the great length of a work such as Thomas
Becon's *The Sick man's salve* derives from the implicit recognition of just

such human fallibility. Suppression of such details, however, does not amount to fabrication. In every other case where Greville is our only source for a particular anecdote, there is sufficient particularity as well as the remnants of circumstantial evidence to leave the facts of the case in no doubt. In this regard the account of the tennis-court quarrel with the Earl of Oxford,[70] and the anecdote concerning Count Hollock's physician are particularly convincing.

Although one cannot fault Greville in his accounts of particular incidents, it is true that elsewhere in the *Dedication* he is trapped into falsification and errors of chronology in what is purported to be Sidney's survey of the state of affairs in Europe, and his proposals for an adequate English foreign policy.[71] Thus at one point Sidney is made to surmise the possibility of a second Armada, at a time when the first had yet to be launched.[72] The anti-Spanish and anti-Catholic opinions expressed in this portion of the *Dedication* are largely Greville's own, prompted by his personal concerns for the state of England at the time of writing; though he may, in part, be recalling private conversations held over a quarter of a century before. What distinguishes this part of Greville's work from the chapters devoted to Sidney's activities in the Netherlands is the fact that in the former Greville is dealing with opinions rather than with events. Over an extended period, ideas and attitudes that are not tied to concrete, personal details will invariably be influenced by the pressing concerns of subsequent occasions. Greville, like most human beings, may have idiosyncratic interpretations of events, and his own preoccupations may influence his memory of interpretations of those events, but he does not invent the events themselves. Given the nature of his commitment to Sidney, it is inconceivable that he would taint his friend's memory by falsifying the essential facts of the case. If his own integrity is not a sufficient guarantee, then it should be remembered that many of the eyewitnesses, as well as close relatives of Sidney, were still alive at the time of writing. Some of them at least would have had access to Greville's manuscript, and it is certain that they would have found a baseless anecdote unacceptable.

Greville's sources for the Low Country anecdotes were very likely verbal ones, since the incidents he records so memorably were remarkable only in retrospect. At the time, Sidney was not expected to die, and so the actions which were subsequently invested with such great significance would not have been regarded as anything extraordinary. They were certainly not the kind of material characteristic of official letters to the Court. When their poignancy was realised, it was too late to report them. The memorial poems which soon appeared were mostly written by people unacquainted with the events of Sidney's last days. The single excep-

tion is George Whetstone, who not only informs us that one Udall helped
Sidney off the battlefield, but also gives us a version of Sidney's parting
words to his brother Robert that is remarkably similar to Greville's:

> Brother (quoth he) to you I must imparte
> Three thinges of waight, impresse them in your Harte,
> *Feare God, and liue: loue well my frendes: and knowe,*
> *That worldly hopes, from vanitie do flowe.*[73]

This is remarkable, but we should not be surprised that Whetstone fails
to produce the kind of detail that would come only from a man who had
sought out every eyewitness he could find to the last days of his beloved
friend.

For slightly different reasons, it is also not surprising to find no
references to the exchange between Sidney and the common soldier in
two other discussions which refer to events in the last months of Sidney's
life. Even if he had known the anecdote, Edmund Molyneux, in his
memoir of Sir Henry and Sir Philip,[74] would have been too constrained
by the chronicle format to expand into the complexity and detail that the
retelling of the tale would require. The incident is also not one which can
be presented as being of remarkable public concern. The personal, intimate and social dimensions of the anecdote which would have made it
the possession of the immediate circle of the family and close friends is
apparent when it is compared with the kind of particular Molyneux
chooses to dwell on. Thus the dying Sidney's desperate letter to Wyer is
quoted in order to demonstrate that Sidney, in the best *ars moriendi* tradition, retained all his faculties to the end, and so, by implication, all
readers would have no doubts as to his salvation; while Sidney's boun-
tiful will is seen as a way of preserving his fame and honour after his
death.[75] There is no straightforward common concern of this kind that
could readily be extracted from the incident recorded by Greville. On the
other hand, it would seem to be admirably suited to Thomas Moffet's
*Nobilis*. Not only was Moffet closely connected with the Sidney circle,[76]
but the work itself was designed to encourage the young William Herbert
to emulate the virtues of his uncle. Moffet's editors outline the work's
concerns:

> piety and love of learning are main themes; Sidney's patriotism and skill
> in dealing with men are next in importance; beyond these we have a half-
> hearted acknowledgement of his poetical ability and some slight emphasis
> upon his martial valor, his friendships, family relations, and noble
> descent.[77]

In this context, an anecdote inviting a response to an act of self-sacrifice,
and gesture of shared human need, would be out of place, especially if

it is remembered that the recipient is a young and rather wilful nobleman.

Once the accretions of various kinds have been removed, there would appear to be an irreducible core of fact underlying Greville's account of Sidney's last days. Like so many of his contemporaries, Sidney was particularly aware that his behaviour, especially his behaviour on recognizably significant occasions, should be conducted in terms of conventions or precedents, or in conformity with some widely held scheme of social values. The facts of this kind of behaviour are naturally difficult to establish, not only because contemporary perceptions of historical events often seem to contaminate the events themselves, but because conventions and values, and so perceptions of conduct determined by them, change. A synchronic view would fail to appreciate the historical and cultural awareness that is as much part of the conduct as the physical activities themselves, while what may be called a homochronic view would reduce the events to whatever is the dominant view of the time— sentimental heroism in the nineteenth, banal cynicism in the twentieth century. A diachronic approach is just as unsatisfactory, since it requires that human perceptions should not be discontinuous, and presupposes some kind of development in human behaviour through time. My method has therefore been what may be called heterochronic, by which I mean that I have attempted to retain an awareness of the disparity of historical perceptions, and so attempted to minimize the falsification of historical incidents that is involved in translating the social behaviour of one culture for the benefit of another. In the process I have found it necessary to diminish the aura of myth of various kinds surrounding Greville's account of Sidney's last days, but have found no evidence for dismissing the account as a mere wishful invention. In consequence the events are made out to be rather ordinary. It may be objected, however, that the lack of contrary evidence is no guarantee that an account is not entirely made up, but such an argument fails to take cognizance of the corroborating evidence gathered in the present essay. More importantly, such scepticism seems to me fundamentally untenable, since it assumes as an epistemological axiom that knowledge is a type of confirmed belief. Following Wittgenstein, philosophers have been telling us that knowledge and belief are different in kind; we can thus return to affirming what lawyers have taken for granted down the centuries, that one accepts what a man claims to know unless there is evidence for doubting him.[78]

## NOTES

1 Sidney's supposed words to the soldier are frequently misquoted, while the vessel containing what is assumed to be water is said to be a cup instead of a bottle; see, for example, William Empson, 'Advanced Thought', *The London Review of Books*, volume 2 number 1 (24 January 1980), 1-2, and the amusing subsequent exchange with Frank Kermode in the following issue (7 February 1980), p. 2; and Sidney (Herbert), 16th Earl of Pembroke *A Catalogue of the Paintings and Drawings in the Collection at Wilton House* (London, 1968), 51-52. Stimulating discussions and generous advice have saved me from my own ignorance and ineptitude in the process of writing this essay. I owe particular debts to Miss Katherine Duncan-Jones, Mrs J. Bromley, and Professor R. Harnett.

2 Wing B4899.

3 See my *The Prose Works of Fulke Greville, Lord Brooke*, Oxford, 1986, 38-41 and notes. This edition is hereafter referred to as *Greville Prose*.

4 See Ronald A. Rebholz, *The Life of Fulke Greville, First Lord Brooke*, Oxford, 1971, 73-74.

5 See below, pp. 71-72. It is unfortunate that my reference to this possible analogue (*TLS*, 19 August 1977, 998) may have prompted Frank Kermode, *The Genesis of Secrecy*, Cambridge, Mass., 1979, 114, to discount the anecdote entirely. My intention then, as now, had been to draw attention to the complexities involved in understanding both human actions and the subsequent reports of those actions. Kermode's views received an immediate riposte form William Empson (see n. 1 above), and an authoritative one from Dame Helen Gardner, *In Defence of Reason*, Oxford, 1982, 126-27.

6 For this reason I have adopted the title of one of the manuscripts of the text: *A Dedication to Sir Philip Sidney*.

7 See below, p. 77.

8 Sidney is often regarded as a kind of Protestant saint, and Greville is frequently cited as the principal hagiographer. In what follows I proceed on the assumption that this view of Greville was inappropriately foisted on him during the nineteenth century.

9 See *MP*, 161-62.

10 Zouch, 266-78. For a modern edition of Gifford's supposed work see *MP*, 166-72.

11 The authenticity of the reference to Lady Rich in one of the manuscripts is, as Katherine Duncan-Jones suggests, questionable; see *MP*, 224. It is possibly a later interpolation.

12 *MP*, 166.

13 Katherine Duncan-Jones has rightly suggested that 'we should probably admire *Sidney's Death* as a work of art rather than a historical document' (*MP*, 164).

14 Some of the more recent studies of the *ars moriendi* tradition are: Kathrine Koller, 'Falstaff and the Art of Dying', *MLN*, LX (1945), 383-86; Beach Langston, 'Essex and the Art of Dying', *HLQ*, XIII (1950), 109-29; Kathrine Koller, 'Art, Rhetoric, and Holy Dying in *The Faerie Queene* with Special Reference to the Despair Canto', *Studies in Philology*, LXI (1964), 128-39, and Nancy Lee Beaty, *The Craft of Dying: A Study in the Literary Tradition of the Ars Moriendi in England*, New Haven, 1970. Langston's claim (p. 113) that only seventeen of the sixteenth-century *ars moriendi* handbooks (in various editions) are known to us, involves a serious underestimation of the situation.

15 *Greville Prose*, 78.

16 *Greville Prose*, 80.

17 *Greville Prose*, 81.

18 *Greville Prose*, 81.

19 *Greville Prose*, 83.

20 Greville (*Greville Prose*, 79) mentions that this took place some time after the sixteenth day, that is, some time after 8 October 1586. Greville is not very precise, and it would be unfair to extract chronology from his account. His point is that at some

stage Sidney, despite his physicians' opinions to the contrary, realised that he would not recover, and so set about the business of preparing for his death.

21  The *Phaedo*, 60D-61B. All quotations from classical works are taken from the *Loeb Classical Library* editions.

22  The *Phaedo*, 84E-85B.

23  Ringler, in a note on *AS* 21.6 (*Poems*, 468), and S. K. Heninger, Jr., 'Sidney and Serranus' Plato', *ELR*, XIII (1983), 146-61, point out that Sidney probably read Plato in the 1578-Henri Estienne edition.

24  *Tusculan Disputations*, I.xxx.73.

25  Plutarch, *Cato*, LXVIII.2.

26  *OA*, 372-73. Jean Robertson's note (p. 480) refers to Walter R. Davis' contention that Duplessis-Mornay's *A Work Concerning the Trueness of the Christian Religion* is the immediate source for the prison scene.

27  *OA*,373-74.

28  Cited by Ruth Hughey ed., *The Arundel Harington Manuscript of Tudor Poetry*, 2 vols, Columbus, Ohio, 1960, II, 73. Waterhouse's seeming disavowal of the 'swansong' convention not only draws attention to his awareness of the usual associations, but confirms the Socratic view that the song is a joyful one (see above, p. 65).

29  See Hughey, I, 12-13 and II, 68-73.

30  For further discussion of the *moriturus* lyric in the Renaissance see my forthcoming article.

31  *Greville Prose*, 82.

32  *Poems*, 276.

33  In Thomas Becon's *The Sick man's salve* (first published in 1561), David is regarded as a type of the repentant sinner, and on two occasions Epaphroditus, the dying man, uses part of Psalm 6 as a prayer; see *Prayers and Other Pieces of Thomas Becon*, ed. John Ayre, Cambridge, 1844, 101, 100 and 155.

34  *Greville Prose*, 76-77.

35  Thomas Moffet, *Nobilis...and Lessus Lugubris*, ed. Virgil B. Heltzel and Hoyt H. Hudson, San Marino, 1940, 102.

36  Moffet, 137.

37  See Thomas Digges, *A Brief report of the military services done in the Low Countries*, 1587, sig. D1.

38  Sir John Smythe, *Certain discourses...concerning the forms and effects of diverse sorts of weapons*, 1590, sig. B3. In quoting from Bodleian Douce S 227 (annotated and corrected by Smythe himself) I have modernized the spelling and punctuation.

39  *CSPFor (Holland and Flanders), 1586-1587*, XXI, Pt II, 151.

40  See *DNB*.

41  I owe this reference to Joaquin Kuhn, who very generously made his unpublished edition of the *Dedication* available to me.

42  *OA*, 289. Katherine Duncan-Jones very kindly drew my attention to this passage.

43  It could be argued that Greville shaped the narrative in the light of his recollection of incidents in the two versions of the *Arcadia*. Such an argument would require us to attribute a subtlety of mind to Greville that he does not exhibit elsewhere.

44  Plutarch, *Themistocles*, III.3-4.

45  *The Countess of Pembroke's Arcadia*, ed. Maurice Evans, Penguin, 1977, 340. Similar examples can be found on 398-99, 503, 527 and 539.

46  Zouch, 383-84.

47  2 Sam 23: 14-17. The anecdote is repeated in 1 Chron 11: 16-19.

48  Lucan, *Civil Wars*, IX.500-10.

49  Plutarch, *Alexander*, XLII.3-6.

50  Luke 16: 19-31.

51  *In Defence of the Imagination*, 127.

52  *Greville Prose*, 77.

53  George Whetstone, *Sir Philip Sidney, his Honourable Life, his Valiant Death, and True Virtues*, ?1587, sig. C1.

54  See Wallace, 379-82.
55  *Greville Prose*, 78-79. The person referred to as Count Hollock was Count Philip of Hohenlohe Langenburg (1550-1606), a habitually quarrelsome man opposed to English involvement in the Netherlands. Greville's remark on reconciled friendship is a direct reference to the many quarrels involving Count Hollock and the English commanders.
56  John Stow, *The Annals of England*, 1592, 1254.
57  John Lothrop Motley, *The History of the United Netherlands*, 4 vols, London, 1869, II, 53.
58  *MP*, 152.
59  Wallace, 201.
60  *MP*, 144-46.
61  Wallace, 179.
62  *CSPFor (Holland and Flanders) 1585-1586*, XX.
63  See *The Works of Sir Philip Sidney*, 3 vols, London, 1725, I, 13-14; *The Works of Sir Philip Sidney*, 3 vols, Dublin, 1739, I, 9; Arthur Collins, *Letters and Memorials of State*, 2 vols, London, 1746, I, 106.
64  Zouch, 256. Zouch's misquotation of Sidney's supposed speech undermines his contention concerning its memorability.
65  See Sidney, 16th Earl of Pembroke, 51-52.
66  Zouch, 385. An early catalogue of West's works lists a painting 'of the Death of Sir Philip Sidney'; see John Galt, *The Life, Studie, and Works of Benjamin West, Esq.*, 2 vols, London, 1820, II, 231.
67  J. Radford Thomson, *Sir Philip Sidney*, New Biographical Series, No. 25, London, 1885, 15; and J. Radford Thomson, 'Sir Philip Sidney', in a collection entitled *Christian Warriors*, London, 1898, 15.
68  Wallace, 387.
69  *MP*, 387.
70  See *Greville Prose*, 38-41 and notes.
71  *Greville Prose*, 47-71.
72  *Greville Prose*, 48.
73  Whetstone, *Sidney*, sig.Cl$^v$. Cf. *Greville Prose*, 83. Whetstone could well be the source for Greville's version of the words.
74  Raphael Holinshed, *Chronicles*, 3 vols, 1587, III, 1548-55.
75  Holinshed, 1554.
76  *Nobilis*, xv.
77  *Nobilis*, xix.
78  In the light of Professor Ringler's article I would certainly want to make some adjustments to my argument, though I do not think that we yet have enough evidence to be as sure as Professor Ringler about either Sidney's motives for not wearing cuisses, or Greville's lack of probity in making up a story of the wounded Sidney's generosity. At best, we can return a Scottish verdict of 'not Proven'. Professor Ringler is not concerned with the conventions and precedents which could have influenced either Sidney's actions or the accounts (fabricated or not) of his actions. Whatever our differences about the interpretation of two details from Greville's account, it seems to me that we share the view both that the sentimentalised image of Sidney cannot be accepted uncritically, and that the two best-known anecdotes concerning Sidney (whatever their status) should not be allowed to distort our understanding of the man.

DOMINIC BAKER-SMITH

# 'GREAT EXPECTATION': SIDNEY'S DEATH
## AND THE POETS

Sidney is such a settled fact in our literary experience that it is a healthy shock to the system to consider the resources of English writing as they appeared to him when composing *A Defence of Poetry*. There is the great founding figure of Chaucer who 'in that misty time could see so clearly', the *Mirror for Magistrates* and Surrey's lyrics 'tasting of a noble birth, and worthy of a noble mind'. *Gorboduc* is listed, already some twenty years in the past, while only *The Shepheardes Calender*, blamed for its archaisms, is yet available to herald the rich developments of the 1580s. The bleakness of the survey hardly points to those developments, though Sidney as critic reveals an austerity of judgement which was happily evaded in his own poetry. It is evident, however, that Sidney's remarkably sophisticated appreciation of the fictional imagination—that quality of the right poet which ranges, 'only reined with learned discretion, into the divine consideration of what may be and should be'—obviously grew out of a richer literary sediment than this vernacular writing could supply.

Here the role of the continental vernaculars, that is to say, French and Italian, is clear enough; yet it needs to be remembered that Latin provided an important resource, not only for those academic communities with which Sidney was associated but also for the whole movement of Northern European humanism. Apart from any other consideration, Latin was the *lingua franca* of international Protestantism. It is, then, particularly significant that Sidney's death was commemorated by the poets not only in the vernacular which he had so enriched but also in the Latin that signalled his academic and political endeavours. The university commemorative volumes guaranteed the Sidney legend a learned audience and, potentially at least, an international one, but the act of embalming his memory in a learned tongue also works to politicize it.

Close on twenty-five years after Sidney's death Robert Burton voiced the perennial complaint of the frustrated scholar:

> ... the Muses are now banished in this bastard age, *ad sordida tuguriola*, the meaner persons, and confined alone to Universities. In those daies, Schollers were highly beloved, honoured and esteemed; as old *Ennius* by *Scipio Africanus*, *Virgil* by *Augustus;* *Horace* by *Mecaenas*: Princes Companions.[1]

It is of course a constant theme for Renaissance authors, from Petrarch in the 'Coronation oration' to Spenser in the 'October' eclogue, but Burton's reference to the universities gives it a specific point. Oxford and Cambridge after the difficult years of Mary's reign had been increasingly drawn into the orbit of government as Elizabeth's ministers tried to build up a cadre of scholars fit for use as secretaries, administrators and, on occasion, diplomats. Leicester's important role in this policy has been studied by Eleanor Rosenberg, but it is clear that Sidney—if only because of his competent Latinity—acted as patron of university men in a far more intimate sense.[2] His death was a serious blow to the academic community and its tributes to his memory draw on the same motifs as 'October' in order to celebrate the union of court and college in Sidney's person.

An earlier generation of patrons exemplified by Burghley, who had become Chancellor of Cambridge in 1559, and by Leicester, who became Chancellor of Oxford five years later, used its powers of patronage freely but without the spirit of participation which marked Sidney. Burghley had been the friend and brother-in-law of John Cheke, the greatest English Grecian, but it is clear that his range of patronage was defined and restricted by the pressures of political life. His rumoured hostility to Spenser may be a case in point. Leicester, while a younger man, was still of the same generation and appears to have lacked the academic polish to move at ease among scholars. Sidney, by contrast, establishes a style of patronage with participation which extends down to Lucius Cary, Viscount Falkland, at Great Tew in the 1630s. Elizabeth's apparent refusal to make adequate use of Sidney's public talents certainly proved beneficial to the arts. An interesting indication of Sidney's status as a model for this new relationship is the fact that Oxford and Cambridge produced verse miscellanies for the first time to mark his death, and thus initiated a tradition of such commemorative volumes.[3]

The new style is handsomely exemplified by Sir Henry Unton, who had studied at Oriel and served under Leicester in the Netherlands where he took part in the fatal skirmish at Zutphen and won praise. His whole public career was devoted to the promotion of an anti-Spanish foreign policy. Unton is best known today for the memorial portrait, possibly painted by a herald, which now hangs in the National Portrait Gallery in London and provides one of our few glimpses of a Tudor masque.[4] The neo-gothic conception of the portrait suggests a link with the chivalric revival in which Sidney shared; equally Unton's challenge to the Duc de Guise for dishonouring Elizabeth's name, issued while on embassy to Henri IV, can be seen as another instance of the anachronistic spirit which the English tried ineffectually to export to the continent.[5] Yet with the medievalism went sophisticated artistic interests: Unton received the dedication of Robert Ashley's Latin version of Du Bartas' *L'Uranie*, he was on friendly terms with prominent dons like John Case the Aristotelian and Matthew Gwinne, Professor of Physick and Latin playwright, while Dowland included 'Sir Henry Umpton's Funerall' in his musical *Lachrimae*. After his death on embassy in France in 1596 Oxford produced a commemorative collection of Latin verses, *Funebria Nobilissimi ac Praestantissimi Equitis, D. Henrici Untoni*. Not only does it have the same printer as the Sidney volume, Joseph Barnes, but the editor, Robert Wright of Trinity College, actually refers to the precedent. Contributors include Case and Gwinne, Thomas Wilson, and that redoubtable champion of stage-plays William Gager who, nine years before, had edited the Oxford tribute to Sidney. Unton, in other words, is Sidney writ small, and the complexion of his interests provides some indication of the public valuation of Sidney. It is surely fitting that one piece should be a dialogue between a courtier and a scholar, 'Aulici et academici dialogus in funere Untoni'.[6] The same theme obviously underlies the memorial portrait which shows both Unton's studies in Oxford and his diplomatic travels, set in a variety of scenes from birth to death; but the scene which catches the eye is his funeral procession of black cowled mourners at Faringdon, in its humble style an evocation of the Lant engraving of Sidney's obsequies which Unton had attended.

At this stage, then, it may reasonably be suggested that *Funebria Untoni* reflects the innovatory significance of the Sidney commemorative volumes. These volumes demonstrate a connection between court and university, between policy and poetics, which is the mature fruit of sixteenth century changes in educational policy and in particular of the new interest of the governing classes in higher education, a ripening which coincides with Sidney's generation. Moreover, when we respond to the classicizing gestures of the commemorative volumes we should set beside them the heraldic icon of Sir Henry Unton with its deliberate 'gothic' character. Both these modes, classical and gothic, are necessary to the interpretation of contemporary cultural life; both are designed to meet the Elizabethan appetite for codified presentation of inner qualities, the sort of conception realised in *imprese*. The episodes from Unton's life in the portrait are not, in the ordinary sense, biographical. They serve to identify the private man with the public role and absorb him into it. In an age when religious life is naturally presented in the form of accommodation to scriptural roles, the definition of self through public types is a secular equivalent, and the function of neo-Latin poetry in elaborating such types deserves wider recognition.

This assimilation to ideal types or 'feigned example', to use Sidney's own term, can certainly explain why the Sidney biographical canon is often problematical. Young Philip Sidney tried to realise himself through roles which he selected, and others proposed roles to him; in life others read him in terms of roles which may not have been his own, while after death the poets conspired to embody in him an ideal type. Throughout his life Sidney was haunted by what he once refers to as 'that friendly foe, great expectation'. The words occur in sonnet 21 of *Astrophil and Stella*, a poem of peculiar moral irony based on the worthy advice of some older friend who warns Astrophil against the snares of love:

> That *Plato* I read for nought, but if he tame
>    Such coltish gyres, that to my birth I owe
> Nobler desires, least else that friendly foe,
>    Great expectation, weare a traine of shame.

The earnest advice builds up to a ponderous adage,

> Sure you say well, your wisdome's golden mine
>    Dig deepe with learning's spade, ...

The trite moralism which sees self-mastery as a product of study collapses in the final line when Astrophil speaks for the first time *in propria persona*,

> ... now tell me this
> Hath this world ought so fair as *Stella* is?

The characteristically humanistic moral scheme is subverted by the blunt call of passion. For our purposes the interesting feature of the poem is Sidney's self-ironic awareness of expectation and all it brought in its train, and it is instructive if we compare the friend's counsel with Languet's own words to Sidney. Writing from Vienna in November 1573, Languet chides Sidney's impetuous curiosity:

> To offend *me* is of little consequence, but reflect how grievously you would be sinning against your excellent Father, who has placed all his hopes in you, and who being now in the flower of life, expects to see the full harvest of those virtues, which your character promises so largely to produce.[7]

If Astrophil's moral guide sounds like Languet it is hardly surprising; what is more interesting is the awareness in Sidney both of what others expected of him, and of the oversimplification that such roles entailed.

   A mythologising tendency helped to shape the conduct of Sidney's life and, even more persistently, to commemorate his death. Such refining of the raw material of life into ideal images was an important aspect of Renaissance public discourse, but one wonders if England were not especially susceptible in view of the carefully manipulated cult of the Virgin Queen. Certainly any examination of Elizabeth's portraits and of the pageantry devised for her reveals the same mythologising tendency which contributed to the creation of the Sidney legend. The unhappy state of Anglo-Dutch relations during Leicester's period of command can be attributed to a variety of causes but two stand out as fundamental: the chivalric ideology deriving from the Accession Day tilts and the commitment to an anti-Spanish Protestant league.[8] The first introduced a spirit of knightly emulation which contributed little to the practical war-effort, while the second subordinated the interests of the United Provinces to an international crusade. The Dutch, fighting for survival as a loose federation of local interests and more concerned with political realities than with dogmatic issues, were quite reasonably suspicious of Leicester's attempts to centralize power and were not over-impressed by military forays which yielded glory rather than practical advantage. Zutphen was no exception. The English had had little practical experience of new military developments since Bosworth, a century before. It is doubly ironical that Sidney's fatal wound was caused by an arquebus, the weapon which had become decisive on continental battlefields since the chivalrous aspirations of Francis I had foundered at Pavia in 1525. Whatever the motives were that prompted Sidney to leave off his cuisses—'unspotted emulation' or the more probable adoption of light cavalry accoutrements—he fell victim to the weapon which brutally exposed anachronism.[9]

Leicester's attempt to impose centralized control on the complex web of Dutch local interests and his furtive assumption of the title of Governor-General suggest that he hoped to salvage something for himself—and thereby for the Calvinist faction—out of the uncertainties created by William of Orange's assassination. His failure lay partly in his personal inadequacies and partly in the incompatibilities of English and Dutch attitudes to the war with Spain; but against that failure it is worth recalling the remarks of P. C. Hooft in the following century:

> And some never doubted but (had he lived) [Sidney's] wisdom and modesty (once time and experience had mollified his passions) would have obliged his uncle, whose intelligence could not compare with his, to discontinue his immature enterprises, which were a humiliation to the States. But others judged, that if he should have used his industry, valour, and ability in undermining liberty (which his insistence, from the very first, that Leicester's governorship should embrace unlimited authority, had given them reason to fear), that this would have disagreed with the country even more than the delusions of Leicester....[10]

The two sentences give a melancholy summary of the English intervention; what is clear is that Sidney had impressed the Dutch, even as a potential opponent. Once his qualities had been lost in death it remained

only for the poets to embalm them in exemplary forms. As Katherine
Duncan-Jones has argued of *Sidney's Death*, attributed to George Gifford,
'we should probably admire *Sidney's Death* as a work of art rather than
a historical monument',[11] so too the poets who commemorate that death
are writing to ensure the survival of his metaphorical presence, active in
the categories of myth. The entire range of idealisation, from laureate to
hero, is compassed in Raleigh's 'Epitaph', printed in the 1595 *Astrophel*:

> That day their *Hanniball* died, our *Scipio* fell,
> *Scipio, Cicero* and *Petrarch* of our time.    (ll. 57-58)

There is a notable precision in the classical allusions, each definitive of
a role: Sidney is a Hannibal to Spain, but to England at once commander
and patron, persuader and poet. The providential victory of Rome over
Carthage celebrated by Petrarch in the *Africa*, becomes a model for the
victory of a Protestant Empire over Spain. Scipio and Ennius represent
in the *Africa* the dynamic interrelation of heroic and literary achievement,
yet Scipio is in himself a familiar type of contemplation and action in
ideal balance.[12] Not only is Sidney a poet and patron of extraordinary
importance but underlying all his endeavours is this Scipionic conjunction of the camp and the schools; it provides the central theme for his
great oration in defence of poetry.

This conjunction is a constant theme of the commemorative poems,
from Thomas Churchyard's 'Epitaph', the earliest to mourn Sidney,[13] to
Spenser's tribute, 'Astrophel', which eventually appeared as part of *Colin
Clouts Come Home Again* in 1595. Spenser's two contributions, the 'Ruines
of Time' in the 1591 *Complaints* and 'Astrophel', are the most distinguished of the vernacular laments. In 'Astrophel' pieces by Matthew
Roydon, Raleigh and (probably) Dyer, which had originally appeared in
*The Phoenix Nest* in 1593, are reprinted with other laments by Lady Mary
Sidney (or, more probably, Spenser) and Ludowick Bryskett to make up
a sequence which is framed by Spenser's own lines. In the pieces by
Bryskett, Roydon and Raleigh one encounters a very similar typology to
that found in the Latin poems; that is, in addition to 'private lack' of 'the
riches of his wit', we are confronted by a political dimension expressed
in military and religious terms. Thus Bryskett's 'Mourning Muse of
Thestylis' both relates Sidney's death to its actual military theatre and
typologically merges Sidney's death in the passion of Christ. It is possible
that these poems were early in date, or at least precede Leicester's own
death (which Spenser's poems do not). What makes them resemble the
Latin commemorative pieces is the way in which they translate Sidney's
personal drama into a public discourse designed to unite the three estates

of court, college, and camp in a poetical statement of the Protestant cause. It is the public discourse that we must now examine.

The four volumes of Latin verse which commemorate Sidney's death originated, unsurprisingly, in universities. The first was the Cambridge contribution, *Academiae Cantabrigiensis Lachrymae Tumulo Nobilissimi Equitis, D. Philippi Sidneij Sacratae*, edited by Alexander Neville of St. John's. Unlike the Oxford volumes which were locally printed, *Lachrymae* was printed in London by John Windet at the expense of Thomas Chard, and to judge by the date of the dedicatory epistle addressed to Leicester it seems to have been intended to coincide with Sidney's funeral at St. Paul's in February 1587. It was followed in September by *Peplus, Illustrissimi Viri D. Philippi Sidnaei Supremus Honoribus Dicatus*, a collection of elegies by twenty-nine members of New College, printed at Oxford by Joseph Barnes. *Peplus* was edited by John Lloyd, fellow of New College, and dedicated to Sidney's brother-in-law Henry Herbert, Earl of Pembroke, and alumnus of the college. Among the contributors were John Owen and John Hoskyns both of whom won literary distinction in later life.[14] *Exequiae illustrissimi Equitis, D. Philippi Sidnaei, gratissimae memoriae ac nomini impensae*, the official Oxford volume, was also printed by Barnes and appeared in November with some apologies for delay. It was edited by William Gager of Christ Church College, an important advocate of stage-plays whose *Meleager* had been presented before Sidney and Leicester and the Polish Prince Albertus Alasco in 1585.[15] The fourth volume, which appeared in the course of 1587, was that associated with the new University of Leiden. The book, entitled *Epitaphia in Mortem Nobilissimi et Fortissimi Viri D. Philippi Sidneij Equitis*, was printed at Leiden by J. Paedts and is made up of twenty epitaphs by Georgius Benedicti (Werteloo). It is not really comparable to the English miscellanies since it is very much a one man effort; rather it belongs with the individual elegies by other Leiden poets like Janus Dousa and Jan van Hout. These men, together with Lipsius, were Sidney's most interesting contacts in Leiden and some of their poems reveal a knowledge of his English writings. Dousa was a friend of Alexander Neville, editor of the Cambridge *Lachrymae*, while the *Epitaphia* is dedicated to Cecil's eldest son Thomas, Governor of The Brill and a potential patron. Despite the different character of the Leiden offering, then, it still fits within the same network of humanistic contacts and literary aspirations.[16]

Nor is this surprising: quite apart from the politico-religious ties between England and the Netherlands, the innovation of publishing university miscellanies of this kind in Cambridge and Oxford must reflect continental influence. Certainly the practice of composing individual verses to commemorate the dead, or major public events, was

common enough and as late as Wordsworth's time at Cambridge
(1787-90) the death of the Master of St. John's was marked by sheets of
verses which were fixed to the coffin and virtually covered it. William
Gager, in the dedication of *Exequiae* to Leicester, Oxford's Chancellor,
states that at first members of the university had written verses to express
their private grief for Sidney before the idea of a university collection was
put forward. How Cambridge came upon that idea we cannot know, nor
whether individuals relieved their feelings in verse. But to take any statement in neo-Latin at its face value is dangerous, and to accept Gager's
pastoral as the whole story would be naive. The Oxford and Cambridge
volumes are probably to be seen as part of a wider political campaign to
exploit Sidney's death in favour of an interventionist policy in the
Netherlands. They give an official stamp to the myth.

The fact that both the Cambridge *Lachrymae* and the Oxford *Exequiae*
were dedicated to Leicester (while *Peplus* was dedicated to the Earl of
Pembroke who had married into the Dudley connection) suggests a concerted scheme to publicize the policy of direct intervention, with its cor-
ollary of a Protestant league against Spain. Such a motive colours
Greville's *Life*; a work which is deeply influenced by Greville's anti-
Catholic and anti-Spanish prejudices. Leicester was a central figure in
the faction which desired Calvinist reform of the Anglican Church and
which looked to a Protestant league in which England would assume an
imperial role. Such a cluster of motives clearly lay behind Leicester's acceptance of the title of Governor-General, a move which infuriated
Elizabeth. Sidney once dead, then his loss could be turned to some account as a theme for propaganda; one must assume that the magnificent
funeral devised for him by Walsingham had such a significance. To
associate the university volumes with this policy does not deny motives
of genuine admiration among those who celebrated Sidney, but it does
give them a practical edge. Leicester's intimate involvement with
patronage in the two universities made such a step logical: ambitious
dons could hope to win attention, the Walsingham-Leicester axis could
gain support and international attention. It is, after all, a point of some
interest that *Lachrymae* is dedicated to Leicester as High Steward of Cambridge University and not to the Chancellor, Burghley. The pragmatic
Burghley did not share Leicester's pan-Protestant ambitions. The
dedication to Leicester, Sidney's uncle, may seem domestic enough but
it needs to be read also in terms of the faction politics which dominated
Tudor government. Sidney's death gave the Leicester faction a martyr,
and that could be more influential at court than Sidney's live interven-
tions had proved to be.

But the mere fact of dedication is not the end of the story; the terms of dedication lend further support to a political interpretation. Leicester had been sworn in as Governor-General on 4 February 1586, and Elizabeth's rage at his presumption followed close on the event. Yet the dedications of the Cambridge *Lachrymae* and of the Oxford *Exequiae*, composed several months later at a time when Leicester's enterprise was foundering, still use the aspiring terms which had earlier given offence. Both go beyond the uncontroversial military title of commander-in-chief to address him as Prefect of the United Provinces, 'Foederatae Belgiae Praefectus', an office with Hapsburg rather than Tudor associations, and Gager in *Exequiae* actually uses the title 'Praecellentissimus', 'Excellency', which Elizabeth had specifically criticised.[17] There is no question of disloyalty to the Queen, but both dedications do surely point to the anxiety of the Leicester faction to restore the flagging momentum of the English intervention.

An apt example of faction at work in an academic context is Dr Lawrence Humphrey, author of a treatise *Of Nobilitye* and a leading contributor to *Exequiae*. A Marian exile at Zurich, Humphrey returned to Oxford, becoming Regius Professor of Divinity in 1560 and master of Magdalen shortly afterwards. He presided over the Convocation which elected Leicester Chancellor, and then led the deputation which offered the dignity. In his turn Leicester appears to have been instrumental in Humphrey's election as Vice-Chancellor in 1571, and when Humphrey was reprimanded for his puritan view of *adiaphora* he looked to Leicester for protection. But we also find Humphrey drawn into the orbit of the court, delivering orations before Elizabeth during her visits to Woodstock in 1572 and 1575. In the second of these orations he refers to the highly political pageants devised by Leicester for the Queen at Kenilworth during that year, and hails the court as a third university.[18] The Kenilworth entertainments were substantially the work of the poet George Gascoigne, and Gascoigne was a close friend of Alexander Neville, editor of the Cambridge *Lachrymae*. Contacts like these may not add up to much in explicit terms, but they surely indicate that in the case of the university volumes, as in much court directed literature, we must be alert to a specific context, one which includes not only religious and political alignments but also the vital interaction between poetic themes and public display.

Both the Oxford volumes and Benedicti's *Epitaphia* have received some attention in recent years, but virtually nothing has been said of the Cambridge *Lachrymae*. Yet, as the first such tribute to appear in England, *Lachrymae* merits some investigation as a fundamental contribution to the Sidney legend. The claim to priority is based on Alexander Neville's prefatory panegyric addressed to Leicester. This is dated 16 February

1586 (i.e. 26 February 1587, new style), the actual day of Sidney's interment at St. Paul's. Yet title-page and colophon give the date 1587, and
the gathering of the volume suggests some change of plan. Thus poems
by sixty-three Cambridge men make up the main body of the book
(pp. 1-86), but they are preceded by an unpaginated section which contains two parts. The first of these (sigs. a-i2) contains Neville's 'Carmen
Consolatorium' and his lengthy panegyric. The second part (sigs. k1-l2),
quite unannounced on the title-page, consists of an English sonnet on
Sidney by King James VI of Scotland, followed by Latin paraphrases of
it by James and several courtiers. Neville's dating of his piece suggests
at least the intention of preparing a volume for presentation purposes,
possibly at the funeral or soon after.[19] Either this was not achieved, or
the arrival of the Scottish material led to a hasty reconsideration of the
book. At least one surviving copy contains the stub of a cancelled title-
page which may indicate such a change of direction.[20]

Alexander Neville (1544-1614) was an appropriate editor, who had
contributed in his own quiet way to the Elizabethan renaissance. As
secretary to Archbishop Parker he had been active in Anglo-Saxon
studies, and he continued to serve Parker's successors Grindal and
Whitgift. As translator Neville produced a version of the *Oedipus* (1563)
which was included in Thomas Newton's influential *Seneca his Tenne
Tragedies*, and he appears also to have tackled Livy. An intimacy with
Barnabe Googe and George Gascoigne, which dated from his time at
Gray's Inn, resulted in contributions to Googe's *Eglogs and Sonnettes*
(1563). Between 1584 and 1586, the period of *Lachrymae*, he was M.P.
for Christchurch. He is representative of those men, humanistically inclined, concerned with expansion of the vernacular, adept at ad-
ministrative duties, who saw in Sidney an important and innovatory
patron. Neville's panegyric in resonant, Ciceronian periods follows a
familiar epideictic pattern, passing from the theme of sorrow, by way of
Sidney's achievement and qualities, to the recognition of his celestial
vocation, 'O nobilissime nunc autem Sanctissimae heros'.[21]

There can be no question, however, that the focus of interest in the
first section of *Lachrymae* is the sonnet by James VI.

> Thou mighty *Mars* the Lord of souldiers brave,
> And thou *Minerve*, that dois in wit excell,
> And thou *Apollo*, that dois knowledge have,
> Of every art that from Parnassus fell
> With all you *Sisters* that thaireon do dwell,
> Lament for him, who duelie serv'd you all
> Whome in you wisely all your arts did mell,
> Bewaile (I say) his inexpected fall,
> I neede not in remembrance for to call

His race, his youth, the hope had of him ay
Since that in him doth cruell death appall
Both manhood, wit and learning every way,
  But yet he doth in bed of *honor* rest,
  And evermore of him shall live the best.[22]

By the standards of C. S. Lewis this would qualify as a modest display
of 'drab' talent, but it does manage to exemplify the typical features of
Sidneian elegy: the diversity of talents personified in rival deities, the
sense of promise blighted, the prospect of a posthumous influence which
will frustrate death.

James's poetic ambitions were guided by Alexander Montgomerie,
and he clearly intended to establish at his court a poetic group comparable to Sidney's own circle. Under his patronage Thomas Hudson
translated du Bartas' *La Judith*, and William Fowler attempted the
Petrarchan *Trionfi* which also drew Mary Sidney's attention. Apart from
his plans for an epic on Lepanto, James had published in 1584 *Essayes
of a Prentice in the Divine Art of Poesie* which contained 'Ane Schort Treatise,
Conteining some Reulis and Cautelis to be observit and eschewit in Scot-
tis Poesie', an essay derived from George Gascoigne's *Certain Notes of Instruction* (1575).[23] James's interest in a specifically Christian poetics was
one of several concerns which he shared with the Sidney circle, another
being the works of George Buchanan. Certainly, Buchanan was admired
by advocates of Calvinist humanism in England, France and the
Netherlands.[24] Like the young Sidney, Buchanan had been profoundly
disturbed by the Saint Bartholomew massacre. The publication of *Bap-
tistes* in London in 1577, under the eye of Thomas Randolph, represents
more than a taste for Latin plays, for Buchanan's literary activity had an
ideological significance for militant humanists which extended to the
'democratic' notions of kingship proposed in the *De iure regni* and the
*Historia*. While Elizabeth was entirely hostile to such notions they were
favourably received within Sidney's own circle and in Leiden.[25] There
are, then, a number of intellectual concerns which can throw light on
James's contribution to *Lachrymae*.

Yet Sidney's interest in James obviously extended beyond literary
sympathy. We have his significant words to Buchanan, 'pedagog to the
kingis Majestie', written at the time of the Alençon affair,

> I haif nocht bene without desire to see you, and kiss the hand of the young
> king, in quhome mony have layd their hopes.

To other Protestant humanists like Duplessis-Mornay, Buchanan's role
as tutor to James gave him the power to mould a new, Protestant Con-
stantine. If Buchanan's royal pupil could appear to some as the governor

of a future Protestant empire—uniting Britain in the process—he had his own more immediate problems to resolve. A month before Sidney's death at Arnhem the Babington conspirators were executed in London. The trial of Mary Queen of Scots opened at Fotheringay on 15 October and, by the time that the solemn funeral cortège recorded by Lant made its way to St. Paul's, the very day that Neville dated his dedication of *Lachrymae*, Mary had been dead for eight days. While James, whose devotion to his mother was less than absolute, might wish to make a gesture on her behalf, a volume in honour of Walsingham's son-in-law was scarcely the place to make it. It is likely that in the long term James saw this contribution to the Sidney hagiography as a chance to commend his own name to those, in England and abroad, who looked for a fit successor to Elizabeth, one equipped to serve the Protestant interest. In the short term it served to confirm James's adherence to the Anglo-Scots alliance which had just been negotiated by Sir Thomas Randolph.[26]

James liked to set his literary friends tasks and this appears to explain the form of the Scottish commemoration of Sidney. The English sonnet is followed by James's own Latin version, and those of several Scottish courtiers, Lord Gray, Sir John Maitland, Colonel James Halkerston, Lord Seton and the Earl of Angus. It is a group of some interest. All that can be said of Halkerston (or Hakerton) is that several of his Latin epigrams were collected in *Delitiae Poetarum Scotorum* where he is described as 'tribunus militum'. Sir John Maitland, who became Chancellor of Scotland in 1587 and won from Burghley the epithet 'the wisest man in Scotland', also appears in the *Delitiae* where his contributions include his verses on Sidney and epigrams on Tycho Brahe.[27] What appears to link the group together is a common complicity in the 1585 plot against James Stewart, Earl of Arran, and commitment to a pro-English policy. Yet none has any connection with Cambridge. Presumably the paginated section of contributions from the University was set up first and the Scottish poems inserted at a late stage, perhaps when the date of Sidney's long-delayed funeral was known. One possible intermediary here would be Sir Thomas Randolph, old student of Buchanan and close friend of Walsingham who, after many years of experience as English emissary in Scottish affairs, had just negotiated the Anglo-Scots alliance.[28] In any case Gray, a 'beautiful, polished and perfidious young man', had been used by James as his intermediary in the discussions over his mother precisely to assure the English government of his continued support for the alliance.[29] The other contributor, Archibald Douglas, Earl of Angus, had fled to England after the fall of his uncle Morton in 1581. There he appears as a frequent companion of Sidney who read to him from the *Arcadia*.[30] So the inclusion of the Scottish contributions is not so arbitrary

as it might seem to be: behind the tributes to Sidney *Lachrymae* promotes
a number of factional interests. Although it is unlikely that the Scottish
courtiers, or even James in his new independence from Buchanan, were
too concerned about the exact religious complexion of English intervention in the Netherlands, yet they would surely share one thing with the
Leicester-Walsingham faction, hostility to Spain. In a sense *Lachrymae* is
a monument not to Sidney alone, but to that Protestant humanism which
he shared with Buchanan, and it clearly establishes the claim that James
VI is that 'King James of Scotland' honoured in *A Defence of Poetry*.[31]

Between them the three university volumes must be the most striking
example of technical virtuosity in Latin writing yet published in
England, and as such they provide an appropriate backdrop for the vernacular experiments of Sidney and his 'Areopagus'. The Cambridge
volume is the least ambitious in its use of verse resources and relies for
the most part on the *carmen funebre* or *epicedium*. While it does contain fourteen Greek poems, and one in Hebrew, it lacks the formal variety of the
Oxford collections. There is no pastoral elegy to compare, for instance,
with John Gifford's 'Lycidas' in *Peplus*, nor with the figure poems such
as John Lloyd's 'altar' in the same volume, or Henry Price's 'wings' in
*Exequiae*. The nearest approach to such mannerist sophistication in
*Lachrymae* is the adoption of single and double acrostic verses.[32] Some
forty-three contributors to the Cambridge volume can be identified with
varying degrees of confidence, and these represent every college. But it
is not surprising to find that the list is dominated by Trinity (10 certain,
1 possible), King's (7 certain, 1 possible) and St. John's (7 certain). St.
John's had its own tradition of classical scholarship, but it is interesting
that all the King's men came from Eton and five of the Trinity men from
Westminster. The youngest identifiable contributor, Joseph Walter, had
entered Trinity from Westminster in 1586. In contrast Dr Humphrey
Tyndall, President of Queens', who matriculated as early as 1555, was
an important representative of Leicester's interest in the University,
having served him as chaplain and officiated at his marriage to Lettice
Knollys in 1578. In its range of contributors *Lachrymae* could be said to
mark the maturity of that Cambridge humanism initiated by Ascham
and Cheke.

It would be interesting to know more about the relationship of these
contributors; how far Neville drew on a conscious network of collaborators, and how far this Cambridge group had continental contacts.
Neville's own friendship with Janus Dousa is suggestive of Dutch affilia-
tions, and Ramism provided another basis for contact abroad. Sidney
was reputed to have Ramist sympathies, and two contributors to
*Lachrymae*, Gabriel Harvey and William Temple, helped to disseminate

Ramist ideas in Cambridge. Temple's annotated edition of the *Dialecticae*, which appeared in 1584, has been claimed as the first publication of the University Press.[33] Among the less formal exercises in the University we can include academic drama and this, fittingly enough, attracted several of those who wrote in honour of Sidney. An important event at Cambridge had been the performance of Thomas Legge's Senecan drama *Ricardus Tertius* at St. John's in 1579. Legge, who became Master of Caius in 1573 and corresponded with Lipsius, did not write for *Lachrymae* but two of his actors did: John Palmer, who had played Richard, and Roger Morrell. Two other names in the cast-list are Abraham Fraunce and Henry Constable. Other contributors who tried their hand at drama were Anthony Wingfield and William Alabaster. Wingfield, a nephew of Bess of Hardwick, was elected Fellow of Trinity in 1576 and later became Public Orator of the University. He is described by Nash as the author of *Pedantius*, a comedy which ridiculed that aspiring Sidneian, Gabriel Harvey. Alabaster was one of the younger contributors who matriculated at Trinity in 1584. Better know today for his English sonnets, he made a name among his contemporaries for his Latin verse; his tragedy *Roxana* was performed at Trinity in 1592, and his unfinished epic *Elisaeis* won enthusiastic praise from Spenser in *Colin Clout*:

Who liues that can match that heroick song.[34]

Two other writers in *Lachrymae* merit special mention, Giles Fletcher and William Temple. Fletcher followed the familiar path to King's from Eton where he had been one of the boys who, in 1563, presented Latin verses to the Queen. He became deputy Orator of the University in 1577, Remembrancer of the City of London ten years later, and ended his career as Master of Requests. Fletcher's literary works ranged from numerous liminary verses to a first-hand account *Of the Russe Common Wealth* (London, 1591) which was suppressed for fear of offending the Czar, and his *Licia or Poemes of Love* (1593). No doubt this activity had its effect on his poet-sons, Giles and Phineas. What is clear is that by 1585, when he entered Parliament, Fletcher was already engaged on diplomatic work since, as we have seen, he accompanied Sir Thomas Randolph on the very embassy to Scotland which may explain King James's inclusion in *Lachrymae*. In contrast to the majority of the contributors who are content to use the familiar persuasions of elegy in a manner which allows little room for personal allusion, Fletcher introduces two elements which make his reference to Sidney highly specific. The first, the location and cause of Sidney's death in the skirmish at Zutphen, is already conveyed by his resonant title: 'In obitum optimi ac praeclarissimi iuvenis, Philippi Sidnaei Equitis aurati, qui in Zutphensi proelio (quod nuper est ad Iselam commissum est, inter Anglos et Hispanos) glande sulphurea ictus interijt.' Sidney is hailed as one who has made the Dutch cause his own and shown exemplary courage, struck down where the waters of the IJssel lap the fields of Zutphen.[35] A certain tension may be sensed behind Fletcher's Latin: the description of Sidney as a foreigner in the struggle (*miles peregrinus*) also carries overtones of knight-errantry, but the explicit brutality of his death, struck down by the leaden bullet of an arquebus (*machina sulphurea*), is a harsh contrast. The second element in the poem which carries a specific interest is an allusion to the chivalric exercises which Sidney knew at first hand and which he describes with such vivacity in *Arcadia*. Fletcher catalogues the emblems of war and of peace which mourn Sidney's passing, among them the 'circus hippodromus' where he had jousted with the lance and schooled the foaming war horses. These direct references to Sidney's career catch the eye in the formalized movement of the elegy as Fletcher lists those institutions which are the poorer for his loss: schools, camp, the court, the forum, and the Church.[36]

Sir William Temple has already been mentioned as a Cambridge Ramist, but his association with Sidney was far more personal than that might seem to imply. He made the move from Eton to King's in 1573 and had already left Cambridge for Lincoln Grammar School when Sidney, on his nomination as Governor of Flushing, made Temple his secretary. He was present at Sidney's death in Arnhem and was a beneficiary under his will. It is not surprising, then, to find that Temple moves beyond a conventional list of attributes and achievements to touch on contemporary worries. Sidney's death is seen as one drastic illustration of the workings of evil, clearly identified with Catholic hostility to Elizabeth, the royal virgin. Catholic plots, Sidney's death, the decline of religious fervour are all traced to the sins of the British people. Beyond the rehearsal of Sidney's literary worth and the final recognition of his place in heaven the elegy gives a degree of urgency to the business in hand: Sidney's example is enshrined in a programme of reform.[37]

The dominant theme of the Sidney elegies, one which we have already met in King James's sonnet, is his Scipionic resolution of conflicting talents. A typical treatment of this theme is John Palmer's 'Martis et Mercurii Contentio'. It was Palmer who acted the part of Richard III in Legge's play and he had previously taken part in disputes before the Queen; so it is fitting enough that he adopts a mythological debate as the governing device of the poem,

> *Mercurio* cum *Marte* gravis contentio nata est,
>   Cuius *Sidneius* sub ditione foret.

> Artes *Mercurius*, Mars arma potentia iactat:
>    *Mercurius* meus est; Mars, meus inquit erit.
> Intererat *Pallas*, iuvenisque accensa decore,
>    Contesta *Iovem*, talia voce refert:
> *Mercurius* belli, *Mars* inscius artis habetur,
>    Hic utrumque tenet, *Pallas* utroque valet;
> Praemia magna Pater, sed praemia debita posco,
>    Sit meus hic miles, debet utrumque mihi.

(A fierce argument arose between Mercury and Mars: under whose sway should Sidney fall? Mercury urged the arts, Mars skill at arms. 'He is mine', claimed Mercury. 'He will be mine', cried Mars. Pallas was standing by and, stirred by the young man's grace, appealed to Jove in this manner: 'Mercury is ignorant of war, Mars of the arts; yet he practices both of them, even as Pallas holds sway in both. I seek a great favour, heavenly father, but one which is my due: that this soldier may be mine, since he owes both talents to me.')[38]

Jove assents, and Mars, in frustrated fury, cuts Sidney's thread of life; Pallas raises the lifeless figure to heaven, and a feud is set between Mars and the followers of Pallas. Clearly Pallas, the armed goddess of wisdom, is a peculiarly apt figure for Sidney's realization of the Scipionic ideal, yet Palmer's device may gain, too, from the association of Pallas with the Queen herself. At Leicester's entry into Utrecht on 1 April 1586, two obelisks were set up with images of Elizabeth as Judith and as Pallas. On the latter was the Latin inscription,

> Ut gladio Pallas Sophiae dea pollet et arte,
> Sic utrisque potens belgas regina tuere.[39]

(As Pallas, goddess of wisdom, prevails with the sword and with art, so the mighty queen defends the Belgae with both.) Here the strands of public mythology join. This theme of a diversity of talents pervades all the commemorative volumes: in essence it is an expression of the general culture proposed by the humanist curriculum and appropriated by the courtier, but in Sidney's case its authentic application is supported by the strong sense of waste which occurs in so many elegies. There is a very particular wistfulness, which even the transparency of the Latin medium cannot disguise, in Alexander Neville's lament on behalf of the University,

> Quod si mors sera fuisset
> O quales fructus aetas matura dedisset
> Dulce decus nostrum, Sydus Sidneae Britannum.

(If only death had come later, what fruits might this paragon, this star of the Sidneys have given to Britain.)[40]

Mythology may serve to dramatize the negative aspects of Sidney's death, the thwarting of expectation, but the final transformation is that of the Christian martyr, 'pro Christo patriaque mori'. Ascent to immortality is a standard feature in elegy, but there is insistence that Sidney's ascent results from a martyr's death—'pro Christi Ecclesiae pugnans'. Not everyone would have seen it that way, certainly not in the Netherlands. Yet it is in perfect accord with that religious policy which Leicester promulgated at Utrecht, a policy of strict Calvinist reform which had no place for the irenical policies inherited from William of Orange.[41]

*Lachrymae* is representative of the commemorative poems not only because it is a compendium of rhetorical themes and devices which constantly recur but because it points to a set of aspirations which were to characterize the Sidney legend. In the case of *Lachrymae*, too, enough external evidence can be brought together to convey a sense of the larger aim it is intended to serve. This is not, of course, to imply that the legend can be explained away as ideology, but the ideology is there and recognition neutralizes it. In T. E. Hulme's sense Sidney's name became 'a word of power', to be utilized in the struggle for military action in the Netherlands. If Sidney was given near mythical stature it was because he invited such canonisation, unlike Leicester who died two years later under the shadow of failure and in changed political circumstance with scarcely a poetic sigh. But if we have the official image of Sidney as a Calvinist martyr we can place against it the tantalizing possibility that just before his death he was moving toward the more liberal position of William of Orange, or even the irenicism of Lipsius.[42] Such private adjustments were outside the range of public grief: that remained firmly set within the established categories,

> Thy countries love, religion, and thy friends:
> Of worthy men, the marks, the lives and ends,
> And her defence, for whom we labor all.[43]

## APPENDIX 1

### King James's contribution to *Cantabrigiensis Lachrymae*

*In Philippi Sidnaei interitum, Illustrissimi Scotorum Regis Carmen.*

Armipotens cui ius in fortia pectora *Mavors*
    Tu *Dea* quae cerebrum perrumpere digna *Tonantis*
Tuque adeo biugae *proles Latonia* rupis
Gloria, deciduae cingunt quam collibus *artes*,
Vos etiam huc lachrymas conferte *Heliconides*, istum

Plangite, quo vestri non observantior alter
Nec fuerat vestris insignior artibus alter,
Plangite talem, inquam, quem fata inopina tulere.
*Cuius* quid memorem, quid carmine persequar altum
Aut genus, aut virides annos, aut quam dederat spem?
Exuit heu rapido mors illaetabilis ictu,
Quo *Mars*, quo *Pallas*, quoque ipsum ornavit *Apollo*,
Sed venerandus *honos*, cineri superinduit urnam,
Parte etiam meliore sui super aethera vivit.

(Lachrymae, sig.k1<sup>r-v</sup>)

*Eiusdem Regis in Eundem Hexastichon*

Vidit ut exanimem tristis *Cytherea Philippum*
    Flevit, et hunc *Martem* credidit esse suum.
Eripuit digitis gemmas, colloque monile,
    *Marti* iterum nunquam ceu placitura foret.
Mortuus humana qui lusit imagine divam,
    Quid faceret iam, si viveret, ille, rogo.

(Lachrymae, sig.k2<sup>v</sup>)

## APPENDIX 2

*In obitum optimi ac praeclarissimi iuvenis, Philippi Sidnaei Equitis aurati, qui in Zutphen-si proelio (quod nuper est ad Iselam commissum est, inter Anglos et Hispanos) glande sulphurea*                   *ictus*                   *interijt.*

Aegid. Fletcher

     Iam tua *Martis* opus spirabat et ardua, virtus,
     Magnanimi proles generosa (*Philippe*) parentis,
     Iamque per afflictos peregrino milite Belgas
     Militiae documenta dabas, ubi Zutphenis arva
5   Alluit irriguo decurrens Isela fluctu:
     Cum te sacra, deum, populos, ius, fasque tuentem,
     Magnanimosque duces, et fortia facta sequutum
     Heroum (dum prima vocas in praelia *Martem*
     Acer et heu fortis nimium in tua fata ruebas)
10  Machina sulphurea traiectum glande peremit.
     Ergo tua pariter deflent in caede peremptas
     Spes (Sidneie) suas, pietas, prudentia, virtus
     Bellica, et immotae custos Constantia mentis,
     Et qui nec falli potuit, neque fallere prudens
15  Candor, et elatam submissa Modestia sortem
     Quae regit, inque tuo deflent sua funera busto.
         Te belli, pacisque decus (generose *Philippe*,)
     Et belli pacisque duces, plebs omnis, et omnis
     Nobilitas, Equitesque gemunt, te iussa sequutum
20  Principis, ipsa dolet Princeps. Nec patria tantum
     Sed locus omnis, et omne solum: te Belgia luget,

Funeris (heu) fatale solum, te SCOTIA, tellus
Itala, teutonicae gentes, te *Gallia* deflet.
Et nisi (saeva licet) sit se crudelior, author
25  Funeris ipsa tuum iam deflet *Iberia* funus.
Nec tantum populique loca sacra, prophana peremptum
Templa, forum luget, rus, curia, castra, Licaeum:
Templa pium, sortemque acies, gymnasia doctum,
Aula comem, rus munificum, lex publica iustum.
30      Te belli pacisque decus (generose *Philippe*)
Ipsa adeo belli, pacisque insignia deflent.
Hasta, libri, calamus, tuba, currus, ephippia, circus
Hippodromus, quo primus equos inferre solebas
Impiger, et longa concurrere fortiter hasta;
35  Inque vicem belli fingens simulachra sub armis
Flectere quadrupedis circo spumantis habenas.
Denique quicquid erat generosum, et amabile, deflet
Et te seque tuo confossum vulnere, solus
Te decus ereptum terris, belloque peremptum,
40  Non moriens, aeternum, et non mutabile mentis
Hospitium, sedesque tuas laetetur Olympus.

(*Lachrymae*, pp. 33-34)

## NOTES

1  R. Burton, *The Anatomy of Melancholy*, Part I, Sect. 2, Memb. 3, Subsec. 15, ed. F. Dell and P. Jordan-Smith, New York, 1927, 273.
2  *Leicester: Patron of Letters*, New York, 1955.
   The relation of Cambridge classical studies to the Elizabethan Church Settlement has been suggestively analysed in Winthrop S. Hudson, *The Cambridge Connection and the Elizabethan Settlement*, Durham, N. C., 1980.
3  Alberta T. Turner, 'Milton and the Convention of the Academic Miscellany', *Yearbook of English Studies*, 5 (1975), 86-93.
4  For a full discussion of Unton's portrait see Roy Strong, *The Cult of Elizabeth*, London, 1977, ch. 3.
5  See J. A. Dop, *Eliza's Knights: Soldiers, Poets and Puritans in the Netherlands, 1572-1586*, Leiden, 1981, which demonstrates the close link between the elaboration of the Eliza cult and a policy of intervention in the Netherlands.
6  *Funebria*, sig. D1. Another thematic thread is Gager's list of great contemporaries, Sidney, Devereux, Leicester, Walsingham, Drake, and Hawkins (sig. B2$^v$), a formidable anti-Spanish roll-call.
7  *The Correspondence of Sir Philip Sidney and Hubert Languet*, trans. Steuart A. Pears, London, 1845; reprint Farnborough, 1971, 2.
8  See Frances A. Yates, 'Elizabethan Chivalry' in *Astraea*, Harmondsworth, 1977, 88-111, and Jean Wilson, *Entertainments for Elizabeth I*, Woodbridge, 1980, for succinct accounts. The implications for actual warfare are brought out by Dop, *Eliza's Knights*, chs III and IV.
9  See Gouws, above pp. 68-69; on the significance of Pavia see R. J. Knecht, *Francis I*, Cambridge, 1982, 171. See also below, n. 36.
10  Cited in J. A. van Dorsten, *Poets, Patrons and Professors*, Leiden, 1962, 167. It is hard to imagine that an Elizabethan aristocrat would appreciate the democratic function of the States, but there is clear evidence of Sidney's sensitive adaption to particular circumstances, witness his dealing with Edmund Campion in Prague.
11  *MP*, 164.

12   Scipio, 'through the poetic and imaginative powers of Petrarch ... was converted into a literary and poetic figure representing an ideal synthesis of the values inherent in history, philosophy and poetry'. A. S. Bernardo, *Petrarch, Scipio and the 'Africa'*, Baltimore, 1962, 110. In addition Petrarch's criticism of the Papacy made him into a Protestant hero.

13   According to John Buxton, *Sir Philip Sidney and the English Renaissance*, 2nd ed., London, 1964, 193.

14   Buxton has described the volume in *Sidney*, 177, and in '*Peplus*: New College Elegies for Sir Philip Sidney', *The Warden's Meeting*, Oxford, 1977, 23-26.

15   *Exequiae* has been discussed briefly by Buxton, *Sidney*, 173-77, and by Rosenberg, *Leicester*, 320. See also J. W. Binns, 'William Gager on the Death of Sir Philip Sidney', *Humanistica Lovaniensia*, XXI (1972), 221-38. In a forthcoming study Dr Binns discusses the university anthologies, including the Sidney volumes, within the context of English Latin writing between 1530 and 1640.

16   See Van Dorsten, *Poets*, 152-66.

17   *Lachrymae*, sig. a2$^r$; *Exequiae*, sig. 2$^r$. On Elizabeth's reaction see R. C. Strong and J. A. van Dorsten, *Leicester's Triumph*, Leiden/Oxford, 1964, 56-57; the title outraged Camden, Hugh Trevor-Roper, *Renaissance Essays*, London, 1985, 142.

18   '... quod Aula tua iam facta est Nova et Tertia Academica', *Oratio in Aula Woodstockiensi habita*, sig, Cij$^r$. Cited by Rosenberg, *Leicester*, 131. On Humphrey's admiration for Chaucer, see David Norbrook, *Poetry and Politics in the English Renaissance*, London, 1984, 71.

19   Dr Alasdair MacDonald has drawn my attention to the price variations for copies recorded in *The Britwell Handlist*, London, 1933, which range from £1 to £105. This may indicate superior presentation copies, though the six copies I have checked are ordinary enough.

20   Cambridge University Library, Bb*.12.13$^1$(F). The cancelled page seems identical to the actual title except that Chard's name is missing. On 2 April 1587 the Privy Council directed certain persons, including Giles Fletcher the elder, to restrain Chard's creditors. Since Fletcher had contact with Walsingham, and accompanied Sir Thomas Randolph on his 1586 embassy to James VI to negotiate a league in defence of the Gospel, he must surely provide the link. His own *Of the Russe Common Wealth* was printed by Chard in 1591. See G. Fletcher, *English Works*, ed. Lloyd E. Berry, Madison, 1964, 20-21.

21   *Lachrymae*, sig. h1.

22   Lachrymae, sig. k1.

23   D. Harris Willson, *King James VI and I*, London, 1956, 58-66. See also Helena Minnie Shire, *Dance and Poetry at the Court of Scotland under James VI*, Cambridge, 1969. Gabriel Harvey owned James's *Poeticall Exercises* and *Essayes of a Prentise* which he considered 'much better then our Gascoignes notes'. His copy of the *Essayes* came from Bartholomew Clerk (1537-90), Dean of the Arches and a close aide of Leicester in the Netherlands; see Virginia F. Stern, 'The *Bibliotheca* of Gabriel Harvey', *Ren.Q.*, XXV (1972), 36-37.

24   James E. Phillips, 'George Buchanan and the Sidney Circle', *HLQ*, XII (1948-49), 23-55.

25   I. D. McFarlane, *Buchanan*, London, 1980, 386-87, 394.

26   Sidney's letter is printed in *The Warrender Papers*, Scottish Historical Society Publications, Series 3, XVIII (1931), I, 146; for Duplessis-Mornay see Buchanan, *Opera*, Leiden, 1725, II, 740. Randolph's negotiations are summarised in Wallace T. McCaffrey, *Queen Elizabeth and the Making of Policy, 1572-88*, Princeton, 1981, 421-27.

27   *Delitiae Poetarum Scotorum*, Amsterdam, J. Blaeu, 1637; for Halkerston see I, 376-77; for Maitland II, 138-43.

28   On Randolph see McFarlane, *Buchanan*, 451-52. Both Randolph and his aide Giles Fletcher (see note (20) above) had literary interests and supported a pan-Protestant alliance. Of particular interest is Fletcher's report to Walsingham, dated March 1586, which refers to both Gray and Maitland, *English Works*, 346-48. For Fletcher's

hostility to Cecil, a stance linked with the Sidney myth, see Norbrook, *Poetry and Politics*, 197.

29 Harris Willson, *James VI and I*, 52-54 and 77. See also G. Donaldson, *All the Queen's Men: Power and Politics in Mary Stuart's Scotland*, London, 1983.

30 Buxton, *Sidney*, 136; *Poems*, 441.

31 *MP*, 59, 110.

32 Gifford, *Peplus*, 27-29; Lloyd, *ibid.*, sig. A3$^r$. Acrostics in *Lachrymae*, 47, 48-49, 58-59.

33 On Cambridge Ramism and Sidney see Walter J. Ong, *Ramus, Method and the Decay of Dialogue*, Cambridge, Mass., 1958, 15-16, 302-04. Temple also wrote a Ramist analysis of Sidney's *Defence*.

34 *Colin Clouts Come Home Again*, 1. 404. On Cambridge drama see F. S. Boas, *University Drama in the Tudor Age*, Oxford, 1914. The actor-list for *Ricardus Tertius* is given on 394-97.

35 *Licia* was edited by A. B. Grosart in 1871; it includes 'The Rising the Crowne of Richard the Third'—another reminiscence of Legge's play?

36 *Lachrymae*, 33-34, see App. 2. The rather arch terms used to describe the fatal gunshot both in Fletcher 1. 10 and in Matthew Roydon's contribution to *Astrophel* ('An Elegie', 11.175-80) suggest the difficulty of assimilating the arquebus into poetic vocabulary. In both cases Mars represents the negative aspects of war. On jousting see 11. 33-36; Sidney's interest in horsemanship is clear from the 'Exordium' to *A Defence of Poetry* (*MP*, 73-74, and note on 186) but Fletcher may well have in mind Dorus's equestrian performance in *Arcadia*, II, 5.

37 *Lachrymae*, 84-85. 'Si Paulus iaceat, fidei si frigeat ardor, / Sabbata publicitus si violata vides: / Esse puta causam populi peccata Britanni, / Dum petitur structis regia nympha dolis.'

38 *Lachrymae*, 21-22 (with modernized punctuation); see Roydon, 'An Elegie', 11. 163-68 for an identical device.

39 Strong and Van Dorsten, *Leicester's Triumph*, 97.

40 *Lachrymae*, sig. 1$^v$.

41 For references to Sidney's martyr-like death see *Lachrymae*, sigs. 92$^r$-h$^r$, pp. 8, 26-27, 30, 45.

42 Roger Howell, jr., 'The Sidney Circle and the Protestant Cause in Elizabethan Foreign Policy', *Medieval and Renaissance Studies*, XIX (1975), 31-46. See also Van Dorsten, 'The Final Year', above p. 23.

43 Raleigh, 'An Epitaph upon .. sir *Philip Sidney*', 11. 30-32, printed in 'Astrophel'.

JOHN BUXTON

## SHAKESPEARE'S *VENUS AND ADONIS* AND SIDNEY

Some years ago, in a short article entitled '*Peplus*: New College Elegies for Sir Philip Sidney',[1] I observed that Spenser's use in *Astrophel* of Bion's Ἀδώνιδος ἐπιτάφιος was especially apposite since Sidney, like Adonis, had died of a wound in the thigh. And I asked, in a parenthesis, 'Did Shakespeare, writing his epyllion on the same myth about the same time, also have Sidney in mind?' Here I propose to consider this question, though with little expectation that I can provide an undisputed answer.

Spenser, in dedicating *The Ruines of Time* to Lady Pembroke in 1591, apologized for his failure hitherto to write in memory of her brother, whom he called 'the hope of all learned men, and the Patron of my young *Muses*'; and he said that 'sithens my late cumming into *England*, some frends of mine (which might much preuaile with me, and indeede commaund me)' had tried to prompt him to do his duty 'by upbraiding me: for that I haue not shewed anie thankefull remembrance towards him'.[2] Spenser had come over from Ireland with Ralegh in the autumn of 1589 to oversee the publication of the first three books of *The Faerie Queene*, and there can be no doubt that Ralegh 'might much prevail with, and indeed command' Spenser to write the elegy which he knew was expected of him. Yet another four years were to pass before Spenser published, in the same volume with *Colin Clouts Come Home Againe*, a collection of elegies on Sidney which his own *Astrophel* served to introduce. Among the other poems in the volume, which was dedicated to Ralegh, were poems by him, by Sir Edward Dyer and by Matthew Roydon which had all been published in 1593 in *The Phoenix Nest*, and two others by Lodowick Bryskett, one of which had been entered in the Stationers' Register as early as 1587. Whether Roydon was an acquaintance of Spenser is not known, but he was a member of Ralegh's circle and therefore probably known to him, and certainly Ralegh, Bryskett and Dyer were Spenser's close friends. Ralegh had commended *The Faerie Queene* on its first publication in two famous sonnets; Bryskett, who had accompanied Sidney on his Grand Tour in 1572-75, knew Spenser well in Ireland and in his *Discourse of Civil Life*[3] described a symposium at which they were both present; and Dyer's name had been coupled with Sidney's by Spenser in a letter of October 1579 where he wrote of 'twoo worthy Gentlemen... who haue me in some vse of familiarity'.[4] Dyer, we may suppose, would be as capable as Ralegh of prevailing with Spenser to

write his elegy both by example and by his intimacy with Sidney, recorded in Sidney's pastoral 'Joyne Mates in mirth to me'.[5] (Fulke Greville,
the other poet whom Sidney there addresses, perhaps surprisingly did not
contribute to *Astrophel*: Grosart's attribution to him of 'Silence
augmenteth griefe' has not been accepted, and Malone's conjecture that
this poem was by Dyer seems certain.)[6] Probably the appearance in *The
Phoenix Nest* of poems in praise of Sidney by three of his friends finally
shamed Spenser into writing *Astrophel*, a poem designed to introduce a
collection. This then became the first volume of English elegies ever published; it had been preceded by three volumes of elegies on Sidney, mostly in Latin, from the two universities, and a fourth from Leiden.[7]

The site of the fatal wound 'upon his thigh three fingers above his
knee'[8] was certain then to recall to any educated person the story of
Adonis, wounded in the thigh by the tusk of a boar while out hunting.
So in *Astrophel* the boar

    with fell tooth accustomed to blood
Launched his thigh with so mischieuous might,
That it both bone and muscles ryued quight. (118-20)[9]

(Whetstone, who was present at Zutphen, says

    The wound was deepe and shivered the bone.)[10]

Bryskett's poem *The Mourning Muse of Thestylis*, which was written in
1587, is placed next after Spenser's poem and *Clorinda's Lay* (which
Spenser, perhaps rightly, attributes to the Countess of Pembroke) in
which the close friendship between Thestylis and Astrophel, Bryskett and
Sidney, is emphasized. In his poem Bryskett compares Sidney to Adonis
slain, but since the poem is largely a paraphrase of Bernardo Tasso's
*Selva nella morte del Signor Aluigi da Gonzaga* the reference might be thought
to be only derivative. But in Bernardo Tasso's poem the allusion to the
story of Venus and Adonis follows immediately after a passage in which
the word 'stella' occurs:

    Allor veduto avresti la sorella
    Coi crini sparsi, e senza leggiadria
    In vista vedovil chiari cristalli
    Versar dal cor per l'una e l'altra stella.
    A Cefalo giammai la bianca Aurora
    Non si mostro si vaga, al dolce Adone,
    Ne al caro Marte suo Vener si bella.[11]

and it follows a section which begins in the English, but not in the Italian,
with the name Stella.

Bryskett was only one of several poets who, in the months following
Sidney's death, made use of the myth of Adonis in mourning him. John

Lloyd, who edited *Peplus*, composed the opening poem, which he designed as an altar and wrote in Greek, intending it, one may suppose, to set
the tone for his collection, as Spenser was to do for *Astrophel*. In it Lloyd
refers to Sidney as another and better Adonis, mourned by Cytherea:

'Ερασμίη Κυθήρη
ἰδοῖσ ' 'Αδώνιν ἄλλον
'Αδωνίστερον ἄλλον
ἀναξίῳ δάμεντα
μόρῳ βέλει Ἀρηος
ὡς αἴλινον στέναξε
θαλερὸν χέοισα δάκρυ
θέον ὄβριμον στύγοισα. (sig. A3ʳ)

(The lovely Cytherea, seeing another Adonis, who seemed more Adonis
than Adonis, undeservedly overcome by a shaft from Ares, sighed
grievously and shed warm tears in her loathing of the powerful god.)
Similarly William Gager ('an excellent poet, especially in the Latin
tongue', in Antony Wood's opinion),[12] who edited the Oxford *Exequiae*,
compared Sidney to Adonis in a pastoral which he contributed to that
volume. Elsewhere in *Exequiae* William Whitlock alludes to the myth of
Venus mourning Adonis, and Henry Price makes direct comparison between Sidney's wound and Adonis':

Quam tibi cum dulci communis Adonide sors est?
   Illi transfodit bellua dente femur...
Sidnaeus nobis, Cytharaeae charus Adonis,
   Interiit simili charus uterque modo. (sig. G3ᵛ)

    In the Cambridge collection, *Academiae Cantabrigiensis Lachrymae* (which
may have preceded the two Oxford volumes), Sidney is again compared
to Adonis in a piece signed R. S. where he calls Venus to come to mourn
him. The identity of this R. S. is not known; neither is that of the R. S.
who six years later edited *The Phoenix Nest*. But the first three poems in
that anthology are the elegies on Sidney by Matthew Roydon, Sir Walter
Ralegh and Sir Edward Dyer; and Sir Edmund Gosse[13] suggested that
'The idea of the compilers of this anthology was, in my opinion, that
although the Phoenix, Poetry, had blazed on the funeral pyre of Sidney,
it was reincarnated in the lyrical work of the young men who had taken
heart of grace to pursue their art since their hero's death', especially
those who contributed to *The Phoenix Nest*. *Englands Helicon*, the pastoral
anthology published in 1600, had the fourth song from *Astrophel and Stella*
in pride of place, and though Francis Davison in the preface to his anthology disclaimed the custom of 'gracing the forefront with Sir Ph.
Sidney's name' yet the first poems in his *Poetical Rhapsody* of 1602 were

'Two Pastoralls, made by Sir Philip Sidney, never yet published', so that his disclaimer is somewhat disingenuous.

Shakespeare's knowledge of Sidney's work and reputation is beyond dispute, but there are two further pieces of evidence which may be considered here, though neither is susceptible of proof. In *Colin Clouts Come Home Againe*, Spenser names among the poets who

> remaine
> Now after *Astrofell* is dead and gone, (448-49)

that is, the company whom *The Phoenix Nest* celebrates, one whom he calls Aetion,

> Whose *Muse* full of high thoughts inuention,
> Doth like himselfe Heroically sound. (446-47)[14]

and Malone [15] long ago suggested that the poet whose name had a heroic sound was Shakespeare. Whoever Aetion is, Spenser here associates him with Astrophel.

More persuasive is Mona Wilson's comment on J. M. Robertson's suggestion that Sonnet 55 is a poem intended to commend a volume of love-poems. If so, she says, the volume it best suits is *Astrophel and Stella*: 'It reads most naturally if we think of the subject as a soldier poet to whom a sumptuous monument has been projected'.[16] The States of Zealand applied to Leicester (who had been appointed by the States-General to be Governor-General of all the provinces of the Netherlands), that they might have the honour of burying Sidney at their expense. They undertook to erect to his memory 'as fair a monument as any Prince had in Christendom even though it should cost half a ton of gold'.[17] To this proposal

> Not marble nor the gilded monuments of princes

seems to refer so precisely that it is difficult to deny the sonnet's reference to Sir Philip Sidney and his poems.

Dover Wilson, in his edition of Shakespeare's Sonnets, points out that sonnet 55 'unlike the other sonnets in Section 1 [nos. 1 to 126] ... seems not to be addressed to Shakespeare's Friend but relates to a dead hero who was at once a lover and a fearless soldier—for that, I take it, is the meaning of

> 'Gainst death, and all-oblivious enmity
> Shall you pace forth—

an imaginary description of how a brave man will behave on the Day of Judgement'. He also says that ll.12-13 'imply a Christian cosmos; all the other Ovidian sonnets are Pythagorean'.[18] I might add that neither of the

most favoured candidates for the role of Shakespeare's fair young man,
the Earls of Southampton and Pembroke, would suit the fearless soldier
of this sonnet: neither was called upon to act that part. The Ovidian sonnets, in addition to 55, are 59, 60, 62 to 68, and 71 to 74. The last eight
lines of 55 derive from the famous conclusion which Ovid wrote to the
*Metamorphoses* (XV.871-9), at the end of the poem in which he had told
the story of Venus and Adonis (X.503-59, 708-28). This, in Golding's
translation, was Shakespeare's source. Venus' team of swans (*cycni*) provided another link to Sidney through the frequently repeated pun on his
name, Sidnaeus, cycneus, which is represented visually in the engraved
portrait before Jean Baudoin's French translation of the *Arcadia*, with the
motto 'Dulcius his cecinit'. Sidney's fatal wound suggested Adonis, and
his name suggested the team of swans which brought Venus to the sight
of his dead body:

> Illa quidem monuit iunctisque per aera cycnis
> carpit iter. (*Metamorphoses*, X.708-09)

In 1593 no one, least of all a young and aspiring poet and dramatist,
could have been unaware of Sidney's reputation as poet and patron of
poets, and of his much lamented death in battle in an age (unlike our
own) when this, at least in England, was altogether exceptional. And the
references in elegies on Sidney show, what might in any event have been
expected, that in the years after his death from a wound in the thigh the
myth of the death of Adonis was often associated with him. If his name
suggested the team of swans which drew Venus about the heavens, then
the story of Venus' love for and grief over Adonis would extend the
mythical association. We do not have to look far to discover why
Shakespeare might have used the myth in relation to the death of Philip
Sidney. That is not to say that the myth might not have been used by
poet or painter without intending any such association. Robert Greene
in *Perimedes the Blacke-Smith* has a reference to the story which has nothing
but narrative interest. And Sidney himself in the *Arcadia* describes
Philoclea, when Amphialus comes to her, in terms of a painting of Venus
'when under the trees she bewailed the murther of Adonis'.[19] But these
are incidental.

It would be odd if Shakespeare devoted a long poem to the myth at that
time without being aware of its association with Sidney by so many of
his contemporaries. *Venus and Adonis* was entered in the Stationers'
Register on 18 April 1593, before the publication of *Astrophel* and probably before its composition, for *The Phoenix Nest* (which I have suggested
helped to prompt Spenser to write his elegy) was not entered until 8 October that year. But the University elegies had been published several

years before, and, though they might not have been known to Shakespeare, the Earl of Southampton, to whom he dedicated *Venus and Adonis*, was up at Cambridge at the time of Sidney's death and at the time when the three volumes of elegies produced by the Universities were being published. He would have been unlikely to miss these, for Sir Henry Danvers, who had been Sidney's page in the Low Countries and who had walked in his funeral procession to St. Paul's, was Southampton's exact contemporary and close friend.[20] Besides, as a member of Essex' circle, he must have been well aware that Essex, who had married Sidney's widow and to whom Sidney left his best sword, modelled himself, especially as a patron of letters, on the example set by Sir Philip. To Southampton, then, a poem on the death of Adonis would inevitably have brought Sidney to mind.

*Venus and Adonis* is not primarily about the death of Adonis, but about the love of Venus for him and her grief at his death. But it would be in character for Shakespeare to exploit the theme of the myth for its own sake without obviously applying it to a particular occasion. Such oblique reference in the treatment of myth is paralleled in his development of Robert Chester's theme in *The Phoenix and Turtle*, about which I have written elsewhere.[21] There Shakespeare, adopting a mythical theme for an occasion with which others had associated it, does not write a poem *about* the occasion but *for* it: he welcomes the opportunity of writing a poem on a myth which was much in men's minds at the time and which was associated with a particular event—the knighthood conferred on Sir John Salisbury which showed that he had restored his family's repute from the destruction brought upon it by his elder brother's treason. So in *Venus and Adonis* he follows many others in associating the myth with the death of Sir Philip Sidney, but his interest is poetic and aesthetic, not commemorative. As I said in my study of *The Phoenix and Turtle*: 'In so far as they [Shakespeare's poems under that title] are ''about'' anything they are about the phoenix and turtle which were the subjects of Chester's clumsily contrived myth... Shakespeare wrote his poems for an occasion and (as he says) about two ''dead birds''.' So with the Greek myth of Venus and Adonis: others had applied it literally to Sidney, because of the coincidence between the fatal wounds received by Adonis and Sidney. Shakespeare wrote on the theme because he saw its possibilities for poetic treatment, not because he wished to lament Sidney. But he could hardly have used the myth at that time without being aware that others had used it in the context of Sidney's death, and he must have known that the patron to whom he dedicated his poem was well aware also of that association, and likely to welcome it.

## NOTES

1 In *The Warden's Meeting: A Tribute to John Sparrow*, Oxford, 1977, 23-26.
2 *The Works of Edmund Spenser: A Variorum Edition*, ed. Edwin Greenlaw, Charles Grosvenor Osgood, Frederick Morgan Padelford, Ray Heffner, 10 vols, Baltimore, 1932-57, II, 35. All Spenser references will be to this edition.
3 In *Lodowick Bryskett: Literary Works*, ed. J. H. P. Pafford, n.p., 1972.
4 Spenser, Variorum Edn, *Prose*, 6.
5 *Poems*, 260-61.
6 Ralph M. Sargent, *At the Court of Queen Elizabeth: The Life and Lyrics of Sir Edward Dyer*, London, 1935, 211-13.
7 They are: *Academiae Cantabrigiensis Lachrymae Tumulo Nobilissimi equitis D Philippi Sidneij Sacratae*, Cambridge, 1586; *Exequiae illustrissimi Equitis, D. Philippi Sidnaei, gratissimae memoriae ac nomini impensae*, Oxford, 1587; *Peplus, Illustrissimi Viri D. Philippi Sidnaei Supremis Honoribus Dicatus*, Oxford, 1587; *Epitaphia in Mortem Nobilissimi et Fortissimi Viri D. Philippi Sidneij Equitis*, Leiden, 1587. See Baker-Smith, above p. 89.
8 Leicester to Burghley, cited by M. W. Wallace, *The Life of Sir Philip Sidney*, Cambridge, 1915, 381.
9 Spenser, Variorum Edn, VII, 182.
10 In *Sir Philip Sidney, his honourable Life, his valiant Death and true Virtues*, London, 1587.
11 Bernardo Tasso, 'Selva nella morte de signor Luigi da Gonzaga', Libro secondo de gli Amori, *Rime di M. Bernardo Tasso*, Bergamo, 1749, II, 1.
12 *Athenae Oxonienses*, 2nd edn, London, 1721, I, col. 366.
13 Quoted without reference by H. E. Rollins in the introduction to his edition of *The Phoenix Nest*, Cambridge, Mass., 1931, xxxvii.
14 Spenser, Variorum Edn, VII, 160.
15 E. Malone, *William Shakespeare*, London, 1821, II, 273-76.
16 Mona Wilson, *Sir Philip Sidney*, London, 1931, 167 n.; her comment is on J. M. Robertson, *The Problems of the Shakespeare Sonnets*, London, 1926.
17 Wallace, 391. (See however pp. 49-50 above.)
18 J. Dover Wilson, ed., *The Sonnets*, Cambridge, 1966, 158.
19 *Arcadia*, III, 1598-edn, 243.
20 G. P. V. Akrigg, *Shakespeare and the Earl of Southampton*, London, 1968, 41-42.
21 In *English Renaissance Studies presented to Dame Helen Gardner*, Oxford, 1980, 44-55.

VICTOR SKRETKOWICZ

# BUILDING SIDNEY'S REPUTATION: TEXTS
# AND EDITORS OF THE *ARCADIA*

There can be few experiences so bruising to an editor as to witness the failure of his contribution to someone else's book, yet such was Fulke Greville's fate in his edition of *The Countess of Pembroke's Arcadia* (1590). His labour in 'The division and summing of the chapters ... adventured by the overseer of the print for the more ease of the readers' turned out to be little more than a poorly executed, futile exercise. One can understand how Greville, after struggling through the huge and heavily corrected manuscript that Sidney left with him, could have anticipated charges of obscurity being levelled against the work. But his steps to safeguard Sidney's reputation by reducing the complexity of the text into digestible portions, each preceded by a summary of the action, backfired upon him. Rather than help to present the author in the best light, when the work was printed these chapter summaries became painfully obvious intrusions, distracting from and fragmenting the natural clarity of the narrative.

In his damning preface to the 1593-edition, Hugh Sanford publicly poured scorn on the presentation of Greville's text, complaining that 'The disfigured face ... wherewith this work not long since appeared to the common view' was covered with 'spots wherewith the beauties thereof were unworthily blemished'. Among these 'spots' the chapter summaries were surely prominent. They must have proved to be a considerable nightmare, for their presentation was almost unbelievably flawed. In the first chapter of the First Book the marginal numeral '2' was omitted, failing to indicate the location in the text of the second topic of the summary, '*The second shipwrack of* Pyrocles *and* Musidorus. *Their strange sauing...*' (sig. B1).[1] This initiated a train of errors which continued right through to the twenty-third chapter of the Third Book, there wrongly described as 'Chap. 17' (sig. Vv8$^v$).

The topics in the summaries were numbered by two methods, but neither arrangement was satisfactorily carried out. In the one, the topics were designated serially, as in the first chapter of the Second Book (sig. O2):

*The loue-complaintes* [1]*of* Gynecia, [2]Zelmane, [3]*and* Basilius. [4]*Her,* [5]*and his wooing of* Zelmane, *and her shifting of both,* [6]*to bemone her selfe.*

The marginal cross-references were intended to be adjusted to correspond to the topics in this list, which does not follow the sequence of events in the story, but were incompletely printed only as 2, 4, 3, and 6. In other instances the marginal numbers were placed in sequence, but the superscriptions juggled in the perversely out-of-order summaries, as in the Third Book, both before the eighth chapter (sig. Mm5ᵛ),

> *The Basilians reembattelled* [1]*first by* Philanax, [4]*then by the blacke Knight.* [2]Ismenus *slaine by* Philanax. [3]Philanax *captiued by* Amphialus. [4]*The blacke Knights exploits.* [5]*His encounter with* Amphialus, *parted by a by-blow.* [6]*The Amphialians retrait, and departure of the blacke Knight.*

and before the twentieth chapter (sig. Tt5ᵛ):

> [2]*The sweete resistance of the true sisters* [1]*to the sower assaultes of their false Aunt. The whipping of* [3]Philoclea [5]*and* Pamela.[4]*The patience of both* [6]*and passions for their louers.*

The extent of this disorganization is most obvious in the sixteenth chapter of the First Book, where the marginal references are not to either of the two topics in the summary (sig. K4ᵛ):

> [1]Phalantus *and* Artesias *pompous entraunce.* [2]*The painted muster of an eleuen conquered beauties.*

Rather, the eleven topics noted in the margin designate each of these beauties as they are mentioned in the narrative, beginning with Andromana and ending with Zelmane, daughter of Plexirtus (sigs. K5-K7).

Not only were these summaries inaccurate and redundant, but their pretentious style smacked of exhibitionism. At times they seemed to mimic and mock rhetorical figures used by the author himself, as in '*Their drawing cuts for tales.* [5]Mopsas *tale of the old cut:* [6]*cut of by the Ladies to returne to their stories*' (sig. Y2ᵛ), or in '[1]Zoilus *the messenger,* [2]*and first offerer of force,* [3]*is forced to flie, and die*' (sig. Zz3ᵛ). Their intruding diction swaggered, vying with the text for attention in unusual usages considerably antedating the earliest examples recorded in the *O.E.D.*: *beleaguered* pp. adj. (1644); *historiology* n. (1616); *Iberian* adj. (1671); *interknowledge* n. (1626); *omniregency* n. (1616); *pathology* n.[2] (1681); *reembattle* v. (1667). Not even John Florio, who on the basis of his colourful language has been posited as the author of the summaries, included such inventions as these in either his *World of Words* (1598) or *Queen Anna's New World of Words* (1611).[2]

Such obvious carelessness in the presentation of his editorial matter wholly belied Greville's integrity towards his task. Further to his purpose in providing a lucid catalogue of principal events, the summaries conveyed to the reader Greville's sense of Sidney's epic structure. This began *in medias res*, as he noted, with '*The second shipwrack of* Pyrocles *and*

Musidorus' (sig. B1), and went on to explain when the reader got there in the Second Book that the oracle was *'the ground of all this storie'* (sig. Ff8). Evidently the summaries were designed to create an impression of the work's thematic unity and artistic structure, with the hope of establishing it as a superior literary achievement in English, and promoting in public this hitherto private side of the author's considerable accomplishments.

Displaying the artistic merit of the work was consistent with Greville's general aim in publishing the 1590 *Arcadia*. This was clearly an attempt to defend and enhance Sidney's reputation. One need only recall his letter to Walsingham of November 1586 to recognize the primacy of this concern: 'I desyre only care to be had of his honor who I fear hathe Caried the honor of thes latter ages w^th him'. Such honour could best initially be guarded, he then suggested, by staying both the unauthorized publication of the *'old' Arcadia*, and, in addition and more radically, of

> monsieur du plessis book agains«t» atheisme, w^ch is since don by an other, [&] so as bothe in respect of the love betwen plessis & him besyds other affinities in ther courses but espetially sr philips uncōparable Iudgement, I think fit ther be made a stej of that mercenary book to.[3]

As news of Sidney's death reached London on 2 November, only three days before the arrival of the corpse on the fifth,[4] by the time Ponsonby approached Greville and he in turn wrote to Walsingham it is highly possible that Thomas Cadnam had already published *A Work Concerning the Trueness of the Christian Religion*, of which he had entered a translation 'by master Arthur Goldinge' in the Stationers' Register on 7 November. But Greville's pique at 'that mercenary book' might even better be understood by recognizing that he would barely have learned of Sidney's death when he would have read on the title-page the sensationalist claim, calculated to promote sales among a devastated London readership, 'Begun to be translated into English by Sir *Philip Sidney* Knight, and at his request finished by *Arthur Golding*'.

Quite apart from Cadnam's advertisement of the book's relationship with the newly-deceased Sidney, Greville's desire to stay this publication of du Plessis 'don by another' appears to have been an attempt to clear away the opposition. By this he could force attention to be focused on the collection of Sidney's religious writings which, he intimated to Walsingham, he would undertake to publish:

> that sr philip might have all thos religous honor w^ch ar worthelj dew to his lyfe & deathe, many other works as bartas his semeyne, *raise as* [40 of] the spalm translated in to myter etc w^chrequyre the care of his frends, not to amend for I think it fales w^th in the reache of no man living, but only to see to the paper & other cōmon errors of mercenary printing.

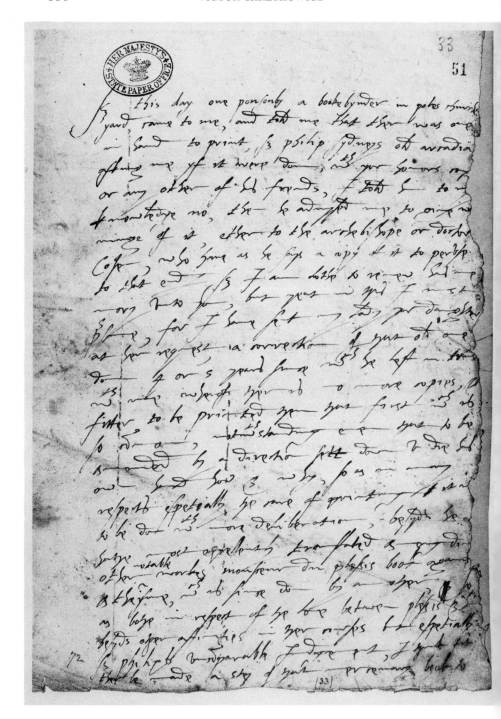

9. Letter, Greville to Walsingham, November 1586 (PRO SP12/195)

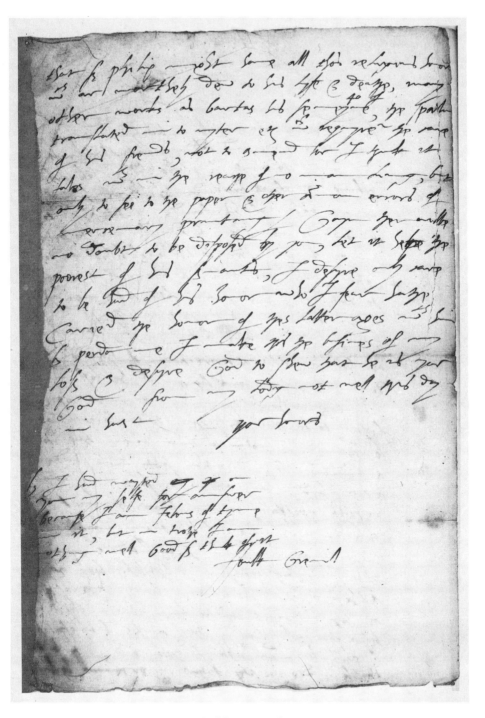

10. Idem, page 2.

Needless to say, this intention to build Sidney's image in the model of a Protestant hero never came off—none of these religious works reached print. But the *Arcadia* which Greville edited did not escape entirely unscathed from this politically associated bias which led him to turn his back on all those secular works which were to be included in the published corpus by 1598, *Astrophil and Stella, Certain Sonnets, A Defence of Poetry* and *The Lady of May*. His urgent plea to Walsingham was designed to prevent publication of the romantic though well polished *'old' Arcadia* and to substitute for it 'a correction of that old one don 4 or 5 years since w$^{ch}$ he left in trus«t» w$^{th}$ me wherof ther is no more copies, & fitter to be printed then that first w$^{ch}$ is so cōmon'. That the early romance was successfully suppressed and the *'new' Arcadia* listed by Greville alongside the religious translations implies that in the *'new' Arcadia* he recognized an adequate poetic sophistication to transmit successfully his own ideals of heroism and virtue.

Incompleteness and omissions from the text seemed not to detract from the general aura connoted by 'fitter to be printed'. Greville made no attempt to supplement these deficiencies while preparing for publication: he left unprinted the first half of a line where there should have been the description of Amphialus' device by which Clitophon recognized his armour (sig. G2); the equivalent of one whole line was left both for what may have been a conventional catalogue of the trees over the River Ladon (sig. V5) and for Lelius' impresa (sig. Cc4); three asterisks indicated a hiatus after OA 73, the lengthy adaptation of the judgement of Paris (sig. Nn3$^{v}$); a decorative border was printed around a blank occupying three-quarters of a page for the epitaph of Argalus and Parthenia (sig. Rr7$^{v}$); and the book was allowed to end unconventionally in the midst of an unfinished sentence (sig. Zz8$^{v}$). But to understand more fully the role played by Greville and the subsequent editors in making public what they judged fit to be presented as *The Countess of Pembroke's Arcadia*, it is necessary first to establish what materials they had to work with, and how far they adhered to or deviated from them.

Although the manuscript that Greville received from Sidney has not survived, comparison of those texts that have—the manuscripts of the *'old' Arcadia*, the Cambridge manuscript of the *'new' Arcadia*, and the editions of 1590 and 1593 (referred to as Cm, 90, and 93)—suggests that in one form or another it contained virtually all of Sidney's work on the *Arcadia*. In composing the *'new' Arcadia*, Sidney reworked a complete copy of the *'old' Arcadia*, altering and adding words, phrases, and sentences, and writing in whole new passages of which the more lengthy were interleaved into that manuscript. Comparison between the appendix to the *'new' Arcadia* which was printed in 93 and the manuscripts of the *'old' Arcadia* reveals that excisions from the early form of the text correspond to materials adapted by the author either for the *'new' Arcadia* or elsewhere in the appendix itself. It therefore becomes clear that while writing the *'new' Arcadia* Sidney was using the same manuscript that was later to become printer's copy for the appendix in 93. Such alterations may be seen in the passage about Menalcas, where Musidorus 'hired him to go into Thessalia, writing by him to a trusty servant of his that he should arrest him until he knew his further pleasure',[5] expanded in 90 but retaining 'hired him to go into Thessalia ... trusty servant ... till he knew my further pleasure' (sig. L7-L7ᵛ); or in the narrative describing how Philanax came to rescue Basilius with the 'principal Arcadian lords' and 'five hundred horse' after he had 'placed garrisons in all the towns and villages anything near the lodges',[6] divided in the *'new' Arcadia* between 'other principal noblemen ... to place such garrisons in all the towns and villages near unto ... his solitary lodge' (sig. Ff8) and 'a hundred horse ... placing garrisons' (sig. Gg1). The more complex form of fragmenting and developing sections of the manuscript occurs near the beginning of the Third Book of the *'new' Arcadia* in 'So that the ground he stood upon being over-high in happiness and slippery through affection' (sig. Ii4ᵛ). This reading originated in the fourth topic of a passage containing 'his heart ... one word ... to discover ... what slippery grounds her hopes stood', from which the first three elements became fused with 'stealing her away ... seaport, under vehement oath ... Thessalia; ... strange humours ... fallen into' in the revised opening section of the appendix:

> *(his heart scarce serving him to come to the point* whereunto his then coming had been wholly directed, as loath in the kindest sort *to discover to his friend his own unkindness)* at length, *one word emboldening another,* made known to Zelmane how Pamela, upon his vehement oath to offer no force unto her till he had invested her in the duchy of Thessalia, had condescended to his stealing her away to the next seaport. That, besides the strange humours she saw her father more and more falling into...[7]

That the author was completely responsible for such alterations as mitigated the sensual intensity of the material printed in 93 may be seen in the deliberate intermingling of references to Pyrocles' plan to return to assist the Helots, anticipated in his promise to them in the *'new' Arcadia* 'that he would, if at any time the Lacedaemonians brake this treaty, come back again and be their captain' (sig. E6ᵛ), with his donning 'a slight undersuit'.[8] Each topic was later independently reiterated, the one when Dametas found Pyrocles in his 'slight undersuit' in Philoclea's bed, and the other during the lengthy description of Euarchus' journey, shipwreck, and landing in Laconia added to the Last Book.[9]

Further substantiation that Greville's manuscript contained the entire working papers of the *Arcadia* lies in the sprinkling of variants from the several states of the *'old' Arcadia* throughout the witnesses to the texts published in 1590 and in 1593. These indicate either that the hand in the manuscript lent itself to independent misreading in several ways, as *imperfections* OA(*ex.* Je),Cm,93; *affections* Je,90; or that there were sometimes two words to choose from, as in *rage* Cl,Le,As,Cm,90,93; *heat* OA(*ex.* Cl,Le,As).[10] Others show that early and late versions were sometimes visible, as *lockes made of* Cm for *laces made of* OA(*ex.* St,Bo) where the later reading was *threads of finest* St,Bo,90,93; or as in the penultimate and final proses of the First Eclogues where the version in 93 *and then ... offered unto it* and *remembering ... hurt* agrees with the earlier manuscripts Je,Hm,Da,Ph,Cl rather than with As,St,Bo or 90.[11] In addition, seven readings agreeing with the first two states of the *'old' Arcadia* and five agreeing with the last two states occur intermingled in close conjunction in the appendix in 93.[12] The manuscript was consistent in both of its parts in reading at times with the *'old' Arcadia* in some names and titles, as *Cleofila* or *Cleophila* in Cm and *Cleofila* in 93;[13] *duke* for *king* in Cm and four times in 93;[14] and *duchess* for *queen* once in Cm and once in 93.[15] Additionally, in the witnesses to the first part of the manuscript, Cm and 90, there remains an indication that it was in Sidney's hand, for *shewed* in Cm,90 (sig. L8ᵛ) was corrected in 93 to *sued*. This error in transcribing as *sh* Sidney's ligature *ss*, misleading in his habit of writing the long *s* in the second position, was frequent in Cm in *eternishe, ishewe,* and *purshewed*.

Not only supporting the hypothesis that Greville's manuscript consisted of the author's working papers for the *'new' Arcadia*, such evidence suggests that this expansion and revision took place in those papers originally used in composing the *'old' Arcadia*. With the exception of a few words in the prose of the eclogues in 90, which the overseer had declared were 'chosen and disposed' by him, and a few more in the version of the eclogues in 93, it appears that the manuscript effectively consisted of the text which was published more or less intact in 1593 and all subsequent editions. But in this single working manuscript of the *Arcadia*, both *'old'* and *'new'* fell into distinct sections: one heavily revised which corresponded to the body of 90, and the other partially revised and marked up with deletions indicating either that material had been re-used or was to be omitted, corresponding to the four eclogues and to the appendix printed in 93.

Such a theory of the text, though differing from that posed by Ringler and Robertson wherein textual transmission was by scribal transcripts and conflation with lost intermediaries, does not argue for literary unity in the 1593 text: far from it. Quite evidently the text printed in 1590 contained only that part of the manuscript which Greville saw had been thoroughly worked up into a coherent and almost completed fragment, while the edition of 1593 reprinted with only minor adjustments that published in 1590, and added that substantial unpublished remnant of the manuscript which had undergone only a minimum of revision and obviously required a great deal more attention before it could be considered as belonging to this new version of the *Arcadia*. Acknowledging this state of affairs, the editors of 93 printed this wholly candid statement before the appendix:

> How this combat ended, how the ladies by the coming of the discovered forces were delivered and restored to Basilius, and how Dorus again returned to his old master Dametas, is altogether unknown. What afterward chanced, out of the Author's own writings and conceits hath been supplied, as followeth.

Once having decided upon which portion of the manuscript was 'fitter to be printed', Greville's task was largely mechanical. In addition to bringing the names and titles of the principal characters from the *'old' Arcadia* into accordance with the changes in the revision, incidentally creating the curious situation of Zelmane commenting upon the picture of the deceased Zelmane at the end of Phalantus' entry procession (sig. K7), there remained to be straightened out such indirection as attested to by Cm over other names which required standardizing, as *Hipponax* for *Amphialus*, *Callias* for *Clinias*, and *Pergamum* for *Phrygia*. Indeed, naïveté on the part of the scribe of Cm has in some instances preserved the shortened form in which Sidney wrote some of the names, leading him to mistranscribe as *y* the abbreviation for the final *-us* in *Musidory, Plexirty, Menelay*, and *Amphialy*.

Besides such practical editorial steps and his explanatory table of contents interspersed throughout in the form of chapter summaries, Greville further indulged his sense of what the book required to give it an aura of completion by preparing from his manuscript his patchwork eclogues. He commented on their incomplete form in the manuscript, saying that

> although they were of Sir Philip Sidney's writing, yet were they not perused by him, but left till the work had been finished, that then choice should have been made which should have been taken and in what manner brought in. At this time they have been chosen and disposed as the overseer thought best. (sig. A4ᵛ)

But if he was to avoid altering the structure of the work, Greville saw that he had to introduce eclogues into his text at the end of the Books where they were required by the narrative: 'the shepherds were ready ... to attend their pastimes' (sig. M5ᵛ), 'the shepherds to begin, whom she saw all ready for them' (sig. Hh1ᵛ). In doing this, he seized the opportunity to enlarge the artistic scope of the *'new' Arcadia* beyond the heroic and to see into print some of Sidney's more important poems, some of them in a version which differed slightly from the form they had taken in the copies of the *'old' Arcadia*. That the tribute to Languet in 'As I my little flock on Ister bank' was brought forward from the Third Eclogues may reflect the poem's importance to Greville who had shared Sidney's relationship with Languet, and who seemed to need to preserve this association between the *Arcadia* and the Protestant cause. But in working from this unrevised portion of the manuscript, he accidentally neglected, with one exception (sig. Ii2ᵛ), to bring the spelling *Klaius* of the *'old' Arcadia* into agreement with Cm,90,93 by changing it to *Claius*.

The editorial policy of the second editors of the *Arcadia* differed considerably from Greville's. In his address 'To the Reader' in 93, Sanford showed his awareness that the Countess of Pembroke was guided by the desire to build a literary monument to her brother which would, and did in 1598, extend beyond the *Arcadia* to include his other works:

> Neither shall these pains be the last (if no unexpected accident cut off her determination) which the everlasting love of her brother will make her consecrate to his memory.

This underlying concept of preserving all of her brother's works of a literary nature almost directly opposed Greville's intention to establish Sidney's reputation on the basis of his epic and religious writings alone. As far as the *Arcadia* was concerned, there can be little doubt that she agreed with Greville's estimation that the manuscript left with him was 'fitter to be printed than that old one', for it was his text of the *'new' Arcadia* as it was published in 1590 that provided the printer's copy for the first part of her expanded edition. Nevertheless, a fundamental objection arose to Greville's limiting the idea of 'fitter' to the completely revised portion of the manuscript. Sanford's address makes it abundantly clear that the Countess of Pembroke,

> in correcting the faults, ended in supplying the defects; by the view of what was ill done guided to the consideration of what was not done. ... as much as was intended, the conclusion, not the perfection of *Arcadia*: and that no further than the author's own writings, or known determinations, could direct. ... the defects being so few, so small, and in no principal part, yet the greatest unlikeness is rather in defect than in deformity.

Although Greville might have objected on grounds of style and structure, the Countess of Pembroke took not only a personal but also a historical view of her brother's *Arcadia*: what existed, however incomplete and with however broken a back, was better then any previous writing of its kind in English and deserved preservation as it stood.

During the course of preparing this edition a modest excess of zeal was expended in polishing Sidney's style and reconstructing Greville's version of the eclogues. Perhaps motivated by a desire to avoid criticism for lack of clarity, their editorial procedure for the 'new' Arcadia included slight embellishment, as in the imitation of the matachin where the protagonists in explanation were specifically given *two adversaries* instead of having just *adversaries* (sig. L2ᵛ). Such good intentions at times detracted from the meaning, for Phalantus became known not because of *his own good* (sig. K2) or goodness but rather only for *his good justing*. Again, Amphialus's earthy challenge to Phalantus that he was *ready to know whether he had anything to him* (sig. Oo7ᵛ) became in 93 the debased *ready to know whether he had anything to say to him*. No doubt such minor tampering, intended specifically to make the narrative more comprehensible, also occurred within the appendix where, having no text like Cm to compare with it, such editorial activity remains undetectable. But as it is evident that Sidney himself was responsible for the alteration of the Third, Fourth, and Last Books of the 'old' Arcadia during the process of revising and developing the narrative, the probability is that the appendix in 93 was just as faithfully reproduced as was the section containing the 'new' Arcadia, where no interference occurred in attempting to supply readings in the three lacunae which fell in the prose: the imprese and the tree catalogue.

Where the editors of 93 did exert their influence, though still in a limited fashion, came at the acknowledged break from textual integrity, in the eclogues. There they exercised their literary faculties in rewriting a few of the prose links between the poems. They altered the selection and order of the verse, having to some extent been freed by their decision to include the remains of the manuscript from the constraints in selection imposed upon Greville. The influence of Sidney's reworking of the Fourth Eclogues was particularly felt, as he had utilized in the body of his new Third Book three of the most significant poems—OA 74, 'Unto a caitiff wretch'; OA 73, 'Now was our heav'nly vault'; and OA 75, 'Since that to death'. The Strephon and Klaius poems, OA 71, 'Ye goatherd gods', and OA 72, 'I joy in grief', having been split between the First and Second Eclogues in 90, were brought back together in the Second Eclogues of 93 as they had been in the Fourth Eclogues of the 'old' Arcadia, and the long poem (OP 4) about their game of barley-break with Urania slipped into the First Eclogues. Two other poems were removed from their places in the eclogues in 90: OA 29, 'And are you there, old Pas?' which from that time onwards was lost entirely, being excluded from 93, and the song by 'a young shepherd who neither danced nor sung with them', OA 66, 'As I my little flock', which was reinstated in the Third Eclogues and sung as it had been in the *'old'* *Arcadia* by Philisides. Commitment to print the remains of the manuscript in 93 reveals an alteration of Sidney's intention, for Greville had filled the gap in the revised part of the manuscript after 'roared out a song of lamentation, which, as well as might be, was gathered up in this form' (sig. Yy2), followed in Cm by a blank space for the poem, by inserting OA 75, 'Since that to death'. The editors of 93, without doubt floundering for substance in their Fourth Eclogues which otherwise contained only OA 76, 'Farewell O sun', lifted OA 75 back from its new context, taking with it and tacitly affirming to be authorial the preceding lines from the *'new'* *Arcadia*. In a similarly cavalier fashion, for the first poem in this set of eclogues being compiled from the rest of the text, they removed OA 70, 'Since wailing is a bud', from the old Fourth Book, again taking along the preceding lines to supply the context. In doing so, they incidentally reproduced from the manuscript not the revised parenthetical remark upon Agelastus, '(the cause of which, as it were too long to tell, so yet the effect of an Athenian senator to become an Arcadian shepherd)' as in St,Bo, but one which agreed with all the manuscripts of the first three states of the development of the *'old'* *Arcadia*, Cl,As,Da,Ph,Je,Hm, which read *wherewith he seemed to despise the works of nature.*[16]

Despite such blunders, these alterations demonstrate the ruthless determination of the editors of 93 to restore balance to the text in having five Books and four Eclogues, motivated by nothing less than a type of integrity to their purpose in elevating Sidney's reputation. When *The Countess of Pembroke's Arcadia* was published in 93 with its new folio format, specially designed title-page, and preface condemning the form in which the work had 'not long since appeared', Sidney could no longer be regarded simply as the author of an uncompleted work of fiction in the renaissance heroic mode. He was being marketed now as the creator of a massive and complex work embracing both the heroic and romance traditions. The manufactured reason given for its lack of cohesion, that 'the father's untimely death prevented the timely birth of the child', was designed to minimize the reader's attention to its unfinished state, encouraging public belief in this edition as a testament to Sidney's unprecedented achievement in possessing, even if not fully executing, the idea or vision of the work in its entirety.

These efforts to promote Sidney's image culminated in 1598 with the first literary collection in English to rival that of the by then old-fashioned Chaucer. That this and all ensuing editions to 1674 were published under the title of *The Countess of Pembroke's Arcadia* with which they opened attests to the success of the editors of the 1593 edition in building and establishing Sidney's position in English letters. It could not be shaken by the little unrest which might have been aroused a decade later by Florio's quibble in the Second Book of Montaigne's *Essays* (1603) that

> this end we see of it, though at first above all, now is not answerable to the precedents: and though it were much easier to mend out of an original and well corrected copy than to make-up so much out of a most corrupt, yet see we more marring that was well, than mending what was amiss.

Such charges, however near the truth of the matter, were left unchallenged and unanswered. Still another decade passed before the expanded note preceding the appendix in 1613 and followed by succeeding editions further obfuscated the reality of the state of Sidney's manuscript at the time of his death and the difficulties facing its original editors:

> Thus far the worthy author had revised or enlarged that first written *Arcadia* of his, which only passed from hand to hand, and was never printed, having a purpose likewise to have new ordered, augmented, and concluded the rest, had he not been prevented by untimely death. So that all which followeth here of this work remained as it was done and sent away in several loose sheets (being never after reviewed, nor so much as seen all together by himself) without any certain disposition or perfect order... and therefore with much labour were the best coherencies that could be gathered out of those scattered papers made and afterwards printed, as now it is, only by her noble care to whose dear hand they were first committed, and for whose delight and entertainment only undertaken.

But by then Sidney's status as a literary hero had been irrevocably established, and the time had now come to offer tributes to the Dowager Countess of Pembroke, who, still enjoying the accolades owing to one of the senior literary figures of the land, gloried in the monument she had so successfully created 'to be a principal ornament to the family of the Sidneys' (sig. A4).

### NOTES

1 Apart from reducing the long 's' I have kept the original spelling and punctuation in the chapter summaries and in Greville's letter to Walsingham. In other quotations the spelling has been modernized. Poems are referred to by the abbreviations given in *Poems* lxxi, and by the numbers assigned to them in that edition.
2 F. A. Yates, *John Florio*, Cambridge, 1934, 203ff.
3 S.P. 12/195/33, reproduced with the kind permission of the Public Record Office, London.
4 M. M. Wallace, *The Life of Sir Philip Sidney*, Cambridge, 1915, 388-92.
5 *OA*, p. 409, 2-4.
6 *OA*, 285, 26-286, 10.
7 *OA*, 174, 5-9; 172, 26-29 *and variant*.

8  *OA*, 217, 2-3 (*variant*).
9  *OA*, 273, 19 (*variant*); 355-57 (*variant*).
10  *OA*, 19, 26; 103, 3 and lxv.
11  *OA*, 238, 8; 88-90.
12  *OA*, 389-96.
13  *OA*, 416, 16 (*variant*).
14  *OA*, 193, 12 (*variant*); 222, 8 (*variant*); 415, 4 (*variant*); 415, 12 (*variant*).
15  *OA*, 193, 19 (*variant*).
16  *OA*, 284, 5-7 *and variant*.

ARTHUR F. KINNEY

# INTIMATIONS OF MORTALITY: SIDNEY'S JOURNEY TO FLUSHING AND ZUTPHEN*

Sir Philip Sidney is now, four hundred years after his death, so obscured by fable and legend, so imprisoned by cultural myths shaping and distorting his untimely fall in battle while in the Netherlands, that understanding the man himself seems forever beyond us. It is one of the most stunning reversals in the whole of Tudor literary history. For during his abbreviated life, no other writer is more persistent than Sidney in placing himself squarely before us if only, by the customary Tudor habit of reading, by implications we discern meaning. Whether as the callow, artistic lover Astrophil later judging himself with wry wit, or the more ardently solemn Philisides, this poet stubbornly dismisses the primary distinctions between life and art. In cunning clues that are unavoidable parts of his meaning, from the mocking irreverence of *Astrophil and Stella* to the serious and committed play of *A Defence of Poetry*, as from the insinuating *Lady of May* to the amazing reach and apparently inexhaustible depths of the later *Arcadia*, he keeps reminding us that the most inspired work of the poetic vision (that of the *vates*) basically remains the simulation of the craftsman (or 'maker'). Continually he shows us that poetic metaphor finds its best networks of references beyond the work in which it is embedded; it finds them in life.

Following the precedent set in *The Lady of May* (where Sidney is barely disguised as the useful, active, ambitious forester), the *persona* of the *Defence*, for instance, steps outside the frame of his essay to remind us that he has studied horsemanship in Italy, to request our sympathy that he is so put upon to defend his art, and to chastise us if we do not instinctively appreciate the practical use and the moving beauty of elegies and epitaphs. Sonnets 24, 35, and 37 of *Astrophil and Stella*, with their prismatic puns on the name of Lord Rich, the present husband of Penelope Devereux, is another case in point. Indeed, Penelope's role as Stella, the star this star-loving, star-studying poet most admires, is carried on into the *'old' Arcadia* where the princesses Philoclea and Pamela, the most virtuous and attractive of women, live in lodges of yellow stone that are star-shaped; Pyrocles especially calls our attention to this by reconceptualizing the two houses, one large and one small, as a comet and a tail.[1] It is even possible that the 1585 Ermine Portrait of Elizabeth I of England deliberately refers to her as the austere Helen, Queen of

Corinth, who is known in the revised *Arcadia* as the bringer of peace and who is championed in the lists by a golden knight, known for his courtesy, who wears an ermine for his device. Where fable had no authentic reference, that is, history could seemingly supply an analogous fiction.

Reading Sidney, then, we, like the Tudors of his first audience, become his collaborators, his conspirators in perceiving fiction-making and factual understanding as indivisible acts. If poetry is actually to function as Sidney prescribes in his *Defence*, then his life must be a part of that poetry just as that poetry is meant to direct his life, to lead him into the continual exercise of virtuous actions. As difficult as this may be to disentangle, I want to suggest how I think Sidney meant us to read the significance of his life as he conveyed it in his poetry. There he has tactically provided us with the ideas that governed his life and that, in turn, help us to understand why it was that a promising young courtier from Penshurst and Wilton came to die on foreign battlefields in Gelderland. The method and meaning of his poetry can, even now, help us to get to the man in spite of the legend and regardless of the myths.

i

Sidney's conspiratorial art, which draws together all of his work in various genres, is easier to grasp when we recall that the entire corpus—from the apprenticeship of *The Lady of May* (1576) to the indelible mastery of the revised *Arcadia* (?1584)—was composed within a brief, compacted eight-year period. It draws with exactitude and finesse on his preceding years at court. It anticipates his actions as governor of Flushing. For Sidney's sense of collaborative art—where poetic metaphor must coordinate, reinforce, and reify historical occurrence—draws on an established rhetorical culture in which poetry-making is indistinguishable from the art of persuasion. If poetry instructs actions, as Sidney tells us in the *Defence* all good poetry must, then its lessons cannot be wholly contained in its fictions. Rather, fiction's connectedness to the lives of actual men and women is the mark the true poet aims for: such connectedness is necessary to complete the *poetic* process.

Such an understanding of poetry stems from the antique learning passed on to Tudor writers like Sidney by the humanist culture that dominated the learning of his time. In Book III of Plato's *Republic*, for instance, one of the main source books for Tudor theories of poetry, Socrates distinguishes between two ways of rendering speech, which he calls *diegesis* and *mimesis*. In the first of these, the poet himself is the speaker (as in Sidney's *Defence*) and never attempts to suggest that anyone else is addressing his audience. In *mimesis*, the poet tries to create the illusion that someone else is speaking (as in *Astrophil and Stella* or, more complexly, in the *Arcadia*) while still advancing suggestions that are his own. It is *mimesis*, through characterization (*prosopopeia*) and place (*prosopographia*), that causes Plato finally to distrust poets and poetry by the time of *Republic X* (and, in the *Ion*, to consider them mad because they are unable to differentiate between the speaking *persona* and the actual author). In his subsequent attempt to rescue poetry from such charges in ways that are both sensible and manageable, Aristotle recognizes the need for such a distinction. By arguing that poets always perform mimetic acts, even when writing first-person narrations, he draws rhetoric to the support of poetics by reasoning that both put forward *ideas*—one by exercising the mind (*diegesis*), the other by emptying the audience of the intermediate, blocking emotions of pity and terror (*katharsis*). Poetry was therefore closely allied to rhetoric in theory for Aristotle, as it had been in practice for Socrates and in theory for Plato. But for Aristotle it is also closely related to logic. The progressive integration of knowledge requires the *patterning* of images, episodes, or ideas (such as the repetitious appeal to stars and starlight in *Astrophil* or the alternating episodes of action and reflection in *Arcadia*) which function (despite their fictive context) as so many enthymemes. It is just this sort of understanding of poetry that caused Tudor schoolmasters like Thomas Ashton, who taught Sidney at Shrewsbury, to instruct rhetoric almost indiscriminately from handbooks, from speeches, from poems, and from plays. This is the understanding conveyed when Tudor poets name women after concepts (such as Daniel's Delia or Spenser's Faerie Queene) or talk of fiction as appealing to the mind (as Lyly and Greene constantly do). Greville, then, is speaking only commonplaces when he remarks of Sidney's *Arcadia* that his friend means 'to limn out such exact pictures, of every posture in the minde, that any man being forced, in the straines of this life, to pass through any straights, or latitudes of good, or ill fortune, might (as in a glasse) see how to set a good countenance upon all the discountenances of adversitie, and a stay upon the exorbitant smilings of chance'.[2]

All of these ideas are central to Sidney's *Defence*—and often they are reinforced by his techniques of writing and his strategies of argument. The *Defence*, for example, harbours the two *prosoposiae* who are the most splendid grotesques he ever created. One is the (individual, particularizing) historian, 'laden with old mouse-eaten records, authorizing himself (for the most part) upon other histories, whose greatest authorities are built upon the notable foundations of hearsay; having much ado to accord differing writers and to pick truth out of their partiality; better ac-

quainted with a thousand years ago than with the present age'.[3] The
others are the group of moral philosophers (numerous because they are
always universalizing): 'I see [them] coming towards me with a sullen
gravity, as though they could not abide vice by daylight, rudely clothed
for to witness outwardly their contempt of outward things, with books in
their hands against glory, whereto they set their names, sophistically
speaking against subtlety, and angry with any man in whom they see the
foul fault of anger' (p. 29). Both are images of the mind, ideas, as well
as types and characters. They are, Sidney implies, caught in a stalemated
disputation. Their irreconciliation prompts Poetry to act as adjudicator,
to make sense of their debate and to draw from it the best lessons that
may be offered. But Poetry is never seen as History and Philosophy
are—we do not even know Poetry's gender—for Poetry is not a grotesque, neither exaggerating nor crippling, restricting nor distorting, reducing nor generalizing the truth.

   Such authorial wit stems from a deliberate disposition of argument as
ongoing dialectic, and one that works two ways simultaneously for the attentive collaborative reader. First, poetry is mediator, uniquely embracing both intellectual activity and rational understanding—or what Sidney
calls *oratio* and *ratio*. Second, poetry's unique pedigree, allowing it to en-
vision and maintain truth through the synthesis of philosophy's concep-
tions and history's applications, allows it further to fuse the ideals of
Platonic thought—such as the perfect Cyrus and the fabulous Cyclops—
by acts of Aristotelian *mimesis* or *imitatio*—as realized, say, in a Pyrocles
(which audibly suggests *peerless*) or Arcadia. 'But even in the most excellent determination of goodness, what philosopher's counsel can so
readily direct a prince, as the feigned Cyrus in Xenophon; or a virtuous
man in all fortunes, as Aeneas in Virgil; or a whole commonwealth, as
the way of Sir Thomas More's *Utopia*?' (p. 33). Asking such questions,
the narrator of the *Defence* reinforces *mimesis* by utilizing *diegesis*.

   By realizing such possibilities, drawn from fact, idea, or imagination,
Sidney tells (and shows) us, the poet becomes a god-like creator, the
maker of an instructive world, like the heavens and the earth of the Lord
Himself. By a further analogy, the reader too, in recognizing the motiva-
tion and purpose of such pleasurable imitations of the imagination as
they instruct him, becomes a third creator in the chain—a second poet,
fashioning his own life after the exemplary thought and behaviour of the
poet's images.

> Certainly, even our Saviour Christ could as well have given the moral com-
> monplaces of uncharitableness and humbleness as the divine narration of
> Dives and Lazarus; or of disobedience and mercy, as that heavenly
> discourse of the lost child and the gracious father; but that His through-

searching wisdom knew the estate of Dives burning in hell, and of Lazarus in Abraham's bosom, would more constantly (as it were) inhabit both the memory and judgement. Truly, for myself, meseems I see before mine eyes the lost child's disdainful prodigality, turned to envy a swine's dinner: which by the learned divines are thought not historical acts, but instructing parables (p. 34).

The Zodiac of such wit—embracing in the metaphor God's heavens and man's astrologies—can unite in its singular universe the beliefs and teachings of the profane and the sacred, through the inspired metaphors of poetry when they are rightly received and wisely understood and applied.

> Infinite proofs of the strange effects of this poetical invention might be alleged; only two shall serve, which are so often remembered as I think all men know them. The one of Menenius Agrippa, who, when the whole people of Rome had resolutely divided themselves from the senate, with apparent show of utter ruin, though he were (for that time) an excellent orator, came not among them upon trust of figurative speeches or cunning insinuations, and much less with far-fet maxims of philosophy, which (especially if they were Platonic) they must have learned geometry before they could well have conceived; but forsooth he behaves himself like a homely and familiar poet. He telleth them a tale, that there was a time when all the parts of the body made a mutinous conspiracy against the belly, which they thought devoured the fruits of each other's labour; they concluded they would let so unprofitable a spender starve. In the end, to be short (for the tale is notorious, and as notorious that it was a tale), with punishing the belly they plagued themselves. This applied by him wrought such effect in the people, as I never read that only words brought forth but then so sudden and so good an alteration; for upon reasonable conditions a perfect reconcilement ensued. The other is of Nathan the prophet, who, when the holy David had so far forsaken God as to confirm adultery with murder, when he was to do the tenderest office of a friend in laying his own shame before his eyes, sent by God to call again so chosen a servant, how doth he it but by telling of a man whose beloved lamb was ungratefully taken from his bosom: the application most divinely true, but the discourse itself feigned; which made David (I speak of the second and instrumental cause) as in a glass see his own filthiness, as that heavenly psalm of mercy well testifieth (pp. 41-42).

Fiction elides into fact; fact slips back here into fiction: poetry *makes us* 'exercise' to 'know'. What Sidney is urging, in this sycretic application of Cicero, Demosthenes, and Quintilian, of the prophets and the apostles, is that the poet, like God, orders, re-forms, and ultimately civilizes men by ordering, rc-forming, and even civilizing the images of the ideas they are meant to figure forth. Sidney's poet, as he emerges from the *Defence*, then, conventionally reforms civilization by instruction *and action* which that instruction is meant to guarantee, as Demosthenes had served Athenian liberty before him and Cicero had defended the

Roman Republic. Sidney's poet is also, following the Tudor commonplace concerning Hercules, one who leads his followers with sweet
and golden chains of language. Such functions are inseparable. Thus the
poet Sidney finds himself obliged to write the Queen about the dangers
inherent in marrying Alençon and obliged himself to fight the Spanish
invaders of the Netherlands; but he must also couch such advice in a
courtly letter and instill patriotism in the battlefield speeches to his men.
Being a poet, as Sidney understood the term, meant doing both. *A Defence
of Poetry* tells us, wittily, eloquently, that as a poet *he had no choice*. Nor,
as readers, can we do less than follow his instruction, for the sake of our
own exercising of knowledge, our own education.

ii

Knowledge and action, the *gnosis* and *praxis* of Sidney's *Defence*, impelled
by a notable use of *energia* ('liveliness') is recaptured in the Platonic *noesis*,
or pure Platonic idea, and the *eikasia*, or imitations of things, that realize
the *Arcadia*. This wider work allows Sidney considerably more room to
pursue the ideas most important to him—as images for poetry and principles for action—by which he meant firmly to inform and persuade his
readers in principles that, I think, came also to direct much of his own
life. In reading the *Arcadia* as Sidney designed it to be read, then, we look
not so much for characters or events as *through* characters and events to
ideas, to the informing texts and principles that the plot realizes through
*mimesis* and we, as conspirators, reconstruct for ourselves. If Sidney's use
of epic history as a containing form recalled for his first Tudor readers
such historians as Xenophon and Thucydides, he also has frequent
recourse in the *Arcadia* to those ideas which emerge as the most important
for him in the philosophic works of Aristotle, especially the *Politics* and
the *Ethics*. Aristotle's thesis in the *Politics* is that 'Man is by nature a
political animal' (*Politics* I.i.9; III.iv.2), one who is distinguished by
reason and by reasoned speech and whose words indicate what is useful
and harmful in society—that is, what is pragmatic—and what is right
and wrong for individual and society—that is, what is moral (I).[4]

> Every state is as we see a sort of partnership, and every partnership is
> formed with a view to some good (since all the actions of all mankind are
> done with a view to what they think to be good). It is therefore evident that,
> while all partnerships aim at some good, the partnership that is the most
> supreme of all and includes all the others does so most of all, and aims at
> the most supreme of all goods; and this is the partnership entitled the state,
> the political association (I.i.1).

The *Arcadia* is a graduated sequence of such partnerships, from the initial
one of Pyrocles and Musidorus through that of the protagonists with

Kalander, with Basilius, Philoclea and Pamela, and Euarchus; it is, *just as vitally*, a partnership of author and reader by way of a rhetorically arranged text.

Sidney's own primary teacher for the *Arcadia* is Aristotle. From *Politics I* and *II* comes much of the political theory of both the old and the new *Arcadia*; from the more practical consequences in *Politics III* and *IV* come many of the incidents. Starting with the premise that 'a good ruler is virtuous and wise' (III.ii,5), Aristotle argues at great length against the deviations from the ideal forms of governments which Sidney tests in poetry (and in life at the English and European courts, as he advises his brother Robert to do):

> tyranny corresponding to kingship, oligarchy to aristocracy, and democracy to constitutional government; for tyranny is monarchy ruling in the interest of the monarch, oligarchy government in the interest of the rich, democracy in the interest of the poor, and none of these forms governs with regard to the profit of the community (III.V.4).

In these Aristotelian terms Sidney meant his educated Tudor audience to recognize, Basilius is a tyrant, for his exile is self-indulgent—and that is precisely how Antiphilus defines him in the *'new' Arcadia* ( II.xxix). Another later addition has Dorus describing to Pamela the origins and faults of oligarchies in his history of Macedon and in his analysis of the government Euarchus inherited before his sense of justice and law made it right again (II.vi). Tyranny is anatomized in his history of Phrygia (II.viii), of Pontus (II.ix), and of Paphlagonia (II.x), while the dangers of democracy, for Sidney that many-headed hydra (II.xxvi), is explained by Clinias (II.xxvii) whose own rebellion, along with that of the Helots (I.v-vii), transforms idea into circumstances, or 'pregnant Images of life', as Greville has it (p. 15). In the later *Arcadia*, Sidney re-emphasizes political theory by further dramatising Aristotle's long and elaborate discussion of the causes of political disorder in *Politics V* (ii-vi) in his characterization of the Paphlagonian King, a good ruler who is easily deceived (II.x), in Antiphilus as a bad ruler who is too easily flattered (II.xxix), in Artaxia who is too militaristic (II.xxix), and in Cecropia who is too selfish and greedy for power (II.v ff.). Of all the bad rulers described in the *Politics*, the worst for Aristotle is just that which is realised in Basilius—'a monarch that exercises irresponsible rule' (IV.viii.3)—while the finest form of government for Aristotle is what in Sidney Euarchus is thought to aspire to: 'the greatest good and good in the highest degree in the most authoritative of all', Aristotle writes, which is 'justice' (III.vii.1). And such praise seems suggestive of Sidney's closing scenes: 'it is preferable for the law to rule rather than any one of the citizens, and according to this same principle, even if it be better for certain men to govern, they

must be appointed as guardians of the laws and in subordination to them'
(III.xi.3). Politics and morality are by nature continually joined in
Aristotle, moreover, so that the *Arcadia*, drawing from it, instructs us that
all forms of government—but most especially monarchy—rely on men
who exercise to know and who know in order to exercise. 'How great
dissipations monarchal governments are subject to', the concern of *Arcadia* IV.vii, stems rather from 'the discoursing sort of men than the active, being a matter more in imagination than practice'.

Aristotle saw the *Politics* and the *Ethics* as necessarily coordinated
works, and Sidney seems to realize this when he also deliberately applies
to his conclusion of the (old) *Arcadia* an independent essay by Aristotle
which the Tudors incorrectly knew as *Ethics V*. There Aristotle is clear
that justice is both a political and a moral concern that, appealing to an
absolute concept, by necessity in action takes on relative form. Aristotle
thus is made accurately to figure Euarchus' predicament and the central
questions raised in *Arcadia* V when he first defines justice: it 'means that
which is lawful and that which is equal or fair' (V.i.8).[5] But *legality* and
*equity* are not always the same thing, as Sidney quickly realizes. Yet,
*philosophically*, Aristotle tells us they *must* be.

> We saw that the law-breaker is unjust and the law-abiding man just. It is
> therefore clear that all lawful things are just in one sense of the word, for
> what is lawful is decided by legislature, and the several decisions of the
> legislature we call rules of justice. Now all the various pronouncements of
> the law aim either at the common interest of all, or at the interest of a ruling
> class determined either by excellence or in some other similar way; so that
> in one of its senses the term 'just' is applied to anything that produces and
> preserves the happiness, or the component parts of the happiness, of the
> political assembly.
>
> And the law prescribes certain conduct; the conduct of a brave man, for
> example not to desert one's post, not to run away, not to throw down one's
> arms; that of a temperate man, for example not to commit adultery or
> outrage; that of a gentle man, for example not to strike, not to speak evil;
> and so with actions exemplifying the rest of the virtues and vices, comman-
> ding these and forbidding those—rightly if the law has been rightly enacted,
> not so well if it has been made at random. Justice then in this sense is per-
> fect Virtue (V.i.12-15).

It is clear that Aristotle wants justice somehow to coordinate law, custom,
class, and suitable conduct while recognizing these may be incongruous.
None of them is so supreme that other considerations are made subor-
dinate or irrelevant. The genus justice has several species—distributive
(V.iii.12), corrective (V.iv.1), natural (V.vi), legal (V.vi), voluntary and
involuntary (V.viii.5). Injustice, too, has many categories (V.ii.6).
Having learned this, Sidney realizes through the *poetry* of the *Arcadia* just
what this means for any Tudor citizen—including himself. But the con-

crete element of poetry, especially when put into dramatic action, shows just how such ideas, broken down, can be misleading or corrupting. So Euarchus refuses to admit conditions and circumstances that might mitigate against law in an (unrealistic) pure state and in doing so his limited learning causes his own behaviour finally to become *im*moral and *un*just. This is confirmed by his notion of an absolute sentence similar in kind to the crime, for Aristotle is emphatic that reciprocity does not make the unjust just (IV.v.2), does not right wrongs. Aristotle's humane conclusion—'Men think that it is in their power to act unjustly, and therefore that it is easy to be just. But really this is not so' (V.ix.14)— gives a further issue to Pyrocles, Musidorus, and Gynecia that Euarchus steadfastly refuses to admit. Yet because justice is the most fundamental union of ethics and politics for Aristotle, it becomes the central subject of his philosophy, as it is the climactic subject for Sidney's most important (prose) poem.

When Sidney extended the lessons taught by his poetry into his own life—when he 'exercised' to 'know' by testing the *prosopopeia* of the *Arcadia*—he felt compelled to such actions as applying to join his father in governing Ireland and advising the Queen against what he saw as a precipitous and ill-informed marriage to Alençon. Both actions, he felt, would forward justice as enlightened partnerships of rulers and subjects. The *Arcadia*, both as initially conceived and as subsequently revised, was neither a retreat from nor a substitute for virtuous action then, but, as the *Defence* laid down, a deliberative examination from which he might determine his own course of action, might also teach himself.

But there was more to Aristotle, as Mary Sidney, Greville, and others in the Sidney, Walsingham, and Leicester circles knew. Aristotle joined the public concern of justice with the private concern of friendship, his other chief interest in the *Ethics* and the one most prominent there (VIII,IX). Sidney also applies this conjunction on nearly every page of the *Arcadia*. First he makes one hero a prince and the other a potential ruler (Prince Pyrocles courts Philoclea; Musidorus courts Princess Pamela); their loves are unavoidably rife with political implication. Such desires and intentions are for Aristotle governed by the intellect (*Ethics VI*) which works through prudence (*phronēsis*) as with Pyrocles and Musidorus, or intuition (*nous*) as with Philoclea, or wisdom (*sophia*) as with Pamela; the four major characters not only allow Sidney variations on justice and friendship through a fundamental chiasmus, but they also allow him to pursue the several ways Aristotle proposes for virtuous knowledge. And whichever we choose, he concludes in *Ethics X*, we will proceed to the highest state of knowledge, the disinterested contemplation of truth, *theoria* (X.vii.1). Sidney works this out deliberately by pro-

ceeding from the soliloquies of Pyrocles and Musidorus in *Arcadia* I (of
the revision) where contemplation seems to lead them to think of appetite, to the debates between Cecropia and Pamela and Philoclea in
revised *Arcadia* III where the life of pure contemplation is defended by the
daughters of Basilius, to the *'old' Arcadia* V where such a state is potentially
possible given the chastening experience of the trial. But pure contemplation of the Deity or the divine is for Aristotle a temporary state since a
moral life also means active political and social engagement.

These informing ideas of both the *'old'* and *'new' Arcadia* are all splen-
didly worked out in the final scenes of the trial in *Arcadia* V. When Euarchus takes up his role of judge, he warns the Arcadians that he is a
stranger, and one who like them suffers the shortcomings of being
human. 'Remember I am a man', he tells them; 'that is to say, a creature
whose reason is often darkened with error'.[6] But, as if anticipating his
later hardening when special conditions ask that his judgement be over-
turned, he adds, 'do not easily judge of your judge; but since you will
have me to command, think it is your part to obey' (p. 365). Despite the
apparent evidence against them, Pyrocles and Musidorus nevertheless
remain calm for they know, as we do, that the case of the prosecution is
only circumstantial. 'We have lived, and have lived to be good to
ourselves and others', Musidorus assures Pyrocles; 'Our souls ... have
achieved the causes of their hither coming ... And to many men (for in
this time, place, and fortune, it is lawful for us to speak gloriously) it hath
been behoveful that we should live' (p. 371). Later, such sentiments,
displaying Musidorus's constancy, are the basis of remarks to Euarchus:

> Therefore, O judge, who I hope dost know what it is to be a judge, that
> your end is to preserve and not to destroy mankind ... since that our doing
> in the extremest interpretion is but a human error, and that of it you may
> make a profitable event (we being of such estate as their parents would not
> have misliked the affinity), you will not, I trust, at the persuasion of this
> brabbler burn your house to make it clean, but like a wise father turn even
> the fault of your children to any good that may come of it, since that is the
> fruit of wisdom and end of all judgments (pp. 402-03).[7]

The warning shrewdly links the paternity of Euarchus with the patriar-
chy of the law he has sworn to uphold and suggests that both family love
and equity might mitigate them. But the redefinition, so carefully prescribed by Aristotle and so thoroughly worked out by Sidney, is seen to
have no effect, just as his contemporaneous letter to Elizabeth I concerning Alençon misfired. Here, too, philosophically and actually, the judge
misjudges, the ruler misrules. Clearly Sidney is using the *Arcadia* to help
understand and explain why—and to teach us at the same time.

Thus only coincidentally, or collaterally, does such a situation as the trial scene of the *Arcadia* relate to romance, the literary form which, through a superficial misreading, has for so long misguided readers. Sidney's major thrust, rather, as we have seen, is to capture human dilemmas in poetic images the better to teach and to exercise us. He does so by examining ideas. And the chief sources of ideas for the *Arcadia*, as for the *Defence*, are Aristotle and Plato, in whose discussions both imitation of human action and ideas of golden worlds actually join. In the *Defence*, Sidney felt he had to answer the challenge of Plato that poetry betrayed man's better ideas and instincts by appealing to his lower passions; he did so by arguing that Plato could see passions aroused by ideas in virtuous ways: that Plato too was a poet, and a good (read *virtuous*, not merely *successful*) poet. That reasoning in Sidney is neither clever nor desperate sophistry, but a thoughtful and logical position that also fused philosophy and poetry with life. He thus returns to this same point at the close of *Arcadia*, since it is so central to his thinking, to his beliefs. For Plato's charge that eroticism conquers reason (*Republic X* 697D-608A) is precisely the issue raised at the trial by Euarchus. He argues that the passion of Pyrocles, Musidorus, and Gynecia has corrupted all three of them and that their perversions should be—must be—punishable by death. In Platonic terms, he means to become (as Sidney means to image) the philosopher king.

> The law ... declares that it is best to keep quiet as far as possible in calamity and not to chafe and repine ... [But] If you would reflect that ... part of the soul that ... in our own misfortunes was forcibly restrained, and that has hungered for tears and a good cry and satisfaction, because it is its nature to desire these things, [this] is the element in us that poets satisfy and delight (*Republic X*, 604B-606A).

In the *Republic*, Plato like Euarchus seeks refuge in what Sidney in the 'old' *Arcadia* terms 'dead pitilesse lawes' (IV.v). But the *Republic* (as Sidney knows) is the first stage in Plato's long trilogy of philosophic works on government. The second, the *Statesman*, transforms Euarchus's position, as essentially preliminary *and wrong*, when it argues that the ruler, not laws, must govern men—'it is clear that lawmaking belongs to the science of kingship; but the best thing is not that the laws be in power, but that the man who is wise and of kingly nature be ruler' (294A) because

> law could never, by determining exactly what is noblest and most just for one and all, enjoin upon them that which is best; for the differences of men and of actions and the fact that nothing, I may say, in human life is ever at rest, forbid any science whatsoever to promulgate any simple rule for everything and for all time (294B).

In Sidney's working out of Plato, Euarchus's skewed scale of values (as demonstrated by his condemnation of the innocent) denies the Greek sense of justice, *dikaiosynēs*, as something *more* than legal, as something *also* ethical, like our word *righteousness*. By insisting on vengeance as the basis for law, moreover (V.vii), Euarchus denies that equity basic to Plato's last discussion of the matter in his *Laws* (where, *on these grounds*, Plato also readmits the poet to a useful function in society). Aristotle is in agreement, in the limitation of law (*Politics* III1 286a; *Ethics* V.i. 13-15), while Cicero also says essentially the same thing in his adaption of Plato's *Laws* (*De Legibus*, I.xii.33-34; I.xv.42) and in his *De Officiis* (III. vii. 33), one of the humanists' favourite and one of the Tudors' most read works. By limiting himself to law, Euarchus relies wholly on what is known. Conversely, by arguing what can be and should be—the common province of poetry and morality in Sidney's *Defence*—Pyrocles and Musidorus must argue from the known and the unknown, must work from logic but also from trust and belief. They are prepared, then, as Euarchus and Philanax are not, for the wondrous miracle of Basilius's recovery, a resurrection that shatters mere case-hardened law. Euarchus, locating constancy in *self*-certainty as in universal and absolute human law, has no capacity for such wonders while Pyrocles and Musidorus, transcending human limitations through love (as Gynecia, Pamela, and Philoclea transcend actuality through prayer and Basilius transcends it through prophecy) *are* prepared. In Basilius's transformation comes all the rest. This, too, is probably derived from Plato—from the conclusion of the *Republic* with its myth of Er; from the ideal portrait of the statesman; and from the concept of the metamorphosing power of law by a Nocturnal Synod set to govern its change. This 'fable', the conclusion of Plato's *Laws* (XII.961 ff.), is parallel to the 'fable' closing the *Republic* and similar to the ending of *Arcadia*.

Such deeply serious ideas, taken up at Oxford and later in study on the Continent and at Wilton, confirm Sidney's continuing prudent interest in classical philosophy. But from the days he began associating with Leicester at Court and from the ineradicable memory of the St. Bartholomew's Day Massacre he witnessed in Paris, Sidney seems also to have been strongly drawn to Christian ideas as well—and their ramifications in the body politic. Just how closely is likewise revealed in the *Arcadia*. The turn of the original *Arcadia* in Book V to thoughts of otherworldliness—later developed in Pamela's prayer in the revision of Book III—points not simply to man's desperate need for consolation in times of fear or distress but to a deeper sense yet of justice—and of equity. Just how close it comes to traditional Christian philosophy may be most easily illustrated, perhaps, by the work of Philip de Mornay, sieur du Plessis-Marly, whose *De la verite de la religion chrestienne* (Antwerp, 1581) Arthur Golding says Sidney later began to translate.[8] Whether or not that is the case, it is surely a work Sidney knew. Many parts of this Protestant apologetics are relevant to *Arcadia*. A particularly important summary chapter is Chapter xviii, 'That God is mans souerein welfare, and therefore that the cheef marke which man should ame at, is to returne againe vnto God' (sigs X1v-Y1). Here Mornay urges man to exercise virtue, 'The calmenesse of our affections' (sig. X7), in achieving policy, 'the right vse of reason in the gouerning of worldly affaires' (sig. X7v) and as the means to wisdom, 'the beholding of God and of things belonging to GOD'. He continues, 'This requireth a man to lift vp himselfe aboue the world, and aboue himselfe, I meane that a man should retyre from all outward things into his owne soule, the Soule vnto her Mynd, and the Mynd vnto God' (sig. X8). 'It remaineth then in the end, that wee must atteine to that by Fayth, which wee cannot atteyne vnto by Reason; that we must mount vp by liuely beleef aboue our vnderstāding, vnto the things whereunto the eye of our mynd is not able to reach' (sig. X8v). The classical philosophers' state of divine or eternal virtue is for Mornay the equivalent of Providence, and although Sidney could not expect all of his readers to know Mornay, he surely means to imply in the *Arcadia* that the pagan philosophy of Book V of his original epic poem is in perfect accord with Christianity. As in the *Defence* where David's Psalms displace the fable of Menenius Agrippa, so in the *Arcadia* poetry allies antique thought with Christian humanism by emphasizing their central shared concerns (with justice and with equity/mercy) as the final moving *idea* in Sidney's grandest *poem*.

### iii

Sidney knew Mornay, and probably they were associated in the minds of many Continental Protestant leaders. In any event, by showing how the classical concern with justice and equity could incorporate ideas of Mornay which were already influencing Leicester, Walsingham, and their powerful friends on the Privy Council and at court, the conclusion of the *'old' Arcadia* unfolds along the very margins of authentic history— and autobiography. In its concern with equity especially, the *Arcadia* makes a poetic case for an enlightened adaptability to circumstance that Sidney had actually already urged on his father as Lord Deputy of Ireland (who, like Euarchus, had been asked to govern in a foreign land).

> So strangely and dyversely goes the cource of the worlde by the enterchanginge humors of those that governe it, that thoughe it be most noble to have allwayes one mynde and one constancy, yet can it not be allwaies directed

to one pointe; but must needes sometymes alter his cource, according to
the force of others changes dryves it ... Particularly to yowr lott, it makes
me change my style, and wryte to your Lordship, that keepinge still yowr
minde in one state of vertuouse quietnes, yow will yet frame yowr cource
according to them. And as they delay yowr honorable rewardinge, so yow
by good meanes to delay your returne, till either that ensue, or fitter tyme
be for this.[9]

The advice is in keeping with the more formal 'Discourse on Irish Affairs' which, written the previous autumn, takes up the same issues.

I must ever have in mind this consideration: That there is no cause, *neither
in reason nor equity*, why her most excellent Majesty should be at such excessive expenses to keep a realm, of which scarcely she hath the
acknowledgement of sovereignty; which cannot possibly be helped, but by
one of these three means: Either by direct conquest to make the country
hers, and so by one great heap of charges to purchase that which indeed
afterwards would well countervail the principal; or else by diminishing that
she doth send thither; or, lastly, with force and gentleness, to raise at least
so much rents, as may serve to quit the same charges. Truly, well may there
be diverse ways, but I think they will fall to one of these heads.[10]

Force may be needed, if reluctantly—Sir Henry Sidney was responsible
for the more humane notion of 'English plantations'—because 'there is
not a nation which live more tyrannously than they do one over the
other' (p. 11) yet he still warns Elizabeth and her Council, as a Pyrocles
might, 'There is no so great injustice, as that which puts on the colour
of demanding justice' (p. 12). For Sir Henry is not to be associated with
Euarchus in the *Arcadia*, finally, as the revision is at pains to make clear
by identifying him instead with Kalander, whose lovely house and
garden in the later text are closely modelled on Penshurst (I.iii).

Such philosophically and politically significant connections between
poetry and action are reinforced by those more obvious references in the
*Arcadia* (such as Parthenia's disfigurement, suggesting that of Sidney's
mother and even Sir Philip himself) which point the way to Sidney's persistently conspiratorial art. The tournaments that swell out in the revision of Book II, for instance, show the thin line between life and art when
we recall that only two or three years previously, in 1581, Sidney himself
had taken just such an extravagant role—may, indeed, have written it for
himself—in 'The Four Foster Children of Desire', staged as 'The tryum-
phe Shewed before the Queene and the French Embassadors' on Monday and Tuesday of Whitsun.

Then proceeded M. Philip Sidney, in very sumptuous maner, with armor
part blewe, & the rest gilt & engraven, with foure spare horses, having
caparisons and furniture veri riche & costly, as one of cloth of gold em-
broidred with pearle, and some embrodred with gold and silver feathers,

very richly & cunningly wrought, he had foure pages that rode on his four spare horses, who had cassock coats & venetian hose al of cloth of silver, layd with gold lace, & hats of the same with golde bands, and white fethers, and eache one a paire of white buskins. Then had he thirtie gentlemen & yeomen, & foure trumpetters, who were all in cassocke coats and venetian hose of yellow velvet, laid with silver lace, yellowe velvet caps with silver bands and white fethers, and every one a paire of white buskins. And they had uppon their coates, a scrowle or bande of silver, which came scarfe wise over the shoulder, and so downe under the arme, with this poesie, or sentence written upon it, both before and behinde, Sic nos non nobis.[11]

But in the later *Arcadia* such performances come into question, wasting as they do the lives of Argalus and Parthenia and needlessly endangering others. There such tournaments are instinctively criticised by Philoclea and cause Pamela to transfer her trust to divinity rather than to human achievement. Her faith in powers unseen is a Christian corrective to Basilius' belief in a pagan oracle, although his ability to trust in things unseen, rather like the horoscope Sidney had cast when he was sixteen,[12] might prove true enough when properly interpreted.

But not all of Sidney's actions need a revised *Arcadia* to reinterpret them. Indeed, the sort of bearing which distinguished him on ceremonial occasions before the court of Elizabeth I was from the start of his adult life, as early as the Grand Tour he made after leaving Oxford, applied with a fine tuning (like the application of equity) to the skilful investigations and negotiations he conducted abroad. From Vienna on 17 December 1574, during the period he was also studying with Languet, he displays the same kind of insight into the affairs of men he will later assign Pyrocles and Musidorus but withhold from Euarchus in a letter to Cecil as Principal Secretary. 'Righte honorable and my singular good Lorde', he writes,

> The Emperour hathe at lengthe obtained his longe desired truice of the greate Turks for 8 yeeres, the grawnte of whiche he hathe undrestoode by a courrier sente by his legier embassadowr ... [The courier] saiethe likewise that there came to Constantinople advertisements that the Belierbei of Egipte hathe latelie overthrowne in a very greate batteil, the Abissines subjectes to Pretre Jhon as we call him. In my simple opinion they have bene provoked by the Portugese to take this matter fur above their forces uppon them, for that the Turke by the redde sea dothe greatlie encroche uppon their Indian traffick. The expectation of these embassadowrs will cawse the Emperowr to delay his journey to Bohemia whiche notwithstandinge he muste necessarily ere it be longe performe they beinge very evill contente, of his so longe absence, in so muche that this yeere they have plainely refused to give certaine greate summes of money, whiche heretofore they had not denied. Besides that he muste please them for to gett his son the crowne for althoughe he do pretende hereditary succession they seeme they will not grawnte it any other waie but in manner of election (pp. 100-01).

Already the ideas of Aristotle and Plato were being put to observation and, in turn, laying the groundwork for the biographies of Pyrocles and Musidorus. Sidney's own skill in translating ideas into actual application is seen again and again in his letters: the correspondence is more concerned with matters of public policy and political action, in fact, than with his personal life or education. For Sidney, the men with whom he spoke and negotiated were (like poetry) concrete examples figuring forth the principles on which he would place chief emphasis. Thus on 22 March 1576, he writes to Walsingham,

> to Prince Casimire I said according to mine Instructions, and to that purpose so much more, as the course of speech, and the framing of the time did give occasion...
> For the second I founde no cause to perswade him to unity with his brother, he being as he saith, fully perswaded so to embrace it as nothing more, yet found I in him great miscontentment that his brother beginnes to make alteration in Religion, for having two principall gover[n]ments the upper Palatinate which lyes in Bavaria, and this which they calle the nether by the Rhine, the Elector hath allready in the upper established Lutheranisme, and as it is feared, is comming shortly to doe the same here (pp. 105-06).

On the same day, Sidney writes a more formal letter to Cecil, but adds a more substantial postscript as well.

> Thus muche I thoughte yowr Lordeshippe woolde be content if I did adde to these former lynes. that as yet the division betwixte the Palatins is not perfittly made, allthoughe the fathers will be sett downe, in so muche that there is some feare there will some jar fall betwixte them that beinge helped on with the diversitie of their religions (p. 108).

Whichever came first, the teachings of Mornay and Languet or the diplomatic missions and investigations, Sidney shows repeatedly in these early letters that for him the force of Protestantism was as powerful a principle in dealing with foreign governments as any other—and perhaps the most powerful of them all. That he is somewhat reluctant to admit this, to others and to himself, is seen in his equivocations in the early letters to Cecil and Walsingham. That he is uncertain of the proper measure of religion in politics is made plain enough by his attempts in the early parts of the 'old' *Arcadia* to retreat to a pagan and pastoral setting where Christianity need not be an issue.

But in life politics and religion, however uneasy they might be at times as bedfellows, would not choose to separate. By May he has had instructions from the Queen herself, prompting yet another letter to Walsingham, this time from Heidelberg.

Hether I came the laste of Aprill, and had Audience the nexte day. I had from her Majestie to condole with him and to perswade him [the Emperor] to unitie withe his brother, he made his vizchancelour to awnswere me, whiche he did in a very longe speeche, withe thanke[s] to her Majestie and prayses of the worthy prince that is dead, the pointe of concorde with his brother he thanked her Majestie for remembringe, and fell into a common place of the necessitie of brothers love, but descended nothinge into his owne particularitie of what he thoughte of him (p. 113).

We can see Sidney, slowly but surely, beginning to translate the lessons of political philosophy into practical politics, and the concerns of a philosopher king into the demands of an increasingly militant Protestantism as the best way to insure virtue. What develops through the subsequent letters collected by Feuillerat is paralleled in the development of the *'old'* *Arcadia*, for by the time of Book V pagan issues are more openly, more obviously, correlated to Puritan concerns as Sidney grew to understand them.

iv

When we place this complex of concerns alongside the revised text of the *Arcadia*, the poem to which Sidney devoted his final months as a poet, we can see a progression of thought that seems accurately to register his own increasing anxieties. The *'old'* *Arcadia*, which Ringler thinks completed by 1582,[13] announces its chief hypothesis at the outset: 'there is nothing so certain as our continual uncertainty' (p. 5). What follows is a debate between Basilius and his subaltern, Philanax, about right rule. Philanax proposes that 'wisdom and virtue be the only destinies appointed to man to follow'. These 'guides' that 'cannot fail' point 'so direct a way of proceeding to prosperity must necessarily ensue' (p. 7). Basilius is concerned, however, with the determining powers of fortune. 'And would you, then, ... that in change of fortune I shall not change my determination, as we do our apparel according to the air, and as the ship doth her course with the wind?' (p. 9). But Philanax remains resolute and inflexible. He still advocates 'a constant virtue, well settled, little subject unto [change]'; 'in great necessity' he would allow alteration and then only actions that are moderate and 'well proportioned' (p. 9). The debate concludes in a stalemate: '"Yet the reeds stand with yielding", said the duke. "And so are they but reeds, most worthy Prince," said Philanax, "but the rocks stand still and are rocks"' (p. 9). A few pages later Musidorus notes an 'alteration' in Pyrocles (p. 13), who is accused of allowing his 'mind to fall asleep' (p. 13) when he too wishes to retreat from the world of action to seek a 'solitariness, the sly enemy that doth most separate a man from well doing' (p. 14). As Richard C. McCoy states, whose argument I have been generally following here,

Musidorus's main point underscores that of Philanax.[14] 'A mind well trained and long exercised in virtue, my sweet and worthy cousin, doth not easily change any course it once undertakes but upon well grounded and well weighted causes ... Even the very countenance and behaviour of such a man doth show forth images of the same constancy by maintaining the right harmony betwixt it and the inward good' (p. 13). Thus in the opening pages the main themes of the *'old' Arcadia* are plainly presented. It will parallel the public responsibilities of a king with the private responsibilities of a prince in love in terms of solitude versus action, right thinking versus right doing. It will test the need for constancy, moreover, and the virtue of flexibility, of 'bending with the wind'.

Such a summary does all right by the first three-fifths of the *'old' Arcadia*, and it will pass for the fourth book as well. But clearly, by the fifth book, it will no longer suffice. Although Euarchus seems set up to harmonize wise thought and just action (by his pronouncements), thus bringing together thought and deed, knowing to exercise and exercising to know, in fact his wisdom misses the mark because he takes apparent truths (such as the death of Basilius and the guilt of Pyrocles and Musidorus) as facts. Thus he is neither wise nor just in actuality. Once he is confronted with mitigating circumstances—his blood relationship to the two young men—he is unable to harmonize the pliability of Basilius, that would allow change of heart and mind, with the rigid stability of Philanax, which has already grown tyrannical in tone and untruthful in statement. There are two possible reasons for this. One, which I think the care of the long *'old' Arcadia* dismisses out of hand, is that Sidney grew careless at the end and dashed off a solution straight from romance literature that might please his sister and her circle of friends reading such works aloud during evenings in the great house. For Sidney has set up crucial concerns of law and justice—crucial concerns, that is, which Plato, Aristotle, and Cicero among others had spent most of their lives thinking and writing about—and he has rather systematically applied them, both in the public and courtly and in the private and pastoral domains; and there is no reason for him to give up at the end, when it were better left unfinished: 'there is nothing so certain as our continual uncertainty' would certainly handle that neatly enough. But the other possibility, and the one which I have been at some pains to explore, is that Sidney changed his mind about the workings of law and justice. He came to understand equity. And equity, which Euarchus cannot hear of, supports Basilius. It also accomodates all the facts—not simply the apparent facts—of *Arcadia* V. Equity admits flexibility and change, but it does not deny justice and stability. Equity was, after all, what Sidney urged on Sir Henry and Ireland in 1580. And by 1584, equity was what the

Netherlands seemed to be struggling for, what his uncle Leicester might advocate, and what Sidney's own youthful talent at negotiation and diplomacy seemed to make him destined to enact. Equity also denied the possibility of tyranny since it existed to make exceptions to just those rules tyrants had to make absolute.

And because Sidney changed his mind, learned as he wrote and as he grew in experience through poetry and politics, he decided to rewrite the *Arcadia*. We have testimony to this change. After Sidney's death Greville sent forth what Victor Skretkowicz, Jr. calls an 'urgent plea to Walsingham [as Sidney's executor] to prevent publication of the romantic though well polished *'old'* *Arcadia* and to substitute for it "a correction of that old one don 4 or 5 years since w^ch he left in trust with me wherof ther is no more copies, & fitter to be printed then that first w^ch is cōm-on"'.[15] Sidney's sister, now the Countess of Pembroke, agreed and, so far as we can tell, destroyed what copies she could of the original. What they published, with great but justifiable pride, was the *'new'* *Arcadia* which is, in many indicative and decisive ways, a very different kind of work. It begins with the disappearance of Urania—of the ideal—so as to leave shepherds and princes alike in a fallen world (already anticipating the original Euarchus). The substantial revisions that follow—first detailed and examined by the Dutch scholar R. W. Zandvoort as long ago as 1929—talk not about 'uncertainty' which no man can respond to adequately, but 'disfigurement', which he can. 'Disfigured minds' follow 'disfigured' bodies and perspectives; from the modified ideal of Kalander's home to the war with the Helots and the long 'captivity episode' of Book III, the *'new'* *Arcadia* traces the minds and actions of men and women who are thwarted in their plans or desires, who thwart others in turn and who, amongst the worst of them, set out with vengeance to rid the world of opposition. The 'disfigurement' of princes posing as a shepherd and an Amazon is no longer a condition of the plot but a consequence of short-sightedness. They betray their stations and themselves to achieve their desires when, by Book V, their actual stations and selves will more than bring them what they seek. But the outer 'disfigurement' of a Musidorus and a Pyrocles and the temporarily misplaced passions of a Gynecia or a Mopsa show the fallibility and foolishness of unrestraint rather than the criminal intention or evil instincts of the more tyrannical. They are curable—obviously so, next to the parade of tyrants in the revised Book II or the unscrupulous behaviour of Cecropia and even Amphialus in the revised Book III.

It has recently been estimated that the *'new'* *Arcadia*, while apparently retaining a dramatic structure for its main plot, weaves into this action hundreds of pages of episodic material' and that 'For Books I and II, the added material alone exceeds the original by almost one-third'.[16] But this too is seen not simply as amplification but as a rethinking, a 're-vision', 'something substantially new'. Here the Phrygian citizens revolt against 'chiefe instruments of Tyrannie' (II.ix) supported by Musidorus who demonstrates what McCoy calls 'sophisticated political insights and principles' (p. 140). In other episodes added to Book II, the blind King of Paphlagonia, also symbolically 'disfigured', misjudges his two sons; Plangus misjudges Andromana; and Pyrocles misjudges Dido. In Book III, Cecropia misjudges Amphialus while the Knight of the Black Tomb is recognized by no one until her death. If these are all 'uncertainties', they also all involve some sort of tyranny, some deep need for equity. Alongside such 'uncertainties', which persist unchecked in the *'old' Arcadia*, Sidney's revision places the trust of the heroes and the faith of Pamela which look forward to the *denouement* already conceived as the *'old' Arcadia* V. (Pamela's theology is now decidedly Calvinistic.) Philoclea, too, is reconceived: 'Though Sidney's basic conception of Philoclea as an example of innocence and natural virtue remains fairly constant, he reworks her character to give increased emphasis to the idea of self-knowledge'.[17] Even Basilius's emotional decision to besiege the castle of Amphialus, despite Kalander's counsel to withdraw and Philanax's argument to seem ready to serve Amphialus' self-interest by offering him pardon, suggests a kind of humanity which might instruct Euarchus if he could only know it. For such are the very feelings which Euarchus lacks, as Sidney tells us.

> The beholders ... most of them examining the matter by their own passions, thought Euarchus (as often extraordinary excellencies, not being rightly conceived, do rather offend than please) an obstinate-hearted man, and such a one, who being pitiless, his dominion must needs be insupportable (p. 414).

But of course Sidney so judges him too. Euarchus' decision hews closely to the rules of deliberative oratory set forth in Aristotle's *Rhetoric*. But we also find, there in that very same *Rhetoric*, this:

> It is equity to pardon human failings, and to look to the lawgiver and not to the law; to the spirit and not to the letter; to the intention and not to the action; to the whole and not to the part; to the character of the actor in the long run and not in the present moment; to remember good rather than evil, and good that one has received rather than good that one has done; to bear being injured; to wish to settle a matter by words rather than by deeds; lastly, to prefer arbitrations to judgment, for the arbitrator sees what is equitable, but the judge only the law, and for this an arbitrator was first appointed, in order that equity might flourish.[18]

Such a position, which Euarchus disavows, is the one which Zelmane sets forth in advising the rebels and Pamela uses in confronting Cecropia in the revised text of *Arcadia*. Thus the solution to *Arcadia* worked out in the original Book V is reinforced and predicted in the revisions of the earlier books. The old Book V still fits in the revision, if a bit disjointedly; Sidney did not feel constrained to complete the revision, because in a sense he already had. It stands complete as a composite work—the way the Countess of Pembroke, Sidney's sister, would publish it and several centuries of readers, avid at least until the time of Samuel Richardson, would read it. It said all he had to say—through both poetic *mimesis* and (through insistent repetition and elaborate expansion of the original) *diegesis* as well. In the *composite text* poet and poetry fully merge.

V

There is another significant reason why the revised *Arcadia* stops in mid-sentence. If Sidney came to a deeper awareness of the need for equity as well as the nature of equity, as I have argued, then having expressed it adequately in the *Arcadia* meant that he had now further to exercise it in active service. An English epic poet much later than Sidney, Words-worth, would argue that intimations of immortality come in contemplation—in *The Prelude* the fact that

> Some intermeddler still is on the watch
> To drive him back, and pound him, like a stray,
> Within the pinfold of his own conceit (V, 334-36)

is a good thing—but this holds no possibility for Sidney. In July 1585 he put aside his writing to take up the post of Master of the Ordnance. By November he was appointed governor of Flushing. He left on 16 November with Thomas Cecil, the new governor of The Brill, for the Netherlands. His landing was not propitious.

> Uppon Thursdai we came into this town [of Flushing] drivn to land at Ramekins becaws the wynd began to ryse in such sort as our masters durst not anker befor[e] the town, and from thence came with as durty a waulk as ever poor governor entred his charge withall.[19]

But he could see the possibilities his new position held for him. 'I must neede[s] sai the better I know it the more I fynd the preciownes of it', especially regarding the opportunities to become a good ruler: 'the peo-ple shew them selves far more carefull then the governors in all thinges touching the publikk' (p. 148). On 10 December Leicester also reached Flushing, and Sidney and the local citizenry welcomed him with fireworks, with salvoes from cannon, with peals of bells, with triumphal arches and allegorical tableaux in Rotterdam, Delft, The Hague, Leiden, and Amsterdam, and with a series of twelve etchings recording the arrival entitled *Delineatio Pompae Triumphalis qua Robertus Dudlaeus comes Leicestrensis Hagae comitis fuit receptus.* Leicester had not really seen battle for two decades; he was growing old and flabby and bald. But what he lacked in experience he supplied in efficiency. He drew up *Laws and Ordinances* for his troops,

> seeing that martial discipline above all things (proper to men of war) is by us at this time most to be followed, as well for the advancement of God's glory, as honourably to govern this army in good order: And lest the evil inclined (pleading simplicity) should cover any wicked fact by ignorance: Therefore these martial Ordinances and Laws following are established and published.[20]

But hereditary Dudley vanity, coupled with the welcome he received, caused Leicester to accept the post of Governor-General of the United Provinces on New Year's Day 1586 causing a serious rupture with the Queen.

This is perhaps not surprising. What is surprising is that Sidney, until now loyal to the Dudley name and to the causes Leicester espoused, began to have his own doubts about the adequacy of Leicester's rule— and the Queen's. Equity and justice were now taking him far afield, into the Netherlands and into the work of the Lord. On 24 March 1586 he writes to Walsingham,

> If her Majesty wear the fowntain I woold fear considring what I daily fynd that we shold wax dry, but she is but a means whom God useth and I know not whether I am deceaved but I am faithfully persuaded that if she shold withdraw her self other springes woold ryse to help this action. For me thinkes I see the great work indeed in hand, against the abusers of the world, wherein it is no greater fault to have confidence in mans power, then it is to hastily to despair of Gods work ... For me I can not promis of my own cource no nor of the my [      ] becaws I know there is a hyer power that must uphold me or els I shall fall, but certainly I trust, I shall not by other mens wantes be drawn from my self (pp. 166-67).

Pamela, and the revised *Arcadia*, had clearly had their effect. Leicester's break with the Queen caused Sidney to part from his uncle whose actions, by now, must have seemed to him similar to those of Amphialus and Euarchus. He writes to Leicester's messenger William Davison,

> COSIN ... For my part I wil for no caws deny (and therefore yow shall have my handwriting to prove I am no acuser of yow), that I was ever of opinion he shold accept it [Governor-Generalship] without delai, becaws of the necessity, without sending to her Majesty becaws of not forcing her in a manner to be furdre engaged then she wold, which had been a peece of an undutiful dutifulnes (p. 169).

He threw himself into what he considered more responsible action; although he took the town of Axel in July, his real energy was given over to diplomacy, to the kind of individual negotiations that all of *Arcadia* means to teach. His trips to and fro across the embattled Low Countries must have been tiring in the extreme; so was the Queen's lack of support—and Leicester's. 'We are now four monthes behynd a thing unsupportable in his place', he tells Walsingham on 14 August, hoping for more support from the Lord Treasurer.

> To complain of my Lord of Lester yow know I mai not but this is the cace if once the souldiours fall to a thorow mutiny this town [i.e. Flushing] is lost in all lykelihod. I did never think our nation had been so apt to go to the Enemy as I fynd them (p. 180).

But he had argued already for principled action in the revised *Arcadia* as he had urged virtuous action so much earlier in the *Defence*, and he stubbornly persisted with his own enlightened government and command of troops in the Netherlands. It was luck that ran against him, not principle. In September the English captured Doesburg, preliminary to the much more important town of Zutphen, key, he thought, to Gelderland. At last the forces of justice and liberty—of Protestantism and individual conscience—were beginning to take hold. The siege of Zutphen began on 13 September; exercising to know once more, Sidney voluntarily joined the battle; on 22 September he fell; in three weeks he was dead.

But by then, the mythmakers and fashioners of legend were already slouching toward Arnhem hoping to see their Sidney reborn. Ironically, they left behind them, as Leicester and the Queen had apparently done long since, the *Defence*, the *Arcadia*, and the pregnant images of life that, like Sidney's behaviour in his final years, could yet teach justice and equity to those who could read life into poetry, and not just poetry into life.

## NOTES

\*   I am grateful to the Sir Thomas Browne Institute, University of Leiden, under whose auspices I was able to conduct much of the research and writing of this essay, and to its Director, Jan van Dorsten, and staff for their constant support. I especially wish to thank as well Professor Dominic Baker-Smith and Marjon Poort whose tough questioning during my course of study helped me to clarify and strengthen what I wanted to say.

1  Thelma N. Greenfield, *The Eye of Judgment: Reading the 'New Arcadia'*, Lewisburg, Pa., 1982, also makes this observation. In addition she cites Plato's account of the creation as 'apposite'.

2  *Sir Fulke Greville's Life of Sir Philip Sidney*, with an introduction by Nowell Smith, Oxford, 1907, 16.

3  *Sidney: A Defence of Poetry*, ed. J. A. van Dorsten (Oxford, 1966), 30. Further citations are to this edition.

4  This and all following citations to Aristotle's *Politics* are to the Loeb translation by H. Rackham.

5   This and subsequent citations to Aristotle's *Nicomachean Ethics* are from the Loeb translation by H. Rackham.

6   This and all subsequent citations to *'old' Arcadia* are from *OA*. This passage is on p. 365.

7   'The Trial of the Princes in the *Arcadia*, Book V', *Review of English Studies*, 8 (1957), 411. For this reference and much of this paragraph, I have drawn on Richard C. McCoy, *Sir Philip Sidney: Rebellion in Arcadia*, New Brunswick, N. J., 1979, 124-27.

8   On the title-page of the English translation he accomplished or completed, *A Woorke concerning the trewnesse of the Christian Religion* (1587).

9   'Correspondence' in *Works*, III, 122. All future references to Sidney's correspondence are to *Works*, III.

10  *MP*, 10; my emphasis.

11  The text is that in Jean Wilson ed., *Entertainments for Elizabeth I*, Woodbridge, 1980, 70.

12  See James M. Osborn, 'Mica mica parva stella: Sidney's horoscope', *Times Literary Supplement*, 1 January 1971, 17.

13  William A. Ringler, Jr., *Poems* 365-66.

14  McCoy, 41-42, 53.

15  See above, p. 116.

16  Nancy Lindheim, *The Structures of Sidney's 'Arcadia'*, Toronto, 1982, 132-33.

17  Lindheim, 58.

18  *Rhethoric* l.xii; 1374b; quoted Lindheim, 159. Lindheim is the only other scholar who has related the classical notion of equity to the *Arcadia*, although her case is quite different from mine.

19  *Works*, III, 147.

20  STC 2788, cited and quoted by Alan Kendall, *Robert Dudley, Earl of Leicester*, London, 1980, 210.

JAN KAREL KOUWENHOVEN

# SIDNEY, LEICESTER, AND *THE FAERIE QUEENE*

i

The Sidney legend was taking shape in the decade after his death in 1586, when Spenser was bringing out his epic (1590, 1596). Have the two events anything to do with each other? Let us state the obvious first: the poem does not present itself as a portrait of Sidney, and so can hardly be canvassed as a formative influence on the legend. Yet it does constitute a huge memorial to Sidney in his legendary capacity. Its relation to him is as specific and definite as it is elusive.

In his Letter to Ralegh, appended to the first instalment of *The Faerie Queene*, Spenser declares that 'the generall end ... of all the booke is to fashion a gentleman or noble person in vertuous and gentle discipline'.[1] Critics such as Nelson have taught us to recognize this as a commonplace of humanist poetics.[2] But we should recognize two other things as well. Until 1590 there had been no native epic in English to which to apply this commonplace. And in the 1580s the commonplace had been developed with unique eloquence by Sidney, in his *Defence of Poetry* (published posthumously in 1595).[3] Given Spenser's early association with Sidney, culminating in the dedication of his *Shepheardes Calender* (1579) to that 'noble and vertuous Gentleman'[4] (who, to judge from the *Defence*, granted it qualified approval),[5] it is just about impossible not to see *The Faerie Queene* as deliberately made to Sidney's specification. And there is something else. To his surviving contemporaries Sidney himself seemed to have embodied as no other the nobility and virtue which, in his view, the heroic poem is calculated to arouse. Hence Spenser's main hero, the youthful Prince Arthur, with his versatility and selfless enthusiasm in doing good, cannot but conjure up Sidney. The poet clinches the matter by his, admittedly incidental, reference to Arthur's death, which immediately follows an account of the martial equipment, including a spectacular shield, made by Merlin

> For this young Prince, when first to armes he fell;
> But when he dyde, the Faerie Queene it brought
> To Faerie lond, where yet it may be seene, if sought.    (I.vii.36.)

These lines more than imply death at an early age and in a foreign country. They evoke the image of Sidney in the Netherlands. The transfer of the armour parallels that of Sidney's body from Flushing to London, to receive a markedly heraldic funeral.[6]

Armour is not, of course, the same thing as a dead body. On the contrary, both literally, in its protective function, and symbolically, as the panoply of God,[7] it stands for the promise of life, as against 'the body of this death'.[8] Spenser often alludes by contrast; but the contrasts are so pointed as to make the allusions unmistakable. There are other examples here. Thus Arthur and Sidney are at one in the magnificence displayed by the former in life (according to the Letter to Ralegh) and lavished upon the latter when dead. Again, the Faerie Queen's exhibition of Arthur's armour equals in reverse England's failure to erect a monument to Sidney's memory.[9]

This negative allusiveness does not characterize Spenser's matter only: it extends to his method. Sidney conceives of poetry as pure invention, because reality is too flawed to serve its purpose, moral suasion.[10] Spenser would seem to comply with a will. He not only chooses a legendary hero, Arthur, whose famous history, it was beginning to be suspected in the sixteenth century, had been thought up by Geoffrey of Monmouth;[11] he even deprives Arthur of this questionable history and makes him the hero of an original fiction instead.[12] Yet this invented Arthur, besides sharing some residual features with the historical Arthur, turns out to portray implicitly the historical Sidney, despite his largely non-biographical career and his resemblance to the Sidney of the legend. Spenser does not quite emancipate himself from history. Sidney also defines poetry in opposition to scholastic moral philosophy, whose normative idealism is too abstract to engage people and move them to virtue.[13] Again Spenser as it were strains to comply, producing fictions that look deceptively like the kind of uplifting stories Sidney envisages. As a matter of fact, however, they do not exemplify virtuous action: they symbolize concepts of virtues. *The Faerie Queene* is a treatise on ethics masquerading as narrative. A riddle from beginning to end—or, to borrow Spenser's own description in the Letter, 'a continued Allegory, or darke conceit'—it belies the literal immediacy which it almost achieves.[14]

Spenser's poem may be said, metaphorically, to entomb Sidney's poetic manifesto: it testifies to the death of what it honours. Only Sidney himself, we are led to infer, could have realized his programme. With his passing there is no future for true poetry. Our conviction that Spenser cannot have thought lightly of his own work does not prove the tribute insincere. It is not as though poetry's praise consists solely in being poetry proper. The Letter to Ralegh does hint that he may not have shared Sidney's apparently passionate faith in fiction. To those who 'had rather have good discipline delivered plainly in way of precepts, or sermoned at large' he will say only that they 'should be satisfide with the use of these dayes'; thus tacitly conceding that they have a point. In light of this scepticism, the extent to which he comes round to Sidney's position measures the substance of his tribute. But let us not be unduly solemn. A touch of *sprezzatura* is required here. Sidney had advanced his beliefs playfully, in the typical Renaissance fashion of *serio ludere*.[15] Spenser has made his conversion in the same spirit.

The view of Sidney as unique exponent of his own poetics justifies our metaphor, which can now be seen to be Spenser's own: *The Faerie Queene* buries Sidney. It effaces him, turning him into another character, one that is notably inconspicuous, for an alleged protagonist. Indeed, it decomposes him, scattering the story of his fictional counterpart across its several Books. Lending him the name of the British king who, as legend has it, lives underground, it sends him into Faerieland, traditionally associated with death.[16] And this name itself suffers funerary deconstruction: unbound as 'Arth-ur' (on the strength of 'Art(h)-egall'), it 'returns' to '*ur*-earth', primal dust.

ii

Sidney had loved Penelope Rich, or at least feigned as much: she had been his star (Stella), and he had been the star worshipper (Astrophil). Spenser's Arthur loves the Faerie Queen, in token of which he wears a '*pretious* stone ... Shapt like a Ladies head', which 'exceeding shone, / Like *Hesperus*', the evening star (I.vii.30). Do the words in italics amount to an allusion? Surely they do, in conjunction with one further point. The Faerie Queen had appeared to Arthur in a dream, vowing that 'her love to him was bent, / *As when just time expired should appeare*' (I.ix.14). Their union is to be long delayed. While he wanders, like another Ulysses, she waits, like another Penelope. As so often, Spenser alludes by contrast: Penelope Devereux, proposed as Sidney's bride-to-be when very young, did not wait for him to fall in love with her and had married a Rich suitor before her attractions were supposedly brought home to him.[17]

However, we have Spenser's word for it, in the Letter to Ralegh, that the Faerie Queen stands for Queen Elizabeth. Now the only person who qualifies as her lover is Leicester; Sidney certainly does not. It would follow that Arthur alludes in two directions. This is awkward. True, Leicester and Sidney were close relatives, uncle and nephew; the latter was even, for a long time, the former's heir presumptive;[18] and in politics they saw eye to eye, on the whole. Yet they bore little likeness to each other. Their public reputations could hardly have been more different. Whereas Sidney obviously adorned the Elizabethan age, Leicester apparently disgraced it. Belonging to the Dudley family, several of whose members had previously scandalized the nation,[19] he was rumoured to have killed his wife to promote his intimacy with the Queen, so as to gain scope for his designs on the state. To many he seemed a ruthless schemer.[20] No doubt Spenser knew better; or thought he did. But he cannot have felt: like nephew, like uncle. Still less can he have hoped to foist off any sameness upon his audience.

Arthur *qua* Leicester is marginal, to be sure, for his love story remains mostly beyond the poem's horizon. Whenever he goes in pursuit of Gloriana, he disappears from the fiction. But the love story is there. We cannot pretend to be rid of the Leicester allusion. What confirms its genuineness is its typically pointed contrariness. In England we have Leicester, who had regular access to Elizabeth yet almost certainly never slept with her: to all intents and purposes she remained the Virgin Queen. In Faerieland we have Arthur, who never finds Gloriana yet almost certainly sleeps with her: his visionary experience is suggestively sexual and suggestively real (I.ix.13-14, 15).

There are external reasons for expecting that Spenser's epic will have a bearing upon Leicester. The poet had been in his employ; and despite a clash, commemorated with obscure wit in *Virgils Gnat*, he not only continued to identify himself with the Earl's cause but connected it with his own poetic mission. In a letter to Gabriel Harvey he refers to *Stemmata Dudleiana*, one of several works mysteriously lost, as his greatest achievement to date. And in the 'October' eclogue of *The Shepheardes Calender* Piers urges Cuddie, 'the perfecte paterne of a Poete', to attempt a heroic poem involving 'fayre Elisa' and 'the worthy whome shee loveth best, / That first the white beare to the stake did bring' (Argument; lines 37-48 and relevant Gloss).[21] Spenser had actually toyed with the idea of dedicating the *Calender* to Leicester before he decided to inscribe it to Sidney instead.[22] Perhaps his move, a matter of prudence betokening no change of allegiance, constitutes a precedent for Sidney's 'ousting' of Leicester in *The Faerie Queene*.

But an external argument cannot be conclusive. To be persuaded that Sidney and Leicester really are two sides of the same Arthurian coin, we need the strongest internal evidence: a turn of the coin. This evidence is provided by a very special Arthur episode, in Cantos x and xi of Book V. It tells how two brothers arrive at the court of Mercilla to complain about the tyrant Geryoneo's oppression of their mother, Lady Belge, and her seventeen sons; and how Arthur, as Mercilla's representative, comes to their rescue. This episode advertises itself as an allusion to England's support of the Netherlands in their revolt against the Spanish yoke, by way of a military intervention in which both Leicester and Sidney played prominent parts. Leicester was its leader; and it is largely because of his uncompromising attitude amidst the variety of Dutch opinion that the venture flopped and he himself had to beat an ignominious retreat.[23] Sidney's official role was a humbler one, but he stole the show: while the disaster of his death was in keeping with the general hopelessness of the enterprise, the manner in which he died, as a paragon of chivalry and piety, irradiated it with a redeeming light.[24] Thus the English mission to the Low Countries crystallized the relation of Leicester and Sidney. In associating them more closely than ever before, it placed them poles apart for all to see.

Naturally English pride chose to remember the Dutch adventure by the bright pole and to forget the dark one. The popular imagination substituted the sweet nephew for the unsavoury uncle—as it could freely do thanks to Leicester's own death in the year after his return to England—and transformed history into myth. Spenser counters the popular imagination. Instead of flaunting its favourite fantasy, Sidney's generous self-sacrifice, in the Belge episode, where it belongs, he hides it in a passing allusion without any context (I.vii.36). The removal is startling. Not so the inference that the episode features Arthur *qua* Leicester. It is blindingly obvious that it does. Nobody has ever thought otherwise, so demonstration would be otiose. All that needs saying is that Spenser does not offer a corrective. Mindful of Sidney's poetics, he pretends to feel England's collective dehistoricizing of the exemplary Sidney as a challenge to go one better and poeticize the unexemplary Leicester. That is why, so far from simply observing the facts, the poet, besides eclipsing Sidney altogether, credits Arthur with a resounding success; for all the world as though Leicester had reversed the fall of Antwerp (1585), which precipitated his mission.

Whereas in *The Faerie Queene* as a whole Arthur virtually transcends his anchorage in Sidney and soars into nearly pure fictionality, in the Belge episode he remains, in spite of his flawless performance, only too obviously tethered to Leicester. Critics, made queasy by its patent topicality, deplore Spenser's flagging imagination.[25] If only they had realized that he is not genuinely floundering but putting on a deliberate act! What proves his control is a meticulous counterhistoricity pervading the episode, exemplified, in fact, by Arthur's triumph. Here are some more examples:

— Belge stands for an area with two synonymous names, 'Netherlands' and 'Low Countries'. Spenser transfers this feature to Spain, representing it by Geryon and Geryoneo, whose names not only look alike and proclaim their identity (Geryoneo = Geryon anew) but variously designate a single mythological character.[26]

— Spenser calls Belge 'mother of a frutefull heritage, / Even seventeene goodly sonnes' (V.x.7); as though there had at one time been a single Netherlandish state, which had subsequently spawned the several Provinces. But the Provinces preceded the state. Indeed, 'heritage' implies this. However, it also reminds us that the Provinces had been legally inherited by Philip II of Spain.

— Geryoneo is a valiant soldier offering his dubious services to Belge after his flight from Spain, where Hercules had clubbed his father to death (x. 9-11). Philip moved in the opposite direction, leaving his northern possessions for good in 1559, a few years after his father's voluntary abdication there; to oppress them from a distance, ultimately from the quasi-contemplative seclusion of the Escorial.[27]

— Belge is a widow, and Geryoneo acts in lieu of her dead husband (x. 11-12). Philip actually was the Netherlands' husband, for countries are symbolically wedded to their sovereigns (as England was to Elizabeth[28]).

— Since Belge's eldest sons are 'of full tender yeares' at the time of their embassy to Mercilla (x. 6), her husband cannot have died long before. One infers that he stands for William of Orange (ob. 1584). But William never was, and emphatically refused to be, sovereign of the Netherlands.[29] Nor did he beget their multiplicity: he fostered their unity, becoming the *pater patriae*.[30]

— Geryoneo succeeds Belge's husband and kills his sons. Philip was succeeded by William and had him, the father of the fatherland, assassinated.

— Belge's children are much of a muchness. The Provinces were vociferously idiosyncratic, insisting on their diverse customs and privileges. And whereas Belge's offspring is masculine, the names of the Provinces are feminine: Hollandia, Zelandia, Frisia, etc..[31]

— Among Belge's children it is the eldest two who go to Mercilla and, by implication, younger ones who have fallen victim to Geryoneo. Among the Provinces it was recent strongholds of the Netherlandish spirit, Holland and Zeeland, that negotiated for England's intervention and pioneering areas of resistance, such as Brabant and Flanders, that submitted to Spain.

— Arthur is on a chance visit to Mercilla's court and happens to hear of Belge's plight. Leicester belonged at Elizabeth's court (no one more so) and had long been engineering the Dutch appeal to England.

— Mercilla 'gladly graunted' the adventure to Arthur, the only knight at all keen to undertake it (x. 15-16). Elizabeth was notoriously reluctant to commit herself to the Dutch cause; while the enthusiasts among her entourage were many: Leicester and Sidney, but also Walsingham, Bedford, Knollys, Mildmay, as well as 'lesser men, such as Davison, Wilson, and Rogers'.[32]

— Geryoneo forces Belge to abandon her cities, so that she welcomes Arthur amidst 'moores and marshes' (x. 18). Leicester enjoyed a notably urban reception.[33]

— Arthur exerts himself repeatedly on Belge's behalf; but when she wants to reward him with sovereignty, he declines (xi. 16-17). Accepting sovereignty was about the first and only thing Leicester ever did, much to his royal mistress's displeasure, to be sure.[34]

— If we were to go by Arthur's authorized defeat of Geryoneo, Elizabeth would have been happy to dispose of Philip. In fact she wished him to relax his strangle-hold on the Netherlands in his own royal interest so as to make her involvement unnecessary. Her whole bent was to have the sanctity of anointed princes respected; witness the crisis brought on by Mary, Queen of Scots (alluded to in Canto ix). It was Philip who had sought to dispose of Elizabeth, ever since the Ridolfi plot (1571). One has only to think of the Armada (1588).

Through its many blatant reversals of this kind the Dutch episode betrays, purposely, what *The Faerie Queene* as a whole manages largely to conceal: namely, that it represents an attempt to rise above history which falls just short of success. Paradoxically it is this Leicestrian section which, in highlighting both the effort and the failure, gestures towards the poem's status as a tribute to Sidney's poetics. Taking perfect aim, it also defines Spenser's frustrated transcendence of moral philosophy. Reversing the Earl in the Netherlands with a vengeance, it literally 'contra-dicts' /lester/ only to produce /retsel/, a possible pronunciation of 'raadsel', Dutch for 'riddle'; in other words, to remain openly caught in allegory. This onomastic significance of 'Leicester' is, of course, improbable, as improbable as that of 'Arthur'. Let us gasp at the names' miraculous fitness, by all means, as long as we acknowledge it as fact which not even the highest degree of improbability can subvert. We shall see that more such incredulous belief is required of us; and why.

### iii

Through Arthur's twofold contrariness the poem divorces even as it marries the outside world. It precludes even as it suggests historical allegory. The separation makes for moral allegory. A selective account of Spenser's conceptual rationale will enable us to appreciate how.

Morality is a provisional manifestation of Man's redemption in Christ. It represents Eternity under the adverse conditions of Time, in which the passive inheritance of grace metamorphoses itself into an active pursuit of goodness and blazing glory is refracted as many-faceted virtue. Rooted in mutually exclusive dispensations, it invites oxymoronic definition as strenuous ease and distracted single-mindedness. Spenser captures just this tension in the overall design of his poem. Of the sedentary Faerie Queen, for whom it is named, symbol of glory eternally enthroned, it contains only tantalizing rumours and glimpses; while to Arthur, symbol of moral perfection, it assigns a quest for her unenacted as such, because moral perfection and glory virtually coincide, but even so completely broken up into a series of exploits under the rubrics of several specific virtues.[35]

Of these we need consider only justice and mercy, since this essay concerns, apart from the poem generally, only the Belge episode, which occurs in the Legend of Justice and centres around Mercilla. Like all the other virtues, these two are different merely in the sense of being different aspects of magnificence (Spenser's term for unspecified virtuousness). They are the same grace in action, seen from two distinct angles. Their treatment in a single Legend asserts their essential identity with particular force. On the face of it this assertion is puzzling, though. For of all the virtues justice and mercy are unique in being incompatible: one cannot act justly and mercifully at once. Indeed, they are total opposites: mercy waives justice, and so amounts to a kind of injustice. How can they nevertheless be understood as identical twins among the several enactments of grace? By recognizing that they coincide in their τέλος, or final cause. Justice, in both its distributive and its retributive aspects, gives every one his due; but it does so in order to 'at-one'. It actually realizes in advance one of the conditions for our eternal merger. However, it also hides this realization, in that it takes for its criterion the rights of individuals. Marking the separateness which it transcends, it obliterates the glory of a union already effected. Mercy is the inverted image of justice so conceived. Its object is, likewise, 'at-onement'. Its arbitrary abstention from punishment flouts justice as a means, so as to flaunt their common end: it proclaims an overriding commitment to reconciliation, without which justice itself would be indistinguishable from private satisfaction. It gestures demonstratively towards the glory of a union not yet effected. The remainder of this essay presupposes a firm grasp of this argument; it is regrettably abstract but necessarily so, because Spenser himself deals in concepts. Again and again the Belge episode will fall into place, to prove a veritable agglomeration of complementary metaphors for mercy. All that needs to be added here is how justice and mercy specify magnificence. As justice, it seems self-generating virtue; while as mercy, it seems divine grace simply passed on, untransformed into action. Jointly the two virtues expose the dual nature of magnificence by polarizing it.[36]

We may now construe the relations between *historia* and *fabula* as moral allegory. The former is 'given' and, in that respect, analogous to grace; while the latter, as a reworking of the former, is analogous to virtue. In the Belge episode fiction conjures up fact through the sheer precision of its contrariness. Spenser's activity is patently minimal: he just 'returns' the gift of events. Compare this with the Legend's main fiction, Grantorto's victimization of Irena and his overthrow by Artegall, at her request. This too contradicts fact. It alludes to Ireland's ardent commitment to the great wrong of Popery and to its persistent rebelliousness, obliterating the reality of its pacification by England.[37] Artegall has always been taken to stand for Lord Grey of Wilton, the Lord Deputy who took Spenser to Ireland as his private secretary. The tradition is sound. But note that his story has the opposite effect to that of Arthur in Cantos x and xi: it makes us completely uncertain of our historical bearings. We are left guessing what particular event it refers to and cannot help wondering whether he may not equally stand for somebody else. The poet gives his identifying attribute not in Book V but in Book III, totally out of context thus 'preventing' identification in both senses of the word. Indeed, in giving he mostly withholds. For the 'couchant Hound' on Artegall's crest (III.ii.25) will not readily trigger off the inference 'Hound, i.e. greyhound, i.e. Lord Grey'.[38] Our inability to clinch Artegall implies no failure of communication. It must be intentional, since it corresponds perfectly with our inability to see in him any special resemblance to Arthur, despite his name, 'Arthur' being Lord Grey's Christian name. The Belge episode and the Irena episode, then, do not illustrate different shades of historical allegory. The contrasting ways in which they counter history symbolise the concepts of mercy and justice. The Belge episode symbolizes mercy also in that it gestures towards the transcendence of Arthur's duality: it alludes to Leicester exclusively, though only to evoke Sidney precisely by failing to do so. However, as part of the Legend of Artegall, which emphasises Arthur's duality by pairing him with a historically allusive *alter ego*, it symbolizes justice.[39]

The episodes discussed in the previous paragraph share an overall polarization of fiction against fact. In *The Faerie Queene* generally, by contrast, Arthur's story positively suggests and contradicts history only marginally, in its Leicester component and in a casual allusion to Sidney in Book I. For all its casualness this allusion—having an impact lacking in the comparably inconspicuous historical identification of Artegall—does make us aware of an overall resemblance between Arthur and Sidney: both epitomize virtue. Although the poet spends all his energy taking Sidney to Arthurian bits, this does not obscure the resemblance. With Arthur we are sure of our historical bearings, as we are not with Artegall. As Sidney transparently decomposed, he symbolizes magnificence, virtue radiant with the grace it laboriously unfolds. The symbolism is enhanced by the marginal nature of Arthur's duality: the Prince's role refers to Sidney and Leicester side by side, but the Leicester reference marks his several exits only, leaving an impression of transcendent singleness almost realized. And there is a further symbolic point. The approximation of fact and fiction we have just observed is not merely a matter of direct, as against inverse, resemblance. It is also a near fusion of modes. The history alluded to is not a datable event, as in the episodes of Book V, but an indefinitely prolonged state of affairs: Sidney's moral excellence and Leicester's favour with the Queen. (The only apparent exception is really an extreme example: Sidney's death, which can, of course, be dated, eternized his virtue.) As for Arthur's story, the sequence of its constituents would suggest development along a time axis, were it not that his several exploits in aid of his peers, each followed by a departure in search of Gloriana, are manifestly variations on the same basic pattern: he spans the poem more than he moves through it. Thus history and story meet in their aspiration to timelessness. Or rather, they break timelessness into temporal fact and temporal fiction without concealing it; and so symbolize magnificence, Eternity recognizable in its refraction by Time.

The correspondence between the terms of the symbol and those of the concept it symbolizes makes for a perspicuous riddle. The allegory reveals its meaning literally. Even so it reminds us of the allegorical status of story and history, so easily overlooked because of the apparent exemplariness of each. Arthur would seem to demonstrate all-round virtue; until we reflect that displaying its several aspects one by one is the very opposite of behaving magnificently. He does not exemplify. Instead his overall performance allegorizes the conceptual structure of magnificence in a clear conceit, rather than in a dark one. Again, Sidney would seem to demonstrate all-round virtue, until we reflect that the poem evokes him not as doing so on any or every occasion but as a man whose virtues were publicly seen to be all of a piece. Thus Sidney too functions allegorically, as a similarly self-unveiling mystery. (That Arthur's pursuit of the Faerie Queen and Leicester's intercourse with Elizabeth are not *exempla* of glory should be too obvious to need arguing.) Story and history, then, are separate symbols coinciding in their meaning. But the poem generally plays down their divorce, in order not to advert to their marriage. Accordingly it deprives Arthur and Sidney both of their allegorical and of their exemplary edge, so to speak, through their perspicuity and their timelessness.

The reverse situation obtains in the Belge episode, where fiction pitches itself against fact, only to expose its anchorage there. Story and history alike are emphatically exemplary; but so perversely so to give away their allegorical status. For neither Arthur's aid to Belge nor Leicester's aid to the Netherlands exemplifies what Mercilla's name tells us she stands for, mercy. Neither Belge nor the Netherlands are culprits being forgiven. On the contrary, they are injured parties being vindicated. Story and history alike exemplify justice. (Sceptics should consider a similar and even more striking perversity: in V.x.4 we learn that the merciful Mercilla of Canto ix had Duessa executed, after all.) The centrality of Mercilla forces us to construe story and history as allegories of mercy. Each demonstratively anticipates the condition of *exemplum* without realizing it; a fact itself symbolic of mercy.

iv

Magnificence equals all the virtues which unfold it. They are distinct aspects rather than distinct entities. To signal this Spenser usually has Arthur emerging in the several Legends to stand in for their titular heroes. In Book V, however, Arthur does not replace Artegall but joins him against the Souldan, in Canto viii. Here his role obliterates a regular equivalence which this companion's name actually clinches. He flaunts separateness, so as to symbolize justice. To redress the balance his role in Cantos x and xi flaunts his single representativeness of all the titular heroes. It recasts in miniature his role in *The Faerie Queene* at large, symbolic of magnificence, glory radiantly refracted, so as to make it symbolic of mercy, glory intimating its wholeness by making its fractures seem gratuitous.

Arthur's mission, uniquely authorized by Mercilla, the queen to whom Belge's eldest sons complain about the one fate that has befallen twelve of their brothers (x. 8), as it were infolds the twelve missions of the titular knights, severally authorized by Gloriana, the queen to whom Una, the Palmer, and so on, complain about the most diverse predicaments. Yet Spenser 'needlessly' forestalls the merger. He has 'two Springals' complaining (x. 6), and he offers the mission they prompt as an instance, 'amongst the rest', of Mercilla 'approving dayly ... Royall examples of her mercies rare' (x. 6, 5) to implement which she has plenty of able-bodied courtiers standing by (x. 14). 'Needlessly' comes between inverted commas because the poet is, of course, constrained by his thematic commitment to the dispensation of Time. He can accommodate only a permutation of the poem's general lay-out. What happens in the Belge episode allegorizes just this necessity of needless separation. Belge's manifold offspring are one, not only in virtue of the single womb which gave them life but also in their utter lack of differentiation in sex, age, and otherwise. They might as well merge. Or so thinks Geryoneo, himself 'three bodies in one wast empight' (x. 8). He devours twelve, a number signifying the fullness of Time as well as its dividedness. However, his unifying belly kills them. Arthur, in opposing Geryoneo, upholds separateness; as he does in preserving five sons. For five is not simply seventeen minus twelve: it is the number of the Legend of Justice, and of justice itself, quintessential virtue, which 'to all people [does] *divide* her dred beheasts' (V Proem 9).[40] He would indeed symbolize justice, rather than mercy, were it not that the likeness of the remaining sons points to a unity which their separateness keeps unrealized. Spenser's conceit proves wholly perspicuous once it is recognized as a conceit. That its perspicuity both presupposes and confirms our sense of its allegorical edge contributes to the symbolism.

It is worth pressing the relationship between the Belge episode and the poem as a whole. First let us see how it compares with the pattern common to the several Legends. All the titular knights have a single task. And all, so far from proceeding to it at once, get distracted by challenges that are irrelevant as well as more or less markedly disconnected amongst themselves. These occupy most of each Book, leaving only a Canto or two for the adventure on which they have set out. One gets the impression of stories 'pourd out in loosnesse' (I. vii. 7) over the length of twelve Cantos. Now consider Arthur's enterprise in aid of Belge. This is composite. The Prince has to tackle not just Geryoneo, himself dubiously single, but also the Seneschal (V. x. 31-3), three knights (x. 34-7), and the monster underneath the altar (xi. 22-32). But he goes out to meet them at once, never gets side-tracked, and gains an inclusive victory in something like the space the titular knights need for carrying out their actual assignment alone. Indeed, one cannot help sensing that really he faces one challenge only, in various guises; for Geryoneo's world is one of *Doppelgänger*. Thus a multiple enterprise belies yet even so conveys unity, in token of mercy. Structural features support this symbolism. For all its striking coherence, the Belge episode is split right down the middle. Cantos x and xi each devote the same number of stanzas to the story proper: x. 6-39 = xi. 2-35. The split is meaningful because Canto xi 'might as well not have been there': Arthur's slaying of Geryoneo, in the first part, 'ought to' have occurred in Canto x, modelled as this action is on Hercules' tenth labour, to which Spenser alludes in x. 10; and Artegall's encounter with Sir Burbon, in the second part, 'ought to' have occurred in Canto xii, to judge from its Argument. Straddling an apparently gratuitous Canto boundary, the episode again conveys the singleness it belies. Also, the number xi, which means mourning and its cessation, qualifies aptly the number x, which means return to divine unity:[41] mourning ceases in pointing to this return, but its cessation does not realize it. The proportion of introductory stanzas, five (x) and one (xi), is similarly significant. Their inverse allocation helps to make the Cantos separately symbolic, as does their common number of narrative stanzas: thirty-four manifestly doubles seventeen, the number of Belge's offspring when it was one, unbroken into twelve and five.

Next let us look again at the titular knights' missions collectively. These missions are disconnected even more markedly than are their constituent adventures. They are 'pourd out in loosnesse' over the length of twelve Books. Their common occasion, Gloriana's feast, lies beyond the horizon. And the one character they all share, Arthur, paradoxically highlights the dissolution. His lack of prominence results in an *Arthuriad* consisting mostly of gaps. Besides, his brief appearances are all distractions from his search for the Faerie Queen, which links them in principle. In fact it gets particularly short shrift. It is also bafflingly directionless: instead of making progress, he seems to be all over the place and none the wiser. Now compare the Belge episode. Here Arthur is dominant to the exclusion of all his peers, as though he contained them all in himself. Yet he does not. The demonstratively 'needless' presence of his virtual namesake, Artegall (x. 4, 15), establishes a vital contrast with the fatal 'Idole' conflating Geryon and Geryoneo (x. 13). Again Arthur is firmly on course. Yet in performing his task he turns his back upon Mercilla, who herself duplicates, even as she materializes the elusive Gloriana, in whom consists the unity of *The Faerie Queene*.

v

Like the fiction of the Belge episode, the history it alludes to functions as a perspicuous conceit presupposing and confirming our sense of its allegorical edge. The Dutch Provinces were united in their commitment to separatism; although their separatist leanings tended to get the better of them. William of Orange had had reason to plead, in his *Apology*: 'Maintain your union: Keep your union, not in words, not by writting only, but in effect also, so that you may execute that which your sheaf of arrows, tied with one band only, doth mean.'[42] In obliterating their oneness they symbolize justice. So do their names, 'Netherlands' and 'Low Countries'. Both, while denoting a single entity, convey multiplicity as well as the inglorious depth of earth, as against the glorious height of heaven. The dual appellation itself testifies to the elusiveness of their existence as a unitary state. However, on closer inspection the symbolic value of history shifts from justice to mercy. The Pacification of Ghent, in which all the Provinces joined (1576), actually proclaimed their unity, a unity soon afterwards becoming demonstratively nominal when North and South parted company to conclude the Unions of Utrecht and Atrecht (1579), both of which invoked the terms of the Pacification.[43] Each symbolizes mercy also on its own: calling themselves 'unions', they advertise an integrity whose reality their designs on each other belie. The numbers of their constituent Provinces, seven and ten, clinch the symbolism. The meaning of ten has already been explained. As for seven, like twelve it suggests both the fullness and the dividedness of Time; but whereas twelve suggests circular, quasi-endless Time, as on a clock, seven suggests linear Time, pointing to Eternity, into which it still has to run out, as in schemes of thought such as 'the seven ages of man' and 'the divine week'. Leicester's role in the Netherlands complements the allegory. He had sailed across to lead the rebelling Provinces in their single-minded opposition to Spain.[44] But his behaviour aroused such contention that his presence, which revealed their hidden alignment, also disrupted it, to become a mere token of unity; it became symbolic, for Spenser's purposes, of mercy. The same meaning reads itself into the Dutch cities' agreeing to hail him with pageantry, each in its own way; and into his adoption of sovereignty, an act which crossed Elizabeth even as it ostensibly united him to her as an extension of her royalty.

Leicester in fact deviated more generally from the single policy towards the Netherlands in which he and the Queen had officially found each other while Elizabeth, for her part, kept reverting to her original half-heartedness. This unreal unanimity makes for another symbol of mercy, as does the position of each in its own right. Leicester, rather than imitating William's efforts to hold together Calvinist theocrats and Erasmian libertinists, allowed himself to be put forward as champion of the Protestant party, which projected the establishment of a small English protectorate, with Utrecht for its centre, as a bridgehead against the onslaught of resurgent Catholicism.[45] The avowed purpose of England's intervention was to support resistance against Philip's tyranny. If it had gone according to plan, it would, in retrospect, have looked like the first experiment in a new foreign policy destined to become standard: a prototype of, say, William III and Marlborough halting Louis XIV, or of Nelson and Wellington countering Napoleon. To the party towards which Leicester was deflected, however, fighting tyranny was a mere war aim by no means coinciding with their cause. As they saw it, Protestantism committed them to the extinction of Catholicism. It was not a belief which, like other beliefs, men have an unalienable right to hold, but the true Catholicism logically intolerant of the false Catholicism it reforms. The construction of a Calvinist enclave around Utrecht, traditionally the 'capital' of the Church in the North, would have been a summary gesture towards the realization of this cause, nationally and, under England's umbrella, internationally, as the core of a single Protestant world empire; symbolizing mercy.

The juncture at which Elizabeth finally gave the go-ahead to Leicester's expedition implies that Antwerp was uppermost in her mind. (That it was also in Spenser's mind can easily be inferred from his fiction. See especially x. 25-30; and compare III. iii. 49.) No doubt she was highly critical of Philip's dealings with his Netherlandish heritage. She would have welcomed a restoration of the ancient order, whereby all the Provinces, while professing allegiance to the King of Spain, went their separate ways (an order symbolic of mercy). But she was realistic enough to see that there was no going back to the good old days. Mediation is what she envisaged for herself, taking her stand upon the right of princes in the hope that Philip would soften enough for the recalcitrant Provinces to repent. The *de facto* assistance to the disloyal North into which she was ultimately drawn highlighted her principles by breaking them (thus symbolizing mercy).[46] Her mind gravitated towards the South. And there she would have been content with a single concession, Antwerp, which, in Spanish hands, and with the northern rebels blocking the Scheldt, presented a direct threat to England's own safety and trade. This projected concession is an exquisite symbol of mercy. For a start, Antwerp, as a severed 'capital', constitutes an unreal epitome of the whole country, much like Utrecht. But there is also the city's name, supposedly derived from 'hand werpen' (to throw hands). An aetiological myth tells how the 'Roman giant, Druon Antigonus ... cut off the hands of those mariners who sailed past his castle without paying toll and threw them in the Scheldt'.[47] Elizabeth fancied an inversion of the myth: raising Antwerp as a single hand cut off from giant Spain. The symbolism resides in the fact that we become aware of this single hand only in the knowledge of the myth's many hands: unity suggests itself through the multiplicity that denies it. Besides, any hand is by its very nature comparably symbolic. Its five fingers, of divisive justice, actually split it up while at the same time conveying its wholeness. Nor is this all. More openly than any other virtue mercy hinges on faith. Instead of doing anything to realize its τέλος, it contemplates it through the sheer intensity of its purely anticipatory belief. Remembering St Paul's metaphor of the *scutum fidei*,[48] we find that 'Scheldt' lies (un)covered behind 'shield' in just this way. What shield? That of the dead Arthur exhibited by Gloriana in Faerieland, 'where yet it may be seene, if sought' (I. vii. 36). We see it: it is the fiction of the Belge episode, Arthur's one consummately Glorianean adventure, and, 'by implication', the entire *Faerie Queene*, shielding its meaning *qua* allegory.[49]

vi

As separate allegories history and story arouse a keen interest, instead of the deathly boredom induced by what was supposed to be historical allegory, fact and fiction 'in one wast empight'. What a relief that we no longer have to think of Spenser as a *weltfremd* idealist, providing a fairy-tale account of reality that would not even qualify as history for toddlers. It is his contemporaries who mythologized history, by plunging Leicester into oblivion. The poet dredges him up and points to his ignominy by a tale too outrageously counterhistorical in its exemplary perfection to be taken as an attempt to gloss it over. This action is impressive, because its honesty must have gone against the grain. Doubtless it was acutely painful for Spenser to remind a public largely indifferent or even hostile to Leicester how his old patron, whose mission ought to have realized, belatedly, his own most cherished ideals, had made a humiliating spectacle of himself on the stage of the world. This is not to say that we should go to the other extreme of thinking Spenser a moral masochist. After all, the need to interpret the Earl's performance allegorically, as it were, suspends the condemnation it demands literally. In prompting his readers to leave it alone in this way, rather than by endorsing their forgetfulness, the poet teaches them the true meaning of mercy, forgiveness. Of course, Leicester was not there any more to know whether or not any readers who got the message were united in mercy towards him in the process. Mercifully, perhaps, God had anticipated them. But if they were, their unity, pointed but unreal because of his absence in death, was the crowning *symbol* of mercy. Or should we reserve 'crowning' for a further allegory? Insofar as Spenser indicts Leicester, he forbears, only too plainly, indicting Elizabeth who, if she had intervened in the Netherlands some ten years earlier, at the time of the Pacification, might well have saved them entire and so prevented the tragically steep decline of the South, for centuries the heartland of culture and industry in Western Europe. In her Dutch policy the Queen belied the glory inherent in her office. Spenser shows, as well as allegorizes, mercy; but the conception of *The Faerie Queene* as a more or less mindless *encomium* of its dedicatee will need refinement.

There is greater excitement ahead. The sheer scale on which undoctored fact turns out to symbolize mercy lends weight to the analogy between history and grace. Not only are both 'given', but the former is 'irresistible' in precisely the sense Luther and Calvin had insisted the latter is: its miraculous fitness captivates the will. Instead of choosing to use history, Spenser could not help using it, one feels. Does it not look as though God had rigged the world of fact specially for the poet's purposes, themselves so divine? That Spenser was thrilled by the 'coincidence' and interpreted it as a sign that the Lord was with him seems, to me, beyond question. The experience must have been particularly invigorating because it came when the poem was already well under way: he had been working on it since 1580 at least. It could be that the events of 1585-87, which led to an episode summing up, as we have seen, its overall design, actually suggested it. The early references to *The Faerie Queene* in the Spenser-Harvey correspondence are too casual for us to decide whether the poet already had in mind the 'fore-conceit' embodied in the work he eventually published. Quite possibly Harvey's dismissive playfulness implies not.[50] What does seem certain is that the end product, 'pourd out in loosnesse', resulted from a process of composition even looser, with the poet writing, and sending round, fragments not always definitely earmarked for his great work.[51] Perhaps history at last proffered a unifying rationale that would make sense of the separateness of the episodes he had been amassing. Even if this speculation should be correct, though, it would not lessen the miraculousness of history's allegorical potential.

However, we need to get the miracle into proper perspective. For the Elizabethans it was an article of faith that God never ceases from acting in history. (That is why they readily inferred the hand of God where later ages would have taken to naturalistic explanation or agnosticism.) What will have startled Spenser is not the idea of God's actual involvement but its revelation. Moreover, the revelation could not have been less substantial. God was believed to govern history not by contriving it from outside but by entering into it and engaging with it in a decisive manner. On the rare occasions when He chose to reveal Himself, He did so literally, in epiphanies of glory, as in His appearance to Moses in the burning bush or, most tellingly, in Christ's transfiguration on the mountain.[52] Seen in this perspective His merely allegorical self-revelation in Leicester's Dutch adventure is pointedly unreal, though none the less breathtaking for that. Glory thus manifestly effaced symbolises mercy, yet again. And the symbol gestures towards another one lurking within it. In their commentaries on Scriptural history Protestant exegetes pressed strongly for literal reading, opposing Catholic indulgence in allegoresis, 'wrong' to them, not because necessarily false but because inevitably centrifugal, like much else in Catholicism.[53] Therefore God, in electing for His habitation an allegory whose unreality is crucial to its meaning, as it were, adds what is at once His personal signature to the Protestant polemic yet also a rider emphatically validating the belief on which Catholics founded their exegesis. By extension He sanctions a Protestantism appreciative of Catholic principles whose perversion it repudiates, such as that of the Church of England.[54] Let there be no mistake here.

It is not as though He ties down His Majesty to Anglicanism. Rather, He upholds distinct confessions as, for all their dividedness, together circumscribing clearly the whereabouts of true Christianity (allegiance to Christ) in order to inspire faith in His control over the century's explosive church history and to discountenance desperate Geryoneonesque compromises, such as the irenic efforts of the syncretist Platonizing pseudo-Christianity made so much of by recent scholarship.[55] So read, God, and the English Church as it reflects Him containing polarized Protestantism and Catholicism, contribute even further to the symbolism of mercy.

The very word 'Catholicism' points demonstratively to what the Church of Rome does not realize, 'catholicism' in its etymological sense of all-inclusive wholeness, and so sums up mode and meaning of both components, factual and fictional, of the Belge episode. In its turn, 'catholicism' advertises itself as an unreal reference to an observation of Sidney's, in his *Defence of Poetry*, determining the comparative usefulness for moral suasion of fact and fiction, an issue which this episode brings to the surface. Sidney, echoing Aristotle, had said that 'poesy dealeth with καθόλου, that is to say, with the universal consideration, and the history with καθέκαστον, the particular'.[56] History as used by Spenser does deal with καθόλου. But it does so not *qua* history but *qua* allegory. Hence on Sidney's ruling this history would qualify for functional incorporation. And, sure enough, the poem 'includes' history not as text alongside its fiction but as event beyond its confines, only the meaning of which gains access. Exclusion, implicit throughout, becomes an emphatic gesture in the Belge episode, whose meaning, mercy, is itself faith's anticipatory insistence on unity (καθόλου) ruling out separateness (καθέκαστον). Here Spenser evokes Sidney the poetician as positively as he does Sidney the man negatively. The two evocations are, in fact, a single one polarized, since honouring the former entails suppressing the latter. However, Spenser sees to it that his almost pedantically scrupulous obeisance does not work. Instead of resulting in pure fiction, it positively evokes Leicester and negatively, as we saw at the end of Section II, 'riddle', also in one stroke, with a symbolic import by now obvious. And this result characterizes Arthur not only in the episode but, *mutatis mutandis*, in the entire poem, of which it is a small-scale permutation.

*The Faerie Queene* as a whole, paying a deliberately approximate tribute to Sidney's conception of poetry, turns the tables on him with admirable delicacy. Sidney had advocated fiction as sheer invention by a poet 'freely ranging only within the zodiac of his own wit'.[57] Spenser, while keeping history out, produces fiction which, in contradicting it, implies its bondage to history. But then, history, unlike fiction, is true; and the truth shall make us free.[58] Spenser celebrates a liberty consisting in enslavement to a grace his own wit could not provide. He ranges laboriously within the zodiac of God's will, under the celestial signs of the twelve virtues. Thus he realizes one aspect of the view he had expressed in his lost book 'called the Englishe Poete', namely that the art of poetry is 'a divine gift and heavenly instinct not to bee gotten by laboure and learning, but adorned with both: and poured into the witte by a certaine ἐνθουσιασμὸς'.[59] *The Faerie Queene* buries Sidney, and his *Defence* with him, though not without using it, like him, as a historical symbol of magnificence: the treatise presents poetry as *sui generis*, in opposition to philosophy and history, only to emphasize its radiant fusion of its rivals' excellencies.[60] The posthumous appearance of the *Defence* preceded by only a year Spenser's overt evocation of it in an episode symbolic of mercy. That it should have received dual publication, by William Ponsonby and Henry Olney, under different titles gesturing towards sameness, supports the symbolism amazingly. Was this just God's doing, or had Spenser himself somehow been instrumental, this time?

## NOTES

1  *Poetical Works*, ed. J. C. Smith and E. de Selincourt, London, 1912; rpt. 1975, 407. In all Spenser quotations the distribution of i/j and u/v has been normalized.
2  *The Poetry of Edmund Spenser: A Study*, New York and London, 1963, 116-23.
3  *MP*, 73-121.
4  See its title page, Spenser, *Works*, 415.
5  *MP*, 112.
6  Malcolm William Wallace, *The Life of Sir Philip Sidney*, Cambridge, 1915, 394-97. See also the article by Sander Bos *e.a.*, 'Sidney's Funeral Portrayed', above, pp. 38-61.
7  Ephesians 6: 13.
8  Romans 7: 24.
9  Wallace, 396.
10  *MP*, 82-94, especially 90.
11  Compare Nelson, 126.
12  'You say *I chose the historye of king Arthure*. But you didn't. There is no Uther in your poem, no Mordred, no Guinevere, no Launcelot, no wars with the Saxons. It was not the history of Arthur you chose, but the bare name.' (C. S. Lewis, *Spenser's Images of Life*, ed. Alastair Fowler, Cambridge, 1967, 137).
13  *MP*, 82-94, especially 85, 91.
14  See further my *Apparent Narrative as Thematic Metaphor: The Organization of 'The Faerie Queene'*, Oxford, 1983, *passim*.
15  Richard Cody, *The Landscape of the Mind: Pastoralism and Platonic Theory in Tasso's 'Aminta' and Shakespeare's Early Comedies*, Oxford, 1969, 153-55.
16  Kouwenhoven, 69-70.
17  *Astrophil and Stella*, Sonnet 33, in *Poems*, 181; and compare Commentary, 436-37. See also James M. Osborn, *Young Philip Sidney, 1572-1577*, New Haven and London, 1972, 346, 424.
18  Wallace, 91; and references in Osborn, Index, *s.v.* 'Sidney, Sir Philip—*Finances*', 561.

19  His brother Guildford, husband to Lady Jane Grey, his father John, Duke of Nor-
    thumberland, and his grandfather Edmund had all been executed for treason
    (Osborn, 6-7).
20  Osborn, 8-9. The year 1584 saw the anonymous appearance of a fierce libel,
    *Leicester's Commonwealth*, which had to be suppressed. Sidney replied with a *Defence
    of the Earl of Leicester* glorifying his Dudley origins. Its publication was probably
    prevented by Leicester himself (*MP*, 129-41, 125).
21  Spenser, *Works*, 486-93, especially the dedicatory sonnet, 612; 457, 458.
22  Alexander C. Judson, *The Life of Edmund Spenser*, Baltimore, 1945, 61.
23  For England's policy towards the Dutch generally see Charles Wilson, *Queen Elizabeth
    and the Revolt of the Netherlands*, London and Basingstoke, 1970. Chapter 5 deals
    specifically with Leicester's mission.
24  Wallace, 377, 379, 385-86, 388.
25  'In the Belgae, Burbon and Irena episodes it is hardly possible to allow that there
    is anything beyond the painfully obvious topical allusion' (headnote to Book V, in
    Edmund Spenser, *The Faerie Queene*, ed. A. C. Hamilton, London and New York,
    1977, 526—a fine survey of criticism's embarrassments).
26  To judge from the Liddell and Scott *Greek-English Lexicon* there are in fact three
    variant forms: Γηρυόνης, as well as Γηρυονεύς (whence Geryoneo) and Γηρυών
    (Geryon); appropriately, for a threefold character. Spenser's doubling—or is it tripl-
    ing? there is also the image of Geryon and Geryoneo (V. x. 13)—contradicts myth
    just as his transfer contradicts history.
27  John Lothrop Motley, *The Rise of the Dutch Republic: A History*, 1856; rpt. London,
    1904, 50-58, 113-14.
28  Paul E. McLane, *Spenser's 'Shepheardes Calender': A Study in Elizabethan Allegory*, Notre
    Dame, Ind., 1961, 39.
29  Motley, 847, 883.
30  To this day the Dutch remember him under this title, inscribed on his tomb (C. V.
    Wedgwood, *William the Silent: William of Nassau, Prince of Orange, 1533-1584*, London,
    1944, 252). But the phrase was applied to him already during his life (Wilson, 51).
31  Accordingly the Provinces were represented by virgins in one of the pageants with
    which The Hague hailed Leicester (Ivan L. Schulze, 'Spenser's Belge episode and
    the Pageants for Leicester in the Low Countries, 1585-86', *Studies in Philology*,
    XXVIII (1931), 236). True, an Utrecht pageant featured men (Schulze, 240); as did
    a medal (R. C. Strong and J. A. van Dorsten, *Leicester's Triumph*, Leiden and Lon-
    don, 1964, Plate 3(c), opposite p. 24). In both cases, though, the men are not
    themselves personifications of the Provinces but mere unindividualized supporters of
    their escutcheons.
32  Strong and Van Dorsten, 5, 8, 18. For Elizabeth's lack of commitment see Wilson,
    31-41, 54-62, 70; and compare his damning Conclusion, 123-36.
33  Schulze, and Strong and Van Dorsten, *passim*.
34  Strong and Van Dorsten, 20-23, 50-59; Wilson, 92-93.
35  See further Kouwenhoven, 16-28.
36  Compare Kouwenhoven, 77, 167.
37  The fiction should not deceive us into thinking that the poet was under any illusion
    about Irish submissiveness. See, for example, the quotations from his, roughly con-
    temporary, *Veue of the Present State of Ireland* in Spenser, *Works*, Introduction, xxxviii.
38  See also Kouwenhoven, 140, 144.
39  That the historical counterparts of Arthur and Artegall are two is equally remark-
    able: according to Walsingham the leadership of the expedition to the Netherlands
    might well have been assigned to Lord Grey (Wilson, 87).
40  For this number symbolism see the passage from *The Garden of Cyrus*, by Sir Thomas
    Browne, quoted in Alastair Fowler, *Spenser and the Numbers of Time*, London, 1964),
    34.
41  'In Pythagorean thought the decad was ... mystically identified with the monad, and
    revered as the number in which the multiplicity of the digits returned to divine unity'

(Fowler, 55). For 'the ancient association of 11 with mourning and specifically with its termination' see Fowler's "'To Shepherd's ear'': the form of Milton's *Lycidas*', in *Silent Poetry: Essays in numerological analysis*, ed. Alastair Fowler, London, 1970, 171.

42  Wedgwood, 223. Compare 36: 'A bundle of arrows with the inscription "L'union fait la force" was a very favourite device of the Netherlands—as pretty a piece of wishful thinking as one could wish to see. Yet it was not, in time of crisis, untrue. For this disunited country was paradoxically united in its love for its own disunity. That was the element of union, the common respect of all for the time-honoured particularities of their neighbours'.

43  Motley, 792-801.

44  Wilson, 92; and compare, 110.

45  Strong and Van Dorsten, 68, 75-76; Wilson, 96-97.

46  The Queen issued a declaration in four languages to justify her departure from the neutrality she favoured all along (Wilson, 86).

47  *Encyclopaedia Britannica* (1969), II. 99.

48  Ephesians 6: 16.

49  This argument is not as far-fetched as it looks. Arthur's 'shield' invites comparison with that of Aeneas, whose lengthy description makes it too an episode. In small compass it pictures prophetically twelve scenes from Roman history (see the diagram in *P. Vergili Maronis Aeneidos Lib. VIII*, ed. Arthur Calvert, London, 1890; rpt. 1953, 38). Naturally these remain mysterious to the Trojan hero: 'miratur, rerumque ignarus imagine gaudet' (line 730) just as, wanting grace, Spenser's readers can only comfort themselves with his fiction, unable to fathom its allegorical rationale. Virgil speaks of the shield's 'non enarrabile textum' (line 625). In one sense Spenser goes against his master: his poem 'tells out', unfolds, the Belge episode. In another sense he conforms: the episode is not narrative. Demonstratively taking diverse cues from a single instruction, he symbolizes mercy.

50  Spenser, *Works*, 628.

51  See also Kouwenhoven, 86, 214 (*n*. 19).

52  Exodus 3: 1-4: 17; Matthew 17: 1-8.

53  See Tyndale, for example, as summarized in C. S. Lewis, *English Literature in the Sixteenth Century, Excluding Drama*, Oxford, 1954, 186-87.

54  Compare Kouwenhoven, 27-28.

55  The reference is to the strand of thought expounded by Frances Yates in works such as *Giordano Bruno and the Hermetic Tradition*, London, 1964. Elsewhere she sums it up as the 'search of the ideal imperial ruler who will save the world from tyranny. The close association in the mind of a Renaissance philosopher between the ideal unified governance of human society and the organization of the physical universe is very clear in Bruno's works, in which the politico-religious message is inseparably combined with the Hermetic religious philosophy.' (*Astraea: The Imperial Theme in the Sixteenth Century*, London and Boston, 1975, xi-xii.) This must strike those aware that ideal rulers will not be forthcoming as a recipe for tyranny.

56  *MP*, 88.

57  *MP*, 78.

58  John 8: 32.

59  See the Argument for 'October', Spenser, *Works*, 456. The poet's self-deprecating *noms de plume*, 'Immerito' and 'Colin Clout', also fall into place now. Contrast Sidney's 'Astrophil' and 'Philisides', which smack of a confident, and quasi-autonomous, 'erected wit'.

60  'Now doth the peerless poet perform both: for whatsoever the philosopher saith should be done, he giveth a perfect picture of it in someone by whom he presupposeth it was done, so as he coupleth the general notion with the particular example' (*MP*, 85).

KATHERINE DUNCAN-JONES

# SIDNEY, STELLA, AND LADY RICH

For the purposes of this essay I shall take it as firmly established that
Sidney's 'Stella' was in some sense based on Penelope Devereux, sister
of the Earl of Essex, who married Robert Lord Rich on 1 November
1582. This identification was so well documented by H. H. Hudson in
1933 that it is unlikely that anyone will now challenge it.[1] Hudson was
originally stimulated to write his article by the preparation of a book by
J. M. Purcell denying any such connexion.[2] So effective was Hudson's
rebuttal, citing a large number of writers such as Sir John Harington,
Gervase Markham, Thomas Campion and John Florio who quite clearly
identified Lady Rich with 'Stella', that Purcell attempted to withdraw his
book for revision, although it was already printed. No one since 1935 has
seriously doubted that Sidney intended the first readers of *Astrophil and
Stella*, whoever they may have been, to link 'Stella' with Lady Rich. The
exact nature of Sidney's relationship with this famous beauty, either in
life or in literature, is another and much more ticklish matter, and it is
this which I wish to explore afresh, by examining first Sidney, then
'Stella', and finally Lady Rich herself, both in life and in literature.

   W. A. Ringler dealt very fully with the documentary evidence in his
great edition of Sidney's *Poems* in 1962.[3] He recognized the question of
biographical truth as important, saying: 'the legitimate procedure is, not
to ignore the biography, but to find out what kind of biography it is.'
After a painstaking survey of Penelope Devereux's movements, her marriage, Sidney's movements, and the various marriage projects on his
behalf, Ringler's conclusion was that *Astrophil and Stella*, though
autobiographical in 'substance', is a highly selective treatment of personal experience: 'mere fact was made subservient to the requirements
of art.' This is cogent, and surely a reasonable view to take of most
'autobiographical' works of art. But Ringler, perhaps sensibly, avoids
considering the question many readers of the sequence persist in asking:
that is, what were Sidney's 'real' feelings for Lady Rich? This is of course
unanswerable. Though Muriel Bradbrook asserts that after Penelope
Devereux's marriage 'Sidney almost immediately fell in love with her',[4]
and P. J. Croft confidently refers to Sidney as 'nourishing an adulterous
passion',[5] there is really no way in which this can be verified. We cannot
hope to *prove* this, any more than we can prove that, as Jack Stillinger
maintained, 'the sonnets were written as complimentary verse ... not as

serious love poems'.[6] I doubt whether even Sidney's closest friends in the years 1581-82 could have shed much light on the question of his 'real' feelings. Very probably even Sidney himself could not have done so, any more than Ralegh could have exposed to us his 'real' feelings for the Queen/Cynthia, Drayton his for Anne Goodyere—or, to open up a wider and more complex perspective, Dante or Petrarch theirs for the ladies on whom Beatrice and Laura were based. We are not dealing here with confessional or diaristic literature, such as Hazlitt's *Liber Amoris* or Wilde's *De Profundis*, but with a sonnet sequence. In the post-Petrarchan age there must always have been an intense self-consciousness and much deliberate re-fashioning in the creation of mistresses addressed in sonnet sequences. A striking example of this is offered by Lorenzo de' Medici, in whom, according to his own account, the determination to write poetry generated a conscious decision to find a 'Petrarchan' object of love:

> A young lady of great personal attractions happened to die in Florence; and as she had been very generally admired and loved, so her death was as generally lamented ... On this occasion all the eloquence and the wit of Florence were exerted in paying due honours to her memory, both in prose and verse. Among the rest I also composed a few sonnets; and, in order to give them greater effect, I tried to convince myself that I too had been deprived of the object of my love and to excite in my own mind all those passions that might enable me to move the passions of others.[7]

Perhaps Sidney's selection of Lady Rich as his poetic mistress was not quite so *voulu* as this. But I think we should bear in mind the possibility that it may have been. Lady Rich was considerably cultivated by court poets in the 1590s, during the high period of her brother's favour with the Queen. Even in 1581, when she was little over eighteen, her beauty, intelligence and family connexions may have made her an obvious choice of poetic mistress for a courtier seeking to serve a poetic apprenticeship through the traditional route. The fact that there had been an abortive scheme to betroth Sidney to her five years earlier would have provided an added dimension of star-crossed love and missed opportunity:

> This could but have happened once
> And we missed it, lost it for ever.
>
> (Browning, 'Youth and Art')

Sidney wrote the *'old' Arcadia* to amuse and distract his newly married sister, the Countess of Pembroke. In it he offered pictures of learned, vigorous young lovers which may have been particularly pleasing to a girl married to a semi-literate husband thirty years older than herself. Could he have written *Astrophil and Stella* in an almost equally relaxed spirit, to amuse another newly married lady who was a family friend? The revised

*Arcadia* offers a conspicuous example of a courtship display undertaken for social and artistic reasons, rather than out of unconquerable passion: Phalantus, 'taking love uppon him like a fashion', challenges all comers to tilt with him in defence of Artesia's beauty, while she plays her own complementary game, calling 'her disdain of him chastitie'.[8] The parallel this phrase offers to AS 32.14 could be a clue to more fundamental similarities.

Against this idea may be set one piece of 'evidence' which has come to light since Ringler's edition of the *Poems*. It appears to illuminate the 'real' relationship between Sidney and Lady Rich, and some later writers on Sidney have given it considerable weight. J. G. Nichols, for instance, finds it 'enough to dispel any doubts that might remain',[9] and M. C. Bradbrook takes it as proof that *Astrophil and Stella* 'was not mere rhetoric'.[10] It calls, therefore, for fairly detailed examination. The 'allusion' was first described by Jean Robertson in 1964.[11] It consists of a five-word sentence in one of two manuscripts of 'The Manner of Sir Philip Sidney's Death', an account apparently written by one of the clergymen who ministered to him, and purporting to describe Sidney's spiritual preparation for death. On the morning of the day on which he was to die, we are told, after a sleepless night, he unburdened himself to the chaplain:

> I had this night a trouble in my mind: for searching myself, methought I had not a full and sure hold in Christ. After I had continued in this perplexity a while, observe how strangely God did deliver me—for indeed it was a strange deliverance that I had! There came to my remembrance a vanity wherein I had taken delight, whereof I had not rid myself. It was my Lady Rich. But I rid myself of it, and presently my joy and comfort returned.[12]

If we could believe in this account, it would of course be extremely significant, suggesting that Sidney's feelings for Lady Rich, and perhaps his actual relations with her, were sufficiently profound and persistent to call for death-bed purgation. Unfortunately, however, for those who cherish the idea of a Sidney 'spotted' by adulterous love,[13] the whole account, though powerfully emotive, is of very doubtful biographical status. It offers a simple dramatization of the dying Sidney's spiritual catharsis which is clearly intended to edify rather than to inform. There can be no doubt of its remoteness from the real events. No reference is made to the physical horrors of death, the 'extraordinary noisom savor' of infection referred to by Greville,[14] or the raging fever and perhaps delirium which accompany a death from septicaemia. Gisbert Enerwitz referred to Sidney on 16 October as having suffered from fever for the previous three days.[15] More tellingly still, in terms of what we can believe in it, 'The Manner of Sidney's Death' presents for the most part a picture of a peaceful one-to-one dialogue, spiritual purification being accomplished through discourse with a single minister. Two chaplains are mentioned in the codicil to Sidney's Will,[16] and two chaplains and a 'preacher' are shown on Lant's *Funeral Roll*. 'The Manner' gives no sense of what must in fact have been a very crowded assembly in the house of Mlle Gruithuissens at Arnhem. The medical men alone were very numerous, and last-minute attempts at resuscitation would surely have been made. Though Greville claims that after the 'sixteenth day' Sidney cast off not only 'all hope', but even 'desire of recovery',[17] this must be a rationalization after the event, or at best a half-truth. Sidney's own last letter shows him as very far from having abandoned 'desire of recovery'. This terrified appeal to the elderly doctor Jan Wyer was written the day before he died, and a good week after, according to Greville, he had given up hope. Though it seems that the letter was never delivered, because it was realized that Sidney was by then beyond cure, it speaks of a desperately persistent will to live:

> Mi Weiere veni, veni, de vita periclitor et te cupio.—Nec vivus nec mortuus ero ingratus. Plura non possum sed obnixe oro ut festines. Vale. Arnemi. Tuus Ph. Sidney.[18]

Though Wyer probably never did come, eight medical men are referred to in the codicil to Sidney's Will, added on the day of his death. In addition, his wife and his two brothers are known to have been present, and would surely not have been far from the bedside. A number of the English gentlemen and noblemen serving with Sidney in the Netherlands may also have been there. If we assume that all those named in the codicil were present, these would number at least seven. Even his uncle, the Earl of Leicester, was of the number, for on 6th October he wrote to Walsingham that he was about to go and visit his nephew. He arrived on 15th October, and in view of his worsening condition he may have decided to stay until the last.[19] Among others present, Sidney is said to have died in the arms of his friend Sir William Temple, the rhetorician.[20] If Sidney's 'much honoured lord the Earl of Essex', to whom he left his 'best sword', was also there, he might have listened with strange emotions to the early morning dialogue in which Sidney dismissed his love for his sister as a troubling 'vanity'.

Actually, however, it seems most unlikely that Sidney ever said 'It was my Lady Rich'. The sentence is a suspect passage in a work in itself of no demonstrable authenticity. It reads very oddly. We are prepared for an account of a 'strange' deliverance from spiritual torment, but are offered instead one of staccato abruptness. How could Sidney in a split second 'rid' himself of Lady Rich, if the persistent thought of her was so troubling that it tormented him all night? It seems like a *Boys' Own Paper* version of the act of perfect contrition—'with one bound Philip was free'. There is something odd about this passage in both MSS of 'The Manner', and the reference to Lady Rich in the Juel-Jensen manuscript cannot be confidently viewed as anything more than a contribution to the Sidney legend. It confirms the view documented by Hudson that writers after Sidney's death saw him, no doubt on the basis of *Astrophil and Stella*, as having been in love with Lady Rich, but it brings us no whit closer to discovering the nature of his 'real' emotions, either in 1581-82 or at the time of his death four years later. Our desire to know the truth behind *Astrophil and Stella* is ultimately a tribute to the *enargeia*, or forcefulness, of Sidney's rhetoric. He has perhaps succeeded in Lorenzo de' Medici's aim 'to excite in my own mind all those passions that might enable me to move the passions of others'; but the emotional process underlying the rhetorical skill may have been as deliberately fuelled as Lorenzo's. We might consider for comparison the mental preparation of an actor about to play the part of Romeo. Like many other Renaissance poets, the young Sidney fashioned a literary myth of himself as lover: 'overmastered by some thoughts, I yielded an inky tribute unto them'.[21] What those 'thoughts' really were, we shall never know. Edward King's death provided the young Milton with an excellent pretext for bursting into poetry when he knew he was not ready for a major work; perhaps Penelope Devereux's 'coming out' at Court, on her marriage to her brother's friend Lord Rich, provided a similar pretext for Sidney, though unlike Milton, he did not venture into print. His 'real' feelings no more offer themselves to our scrutiny than do those of Milton.

What we can do more fruitfully is to examine the image of Lady Rich in literature. First of all, we can look closely at *Astrophil and Stella* itself, which offers more suggestions of Stella's position in the relationship than has been generally recognized. Ringler saw the sonnets as 'verse epistles', but epistles which are not even to be imagined as seen by Stella herself—'indeed, many of them were inappropriate for her eyes'.[22] According to Ringler, they are in effect solitary meditations: 'a series of conversations or monologues which the reader overhears'. Leaving aside the question of whether the sonnets were *really* shown to Lady Rich, and limiting ourselves strictly to the fiction within the sequence, this is scarcely the picture the poet gives us. In line 3 of Sonnet 1 he states his intention that 'Pleasure might cause her read', and as the sequence proceeds we are shown an Astrophil who is frequently responding to words and actions of Stella, and who himself stimulates responses in her. His love is based on 'knowne worth' (Sonnet 2), not on a single vision or epiphany. Though we have no great sense of what she is like, apart from having

dark eyes, fair hair and a good singing voice (Sonnet 36 is the first
celebration of her Orphic power), if the sonnets were to be read by
Stella/Penelope, it would not be necessary to describe her. Affirmation,
not description, is the sonneteer's task. We have a frequent sense of her
presence and her speech, as a detailed survey (based on the assumption
that the 1598 arrangement of the sequence represents Sidney's intentions) will show. I make no apology for what may seem a naively literal
account of the 'story' in *Astrophil and Stella*. Many critics have written well
on Sidney's complex approaches to the reader, his shifting persona and
his self-reflexive ironies,[23] but since Mona Wilson's extremely sentimentalized summary in 1950[24] I believe that the narrative element has been
unduly neglected. It is best explored by J. G. Nichols,[25] but even he finds
the sequence more discontinuous than I do, and discusses it piecemeal
rather than *seriatim*.

Stella first makes her presence definitely felt just over a third of the way
through the sequence. In Sonnet 41 Astrophil does well in a tournament
before English courtiers and French ambassadors because '*Stella* lookt
on'; and in the next sonnet she is still looking on, and he begs her to continue. In 44 she 'heares' Astrophil's words, though she fails to pity him;
in 45 she both sees him and hears him unmoved, but weeps at a fictional
account of 'Lovers never knowne'. (It would be pleasing if we could here
imagine Sidney reading aloud from Book 4 of the 'old' *Arcadia*, with its
painful account of Pyrocles's attempted suicide). In 47 an attempt to
shake off the yoke of love is abandoned on the imminent arrival of Stella
herself—'Soft, but here she comes'. This is the first hint of a theme
developed later, that Astrophil is weary of the affair, but is held to it, un-
consciously or deliberately, by Stella. In 48 he again beseeches her to go
on looking at him. In 52 (almost half way through the sequence)
Astrophil first shows himself explicitly as an un-Petrarchanly physical
lover, praying

That *Vertue* but that body graunt to us.

Where Petrarch's sonnets often represent a journey through time to
achieve grace by recollection of the dead or unattainable Laura, Sidney's
Astrophil is an urgent present-tense lover of a girl who is often physically
present with him, and even at moments seemingly 'available'. Perhaps
the emergence of sexuality in 52 is signalled further in 53, another tournament scene, but this time with Astrophil paralysed and distracted by
Stella gazing on him from a window and blushing—'One hand forgott
to rule, th'other to fight'. His failure to 'rule', or manage his horse, may
image a failure to rein in his own lust. A definite understanding between

the lovers is suggested by 54, in which court ladies believe Astrophil incapable of love because incapable of flirtation:

> And think so stille, so *Stella* know my mind.

56 suggests frequent habitual meetings between the lovers, for Astrophil protests at 'a whole weeke without one peece of looke'. After this brief separation, 57 denotes a striking level of reciprocity, for Stella hears Astrophil's 'plaints'—presumably songs from the very sequence we are reading—and sings them to him; and in 58 she reads him 'Th'anatomy of all my woes'. These sonnets make Stella an integral part of the artistic process; not only does Astrophil's poetic skill 'cause her reade', but she reads his sonnets back to him and sings his songs, improving them in the process. (We might note that this would entail a change of gender reminiscent of many of the early scenes in the 'old' *Arcadia*). The fiction of urgent courtship is metamorphosed into one of sophisticated courtly entertainment—what C. S. Lewis called 'a little music after supper'. In 59 Astrophil puts himself forward as a rival to Stella's lap-dog, a proposal that suggests considerable physical proximity. In 60 he reflects on Stella's capriciousness in disdaining him when present, but showing 'love and pitie' to him when he is absent. It is not clear whether we are here to imagine that Stella speaks kindly to him when he is about to leave her; or that he hears reports that she speaks well of him; or even possibly that she sends him kind letters. In 61 they have been together again, for she has preached him a 'sweet breath'd' sermon on the unselfish nature of true love. 62 represents a misunderstanding and reconciliation; Astrophil, 'tyr'd with wo', has called Stella unkind, and she has brought him back to heel with an assurance of 'true love', virtuous love. 63 represents the first of several seduction attempts:

> I crav'd the thing which ever she denies.

Afterwards, Astrophil tries to persuade himself, by 'Grammer rules', that Stella's 'No, no' was really a 'Yes'. The First song culminates in a celebration of Stella's voice, and Sonnet 64 seems to reflect further discussion, for he is reflecting on her 'counsels'. 66 is exceptionally anecdotal: 'last faire night', i.e. 'the other evening', Astrophil was aware of Stella looking at him, 'while I lookt other way', and when he looked back at her, her eyes 'fled with blush, which guiltie seem'd of love'. In 67 he reflects further on the meaning of her look and her blush. In 68 he listens to Stella speaking 'choisest words', but the more virtuous her speech, the more he thinks, with explicit sexual reference,

> what paradise of joy
> It is, so faire a Vertue to enjoy.

69 and 70 represent what appears to be a high point of happy mutuality, however over-interpreted by Astrophil:

> *Stella* hath with words where faith doth shine,
> Of her high heart giv'n me the monarchie,

and his Muse is turned, first to happy notes, and then to 'Wise silence', reflecting a moment of specious fulfilment when Astrophil thinks poetry at last redundant. 70 is something of a watershed in the sequence, analogous to the pivotal seduction scene in Book 3 of the *'old' Arcadia.* From 71 onwards Astrophil is never again wholly successful in persuading himself that virtuous love is bliss:

> So while thy beautie drawes the heart to love,
>   As fast thy Virtue bends that love to good:
>   'But ah', Desire still cries, 'give me some food'.

Thomas P. Roche's numerological analysis would support my purely narrative one, for he points out that these lines 'are literally at the midpoint, or heart of the whole sequence'.[26] The failure of Astrophil's attempt, declared in 72, to banish Desire, is manifested in the Second song, in which he steals a kiss from the sleeping Stella, wakes her, and curses himself 'for no more taking'. 73 shows Stella still angry, but Astrophil still bent on kissing—whether in imagination or actuality is not clear. 74 celebrates the inspiration instilled into Astrophil by the kiss, and in 76, swelling into excited six-foot lines, he prepares for a fresh encounter with Stella, in no condition for virtuous love:

>             what helpe then in my case,
> But with short breath, long lookes, staid feet and walking hed,
> Pray that my sunne go downe with meeker beames to bed.

77 builds on this: her presence and 'conversation sweet' should satisfy him, he knows, but they do not. The anatomy of jealousy in 78 lowers the tone yet further with the coarse suggestion that Stella's jealous husband thoroughly deserves to be cuckolded. In 79, 80, 81 and 82 Astrophil expatiates further on the stolen kiss, pleading for more; in 83 he tries to banish his rival the lecherous sparrow from Stella's lips to make room for the human but equally lecherous *'Phip'.* Closeness continues in the Third song, celebrating Stella's beauty as she sings. In 84 and 85 Astrophil, in a state of painful excitement, is on his way to the house where Stella is, and in the Fourth song they are together indoors at night. After verbal pleas, Astrophil makes another attempt to embrace her—'Sweet alas, why strive you thus?' Rejection and 'change of lookes' in 86 are perhaps predictable after this, and the Fifth Song, written in rather old-fashioned diction and six-foot lines, is Astrophil's poetic revenge. Not only does he

abuse Stella as a thief, murderer, tyrant, rebel, deserter, witch and devil, but he insults her by presenting her with a poem which is deliberately inelegant and repetitive.[27] Punishing her for her rejection of him by sending her a bad poem, he promises that he can nevertheless do better if *she* does better:

> mend yet your froward mind,
> And such skill in my Muse you reconcil'd shall find,
> That all these cruell words your praises shall be proved.

The Sixth Song is a celebration of the rival attractions of Stella's face and her (singing) voice. We seem in these three songs to have a reversal of rôles, with Astrophil a rather clumsy poet attempting laboriously to reach after the harmony of Stella's 'soul-invading' voice and 'sacred tunes', as if she, not he, were the true maker of harmony.

The Eighth Song has been very extensively discussed. Whatever we think of its role in the sequence as a whole, there can be no doubt that it presents us with a Stella who is definitely present with Astrophil, not far off and dimly perceived. She not only rejects him physically:

> her hands his hands repelling
> Gave repulse all grace excelling,

but also verbally in a speech of twenty-eight lines, which makes her attitude to him clearer than in any of the sonnets, where it has been seen only as refracted through the excited responses of Astrophil. If we take this song, not as a fantasy or dream of Astrophil's, but as a narrative which Sidney intended readers of the sequence to accept as revelatory, it gives a perhaps rather surprising account of Stella's position. She loves him, she says, and suffers in loving him:

> 'Trust me, while I thee deny,
> In my selfe the smart I try,
> Tyran honour thus doth use thee,
> *Stella's* selfe might not refuse thee.
>
> 'Therefore, Deere, this no more move,
> Least, though I leave not thy love,
> Which too deep in me is framed,
> I should blush when thou art named'.

'Tyran honour' seems here to refer more to reputation and social image than to any moral idea of chastity. By a quibble worthy of Astrophil himself, Stella establishes a position in which her 'selfe' loves Astrophil, but her 'honour' must reject him, fear of embarrassment—'I should blush'—being in the end the insuperable barrier to fruition. The pastoral setting of the Eight Song is developed into a fully pastoral mode in the Ninth, with a whimsically rustic Astrophil bidding farewell to his flock

as he meditates on the paradox of Stella's attitude in claiming to love him
and yet casting him off:

> Is that love? forsooth I trow,
> If I saw my good dog grieved,
> And a helpe for him did know,
> My love should not be beleeved,
> But he were by me releeved.

Since Sonnet 70, then, we have seen a decline and disintegration in
Astrophil. From a highly sophisticated court poet he has become a trivial
seducer and a laborious versifier, and now adopts a childish pastoral persona as he struggles to come to terms with unambiguous rejection.
Reversals continue: in 87 Astrophil is called away from Stella by 'iron
lawes of dutye', and weeps more for Stella's grief than for his own—'I
saw that teares did in her eyes appeare'. In 88, absent from Stella, he is
tempted by another lady 'From my deare Captainesse to run away', and
only by a deliberate act of inward recollection retains Stella's image in
its supremacy. 89, using only the two end words 'night' and 'day', is an
exercise in poetic paradox, and in 90 Astrophil reassures Stella that his
poetical endeavours have no goal but her. However, 91 marks a fresh
temptation to unfaithfulness in absence, and this time the evident relish
with which the other ladies' beauties are catalogued makes the final
reassurance rather unconvincing:

> If this darke place yet shew like candle light,
>   Some beautie's peece, as amber colourd hed,
>   Milke hands, rose cheeks, or lips, more sweet, more red,
> Or seeing jets, blacke, but in blacknesse bright,
>   They please, I do confesse, they please mine eyes.

Still absent, in Sonnet 92 Astrophil asks for vivid news of Stella—'How
cloth'd, how waited on, sighd she or smilde'—and in the Tenth song
sends his 'Thought' off on a journey of sexual exploration which in a
fleshly encounter would never have got so far:[28]

> Thinke of my most Princely power,
>   When I blessed shall devower,
>   With my greedy licorous sences,
>   Beauty, musicke, sweetnesse, love
> While she doth against me prove
> Her strong darts, but weake defences.

Even in absence, it seems, Astrophil has the capacity to overstep the
mark and antagonize Stella, for in 93 she is 'vexed' with him, for reasons
that are rather obscure—'wit confus'd with too much care did misse'.
The most obvious gloss, given Stella's concern for her 'honour', is that

he has injured her reputation. 94, 95 and 96 are miserable meditations in solitude, and 97 is the third recurrence of the theme of unfaithfulness, with 'a Lady *Dian*'s peere' trying to cheer Astrophil up. 98 and 99 comment on wretched sleepless nights, but in 100 it is again (as in 87) Stella, not Astrophil, who is weeping—'O Teares, no teares, but raine from beautie's skies'—and there is a revival of sensuousness in the evocation of her 'honied sighs', 'whose pants do make unspilling creame to flow'. A different kind of panting succeeds in 101 and 102, with Stella ill. In 103 Stella travels Cleopatra-like on the Thames, and we have a recollection of the 'blush, which guiltie seem'd of love' in 66, but here it is stimulated only by the 'wanton winds', as Astrophil all unseen looks on from a window. In the Eleventh song he pleads under Stella's window in the last encounter definitely imaged in the sequence. As in Sonnet 91, he has to reassure her that he will not be unfaithful:

> 'What if you new beauties see,
> Will not they stir new affection?'
> I will think theye pictures be,
> (Image like of Saints' perfection)
> Poorely counterfeting thee.

The ending of this last meeting is brought about by social pressure—'I thinke that some give eare'—and it is 'louts', not Stella herself, who drive him finally from her window. The obscure 105 evokes a missed glimpse of Stella driving by in a coach—'Curst be the page from whome the bad torch fell'; and in 106 Astrophil seems to be persuading himself, not Stella, that he cannot be effectively consoled by the 'store of faire Ladies' who beguile him 'with charme of conversation sweete'—a phrase that had been used of Stella in Sonnet 77. Most telling of all, in terms of our final image of Stella, is the penultimate sonnet, 107. Here Astrophil pleads to be released from poetic and emotional servitude—'Sweete, for a while give respite to my hart'. He wants to proceed with 'this great cause, which needs both use and art'. Stella, it appears, is an exacting audience for Astrophil's poetry, but he wants to move on:

> as a Queene, who from her presence sends
> Whom she imploves, dismisse from thee my wit,
> Till it have wrought what thy owne will attends.

The word 'wit', and the suggestion that Stella herself is eager for the fruits of this new 'cause', seem to point to a literary project rather than a political duty, or, as Ringler suggested, 'public service in general'.[29] The implication seems to be that if Stella will now release Astrophil from the labour of writing sonnets for her he can get on with writing something more important which she will herself enjoy—perhaps a work com-

parable with the 'graver labour' promised by Shakespeare to the Earl of
Southampton in the dedication of *Venus and Adonis*. This can be only
speculation; but what is clear is that the penultimate sonnet suggests that
the only reason Astrophil is still writing sonnets for Stella is that she
demands them. Honour is satisfied, and the myth concluded, with the
final sonnet, in which Astrophil is alone again and imprisoned in the
oxymoronic toils of love. But the revelation to the reader that it is Stella,
not Astrophil, who has been protracting the poetic love affair removes all
further poetic impetus. Though the sequence has been almost universally
viewed as 'inconclusive',[30] Sonnet 107 surely does provide at least a sign-
ing off, a clear indication to the reader that we shall have no more in this
vein. Both lovers are concerned about their reputation, and further
continuance could bring them into disgrace:

> O let not fooles in me thy works reprove,
> And scorning say, See what it is to love.

Like a persuasive actor who steps out of his part to speak the Epilogue,
Sidney takes away the illusion he has so brilliantly created by revealing
to us that Stella has all along been Astrophil's accomplice in an elaborate
game of love.

Where does this survey leave us, in reconsidering the literary image
of Stella/Penelope? Close reading suggests, or at least mine does, that
Sidney's Stella is no quixotic Dulcinea. She is intelligent, self-aware,
probably verbally adept, certainly musical. She receives Sidney/
Astrophil's poems appreciatively, and enhances them by reading and
singing them back to him. Far from being remote and unattainable, as
Ringler suggested—'He may never have known her very well—all
stars are distant and only dimly apprehensible'— she is shown explicitly
as returning Astrophil's love, or at least affection, and implicitly as acting
out a conscious role in the stage-play of love. She is no dumb blonde, but
a lively audience for Astrophil's verses who probably understands what
is 'really' going on as well as Pamela in the *Arcadia* understands
Musidorus's veiled courtship of her through the doltish Mopsa. Sidney
was a highly original writer, and no doubt the unique suggestions in his
sonnet sequence of 'comeback' from the beloved were part of a deliberate
strategy for increasing the poems' 'forcibleness'. But it seems possible
also that Penelope Devereux's real-life qualities offered him considerable
stimulus in fashioning Stella. A necessarily brief examination of her life
and literary connexions may support this possibility. I do not mean to
imply that *Astrophil and Stella* is a diaristic chronicle of real feelings and
events. But given that Sidney was not fashioning a beloved out of a dead
woman or one he had never met, but one with whom he was surely at

least reasonably well acquainted, her actual qualities may have contributed rather more to 'Stella' than did, for instance, those of Beatrice Portinari to Dante's Beatrice.

Penelope Devereux was born about 1563, the eldest child of Walter Devereux, first Earl of Essex. Her mother was the beautiful and spirited Lettice Knollys, who was to marry two more husbands, the second of them Sidney's uncle the Earl of Leicester, and live to the age of ninety-five. Walter Devereux died of dysentery in Ireland in 1576 (though some said Leicester had poisoned him to free his wife), and expressed a death-bed wish that Penelope might marry Philip Sidney, who was in Ireland at the time. He expressed his love for him by calling him 'son' in anticipation of this match.[31] He also made the Earl of Huntingdon responsible for the maintenance of Penelope, Dorothy, and his younger son Walter; Robert, the heir, was made Burghley's charge. Ringler deduced from this that Penelope spent the years 1576-81 continuously in the Huntingdon household at Ashby-de-la-Zouch, perhaps at times even going as far North as York.[32] This would mean that Sidney and Penelope could not have met until she arrived in London in 1581. However, after her mother married Sidney's uncle Lord Leicester in September 1578 it is surely possible that the Devereux children occasionally came to Wanstead. Records of the movements of the children in these years do not appear to survive; but once their widowed mother became again, as Countess of Leicester, mistress of a large house, it seems reasonable to imagine that she may have resumed custody of her children for at least part of each year. In later years she clearly maintained close relations with all her children; I find it hard to imagine that she would have allowed five years of their adolescence to pass away without seeing them. This hypothesis—and it is no more—would allow for the intriguing further possibility of Penelope Devereux's presence at Wanstead when Sidney's *Lady of May* was performed for the Queen there in 1578 or 1579. However, we are not on firm ground in tracing her movements until January 1580/1, when she came to Court under the tutelage of the Countess of Huntingdon. She had been in London only a month when the second Lord Rich died, and the Earl of Huntingdon wrote to Burghley of his heir, the young Lord Rich, as 'a propper gentleman and one in yeares verry fytte for my lady penelope devereux'.[33] The marriage took place on 1st November 1582. Though it was claimed twenty-five years later that she was married against her will and had already been contracted to the man who was later to become her lover, Charles Blount, there seems to be no contemporary document which supports this. Indeed, an early meeting between Penelope Devereux and Charles Blount is even harder to establish than one between her and Sidney, since it is not clear that Blount was at Court before 1583.[34] Whether the Rich marriage was as unsatisfactory initially as it was later to become we have no means of knowing. It would certainly be most unsafe to use *Astrophil and Stella* itself as evidence here. J. G. Nichols has even suggested refreshingly, that Sidney and Lord Rich may have been 'very friendly', and the attack on 'Rich fooles' in Sonnet 24 no more than comradely banter.[35] Though it can never be proved either way, such a reading seems to make more allowance for the layers of irony and paradox in which Sidney habitually enfolded himself than does a literal acceptance of *Astrophil and Stella* as evidence that Penelope Devereux's marriage was from the outset a 'foul yoke'.

All we can say for certain of her early married life is that between 1583 and 1590 Penelope bore her husband five children. Henry Constable wrote two sonnets on the fourth, a shortlived girl born in the Armada year.[36] But from 1590 onwards Charles Blount seems to have been openly acknowledged as her lover. Peele so described him in *Polyhymnia*:

> Comes Sir Charles Blunt in Or and Azure dight,
> Rich in his colours, richer in his thoughts,
> Rich in his Fortune, Honor, Armes and Arte.[37]

Gold and azure, we should perhaps remember, were the colours Sidney had worn in the splendid *Four Foster Children of Desire* tournament in May 1581, and they are also the colours worn by Pyrocles on his first appearance in the revised *Arcadia*. 1590 seems to be the turning point in Penelope Devereux's life. After this date, despite her liaison with Blount, her fortunes seem to have risen in tandem with those of her brother, the Earl of Essex, and it is in the years of his greatest fame that she emerges as a literary patroness. Despite unwise intervention on his behalf, she weathered the storm of his disgrace and execution, surviving to become a Lady of the Bedchamber to Queen Anne and to take part in court masques by Daniel and Jonson. Her final disgrace did not come about through her brother's rebellion, but through her marriage to Blount in 1605 after a legal separation from Lord Rich which had specifically forbidden re-marriage. Blount did not long survive the marriage, and Daniel, Ford and John Cooper wrote poems vigorously defending the dead Earl (as he was by then) and his controversial match.[38]

This may seem to take us far away from the subject of Penelope Devereux's relations with Sidney more than twenty years earlier. But a selective analysis of the literary documents linked with her from 1590 onwards yields a surprising number of details which appear to shed light back on *Astrophil and Stella*, not all of which can be explained away as a continuance of traditions established by Sidney himself. For instance, I have suggested that Sidney and Penelope may have been engaged in a deliberate game of love. Some of her later correspondence indicates that she had a marked taste for such games. Two 'fantastical' letters from Essex to his sister, apparently written at her request, suggest that she certainly derived amusement from playing such games with him. Though in both letters he adopts a pose of detachment from passion and intrigue, he does so in a manner reflecting the conflicting emotions of Petrarchan love poetry:

> I am malencholy, mery, some tymes happy and often unfortunate. The Court of as many humors as the rayne bow hath cullores. the tyme wherein we live, more unconstant then womens thoughts, more miserable then old age itself and breedeth both people and occasions like to itself that is violent, desperate and fantastical.[39]

Essex's letters are, like Sidney's love sonnets, self-revelations so mannered that it is impossible to tell what, if anything, is being revealed. Arthur Freeman, who edited these letters, suggests that they fall between the years 1596 and 1599; but I would be inclined to assign them rather to the late 1580s, when Lady Rich was largely resident at the Rich house, Leighs, to which they are addressed, and perhaps in much need of diversion. Another 'fantastical' correspondence which was more explicitly flirtatious consists of letters to her from Antonio Pérez, the former secretary to Philip II of Spain who was exiled in London in the mid-1590s. Six of them survive, written in Spanish.[40] They not only indicate that Penelope was fluent in Spanish, and well able to communicate the contents of these letters to her mother, sister and sister-in-law, but also that her attention could be gained by the use of elaborate love conceits verging on the grotesque. For instance, Sidney's Astrophil had compared himself with Stella's dog (Sonnet 59); Pérez goes one better than this, for in offering Penelope a pair of dog-skin gloves he wishes that he might flay his own skin to make gloves for her. Sidney had played on the name he shared with 'Philip' sparrow (Sonnet 83); Pérez plays here on the resemblance of his name to *perro*, 'dog'. Clearly he knew *Astrophil and Stella* and was consciously elaborating some of Sidney's conceits, but what is striking is that he thought this an effective way of seeking, through Penelope, the protection of Essex. Clearly the Queen was not unique in conducting political manouevres in amorous language. The letters of Pérez indicate that he discerned in their recipient both linguistic skills and a sophistication of taste bordering on decadence. Published works dedicated to Lady Rich expand these qualities further.

The earliest printed book dedicated to Lady Rich seems to be Richard Barnfield's *The Affectionate Shepheard*, 1594.[41] This is a two-part poem

describing the rustic courtship of the 'sweet-fac'd Boy' Ganimede by the
shepherd Daphnis. He has a female rival, 'the faire Queen *Guendolen*'
who had previously loved 'a lustie youth/That now was dead', and has
been seen as an image of Penelope Rich herself, lover of the dead
Sidney.[42] This is open to question. Sidney is explicitly elegized in 'The
Shepheards content', an appended poem presenting love as the only foe
to pastoral happiness—'By thee sweet *Astrophel* forwent his joy'—and
recalling Sidney as 'The Syren of this latter Age'. What is striking is that
Barnfield considered Penelope Rich an appropriate dedicatee for a work
celebrating 'disorderly love, which the learned call *paederastice*', as E.K.
called it.[43] Evidently *The Affectionate Shepheard* excited some disapproval on
these lines, for in his next collection of poems, *Cynthia, with certaine Sonnets*, 1595, Barnfield felt constrained to defend the earlier poem, rather
unconvincingly, as 'nothing else, but an imitation of *Virgill*'.[44] From his
two-stanza dedication in *The Affectionate Shepheard* there seems no way of
telling whether Barnfield actually knew Lady Rich and discerned in her
a sympathetic patroness. In praising her eyes and speech he may have
been merely echoing *Astrophil and Stella*:

> Fayre lovely Ladie, whose Angelique eyes
> Are Vestall Candles of sweet Beauties Treasure,
> Whose Speech is able to inchaunt the wise,
> Converting Joy to Paine, and Paine to Pleasure.

Barnfield's poetic career spanned only four years, during which he published seven books, before retreating to his native Staffordshire. But he
may have been, or have hoped to be, a protégé of the Devereux family,
whose seat of Chartley was not far from Darlaston, where Barnfield
seems to have lived.[45]

There seems little doubt that Lady Rich was personally known to
Charles Tessier, who dedicated his *Le premier livre de chansons* to her in
February 1596.[46] It is a volume of thirty-five part songs in French and
Italian. Like Antonio Pérez, Tessier was a visiting member of the
Essex/Bacon circle, who had perhaps met Antony Bacon in France some
ten years earlier. He arrived in London late in 1596.[47] Where Barnfield
had merely praised Lady Rich's 'speech', Tessier in his dedication (written in Italian) suggests that she has good musical judgement, and in
Chanson VI, a song specifically addressed 'A Madame Riche', he
ascribes to her more than Apollonian musical skill. Addressing Apollo,
he says:

> Aussy bien ta harpe n'a pas
> Tant que son luth de doux appas
> Et puis tes chansons desliennes
> Ne sont si belles que les siennes.

If Tessier made an accurate assessment of Lady Rich's tastes, the content of many of his lyrics is quite revealing. For instance, Chanson IV recalls Sidney's Fourth song, evoking a meeting of lovers by night in the house of the girl's mother, and using her refusal as a refrain:

> Laisses cela he bien he bien
> aussi bien ne gagnes vous rien.

But here the seduction is successfully accomplished: 'Puisque c'est faict je le veux bien', the lady finally sings. Many other songs are striking: one of the most distinctive, Chanson XVIII, celebrates the passionate love of a sister for her brother. She begs him to consummate their mutual affection:

> Junon de pareille flame
> Son frere ayme come moy
> Cela point l'amour n'offence
> Nature force la loy.
>
> Sans craindre pere ny mere
> Prenons la comodite
> Car le nom de ses deux freres
> Emporte grand privaute.

It may be pure coincidence that in the mid-1590s Lady Rich was the recipient of celebrations both of pederastic and incestuous love—not to mention the contorted masochistic conceits of Pérez; but it does seem possible that she was known to enjoy such unconventional expressions of feeling.

We are on safer ground, however, in exploring Lady Rich's musical tastes, which would reward more expert study than mine. There are, for instance, various versions of 'Lady Rich's Galliard',[48] and her participation in Daniel's *Vision of the Twelve Goddesses* (as Venus) in 1604 and in Jonson's *Masque of Blacknesse* (as the nymph Ocyte) in 1605 suggests that even in middle age she was a good dancer. Making all allowance for flattery, there still seems little doubt that she was genuinely musical and had a good singing voice. Sidney commanded Edward Denny in May 1580 'that you remember with your good voyce, to singe my songes for they will one well become an other'.[49] When a couple of years later he wrote, for instance in Sonnet 57, of Stella singing his songs, he probably knew that Lady Rich, too, was well able to do this. The Denny reference suggests that some of Sidney's poems were set to music very early, or else written to fit existing tunes. Though none of the settings listed by Ringler[50] seems to go back to Sidney's lifetime, it seems reasonable to conjecture that earlier ones existed. Renewed confirmation of Lady Rich's ability to sing comes in the last year of her life, with John Cooper's *Funeral Teares for the Earl of Devonshire* (1606).[51] This is a sequence of seven songs lamenting the sudden death of Lady Rich's second husband, who had been created Earl of Devonshire in 1603, contracted his illegal marriage in December 1605, and died of pneumonia only three months later. Cooper's declaration of support for the marriage is even more confident than those of Ford and Daniel. His military career, his statesmanship and his learning are seen as entitling the dead Earl to place his heart where he wished:

> Did Mountjoy love? and did not Mountjoyes sword
>> When he marcht arm'd with pallace dreadful helme
> The rough unquiet Irish rebels curbe?
>> And the invading Spaniards overwhelme?
> Lov'd he? and did he not nathlesse assist
>> Great Brittaines counsels, and in secret cells
> The Muses visite? and alone untwist
>> The riddles of deepe Philosophick spels?
> Did Dev'nshire love? and lov'd not Dev'nshire so
>> As if all beauties had for him beene fram'd?
> For beautie more adorn'd no age shall know
>> Then hers whom he his once for ever nam'd.

Incidentally, Cooper's reference to Mountjoy's visits to the Muses is one of several pieces of evidence that he was a poet.[52] If his poems survive anywhere, they would be a remarkable trouvaille, and might give us yet more poetic images, to set beside Sidney's, of Lady Rich. Mountjoy and Sidney run strangely parallel: both poets, both 'lovers' of Lady Rich, though perhaps in different senses, both wounded in the leg at Zutphen. But to return to the *Funeral Teares*: as striking as Cooper's loyalty to the dead Earl is his confidence that the widowed Countess will be able to sing the songs herself. Six out of the seven are set so that they can be sung 'by a treble voice alone to the Lute and Base Viole', and Cooper makes it abundantly clear that he expects them to be sung by the lady whose grief they express:

> Sing Lady, sing thy Dev'nshires funerals,
> And charme the Ayre with thy delightfull voyce,
>> Let lighter spirits grace their Madrigals,
> Sorrow doth in the saddest notes rejoyce.
>> Fairest of Ladies since these Songs are thine,
>> Now make them as thou art thyselfe, divine.

The first song, addressing the air, presents her as a habitual singer, now changing her tune:

> Oft thou hast with greedy eare,
> Drunke my notes and wordes of pleasure,
> In affections equall measure,
>> Now my songs of sorrow heare.

> Since from thee my griefs doe grow
> Whome alive I pris'd so deare:
> The more my joy, the more my woe.

In each of the first six songs punning reference is made to the Countess's lost 'joy' ( = Mountjoy); the sixth, in which 'My ioyes faire image carv'd in shades I see', seems to be a meditation on a portrait or funeral effigy.[53] The seventh and last song requires a second voice, an alto, and consists of a short dialogue assuring the widow of her husband's immortal life and true fame. Cooper's boldness in furnishing her with these semi-dramatic songs of grief suggests that he knew that music was a habitual form of expression for her. Possibly he acted as music tutor to some of her children, as he did later to Henry Lawes, who in turn was to teach Milton's patrons the Egertons.[54] One intriguing feature of the *Funeral Teares* has been pointed out by Vincent Duckles. The instrumental introduction to the best known lyric, 'In darkness let me dwell' (IV), 'gives a clear quotation of one of Ophelia's best known songs from *Hamlet* ... Here is an allusion that no contemporary could miss, an elegy within an elegy, linking the sorrow of Devonshire's widow with the pathetic grief of Polonius's daughter'.[55] If this is right, the presentation of Lady Rich as an Ophelia figure adds yet another dimension to her literary image.

The evidence that Lady Rich could sing fits in well with Sidney's Sonnet 57 and the Third, Sixth and Seventh songs. But musical accomplishments were widely developed in Elizabethan noblewomen, and in her singing and (if we believe Tessier) lute playing Lady Rich may not have been very unusual. Much more remarkable were her verbal skills. The 'golden chaine' of rhetoric was associated with Stella in Sonnet 58, and such an image would have been quite applicable also to Lady Rich. Whether she was well schooled in languages in the Huntingdon household, or developed these skills early in her married life, perhaps with the help of John Florio,[56] there is no doubt that Penelope Rich was not only verbally adept in her own language, but also fluent in French, Italian and Spanish. Not every Elizabethan noblewoman was capable of spending the evening writing letters, as Stella is supposed to be doing in the Fourth Song: but Lady Rich must often have done so. Enough of her letters survive to show that she expressed herself in a lively and forceful manner. One of them, her plea to the Queen for her imprisoned brother, achieved very wide MS circulation, and was also printed.[57] We have evidence that she consistently used letters for political ends. In 1589, for instance, she was writing letters to Mr Richard Douglas which were intended for the eyes of King James:

> whereby she remembers him of his charge for his friends, & a nickname for
> every one that is a partaker in the matter... She is very pleasant in her let-

ters, and writes the most part thereof in her brother's behalf, so as they shall be showed to the King ('Victor') which they were, and the dark parts thereof expounded to him. He commended much the fineness of her wit, the invention and well writing ... Lady Riche writes almost every weeke.[58]

This was not mere flirtatious chit-chat, but a dangerous secret correspondence in which Lady Rich ('Ryalta') and her husband ('Richardo')—who seems to have been no ready writer, since letters from him were expected but did not materialize—were promoting Essex's interests with the King, in mistaken anticipation of the Queen's shortly approaching demise. Lady Rich's speedy promotion to Lady of the Bedchamber to Queen Anne, fourteen years later, when Queen Elizabeth finally had shuffled off her virgin and mortal coil, was presumably the fruit of many years of undercover cultivation of the Scottish King.

Lady Rich's skill as a linguist has been suggested through the fact that she received letters in Spanish and French and songs in French and Italian. Bartholomew Yong paid tribute to her as such in the dedication of his translation of Montemayor's *Diana* in 1598. He recalls:

certaine yeares past ... in a publike shewe at the Middle Temple ... it befell to my lot in that worthie assemblie, unwoorthily to performe the part of a French Oratour by a deducted speech in the same toong, and that amongst so many good conceits and such general skill in toongs, all the while I was rehearsing it, there was not any, whose mature judgement and censure in that language I feared and suspected more then your Ladiships, whose attentive eare and eie daunted my imagination with the apprehension of my disabilitie, and your Ladiships perfect knowledge in the name.[59]

He goes on to refer to the Spanish language in general and Montemayor's romance in particular as already 'so well knowen to your Ladiship'. With the confirming evidence of Lady Rich's ability to correspond in French and Spanish, and in ciphers and riddles in English, we do not need to subtract much from Yong's praise of her linguistic ability.

Lady Rich was a remarkable woman, whose distinctive talents and personality cannot be explained away as the creation of those who sought her favour, or that of her brother. Though we have no literary works written by her, the evidence of her cultivation and intelligence is inescapable. Playful, but with serious, even sinister political intent underlying her play (as in the 'Ryalta' correspondence) she offers parallels to Sidney himself. Her role in the rise and fall of Essex, and so in the whole course of the last ten years of Elizabeth's reign, was probably crucial. For Ringler's picture of Stella as based on a woman 'distant and only dimly apprehensible', I would like to substitute one of Lady Rich as a woman whose personality was so vivid that Sidney cannot have failed to apprehend her. Whether or in what sense he loved her, we shall never know. But there can be little doubt that as a model for 'Stella', she was considerably more than a lay-figure.

## NOTES

1  Hoyt H. Hudson, 'Penelope Devereux as Sidney's Stella', *Huntington Library Bulletin*, VII (1935), 89-129.
2  James M. Purcell, *Sidney's Stella*, New York and London, 1934.
3  *Poems*, 440-47.
4  M. C. Bradbrook, *John Webster, Citizen and Dramatist*, London, 1980, 54. An even more credulous reading of the sequence is offered by Sylvia Freedman in her otherwise useful book *Poor Penelope: An Elizabethan Woman*, Windsor, Berks., 1983, 50-57.
5  P. J. Croft, ed., *Poems of Robert Sidney*, Oxford, 1984, 62.
6  Jack Stillinger, 'The Biographical Problems of *Astrophil and Stella*', *JEGP*, LIX (1960), 617-39.
7  Quoted in Hugh Ross Williamson, *Lorenzo the Magnificent*, London, 1974, 93.
8  *Works*, I, 98.
9  J. G. Nichols, *The Poetry of Sir Philip Sidney: An Interpretation in the Context of his Life and Times*, Liverpool, 1974, 62-63. Alan Hager, in 'The Exemplary Mirage' *ELH*, XLVIII (1981), 11, misunderstands my account of 'The Manner of Sir Philip Sidney's Death'. It was I, not Van Dorsten, who edited this text, and I did not suggest that 'it seems to have been doctored to remove Sidney's last words on the subject', but that a longer passage had dropped out, 'whether of a more or a less compromising nature is impossible to conjecture'. The passage is even more uncritically accepted by Sylvia Freedman, 59-61.
10  Bradbrook, 54.
11  Jean Robertson, 'Sir Philip Sidney and Lady Penelope Rich', *RES*, XV (1964), 296-97.
12  *MP*, 169.
13  Hager, 13-14.
14  Fulke Greville, *Life of Sir Philip Sidney*, ed. Nowell Smith, Oxford, 1907, 133.
15  Letter printed in G. F. Beltz, 'Memorials of the Last Achievement, Illness and Death of Sir Philip Sidney', *Archaeologia*, XXVIII (1840), 27-37.
16  *MP*, 152.
17  Greville, 135.
18  CSPFor (Holland), X; printed in *Works*, III, 183.
19  John Bruce, ed., *The Leycester Correspondence*, Camden Society, vol. XXVII, London, 1844, 423; BL MS Add. 48014, f. 163.
20  *MP*, 221.
21  *MP*, 111.
22  *Poems*, p. xliv.
23  See for instance Hallett Smith, *Elizabethan Poetry*, Cambridge Mass., 1952, 142-57; John Buxton, *Elizabethan Taste*, London, 1963, 269-94; David Kalstone, *Sidney's Poetry: Contexts and Interpretations*, Cambridge Mass., 1965, *passim*; Rosalie Colie, *Paradoxia Epidemica*, Princeton N.J., 1966, 89-95; A. C. Hamilton, *Sir Philip Sidney: A Study of his Life and Works*, Cambridge, 1977, 79-106; Thomas P. Roche, '*Astrophil and Stella*: A Radical Reading', *Spenser Studies*, III (1982), 139-91.
24  Mona Wilson, *Sir Philip Sidney*, London, 1950, 167-206.
25  Nichols, 65-113.
26  Roche, 144 and 186. I had already decided that these lines formed a narrative midpoint before I had read Roche's article, so I think they may be sensed as such even by readers unaware of the numerical underpinning.
27  *Poems*, 484, suggests that this song was written early, perhaps originally forming part of the Philisides-Mira sequence. Taking the 1598 order as probably authoritative, its placing here suggests that Sidney could make resourceful use of his own juvenilia.

28 This song seems to be answered in Fulke Greville's *Caelica* xlv, also a song on absence:

> But thoughts be not so brave
> With absent joy:
> For you with that you have
> Your selfe destroy:
> The absence which you glory,
> Is that which make you sorry,
> And burne in vaine:
> For thought is not the weapon
> Wherewith *thoughts-ease* men cheapen,
> *Absence is paine.*

(cheapen = purchase).
29 *Poems*, 490.
30 See for instance Nichols, 113; Roche, 142.
31 M. W. Wallace, *Life of Sidney*, Cambridge, 1915, 169. See also D. E. Baughan, 'Sir Philip Sidney and the Matchmakers', *MLR*, XXXIII (1938), 506-19.
32 *Poems*, 437.
33 *Poems*, 438.
34 See Cyril Bentham Falls, *Mountjoy: Elizabethan General*, London, 1955, 21.
35 Nichols, 96.
36 Joan Grundy ed., *The Poems of Henry Constable*, Liverpool, 1960, 157 and 170. Sylvia Freedman gives a useful account of the number and paternity of Lady Rich's children, including one, Scipio, born at the end of 1597, not hitherto recorded, p. 89.
37 D. H. Horne, ed., *The Life and Minor Works of George Peele*, Yale, 1952, 237.
38 John Ford, *Fames memoriall, or the Earle of Devonshire deceased*, London, 1606; Samuel Daniel, *A funerall poeme uppon the death of the late noble Earle of Devonshire*, London, 1606; John Cooper (alias Giovanni Coprario), *Funeral Teares for the Earl of Devonshire*, London, 1606. Ford also paid tribute to the Devonshire marriage in his *Honor Triumphant*, and also possibly recalled it in some of his plays; cf. K. Duncan-Jones, 'Ford and the Earl of Devonshire', *RES*, XXIX (1978), 447-52; cf. also *RES*, XXX (1979), 332.
39 Arthur Freeman, 'Essex to Stella: Two letters from the Earl of Essex to Penelope Rich', *ELR*, III (1973), between pages 248 and 249. It is a pity that no information is given about the paper and watermark, which might have given some clue to dating. The letters are reproduced in facsimile.
40 Gustav Ungerer, *A Spaniard in Elizabethan England: The Correspondence of Antonio Pérez's Exile*, London, 1974, vol. I, nos 41, 42, 44, 45, 48 and 50.
41 [Richard Barnfield], *The Affectionate Shepheard. Containing the complaint of Daphnis for the Love of Ganymede*, London, 1594.
42 Hudson, 93. Harry Morris, *Richard Barnfield: Colin's Child*, Tallahassee, 1963, 41, rightly questions Hudson's reading of the poem as personal allegory.
43 Spenser, *The Shepheardes Calender*, London, 1579, gloss on line 59 of the January Eclogue.
44 Richard Barnfield, *Cynthia, With Certaine Sonnets, and the Legend of Cassandra*, London, 1595, sig. A3.
45 Cf. Harry Morris, 11-13 and *passim.*
46 Charles Tessier, *Le premier livre de chansons*, London, 1597.
47 Cf. Gustav Ungerer, 'The French Lutenist Charles Tessier and the Essex Circle', *Ren. Q.*, XXVIII (1975), 190-203.
48 Cf. Diana Poulton, *John Dowland*, London, 1972, 156.
49 James M. Osborn, *Young Philip Sidney*, Yale, 1972, 540.
50 *Poems*, 566-68.
51 Giovanni Coprario, *Funeral Teares*. Only four copies of this book appear to survive, but the text is reproduced in Edward Doughtie, *Lyrics from English Airs*, Cambridge Mass., 1970, 251-58. His works are listed by Richard Charteris, *John Coprario: A Thematic Catalogue of his Music, with a Biographical Introduction*, New York, 1977.

52  As early as 1589 one I.L., translating D.F.R. de M.'s *An Answer to the Untruthes, published and printed in Spaine*, p. 52, praised Charles Blount as one who was a poet before he became an Armada hero:

> From foorth the *Oxens* tract, to courtly state,
> I see the treasure of all Science come:
> Whose pen of yore, the Muses stile did mate,
> Whose sword is now unsheathd to follow drumbe,
> *Parnassus* knowes my Poet by his looke,
> *Charles Blount*, the pride of war, and friend of booke.

53  Diana Poulton's attempt (pp. 256, 317-18) to attribute 'In darknesse let me dwell' wholly to Dowland is not convincing. Everything points to these seven songs as original and specifically written for the occasion of Devonshire's death; though it may still be the case, of course, that Dowland's setting of the first stanza is musically superior to anything Cooper could do.

54  For an account of what little is known of Cooper's career, see Manfred F. Bukofzer ed., Giovanni Coperario, *Rules how to Compose: a facsimile edition of a manuscript from the library of the Earl of Bridgewater (circa 1610) now in the Huntington Library*, Los Angeles, 1951.

55  Vincent Duckles, 'The English Musical Elegy of the Late Renaissance', in *Aspects of Mediaeval and Renaissance Music: A Birthday Offering to Gustave Reese*, New York, 1967, 134-53.

56  John Florio's dedicatory letter to Lady Rich and the Countess of Rutland (Sidney's daughter) in the second book of his translation of Montaigne's *Essayes*, 1603, sigs R2-R3, suggests considerable intimacy with both ladies.

57  Among many MS copies of this letter—probably at least two dozen—one which has been recently printed is in Folger MS V.a.321, fols 6$^v$-7$^v$, edited by A. R. Braunmuller as *A Seventeenth-Century Letter-Book*, London and Toronto, 1983. The Huntington Library copy of *An apologie of the Earle of Essex* (STC films 275) includes a printed version of Lady Rich's letter on sig. A2, apparently on an insert; none of the other copies of the printed version of Essex's *Apologie* that I have seen includes it.

58  H. M. C. Salisbury MSS, vol. III, 435. Others involved in this intrigue included the poet Henry Constable (who wrote over twenty sonnets to Lady Rich) and Leicester's secretary Jean Hotman, to whom Lady Rich wrote at least one letter in French. Cf. Grundy, 26-31; Ruth Hughey, ed., *The Arundel Harington Manuscript of Tudor Poetry*, Columbus, I, 244-52.

59  Bartholomew Yong trans., *Diana of George of Montemayor*, London, 1598, sig a2; cf. also the modern edition of this book by Judith M. Kennedy, London, 1968, 3-4.

SETH WEINER

# THE QUANTITATIVE POEMS AND
# THE PSALM TRANSLATIONS:
# THE PLACE OF SIDNEY'S EXPERIMENTAL
# VERSE IN THE LEGEND

'All things in my former life have been vain, vain, vain'. Such was
Sidney's dying pronouncement, at least according to George Gifford,
one of the ministers present at his death.[1] Words like these coming from
a dying man should surprise no one and need not, of course, refer to
anything specific, least of all to Sidney's poetry. Yet ever since Fulke
Greville and Thomas Moffet penned their accounts of the death, the idea
of the repudiation of literary vanities has become canonical in that
strange blend of fact and myth known as the Sidney legend. Indeed, from
a literary as well as from a political point of view, Sidney's whole last year
becomes something of a preparation for his 'good death'.[2] Even before
taking up his responsibilities in the Low Countries, he had renounced his
poetic toys, said farewell to the love that reachest but to dust, and concen-
trated his literary energies on the translation of devotional treatises and
of the psalms of David.[3]

The psalms are particularly interesting because they constitute a direct
challenge to Sidney's earlier poetry. Of course, psalms, as examples of
the Divine poetry that Sidney sets apart from all other kinds in the
*Defence*,[4] were a traditional antidote to the bawdy songs and lecherous
lays with which courtiers were held to amuse themselves. But the forty-
three psalms that Sidney completed (the remaining one hundred and
seven were translated after his death by the Countess of Pembroke)
answer his earlier poems formally as well as doctrinally: each is clothed
in a different (and sometimes *recherché*) metre and rhyme scheme, reminding one strongly of the bold experimental verse in the 'old' *Arcadia* and
in *Certain Sonnets*. Of these earlier poems, the most overtly experimental
in nature are surely the thirteen that attempt to employ the quantitative
structures of Greek and Latin poetry in the writing of English verses. In
terms of prosodic oddity alone, these poems deserve to be singled out and
set over against the psalms.

Yet, unlike the psalms, the quantitative poems have been accorded no
special place in biographies of Sidney, legendary or otherwise. They are
seen, if at all, as nothing more than a minor series of failed technical experiments, sensibly and quickly abandoned. In deference to Sidney
himself (who gives equal weight to quantitative and to native, stress-

based poetry in the *Defence*) and in light of the fact that the Elizabethan prosodists divide their attentions in about the same proportion, I should like to suggest otherwise. To be sure, Sidney's thirteen quantitative experiments merit little acclaim as poems. But, few and slight as they are, they bear witness both to Sidney's humanistic interests and to the enthusiasm he shared with many intellectuals on the continent who thought that the reformation of poetry could somehow inspire men to better their spiritual (and consequently their political) lives. Considered, then, not as poems but, rather, in terms of the humanistic concerns that produced them, the quantitative experiments can be seen as part of a process of developing poetic purpose culminating logically in the psalm translations.

The sequence I am suggesting here implies, of course, that Sidney's poetic toys are susceptible of didactic purpose. What, then, are we to make of the death-bed misgivings, not to mention the disclaimers and protestations to be found in the *oeuvre* itself? It has been suggested that such rhetorical gestures have a grain of truth in them: Sidney never grew old enough to leave the chamber of maiden thought so that, by comparison with the great scenes of virtue in action that he wrote of in the *Defence of Poetry*, his own productions must have seemed to him somewhat trifling at best.[5] While I agree with the notion that rhetorical gesture can co-exist happily with real life, I also think that poetry about profane love need not fall short of the moral purposes Sidney argued for in the *Defence*. I might add that Fulke Greville and Thomas Moffet thought the same thing. To be sure, they express great approbation when the dying Sidney, Virgil-like, consigns the *Arcadia* to the flames or arranges to have the 'Anacreontics' suppressed, but they also defend the *Arcadia* as a book of political wisdom (Greville) or as a useful exposé of cupidity in its various guises (Moffet).[6] The resolution to the difficulty here is suggested by Greville's observation that the *Arcadia* has been spared a fiery fate (Greville himself helped edit it) only 'untill the world hath purged away all her more gross corruptions'.[7] The *Arcadia*, in other words, is ultimately vain, but provisionally useful in a fallen world. What we see through a glass darkly is not necessarily vain in itself, but is most assuredly vain in comparison to what we see face to face. This is the idea, so fitting both to the man and to the myth, in terms of which I shall discuss the prosodic experiments—first the neglected poems in quantitative metres, and then the psalm translations.

### i. *'A Kind of Secret Music'*

Before discussing Sidney's reasons for performing his quantitative verse experiments, it might be a good idea to review, from a technical standpoint, exactly what they are and what they are not.[8] They are not mere attempts, like Longfellow's *Evangeline*, to produce facsimiles of classical metres by substituting stressed and unstressed syllables for long and short ones. They are concerted attempts to base English verses on syllabic duration—to make them behave just like verses in Latin. To this end, Sidney and others who succeeded him in this enterprise, used Latin prosodic rules, paramountly that of position (a syllable with a lax, or 'short' vowel followed by two consonants is long), while composing in English. Here is an example—the first four lines of OA 13, an experiment in dactyllic hexameters, the simplest and most common of Latin metres:

> Lādў, rĕsērvd bў thĕ hēav'ns tŏ dŏ pāstōrs' cōmpănў hōnnŏr
> Jōynīng yōur sweēte vōıce tŏ thĕ rūrāll mūse ŏf ă dēsērte,
> Hēre yōu fūllў dŏ fīnde thīs strānge ŏpĕrātiŏn ŏf lōve,
> Hōw tŏ thĕ wōods lōve rūnnes ās wĕll ās rўdes tŏ thĕ Pāllăce.

Sidney took more pains than most other Elizabethan experimenters to adapt his quantitative verse to the realities of English pronunciation. Thus, while what we would call 'stress' in no way determines syllabic length, one can observe in the lines quoted a high degree of coincidence between stressed syllables and *ictus* (a vocal beat or pulse on the first long syllable of each foot). Most of the quantities can be justified in terms of vowel tenseness (e.g., *Lādў*), diphthong (e.g., *vōıce*), position (several examples) or the rule stating that vowel before vowel is always short (*operatiŏn*). Monosyllabic words are indifferent (long or short) unless they must be long by position (e.g., *ās well*). A clash of requirements occurs in a word like *Pāllace*, where the lax vowel wants to be scanned short, but Sidney wants a long syllable here to coincide with the *ictus*. His solution is to double the consonant so the syllable becomes long by position.[9] The only real violation of the ear—and this is a feature typical of all English quantitative verse—is the lengthening by position of the final unstressed syllables of certain words (e.g., *joynīng*).

Fulfilling the requirements of the classical rules for determining syllabic quantity, accommodating these rules to English so that stress matches *ictus*, and making syntactic sense all at once no doubt demand considerable ingenuity. But one cannot escape the conclusion, if OA 13 is at all typical, that Latin feet march rather lamely in English, and that Sidney's quantitative experiments are, in fact, his least eloquent poems.[10] The paradox I want to emphasise in this essay is that in theory, facts notwithstanding, they are the *most* eloquent poems, possessed of a harmony that surpassed that of which native, stress-based verse was supposedly capable.

Indeed, on both occasions when Sidney writes about quantitative poetry, music is his theme. The best known instance occurs toward the end of *A Defence of Poetry* where he distinguishes between ancient or classical verse based on quantities, and modern or vernacular verse based on 'number' (syllable count), rhyme, and on 'some regard of the accent' (by which he means the total quality of pronunciation in the vernacular, and not just stress).[11] He goes on:

> Whether of these be the more excellent, would bear many speeches: the ancient (no doubt) more fit for music, both words and time observing quantity, and more fit lively to express diverse passions, by the low or lofty sound of the well-weighed syllable; the latter likewise, with his rhyme, striketh a certain music to the ear, and, in fine, since it doth delight, though by another way, it obtains the same purpose: there being in either sweetness, and wanting in neither majesty.[12]

Sidney's remarks here are not original; they corroborate what many others were saying, both in England and on the continent, the chief difference being that Sidney is more generous than most in his assessment of vernacular metres. The major point is that quantitative verse is, in a precise and technical way, closer to music than is the native variety. Like music, quantitative metres divide time into proportional units (allowing for the ancient convention that a long syllable has just twice the duration of a short one). Different proportional relationships produce different kinds of motion, each kind appropriate to some particular passion, whether low or lofty. Sidney's use of these last two terms is significant in that they suggest not only different levels of style, but also different (and corresponding) levels of pitch. To compose or to recite a quantitative poem, that is, requires that one consider, or weigh, each syllable with respect not only to duration but also to the vocal range most suitable to the poem's subject. Theoretically, then, a quantitative poem should provide a fairly precise blueprint for its musical setting. But is it really musical setting that Sidney has in mind? To find out, we must consult his other passage on the subject.

This is an earlier version of the one we have been considering and occurs in two MSS of the *'old' Arcadia*. According to Ringler's guess it was cancelled when the discussion in the *Defence* superseded it.[13] Sidney begins with the rather sweeping (and problematic) assertion that all verses have 'ther chefe ornament, if not eand, in musike'. With regard to quantitative verse, this chief ornament and end is clearly not a musical setting. Such verse, we learn,

> hath in it self a kind (as a man may well call it) of secret musicke, since by the measure one may perceave some verses running with a high note fitt for great matters, some with a light foote fitt for no greater than amorous conceytes.

Interestingly enough, it is only when we consider native verse forms that the idea of the relationship between words and music takes on the practical aspect of providing a setting: since poetry in vernacular metres carries no secret music of its own, it can acquire the 'measured quantity' that music brings only by being set. By contrast, the relationship of words to music becomes a complex and vague concept when applied to quantitative poems. Their mere recitation seems instinct with music: they need not be sung to produce the proper stylistic sound effects (the 'high note' or the 'light foote').

It is difficult to learn anything about this curious idea of musical recitation because neither Sidney himself, nor any other Englishman of the sixteenth century, elaborates on it. To be sure, Sidney specifies an instrumental accompaniment for many poems in the *'old' Arcadia* (both quantitative and rhymed), but such fictional music just compounds the mystery. Suggestive scattered remarks on the importance of quantitative poetry, and sometimes on its musicality, can be found in the prosodic speculations of such authors as Ascham, Spenser, Harvey, Stanyhurst, Webbe, Puttenham, Campion, and several others, but these passages prove just as cryptic as Sidney's.[14] For more explicit commentary, we must turn to continental sources.

France is the obvious place to look first, for there are demonstrable links between Sidney and a number of men connected with the *Pléiade* and, later on, with the *Académie de Poésie et de Musique*, founded in Paris in 1570 by the poet Jean Antoine de Baïf and the musician Joachim Thibault de Courville.[15] Sidney was in Paris at a time when he could well have attended one of Baïf's learned *soirées* and heard specimens of *vers* and *musique mesurée*, that is, choral settings of French quantitative poetry.[16]

The general aims of the French academicians, and the place occupied by quantitative verse in their programme, have been described thoroughly and definitively by Frances Yates and need not be rehearsed here.[17] We are interested solely in pursuing the concept of musical recitation and the ideas tributary to that concept. The musical theorist closest to Baïf's *Académie* in time and place is Pontus de Tyard. Aside from his activities as a poet of the *Pléiade*, Tyard produced a series of philosophical discourses, the first two of which (named after the Solitary, a character who acts as Tyard's spokesman) treat poetry and music, respectively. We shall be concerned with the *Solitaire Second*. Of the two ancient divisions of music, harmonics and rhythmics, this treatise concentrates mostly on the first. Like all musical humanists (a term by which modern scholars designate those who sought to recapture the quasi-legendary union of music and poetry inherent in ancient Greek *mousike*) Tyard devotes a good deal of space to describing the affective powers of the traditional

melodic scales, or modes, a notion insisted on by the theorists of antiqui-
ty.[18] When Tyard writes of the union of music and poetry, then he usually has actual singing in mind, though, as we shall see, the modes were
sometimes thought to be suggested by the speaking voice as well. Tyard
imagines a species of monodic chant—'the simple solo voice, flowing
sweetly, and moving in accord with the dictates of a mode chosen to
match the nature of the verse'—and finds in this 'a secret and wonderful
power'.[19] Yet, the secret is not in the modes alone; part of it, like
Sidney's 'secret kind of music', lies in a carefully contrived rhythmic motion. Tyard does not advocate strict quantitative verse in accordance with
Latin rules, nor does he find it necessary to abolish rhyme; but he surely
anticipates the insistence of the quantitative experimenters, both French
and English, on the quality of measurement:

> in imitation of the ancients (since their spondees, trochees, military
> measures, orthees, and so on, are far removed from common usage and
> known only to a few) our songs should employ certain prescribed line
> lengths (following or mingled with the rhymes and the melodic mode) in ac-
> cordance with the nature of the subject treated by the poet. The latter,
> observing in his verses double or triple proportions, as well as those
> diminished by halves or by thirds, and, in addition, insuring that these pro-
> portions line up properly with the consonances, will be a worthy poet-
> musician and will bear witness to the fact that harmony and rhyme prac-
> tically share the same essential being, and that without the marriage of the
> two, both poet and musician will continue to enjoy less of the grace they
> seek to acquire.[20]

Though Tyard is writing here, as usual, of sung poetry, he does suggest
that different rhythmic patterns in themselves have affective powers that
correspond to those of the various modes. This idea approaches what
Sidney says of quantitative measures (even though Tyard's discussion is
hardly confined to these). When Tyard speaks in this passage of rhyme,
he means not only rhyme-scheme or rhymed poetry, but any poetry with
a determinate and carefully measured rhythmic pattern.[21] Such poetry,
he tells us, is almost the same thing as harmony.

If we are to get closer than this last statement of Tyard's to Sidney's
notion of musical recitation, we must consult a detailed treatise on
rhythmics. We can find one included in the massive *Harmonie Universelle*
(1636) of Marin Mersenne. Mersenne was born two years after Sidney
died and wrote his works on musical theory after the last of the original
academicians had been laid to rest. But in his youth he knew various per-
sonalities in Baïf's circle and was particularly good friends with the com-
poser Jacques Mauduit. He wrote a great deal about the *Académie* and is
an invaluable source about the group's activities and aims.[22] His account
of rhythmics (in which one finds Baïf mentioned often) thus bears directly

on the issue of measuring verse and on why such measurement was so important to the poetic reformers of the late sixteenth century.

Mersenne attempts a much fuller account than Tyard of the metric ethea: he actually recommends specific metres to go with the various modes.[23] Thus, if one wants to induce a sense of peace and tranquillity, one employs the Dorian mode with a spondaic measure. By contrast, a sense of turbulence can be evoked by the Phrygian mode in conjunction with an iambic or trochaic measure—one in which the downbeat (*thesis*) lasts twice as long as the upbeat (*arsis*). But, oddly enough, Mersenne cannot, in the end, be much more specific or illuminating than Sidney or Tyard on this subject. He complains that it is difficult to match every metric foot with its appropriate passion because poets have been inconsistent in their practice: they have used every available verse form in an apparently indiscriminate way to evoke every conceivable emotional effect.[24] Faced with this insurmountable problem, Mersenne throws up his hands:

> If anyone thinks himself sufficiently perspicacious in the study of antiquity to offer some decisive solutions to these problems without running into the dangers I have cited, he will oblige the public by sharing them, and, particularly, those who enjoy poetry and harmony.[25]

Given Mersenne's failure, we too must despair of showing precisely how a quantitative poem by Baïf, Sidney, or anyone else embodies the concept of metrical ethos. I do not think that Sidney himself could have done so. Mersenne draws the limits of discourse for us. All we can really talk about is the general significance of associating the metrical ethea with quantitative verse.

We can approach this last issue through a related discussion by Mersenne of what he calls the accents of passion.[26] He defines the term in the rubric to proposition xi of Book VI:

> Accent, our topic here, is an inflexion or modification of the voice, generally, or of the speaking voice, through which we express the passions and emotions, either naturally or by means of artifice.

To aid the artist who wishes to imitate nature, Mersenne actually attempts, in propositions xii—xiv, to calculate the pitch and speed of the speaking voice at various levels of emotional intensity, basing his estimates on the way the pulse-rate fluctuates as the three basic passions (which he identifies as love, anger, and sadness) ebb and flow and combine in all sorts of permutations and combinations.

In the face of this drive to quantify and categorise, it is a little odd, and therefore noteworthy, that Mersenne makes no effort to distinguish clearly between the singing and the speaking voices. He entitles his discourse 'Of Accentual Music' and gives detailed advice to musicians on how to apply the facts about proportional pulse-rates to their art.[27] Then he offers similar advice to preachers and other orators, so his focus has obviously turned from singing to speaking. But his first recommendation to the would-be orator is to test his vocal range to see whether or not he can produce all the intervals contained in the diapason, or octave, so that they can be clearly heard and distinguished.[28] Here 'accentual music' seems almost to include a kind of proto-*Sprechgesang* as well as proper singing. Mersenne says as much himself:

> the octave is divided into five tones and two semi-tones when we sing diatonically; but each semi-tone is subdivided further by the speaking voice into an infinity of tiny intervals, which are often imperceptible. And each division can change the accent.[29]

The distinction (or, perhaps, conflation) Mersenne makes here is enunciated more starkly by the important Italian musical humanist, Gioseffo Zarlino, whose works, judging from the way he is mentioned in the *Harmonie Universelle*, Mersenne knew well and admired. Zarlino divides recitation into two categories: *continuous* and *intervallic*. The latter is really singing because the voice leaps from pitch to pitch, thereby producing discrete intervals. In the former, the voice slides between pitches. But both kinds of recitation are species of 'accentual music'.[30] Indeed, in his last treatise on music, Zarlino returns to this subject and analyses lines of Virgil and Horace and even extracts from orations by Cicero in terms of the intervals traversed by the 'continuous voice' in reciting them. On the basis of this analysis, he classifies the passages according to musical mode (Dorian, Phrygian, etc.) as well as species of tetrachord (diatonic, chromatic, enharmonic).[31] With this passage in mind, Mersenne's advice to preachers hardly seems very radical. When a Renaissance theorist treats accent and rhythm, words like 'music', 'mode', 'diapason', and the like simultaneously have a literal meaning applied to singing and a more or less figurative one applied to speech. In its broadest sense, Mersenne's phrase 'accentual music' describes an abstraction—the shape or form of any utterance of whatever kind. In fact, Mersenne goes so far as to suggest that every language is defined by its own 'accentual music', or form, by which it can be identified (at least theoretically) even in the absence of any actual words or characteristic idiomatic expressions.[32]

The idea of accent as form approaches the concept of rhythm as we meet it in the oft-repeated distinction between rhythm and metre. For the Renaissance, the *locus classicus* is Quintilian:

though both rhythm and metre consist of feet, they differ in more than one respect. For in the first place rhythm consists of certain lengths of time, while metre is determined by the order in which these lengths are arranged. Consequently the one seems to be concerned with quantity and the other with quality ... [Rhythm employs various feet like *dactyls, paeans, iambs*, etc.] ... these same feet are also employed by metre, but with this difference, that in rhythm it does not matter whether the two shorts of the *dactyl* precede or follow the long; for rhythm merely takes into account the measurement of the time, that is to say, it insists on the time taken from [the voice's] rise to its fall being the same.[33]

In this formulation, rhythmic feet are little more than ratios established by dividing a given unit of time and comparing the parts; the order of long and short syllables is immaterial. Such feet are like patterns or blueprints for metric feet. If we were to take Quintilian a step further, we might say that rhythmic feet define the form of motion that may then be incarnated in a given metre. This step is actually taken by St. Augustine in his *De musica*, a treatise cited often by Renaissance theorists of music and oratory. For Augustine, the traditional classical feet eventually become nothing but a convenient means for talking about the ratios that define measured motion of any kind—from poetic to cosmic.[34] Mersenne closes his discussions of rhythm with a detailed summary of Augustine's *De musica*, evidently considering that treatise an apt retrospective on the whole subject.[35] And his opening remarks, defining the scope and significance of the study of rhythm, are surely also to be understood in an Augustinian light:

> The art of rhythm encompasses the study of number as it applies to the objects of sight, sound, and touch; for the inquiring mind that considers intellectual numbers in their purity, descends to the matter that accompanies them and renders them perceptible, in order to raise itself, somehow, to an intellectual and rational plain and disengage itself from change, mutability, and corruption.[36]

It is a long way, perhaps, from Mersenne's *o altitudo* to the nuts and bolts of Sidney's quantitative verse experiments; no one, I am sure, would want to argue that Sidney was constantly trying to disengage his mind from it pre-occupation with the mutable world as he wrote them. The passages from Mersenne and Tyard simply illustrate something of the nexus of ideas that certain Renaissance intellectuals (aptly chosen with regard to Sidney) could have generated starting with the notion that measured poetry somehow contains 'a kind of secret music'. The advantage of writing quantitative verse, it would seem, is simply that it insures measurement. As the Venerable Bede, following St. Augustine, had long ago stated in a passage well-known in the Renaissance: 'Rhythm can exist without metre, but metre cannot exist without rhythm'.[37] Judging from the rhetoric of most Elizabethan poetic reformers, rhymed poetry, which falls into the category of rhythm without metre, was all too often only a travesty of what rhythm could and should be. It was not the art of which Mersenne speaks, but, rather, the doggerel huddled up by ignorant ale-house fiddlers who counted up to fourteen and looked for a rhyme-word. Given this outlook, much effort went into finding some way of using rhyme-scheme as a measuring device that would be more sophisticated than the mere counting of syllables and would thereby confer a new respectability on non-quantitative verse.[38] Sidney not only experimented with this last technique, employing a vast array of complex stanzaic forms, but also wrote rhymed poems to pre-existing tunes so that they would embody the measure of the music.[39] He practised both techniques in his psalm translations.

Bede is illuminating with reference to another point that, in moving to the psalms, we must touch on. Though rhythm in its Augustinian sense was a lofty concept, purely rhythmic poetry had also long been associated with lack of learning. Bede, who bases his account on Augustine's *De musica*, yet holds with this view. But an unlearned rhythmic poem with no metre need not be the kind of thing the Elizabethans complained about; it could yet have order and beauty and measure. Bede quotes two hymns, one Ambrosian and one Prudentian, to prove the point. Indeed, in quoting these hymns, Bede rather suggests that they are inspired in a way that learned metrical verse is not. There is something that we might call 'original' about them.[40]

The concept of 'original poetry' was popular in the Renaissance. Everyone is familiar with the orisons of Milton's Adam and Eve, delivered in Prose or numerous Verse

> More tuneable then needed Lute or Harp
> To add more sweetness.[41]

Here is a more formal statement of the idea by the important Italian critic, Antonio Sebastiano Minturno:

> No sooner were men born, then they wanted to imitate the way of those who live in heaven, either because they could better perceive the divine ordering of nature (their heavenly origin being fresh and new), or (as Plato thought) because they still remembered their other life, which was celestial. We can surmise that they elected to honour God in no other way than with music and poetry ... singing words according to a fixed musical law of linked and regimented feet.[42]

The context here suggests that Minturno is speaking of rhythmic rather than metric feet. Exactly who his first spontaneous rhythmists were, however, remains something of a mystery. But since Minturno's statements are drawn from a set of commonplace ideas that recur in varying combinations, the answer can easily be found by consulting another theorist whose emphasis is slightly different. One particularly close to Sidney in time and provenance is Richard Willes, whose *De re poetica* (1573) is the first apology for poetry to be printed in England. Willes makes all the expected points about the divine origin of the rhythmic faculty and then, following Eusebius, tells us directly who the first poets were:

> Certainly the practice of poetry, you may have it on good authority (if you are content with Eusebius' authority), first existed and flourished among the earliest Hebrews, who were poets long before the Greeks.[43]

The Greek poets mentioned by Willes—and later the Romans—were commonly held to have corrupted the inheritance they had received. As Sidney put it in the *Defence*, going over the same old territory:

> The chief [poets] both in antiquity and excellency, were they that did imitate the unconceivable excellencies of God. Such were David in his Psalms; Solomon in his Song of Songs, in his Ecclesiastes, and Proverbs; Moses and Deborah in their Hymns; and the writer of Job: which, beside other, the learned Emanuel Tremellius and Franciscus Junius do entitle the poetical part of the Scripture. Against these none will speak that hath the Holy Ghost in due holy reverence. (In this kind, though in a full wrong divinity, were Orpheus, Amphion, Homer in his Hymns, and many other, both Greeks and Romans). And this poesy must be used by whosoever will follow St. James's counsel in singing psalms when they are merry, and I know is used with the fruit of comfort by some, when, in sorrowful pangs of their death-bringing sins, they find the consolation of the never-leaving goodness.[44]

This passage suggests something of the personal and cultural value that Sidney might well have attached to the project of translating the psalms. For one thing, psalm translation into measured English verse provided a more effective means than the quantitative poems of recapturing the rhythms of those who imitated Godhead directly and worshipped with a right divinity. Sidney could thus attune himself and his language more closely to the wisdom of the ancients. He could achieve, in the broadest theoretical sense, the perfect union of music and poetry.

## ii. *'A Heavenly Poesy'*

A good transition between the idea of rhythm in classical verse and the idea of Hebrew poetry is provided by a passage in the *Sopplimenti Musicali* (1588) of Gioseffo Zarlino, one of the so-called musical humanists already mentioned in relation to Mersenne. Zarlino was *maestro di capella* at St. Mark's in Venice when Sidney visited that city toward the end of 1573, but there is no evidence that Sidney met him or knew of him. And

in any event, the passage in question postdates Sidney's death. I include
it because it shows very explicitly some of the areas of discourse an informed intelligence of the late sixteenth century might have considered
to go together and bear powerfully on each other.

   Zarlino's discussion concerns accentuation in the broad sense of pronunciation or recitation. This last is, not surprisingly, a branch of
*melopoiea*, or the union of words and music. So far, we are on familiar
ground, a fact underscored by Zarlino's referring to *melopoiea* as the 'dark
and secret power of pronunciation', a phrase that recalls Tyard's 'secret
and wonderful power' and Sidney's 'secret music'.[45] As usual, this
elusive power encompasses both actual singing and also unsung recitation informed by the idea of music. What sets Zarlino apart from the
others here is his attempt to project the idea of the union of music and
poetry against a background of Rabbinic lore. He distinguishes three
kinds of recitation, or accent: the grammatical, the rhetorical, and the
musical.[46]

> They [the Hebrews] call the grammatical accent *Taham*, that is, taste',
> because the utterance of every word seeks after it, and by its means the
> voice resounds more pre-eminently. They call the rhetorical accent *Metheg*,
> that is 'obstacle' or 'net' or 'bridle', because by its means they achieve an
> ornamented pronunciation of a text. But the musical accent they call
> *Neginah*, that is, 'harmony', since by its means they are enabled to pro-
> nounce words with a measured motion.[47]

The combination of the three accents in any language—Hebrew, Latin,
or one of the vulgar tongues—would consist of that language's
characteristic deployment of syllabic emphasis (grammatical accent) or-
namented and enhanced in accordance with the emotional content of
whatever is being said (rhetorical accent) and fitted into some scheme of
measurement (musical accent).[48] Zarlino finds this system quite as applicable to Latin as it is to Hebrew:

> In order to shed some light on what has been said for our musicians, we
> shall choose from our Latin tongue these words of the most eminent Virgil:
>     Mānēt āltā měntě rěpōstūm iūdǐcǐūm Pǎrǐdīs.
> Here the grammatical accent doubtless falls where the wording of this
> member or period requires. But the musical accent dominates only in the
> words *alta* and *Paridis*, and in their first syllables, so that the verse will re-
> sound as follows:
>     Mànet álta mènte repòstum iudicium Páridis.
> The accentuation, then, consists first of a grave accent on the word *Mànet*,
> which the Hebrews would have called its 'minister', likening it to those who
> go before the Prince in pompous display and are followed after by his
> Gentlemen. In a sense, the word *Alta* has two ministers: the one, truly
> called minister, preceding in the word *Mànet*; and the other following in the
> word *Mènte*.[49]

Zarlino claims implicitly here that the grammatical and musical accents, expressed in terms of the Hebrew system of kings and ministers, can be found in the Latin poetry known to every schoolboy and can also profit the practising musician who wishes to set a text. Locating the accents in a familiar Latin poem like *The Aeneid*, or composing a vernacular poem with the accents in mind, or being aware of them while setting a poem to music would all be ways of getting back in touch with one's original and God-given cultural inheritance. After all, the system of Hebrew accentuation (the so-called *te'amim*), of which Zarlino's three accents are the constituent parts, is the key to understanding God's word, for it influenced the grammatical meaning as well as determining the inflectional emphases of scripture. The ancient rabbis had encoded instructions for the proper accentuation of the Bible (called *Masorah* or 'tradition') in cryptic 'masoretic' notes.[50] One of the most important interpreters of these notes, and hence of the literal meaning of the scriptural text, was the Jewish grammarian Elijah Levita (1469-1549), whose definitive *Massoreth Ha-Massoreth* appeared in Venice in 1538.[51] It was immediately made available to Christian scholars by the great cartographer and Hebraist, Sebastian Münster, who published it at Basle with a facing Latin translation in 1539. According to one of his early biographers, Zarlino had actually studied Hebrew with a nephew of Levita.[52] In any event, he knew of the *Massoreth Ha-Massoreth*, for he cites it and quotes from its introduction in his chapter on the three accents. Zarlino can thus move freely from Levita and the *te'amim* to Virgil to *melopoeia* to the modern poet and musician. All are encompassed by the subject of rhythm, or the dark and secret power of pronunciation.

The practical implications of what Zarlino says for the translator of psalms, or any other 'poetical' part of the Bible, would be to employ rhythmic vernacular poetry rather than quantitative verse. It seems rather odd, then, that Zarlino quotes approvingly from St. Jerome's introduction to the book of Job, in which St. Jerome contends that Biblical poetry is quantitative:

> the verses are Hexameters, running in dactyls and spondees, but according to the language and idiom, frequently receiving other feet, not of the same syllabic structure, but of the same durations (*eorundem temporum*). Occasionally the rhythm itself, sweet and ringing, is borne by measurements (*numeris*) free from feet, which those educated in metre will understand better than the ordinary reader.[53]

This passage of Jerome's, and another of the same sort that he wrote on the psalms, carry the weight of patristic authority. One is likely to find one or both of them, sometimes cited accurately and sometimes butchered, whenever the subject of Hebrew poetics comes up. Willes, for example, in the continuation of the passage quoted above, paraphrases from both and even repeats a dictum of Josephus (one of Jerome's sources) to the effect that Moses's song in *Exodus*, 15 is composed in hexameters. Similar instances can be found in the preface to Barnaby Googe's *Eclogues, Epytaphes, and Sonetes* (1563), or in Thomas Lodge's *Defense of Poetry* (1579).[54] In all these cases, Jerome's words are cited uncritically as proof that Biblical poetry was metrically comparable to that written by the ancient Greeks and Romans.

But such uncritical thinking was not possible for those in closer touch with Hebraic scholarship. Few in the Renaissance were willing simply to dispose of Jerome, but among Christian Hebraists, his dicta were subject to continual re-evaluation. The extract given by Zarlino, for instance, is not as odd in context as might at first appear. It could easily support the notion that Jerome is really talking about rhythm rather than metre: he surely admits rhythmic feet, as Quintilian had defined them, into the discussion. And the idea that the Hebrew rhythms were occasionally free from feet altogether[55] could be made to square with the notion that something other than quantity, like the musical accent, for instance, gave Hebrew verse its standard of measurement. But neither Zarlino nor anyone else can tell us precisely how Hebrew poetry is to be scanned. The point here is that there is no definitive statement to substitute for Jerome's once his meaning has been called into question.

In this context of uncertainty, we may profitably view Sidney's brief remarks on the subject:

> And may not I presume a little further, to show the reasonableness of this word *vates*, and say that the holy David's Psalms are a divine poem? If I do, I shall not do it without the testimony of great learned men, both ancient and modern. But even the name of Psalms will speak for me, which being interpreted, is nothing but songs; then that it is fully written in metre, as all learned hebricians agree, although the rules be not yet fully found.[56]

Sidney's use of 'metre' here could be a distant echo of Jerome's time-honored quantitative theory, or it could simply mean, loosely speaking, that the psalms are written in verse rather than in prose. The important point, though, is that 'the rules be not yet fully found'. Perhaps that statement is not in itself terribly revealing; Sidney was not, after all, a Hebraist. What is remarkable, though, is that he was in touch with the most up-to-date and informed scholarly opinion on Biblical versification: he does not hold the uncritical attitude of men like Willes, Lodge, or Googe.[57] Who, then, were some of the 'learned hebricians' who might have been responsible for Sidney's uncertainty?

The two who must head the list are undoubtedly Emanuel Tremellius and Franciscus Junius, for Sidney mentions them in the passage quoted above on the most ancient and excellent Biblical poets. On the title page to Part III of their Latin Old Testament (1575-79, many subsequent edn.), translated out of the Hebrew and copiously annotated, Tremellius and Junius distinguish five books as 'poetical': Job, Psalms, Proverbs, Ecclesiastes, and the Song of Songs. Sidney mentions the same five books, but he evidently saw more than just the title page, for he also lists two smaller poems (the Songs of Moses and Deborah) that are not in any of the five books, and that Tremellius and Junius designate (with a few others) only in their preface to Part III.[58] Here is the relevant passage (the translators are defining the word 'psalm'):

> We ordinarily call all those books 'psalms' that are rhythmical and not written in the language of prose, as are the rest (though interspersed even in these, there stand out certain quite exquisite canticles by Moses, Deborah, David, Isaiah, Hezekiah, Jeremiah, and Habbakuk) but are rather, regimented according to number (*numeris adstricti*) for the convenience of memory and of singing.[59]

Remarks as brief as this offer no opportunity for advancing an elaborate theory of versification. But the vocabulary here strongly suggests that Tremellius and Junius considered the form of the poetic sections of the Bible to be rhythm without metre. At the very least, they leave the issue open and are unwilling to opt for a specifically quantitative system.[60]

The annotations on the individual psalms offer no further clues about the details of poetic form. There are, however, some rather elaborate and interesting glosses to the psalm inscriptions, especially those concerning music. They contain much more information than the analogues Sidney would have seen in the *Geneva Bible*. Occasionally, they even relate the psalms to the concerns of the musical humanists discussed above. The inscription to *Psalm* 6 provides a case in point:

> To the master of harmonious strings, with low sonority,
>     a psalm of David.[61]

*Geneva* reads:

> *To him that excelleth on Negin'oth upon the eight tune. A Psalm of David.*

The 'eight tune' here is no more informative a phrase than St. Jerome's '*pro octava*' in the Vulgate. Junius and Tremellius say much more. They refer us to another of their notes, that on *I Chronicles* 15.21, where the term 'low sonority' had previously occurred. (For this passage too, the gloss in *Geneva* simply mentions the eighth tone.) Here is what Tremellius and Junius have to say:

> this [grave sonority] is what ordinary musicians call bass and tenor, or what the ancients call *hypaton* and *meson*, or sounds of low and middle range. It

is approximately that species of song in its harmony that was placed with the third genus of music.[62]

On the face of it, this passage might strike one as longer but no more meaningful than 'the eight tune', though it is certainly more interesting if only because it sounds like something out of a musical humanist's treatise. *Hypaton* and *meson* are pitches on the ancient Greek scale (the Greater Perfect System). *Meson* is the middle 'note', which also happens to be the eighth tone. The characterisation of the harmonic species as the 'third genus of music' is less clear. It could mean that the melodic structure of the psalm is chromatic,[63] though it could likewise refer to the third, or Lydian, mode.[64] In either case, the melodic type would be traditionally associated with a wanton and lascivious mood and also with grief and lamentation. Since the music being described is that for the first of the penitential psalms, often seen in the Renaissance as the record of David's penance for having caused the death of Bathsheba's husband, either the Lydian mode or the chromatic genus would be most appropriate.

One cannot, of course, prove that Sidney thought any of these things, or even that he pored over Tremellius' and Junius' annotations. But we can at least be sure that their concerns were important to him. Junius himself seemed to think so, at any rate, for in 1580, he dedicated his *Grammatica Hebraeae Linguae* to Sidney. In the dedicatory epistle, he testifies to the considerable scholarly interest in Hebrew he finds among Englishmen and mentions a service Sidney had performed for him. J. A. van Dorsten has found evidence to suggest that Sidney may well have met Junius at Heidelberg in 1577, when he was working on the Bible with Tremellius.[65] At the time, Part III (containing the poetical books) was quite likely available in some form in which it could have been presented to Sidney, in the capacity of English Protestant ambassador, as a religious and political gesture. Sidney's service would then have been to present what was considered to be the Protestant League Bible to his countrymen. In this connection, there is an appropriate passage in the introductory encomium to the psalms, praising the power of their music to allay devisive passions and produce an integrated and virtuous order:

> [the book of psalms] masters ... the passions that dominate the minds of men in this life, by conducting the mind, as it were, musically and with a delight that brings back and rules our virtuous thoughts.[66]

Perhaps Sidney was thinking of this musical power when he wrote (in the *Defence*) of the Psalmist's ability to mediate between earthly and divine passion. The psalms are a kind of heavenly poesy, wherein almost he showeth himself a passionate lover of that unspeakable and everlasting beauty to be seen by the eyes of the mind, only cleared by faith.[67]

The theme of integration here minimizes the importance of the fact that Sidney speaks in terms of sight rather than sound. Whatever he may have read of Tremellius' and Junius' introductions and annotations would doubtless have supported his notion that the psalms are 'nothing but songs', and may well have confirmed him in his decision to base a good number of the stanzaic forms in his translations (nineteen out of forty-three) on pre-existing pieces of music, specifically, the tunes in the French Huguenot Psalter.

The French Psalter calls to mind other 'learned hebricians' with whose views Sidney may have been familiar. Late in 1573, at Venice, he met the Huguenot François Perrot de Mésières, then working on a translation of the psalms into Italian.[68] Like Sidney, Perrot held the French Psalter in high esteem; he based all, not just some, of his psalm stanzas on the French tunes. Unlike Sidney, Perrot had studied Hebrew. If he had any exact knowledge of current views on Biblical versification that he might have imparted to Sidney, they would most likely tally with those of the French translators, Clément Marot and Theodore Beza. Sidney was later to know Beza's views directly. Seven years after the meeting with Perrot, Beza brought out his *Psalmorum Davidis et Aliorum Prophetarum Libri Quinque, Augmentis & Latina paraphrasi illustrati*, dedicated to Henry, Earl of Huntington, and published in London. For each psalm, Beza supplies an argument, a translation, a paraphrase, and a version in some quantitative metre. But Beza was more of a skeptic than a believer in the quantitative theory. In the preface, he tells us that his metrical Latin exercises are the product of continued meditation on the psalms and are intended to complement his French rhythmic versions (*Gallaci rithmi*) in the psalter. He cites as one of his chief models the Hebraist Henricus Mollerus, who held that our lack of knowledge about Hebrew music was connected to our ignorance about the system of Hebrew poetry.[69] Thus, when Beza says that he has omitted the musical inscriptions from his paraphrases because their practical applications 'are to us thus far unknown', he is also admitting that he is unsure about the particulars of Hebrew versification.

Unlike Beza, Marot produced no scholarship on Hebraic subjects, but he studied with the renowned Franciscus Vatablus (c. 1490-1547), the first to occupy the regius chair of Hebrew at the Collège de France.[70] According to his student and successor in the chair, Joannus Mercerus, Vatablus had laid it down that Hebrew syllabic quantities could not be influenced by position and that the Schewa (a sign denoting a non-vocalic

consonant that is sometimes silent and sometimes to by articulated with
the neutral sound of ə) counted for nothing.[71] In the first part of the
seventeenth century, Franciscus Gomarus was to use these rules to support an elaborate array of quantitative scansions of Biblical poems.[72] But
Mercerus, writing in 1551, was unable to extrapolate a poetic system
from Vatablus' rules. Like Sidney later on, he feels that there *is* a system,
but that it has not yet been discovered. The most one can deduce from
the Vatablus connection, then, is that it may have suggested a non-
dogmatic quantitative approach to Biblical poetry that could be set over
against the more purely rhythmic idea contained in the Tremellius—
Junius commentary.

We must not, of course, assume for a moment that Tremellius and
Junius were in any way opposed to Vatablus and Mercerus. They were
all part of a European community of Hebraic scholars. One of Vatablus'
most prominent pupils, for instance, was Antonius Cevallerus, or Antoine Chevalier (1523-72), who was also the son-in-law of Tremellius.
In the early 1550s Cevallerus stayed with Tremellius at Cambridge and
lectured unofficially there. Tremellius himself had been invited by
Cranmer to lecture in place of the official regius professor, Thomas
Wakefield, who, presumably, had troubles because of his refusal to con-
vert to Protestantism. In 1568, Cevallerus was back in England after
holding a post at Strassbourg during the reign of Queen Mary. He lectured at St. Paul's Cathedral and then, in 1569, became the new regius
professor at Cambridge.[73] One presumes that he brought the teachings
of Vatablus to England, but also that he learned from Tremellius. He left
no writings on Hebrew versification. We have his commentaries on the
prophets and a few basic text books. Among these (aside from his
*Rudimenta hebraicae linguae'*, Geneva, 1567), there survives a quite elemen-
tary treatise on the Hebrew alphabet, vowel pointings, and system of
scriptural accentuation culled, as the title page informs us, from the
researches of Antonius Cevallerus. It was printed at Geneva in 1566 by
Sidney's friend Henricus Stephanus.[74] The contents, all commonplace
enough to be grasped by the interested amateur as well as by the professional Hebraist, could support either a quantitative or a rhythmic interpretation of Hebrew poetry. The vocalic sounds are classified according
to their tenseness or laxness as long, short, or very short (*raptae*).[75] On
the other hand, the book supplies a table of the various classes of
accent—the kings and ministers to which Zarlino alludes—and also gives
brief mention to two kinds of rhetorical accent—the already familiar
*Metheg*, a retension or bridling of the breath similar to a glottal stop, and
*Makkáph*, presumably analogous to elision in Latin. The chief importance
of Cevallerus' little book for this study is that it is concerned entirely with

the pronunciation of scriptural language. While it offers no solution to the problem of form in Biblical poetry and, in fact, is just as applicable to prose, it underscores the centrality of recitation as an idea. It takes us back to Zarlino's concept of *Melopoeia* or Mersenne's discourse on the accents of passion or Sidney's secret music.

One could go on expanding the network of Hebraists whose views may have figured in discussions Sidney had with Perrot or who were known to other learned men he met on his travels or whose commentaries appeared in various well-known polyglot Bibles of the period. The point is not that Sidney, who knew no Hebrew, had read and assimilated the works of any professional Hebraist, but rather, that he moved in circles where men like Vatablus, Mercerus, Cevallerus, and others were discussed. Indeed, his *direct* sources for the psalm translations have long been known, and need not be described here. To those usually mentioned,[76] I should like to add the Latin translation of the psalms from Sebastian Münster's *Old Testament* (1534-35), because this psalter was appended to the Latin *Book of Common Prayer* commissioned by Queen Elizabeth in 1560 for use in college chapels at Oxford and Cambridge.[77] Münster, we recall, had made the work of Elijah Levita on the masoretic notes available to western Christendom. His reputation as a Hebraist was strong in England. In fact, Archbishop Parker had recommended his *Old Testament*, together with that of Sanctes Pagninus, to the translators of the Bishops' Bible.[78] To an extent, Münster also influenced Coverdale's work on the Great Bible, and hence lies behind the traditional English Psalter.[79] But the Bishops and Coverdale had followed Münster's text inaccurately and inconsistently. Consulting the original Latin was still an important step for anyone interested in reproducing the Hebrew meaning accurately.[80]

The problem of applying what we know of either the theory of rhythm or the climate of Hebrew scholarship to the specific criticism of Sidney's collection of psalms is, of course, immense. What, for instance, was the rationale—or was there a rationale—for each choice of stanzaic form? One can only speculate. The nineteen stanzas based on tunes from the French psalter are doubtless meant to be informed by a musical moment or factor. Interestingly enough, though, some of them cannot be sung to their tune: Psalm 1, for example, contains an extra half-stanza that would cause it to end at a musically inappropriate medial cadence.[81] It appears that Sidney was interested more in appropriating the measure of the music than in the music itself. Matching his syllables to the notes of the French tunes, that is, was one way of insuring that non-quantitative poems could yet embody 'a kind of secret music'.[82]

The form of Psalm 6, the first of the penitentials, provides a more ob-

viously interesting opportunity for prosodic commentary. I quote the last
three stanzas:

> Woe, lyke a moth, my face's beauty eates
> And age pull'd on with paines all freshness fretteth:
> The while a swarm of foes with vexing feates
>     My life besetteth.
> Get hence you ev'ill, who in my ev'ill rejoyce,
> In all whose workes vainess is ever raigning:
> For God hath heard the weeping sobbing voice
>     Of my complaining.
> The lord my suite did heare, and gently heare,
> They shall be sham'd and vext, that breed my crying,
> And turn their backs, and strait on backs appeare
>     Their shamefull flying.

Sidney's form here is the accentual sapphic. The only other poem in
which he used this stanza is OA 59, in which Basilius, thinking incorrectly that he is on his way to meet Cleophila, celebrates the prospect of sinful
lovemaking. Like the psalmist, he bids his complaint adieu:

> Get hence foule Griefe, the canker of the minde:
> Farewell Complaint, the miser's only pleasure:
> Away vayne Cares, by which fewe men do finde
>     Their sought-for treasure.

In form and in diction, then, Psalm 6 resembles the sapphic love song
in the 'old' *Arcadia*. It also recalls the proto-madrigalian verse of CS 3 and
CS 4 in feminine rhymes like raigning/complaining and crying/flying.
The Psalm is a sort of formal lover's complaint, a point Sidney enforces
by departing from the words of the Psalter and the Geneva Bible (both
of which read 'weeping' rather than 'complaining') and following Sternhold and Hopkins, who are seconded here by the far more respectable
Marot. Or, perhaps Sidney thought of Wyatt, who also used 'complaint'.
Wyatt had emphasized that this and the other penitential psalms recorded
David's penance for the sins he had committed in promoting his love for
Bathsheba. Sidney's casting the psalm as a courtly complaint recalls this
interpretation. The sapphic form with the madrigalian rhyming becomes
a rhythmic analogue for the chromatic music (or, perhaps, the Lydian
mode) with which Tremellius and Junius seem to associate the psalm.
But unlike Basilius' song, the Psalmist's complaint is an antidote to sinful
love: the love song becomes a song of reconciliation with God. It is worth
noting, in this connection, that Sidney's friend Du Plessis
Mornay, in his treatise on *The Trewnesse of the Christian Religion*, had related
the separation of love songs from sacred songs to the general fragmenta-
tion that occurred at the Fall.[83] Sidney, who began a translation of Mornay's work, was likely to know the passage well. In its light, Psalm 6 can

be seen (in terms of its formal counterpart, OA 59) as an attempt to re-integrate the poet of love with the divine and with the philosopher. The process of re-integration accompanies the transformation of the vain lover of God's creature into the 'passionate lover of that unspeakable and everlasting beauty to be seen by the eye of the mind, only cleared by faith'.

With this idea of re-integration, we have made our circle just, for we are face to face once more with the truth of the Sidney legend, a truth that enhances and transcends the actual facts. Appropriately enough, one scholar has suggested that Psalm 6 may have been the 'song' that Greville reports Sidney called for on his death bed and named *La Cuisse rompue.*[84] Whether or not this is literally true, Sidney's (or perhaps Greville's) brilliant rhetorical gesture certainly enforces what we have said of the psalm. It calls attention to the thigh wound, thereby invoking a long and venerable tradition of Biblical exegesis that associates such wounds, the first of which was received by Jacob when he wrestled with the angel at Peniel (Genesis 32:24-32), with a paradoxical 'good eunuchry': one 'cuts off' the vain pleasures of the flesh in order to be fruitful in multiplying spiritual goods.[85] How appropriate that this re-dedication of one's vital energies should find poetic expression in a penitential psalm. And how fitting that a psalm should mark the point where a man about to die chooses to view literal facts of his life (his broken thigh, for instance) in terms that rescue them from vanity by revealing their final meaning.

Posterity, certainly, has done little to rescue Sidney's experimental verse: of the quantitative poems, only the echo poem, OA 31, was anthologized, and that did not happen until 1638.[86] As a quantitative poet, Sidney was simply the model and mentor for other quantitative poets. The psalms have fared slightly better as estimable poems, but even they are frequently passed by as 'not particularly promising'.[87] As a psalmist, Sidney's influence was minimized by the fact that the translations were not printed until 1823. To be sure, certain important poets knew the psalms in manuscript and appreciated their merit and their potential significance to the nation. John Donne, for one, wrote a poem in which he expressed the hope that they would come out of private chambers and inspire men to improve the forms of public worship:

> I must not rejoice as I would doe
> When I behold that these Psalms are become
> So well attyr'd abroad, so ill at home,
> So well in Chambers, in thy Church so ill,
> As I can scarce call that reform'd untill
> This be reform'd; Would a whole state present
> A lesser gift than some one man hath sent?[88]

Even if that one man's gift remained little known, his effort in making it has more national significance than Donne, perhaps, suspected in the early years of the seventeenth century. With hindsight, the psalms—and the quantitative poems, too—can be properly assessed against a background of European scholarship concerning the relationship of words to music and the nature of Biblical poetry. That scholarship, though often concerned with minutiae, yet had profound spiritual and political ends: it sought unity and integration by finding out the origins of things. Sidney's experimental verse is an exercise in reverse *translatio studii*. The musical humanistic theories that guided the writing of quantitative poetry find their logical fulfillment in psalm translation. And if Sidney's psalms had little direct impact on English poetry, they can yet be seen as symptomatic of the kind of scholarship and scholarly attitudes that would result, a short time later, in the King James Bible.

## NOTES

1  *The Manner of Sir Philip Sidney's Death* in *MP*, 171. Gifford's authorship is by no means certain: see the introduction by Duncan-Jones, 161-65.
2  For a discussion of this convention, see the article by John Gouws in this volume.
3  I am accepting Ringler's suggestion (see discussion in *Poems*, 500-01) that the psalms are late work—perhaps begun not long before Sidney's departure for the Netherlands in 1585. I use Ringler's edition of the poems throughout this essay and employ his abbreviations.
4  *MP*, 88.
5  See, e.g., J. A. van Dorsten, 'The Final Year', in this volume, and Duncan-Jones, 'Philip Sidney's Toys', *Proceedings of the British Academy*, LXVI (1980), 161-78. For further treatment of the complex relationship between man and myth, see, aside from various essays in this volume, Richard Lanham, 'Sidney: The Ornament of his Age', *Southern Review*, II (1967), 319-40; and Richard Helgerson, *The Elizabethan Prodigals*, Berkeley, Calif., 1976, 124-55.
6  *Sir Fulke Greville's Life of Sir Philip Sidney*, ed. Nowell Smith, Oxford, 1907, 16-17 (Sidney rejects *Arcadia*); 11-16 (*Arcadia* defended). Thomas Moffet, *Nobilis, or a View of the Life and Death of Sidney*, ed. and tr. Virgil B. Heltzel and Hoyt H. Hudson, San Marino, Calif., 1940, 41 and 91 (Anacreontics rejected); 11 and 74 (*Arcadia* defended).
7  *Life*, 17.
8  My discussion here is based squarely on that of Derek Attridge, *Well-weighed Syllables: Elizabethan Verse in Classical Metres*, Cambridge, 1974, 173-87. The reader desiring a full and detailed analysis of the various techniques of writing quantitative verse in English should consult Attridge.
9  See Attridge, 180. For a list of the rules Sidney used in composing quantitative poetry (called Drant's rules, after their compiler, Thomas Drant, Archdeacon of Lewes) see *Poems*, 391. These rules are appended to OA 11 in a single MS of the *Arcadia*.
10  It is only fair to point out, however, that Sidney's quantitative verse is considerably less awkward than that of his contemporaries, including Spenser. For a wide sampling, see Attridge, *passim*. See also my essay, 'Spenser's Study of English Syllables and Its Completion by Thomas Campion', *Spenser Studies*, III (1982), ed. P. Cullen and Thomas P. Roche, 7-25.

11 Latin *accentus* translates Greek *prosodia*, which means 'pronunciation', broadly applied, and the melodic, or 'pitch' characteristics of words, more narrowly applied. See W. S. Allen, *Accent and Rhythm: Prosodic Features of Latin and Greek: A Study in Theory and Reconstruction*, Cambridge, 1973, 86. In the Renaissance, the word *accent* carries both of these related meanings.

12 *MP*, 119-20.

13 *Poems*, 389. Ringler prints the passage on 389-90.

14 For a detailed consideration of all these theorists in the light of *musical/poesis speculative*, see my 'Renaissance Prosodic Thought as a Branch of *Musica Speculativa*', diss., Princeton, 1981, chap. 3.

15 See James E. Philips, 'Daniel Rogers: A Neo-Latin Link Between the Pléiade and Sidney's "Areopagus"', in *Neo-Latin Poetry of the Sixteenth and Seventeenth Centuries*, Los Angeles, 1965, 5-28; J. A. van Dorsten, *Poets, Patrons, and Professors: Sir Philip Sidney, Daniel Rogers, and the Leiden Humanists*, Leiden, 1962; and *The Radical Arts: First Decade of an Elizabethan Renaissance*, Leiden, 1970.

16 The so-called *musique mesurée* allowed every long syllable a minim and every short syllable a crotchet. Unlike the hypothetical songs in OA, the French pieces are set for *a capella* choir and not for solo voice with instrumental accompaniment. The part writing is kept severely homophonic so that the quantitative pattern can be heard. For specimens see F. A. Yates, *The French Academies of the Sixteenth Century*, London, 1947, App. VIII.

17 *French Academies*, chaps. 3 and 4.

18 The standard work to consult on the technical aspects of musical humanism is D. P. Walker, 'Musical Humanism in the 16th and Early 17th Centuries', *The Music Review*, II (1941), 1-13, 111-21, 220-27, 288-308; III (1942), 55-71.

19 *Solitaire Second*, ed. Cathy M. Yandell, Geneva, 1980, 214.

20 *Solitaire Second*, 244:
> Je requerrois donq (veu-je dire) qu'à l'image des Anciens (si bien leurs Spondées, Trochées, Embateries, Orthies, et telles autres façons sont loin de l'usage de tous, et de la cognoissance de peu) noz chants ussent quelques manieres ordonnées de longueur de vers, de suite ou entremellement de Rimes et de Mode de chanter, selon le merite de la matiere entreprise par le Poëte, qui observant en ses vers les proportions doubles, triples, d'autant et demi, d'autant et tiers, aussi bien qu'elles sont rencontrées aux consonances, seroit digne Poëte-musicien, et tesmoigneroit que la harmonie et les Rimes sont presque d'une mesme essence, et que sans le mariage de ces deux, le Poëte et le Musicien demeurent moins jouissans de la grace qu'ils cherchent aquerir.

21 There was widespread ambivalence about the word *rhyme* (etymologically linked to *rhythm*) in the Renaissance. On the one hand, it could refer to the large body of vernacular poetry that had supposedly descended from accentual (i.e., stress-based) Medieval Latin poems called *rithmi* (to distinguish them from classical, quantitative verse). On the other hand, *rhyme* meant *Rhythmos*, that is, the measured quality of ancient Greek *mousike* (the perfect blend of word and tone). The word could thus be used disparagingly or reverentially. See Attridge, 94-96.

22 Mersenne deals most squarely with the *Academie* in *Quaestiones Celeberrimae in Genesim*, Paris, 1623, Qu. 57. *Harmonie Universelle* is more complete on the subject of rhythmics.

23 VI, xxvi.

24 Prop. xxvi, 402. Walker, 1941, 296, quotes the entire passage to which I refer and comments that Mersenne's complaint explains the relative silence of other musical humanists on the issue of the metric ethea. If Walker is right about this silence, then Sidney's remarks in the cancelled OA passage reflect an esoteric strain in musical humanistic theory rather than a mere commonplace.

25 VI, xxxii, 424:
> Si quelqu'vn se croid assez clairuoyant dans l'antiquité pour donner des raisons peremptoires de ces difficultez sans recourir au hazard, & à ce que i'ay dit ici,

il obligera la public s'il luy en fait part, & particulierement tous ceux qui se plaisent à la Poësie, ou à l'Harmonie.

26  VI, Part iii (props. ix-xi): *De la Musique Accentuelle*. Rubric to prop. xi:
   *L'accent, dont nous parlons icy, est une inflexion ou modification de la voix, ou de la parole, par laquelle l'on exprime les passions & les affections naturellement, ou par artifice.*

27  VI, xv.

28  xvi, 373.

29  ix, 365:
   l'Octaue se deuise seulement en 5. tons & deux demi-tons, quand on chante diatoniquement, neantmoins chaque demi-ton se subdiuise encore par la parole en vne infinité de petits interualles qui sont souuent insensibles: Et chaque diuision peut changer l'accent.

30  *Le Istitutioni Harmoniche*, Venice, 1573 (1558), 95.

31  *Sopplimenti Musicali*, Venice, 1588, 266-68. Zarlino borrows here from Antonius Lullius, *De Oratione Libri Septem*, Basle, 1558, 406-10. Lullius' work, generally, draws heavily on that of the ancient Greek rhetorician, Hermogenes of Tarsus (fl. 161-180 A.D.).

32  x, p. 366.

33  *Institutio Oratoria*, ed. and tr. H. E. Butler, Camb., Mass. (Loeb Classical Library), 1921, IX.iv.45-48.

34  See Bk. VI for the discussion of cosmic rhythms. Augustine describes the classical feet in Bk. II. There, *arsis* and *thesis* have no perceptible vocal qualities. They are just arithmetical divisions of the foot. See Henri-Irénée Marrou, *Saint Augustine et la Fin de la Culture Antique*, Paris, 1958 (1938), 272.

35  Prop. xxxiii. This comes just before the corollaries to Book VI, the treatise on Rhythm. There is an extra proposition on chromatic and enharmonic *genera* following the corollaries, but this is more of an afterthought than a proper conclusion to Book VI.

36  Intro to Book VI, part iv, 374:
   l'Art Rythmique a son estenduë aussi grande que les nombres appliquez aux objets de la vûe, de l'oüye, & du toucher; de maniere que l'entendement qui considere les nombres intellectuels dans leur pureté, descend à la matiere qui les accompagne, & qui les rend sensibles, afin de l'éleuer en quelque façon à vn estre intellectuel & raisonnant, & de la degager de l'alteration, de la mutabilité, & de la corruption.

37  *De Arte Metrica* in *Patrologia Latina*, ed. Migne, vol. 90, Paris, 1862, col. 173:
   rhythmus sine metro esse potest, metrum vero sine rhythmo esse non potest.

38  See, for example, the second part of George Puttenham's *The Arte of English Poesie* (1589), 'Of Proportion Poetical', in *Elizabethan Critical Essays*, ed. Smith, II, esp. 88-95, 'Of Proportion by Situation'. See also Samuel Daniel, *A Defence of Ryme*, Smith, II, 359-60. Daniel is not specific, as is Puttenham, about technical matters, but, rather, describes rhymed poetry in the language usually applied to rhythm in continental treatises on the subject (words like 'number', 'harmony', 'measure', 'quantity', and 'proportion' abound). Daniel, that is, sees rhyme as a sophisticated measuring device.

39  See e.g., CS 3, 4, 6, 7, 23, 24, 26, 27. Some of these, notably 3 and 4, anticipate a kind of verse that would become very popular in the 1590s with the advent of the Italianate English madrigal. Such verse is characterized by lines of seven and eleven syllables with frequent feminine rhyme. The book that started the vogue was *Musica Transalpina*, an anthology of Italian madrigals with the words translated into English and then fitted to the original music. It was not published until 1588, two years after Sidney's death.

40  *Patrologia Latina*, 90, col. 174. If one is hesitant about this conclusion with regard to *De Arte Metrica*, one has only to think of Bede's later account of Caedmon's Hymn in the *Historia Ecclesiastica Gentis Anglorum*.

41  *Paradise Lost*, V, 150-52.

42  *L'Arte Poetica*, Naples, 1564, 167:

> E tosto che nacquero gli hyomini; ò che per divina ragione di natura, quanto
> l'origine loro, che dal cielo haveano, era piû fresca e nuova, tanto meglio
> vedessero il migliore; ò che riducendo è memoria l'altra lor vita, che fù celeste,
> qual fù l'openione di Platone, il costume di coloro, che nel cielo habitano,
> volessero imitare: stimar possiamo, che non d'altro modo elessero d'honorar
> Dio, che con la Musica, e con la Poesia ... cantando parole sotto certa Musica
> legge di piedi legate e ristrette.

43  Ed. and tr. A. D. S. Fowler, Oxford, 1958, 65.
44  *MP*, 80.
45  Zarlino actually lifts his phrase from Antonius Lullius, *De Oratione*, 404: 'Est autem
   in oratione latens quaedam obscuráque pronunciationis vis'.
46  These terms are not rare in Renaissance musical treatises; they appear especially in
   discussions of ecclesiastical chant, e.g., in Ornithoparcus' popular *Musicae activae
   micrologus libris quator digestus*, Leipzig, 1517, tr. John Dowland, London, 1609, 69.
   But the terms are also associated commonly with the study of Hebrew versification
   and cantillation, a point made not only by Zarlino, but by Mersenne, who notes that
   while the Greeks and Latins have the grave, acute, and circumflex accents, the
   Hebrews have the grammatical, the rhetorical, and the musical (*Harmonie Universelle*,
   VI, ix, 365-66).
47  Pp. 322-23:

> Chiamano però l'Accento Grammatico טַעַם; Taham; cioè, Gusto; percioche
> ogni prolatione di ciascuna Dittione lo ricerca; mediante ilquale la voce risona
> più eminentemente. Chiamano dopoi l'accento Rhetorico מֶתֶג; Metheg; cioè
> Retenimento, ò Retinaculo ò Freno; percioche con quello ornatamente vengono
> à pronunciar la parola. Ma l'accento Musico chiamano נְגִינָה; Neginàh; cioè,
> Harmonia; essendoche col suo mezo vengono à pronunciar le parole con
> modulatione. Zarlino translates this passage *verbatim* from Sebastian Münster,
> *Opus Grammaticum Consummatum*, Basle, 1541, 247.

48  The interpretation given here of grammatical accent requires some explanation. All
   of Zarlino's examples of the accents are in Latin. He tells us that the grammatical
   accent 'follows the long and short time in the quantity of the syllables' (*Sopplimenti*,
   323). This would seem to indicate the stressed-ictus reading commonly practiced in
   grammar schools to highlight poetic metre. But Zarlino also says, several times, that
   grammatical and musical accents must coincide. The musical accent is clearly a question of syllabic emphasis, what we would call 'stress'. Ictus and 'stress' do not always
   coincide in Latin verse. The only interpretation that fits all of Zarlino's statements
   and examples is that the grammatical accent follows the ordinary stress patterns of
   the language. In Latin, the so-called penultimate rule (words of more than two
   syllables are accented on the Penult if that is long and otherwise on the Antepenult
   [Allen and Greenough, *New Latin Grammar*, Rev. edn, Boston, 1931, 7])provides
   the required link between quantity and 'stress'. I owe this explanation to Professor
   Edward R. Weismiller.
49  *Sopplimenti*, 324:

> Et per dar qualche lume di quello che si è detto à i nostri Musici, pigliaremo
> nella nostra lingua Latina da Virgillio in prestanza queste parole: *Mānĕt āltā
> mēntĕ rĕpōstūm iūdĭcĭūm Părĭdīs*: nellequali (senza dubio) l'accento Grammatico è
> in qual si voglia dittione di questro membro ò periodo; ma l'accento Musico
> domina solamente nelle dittioni, *Alta*, & *Páridis*, & nelle loro Prime sillabe; di
> modo che'l Verso resonerà in questo modo: *Mànet álta mènte repòstum iudìcium
> Páridis*. L'Accento adunque havrà il precedente accento grave nel verbo *Manet*;
> ilquale da gli Hebrei sarà detto suo ministro, alla guisa di quelli, che come
> ministeriali nella Pompa precedono prima il Prencipe; seguendo poi i suoi Gen-
> til'huomini; onde la dittione *Álta* ha due ministri ad un certo modo: l'uno
> veramente detto ministro, precedente nel verbo *Mànet*; l'altro seguente nella

parola *Mènte*. Zarlino translates this passage *verbatim* from Johannes Reuchlin, *De accentibus et orthographia linguae hebraicae*, Hagenoae, 1518, fol. LXXII. Zarlino or his compositor has scanned *Mănĕt* incorrectly as *Mānēt*.

50  For a general introduction to the *te'amim*, the masoretic notes, and the raging debate in the Renaissance about when the notes were written, see James Kugel, *The Idea of Biblical Poetry*, New Haven, 1981, 109-16, 258-59, and 261-64. The debate included the issue of whether the *te'amim* were originally only grammatical (the word derives from *taham*, 'sense' or 'taste', which Zarlino says denoted the grammatical accent) or whether they comprised a system of musical notation as well.

51  On Levita, see Gérard E. Weil, *Élie Lévita: Humaniste et Massorète*, Leiden, 1963; intro. to C. D. Ginsburg, ed. and tr., *Massoreth Ha-Massoreth*, London, 1867, reissued, New York, 1968, ed. Harry M. Orlinsky.

52  Baldi, cited by Claude Palisca in *New Groves Dictionary of Music* under 'Zarlino'.

53  As quoted in *Sopplimenti*, 325:
    Hexametri versus sunt, Dactylo; Spondeoque currentes: & propter lingua & idioma, crebro recipientes & alios pedes; non earundem syllabarum; sed eorundem temporum. Interdum quoque Rhythmus ipse dulcis & tinnulus fertur numeris pedum solutis, quod metrici magis, quam simplex lector intelligat.

54  For a convenient catalogue of English passages on Hebrew versification, see Israel Baroway, 'The Bible in the English Renaissance: An Introduction', *JEGP*, xxxii (1933), 473-74.

55  Zarlino misquotes Jerome here, substituting *numeris pedum solutis* for *numeris lege metri solutis*. The error was common in the Middle Ages and Renaissance (see Kugel, *Idea of Biblical Poetry*, 252, n. 112). Jerome himself borrowed the phrase from Horace's characterization of Pindar's verse (*Odes*, iv, 2; see Kugel, 234-35). Pindar and Horace were commonly held to be the Greek and Latin inheritors of the ancient Hebraic rhythms.

56  *MP*, 77.

57  Another informed, critical statement is that of George Puttenham, *The Arte of English Poesie* (1589), in Smith, *Elizabethan Critical Essays*, II, p. 10. Puttenham contends that ancient Hebrew and Chaldean verse had a 'maner of rime, as hath bene of late obserued by learned men'. On these men and their theories, see Kugel, 237-39. Harington (Smith, II, 207) seems to be informed as well but, in fact, is simply paraphrasing Sidney.

58  See I. Baroway, 'Tremellius, Sidney and Biblical Verse', *MLN*, XLIX (1934), 245-49.

59  *Testamenti Veteris Biblia Sacra*, London, 1579-80, III, 4:
    hos libros omnes communiter vocamus Psalmos, quia sunt rythmici; non prosa oratione scripti, ut omnes alii (etsi in his Cantica quedam extant elegantissima Moschis, Deborae, Davidis, Ieschahhjae, Iechizkijae, Iirmejae, & Chabbakuki inspersa) sed numeris adstricti ad commoditatem memoriae & cantus.

60  I. Baroway, 'The Accentual Theory of Hebrew Prosody', *ELH*, XVII (1950), 120; Kugel, 251.

61  Magistro symphoniae fidium, ad gravem symphoniam; psalmus Davidis.

62  id [gravis symphonia] est, ut vulgus musicorum vocat basso & Tenore, sive ut veteres, Hypatis & Mesis.i.imis & mediis sonis: quod genus cantionum ferè in harmonia, tertio genere musices, positum est.

63  The different species of tetrachord (diatonic, chromatic, or enharmonic) are called *genera*. In classifying them, Tyard (following Aristoxenes and Boethius) divides the diatonic tetrachord into two sub-genera, and the chromatic, into three. The enharmonic is indivisible. According to this classification, 'la troisiesme mutation de Musique est la Chromatique entonnée' (*Solitaire Second*, 175).

64  I follow the traditional ordering of the modes: I: Dorian and Hypodorian; II: Phrygian and Hypophrygian; III: Lydian and Hypolydian; IV: Mixolydian and Hypomixolydian.

65  'Sidney and Franciscus Junius the Elder', *HLQ*, 42 (1978-79), 1-13.

66 Tr. van Dorsten, *art. cit.*, 9-10.

67 *MP*, 77.

68 James M. Osborn, *Young Philip Sidney*, New Haven, 1972, 112-13; Martha Winburn England, 'Sir Philip Sidney and Francois Perrot de Messieres: Their Verse Versions of the Psalms', *Bulletin of the New York Public Library*, 75 (1971), 30-54; 101-110.

69 On Mollerus, see Kugel, 255.

70 On Vatablus and Marot see Orentin Douen, *Clément Marot et le Psautier Huguenot*, Paris, 1878, I, 164; 281-83.

71 Kugel, 252.

72 I. Baroway, '*The Lyre of David*: A Further Study in Renaissance Interpretation of Biblical Form', *ELH*, 8 (1941), 119-42.

73 David Daiches, *The King James Version of the English Bible*, Chicago, 1941, 144-45; 150; J. B. Mullinger, *The University of Cambridge from the Royal Injunctions of 1535 to the Accession of Charles the First*, Cambridge, 1884, 172, n.4 and 416. A very learned study has recently appeared on the subject of Hebraic studies in England. Among other things, it is particularly excellent on who was where when and who knew whose work. See G. Lloyd Jones, *The Discovery of Hebrew in Tudor England: A Third Language*, Manchester, 1983.

74 *Alphabetvm Hebriacum, In quo literae Hebraicae describuntur, punctorum vocalium, accentuum forme & vis: cum appellatione syllabarum & dictionum Hebraicarum.* Ex Antonii Ceuallerii Hebraicarum literarum professoris recognitione, Geneva, 1566. The copy in the Huntington Library in San Marino, Calif., is interesting. It is bound (in a seventeenth century binding) with a little treatise on the Greek alphabet and system of pronunciation by Beza (Geneva, 1600), with a Greek grammar, London, 1633, and with a copy of *Lily's Grammar*, Oxford, 1636. The order is Lily, Greek grammar, Greek alphabet and pronunciation, Hebrew alphabet and pronunciation. Someone in the seventeenth century was evidently interested in collecting grammars and binding them so as to illustrate the concept of *translatio studii*.

75 One wonders whether there is any connection between the Hebrew 'very short' syllables and Drant's rule 7: 'Some wordes especially short'.

76 The Miles Coverdale translation from the Great Bible (which had become the standard psalter printed with the *Book of Common Prayer*) and the Geneva Bible of 1560 provided him with most of his phrasing. He took some hints from the jog-trot psalms of Sternhold and Hopkins, sung in churches throughout England, and borrowed ideas, both verbal and formal, from the Huguenot Psalter. He supplemented these popular versions with a variety of books somewhat more specialized and overtly learned in nature—Beza's paraphrase already mentioned in the text, possibly the *Paraphrasis Psalmorum Davidis* (1566; 1580 English ed.) by the Scottish humanist, George Buchanan, and the Tremellius-Junius version discussed in the text above.

77 On the Latin Prayer Book, see William Haugaard, *Elizabeth and the English Reformation*, Cambridge, 1968, 113-19; Norman L. Jones, 'Elizabeth, Edification, and the Latin Prayer Book of 1560', *Church History*, 53 (1984), 174-86.

78 A. W. Pollard, ed., *Records of the English Bible*, Oxford, 1911, 297.

79 Daiches, *King James Bible*, 177; Hallet Smith, 'English Metrical Psalms in the Sixteenth Century and their Literary Significance', *HLQ*, 9 (1946), 260.

80 Part of my reason for suspecting that the Sidneys consulted Münster concerns verb tense. Hebrew has only a perfect and imperfect tense and a variety of participial constructions. Translating into our past, present, and future is often a tricky business: it is no surprise, for example, that a Hebraist like Vatablus should include virtually hundreds of notes on tense in his commentary on Sanctes Pagninus' translation of the psalms (printed by Robert Stephanus in 1556). Both Sidney and his sister depart from their usual sources in verb tense a number of times and seem to follow the tense suggested by Münster's version. Psalm 3 provides some ready examples, but they are too long and technical for inclusion here.

81 The music is printed in modern notation by Waldo Selden Pratt, *The Music of the French Psalter of 1562*, New York, 1939; and in old notation with the first stanza

underlaid by Pierre Pidoux, *Le Psautier Huguenot du XVI<sup>e</sup> Siècle: Melodies et Documents*, I, Basle, 1962.

82  I am convinced that there is *some* explanation for each stanzaic choice that can at least be guessed at. A few forms may have been suggested by Beza and Buchanan. Thus, Psalms 15 and 18 are in alexandrines, and while I cannot account for the different rhyme schemes of these poems, I am impressed by the fact that Beza's 15 and Buchanan's 18 are in heroic hexameters, for which alexandrines are a logical analogue. The odd form of Psalm 2 (an alexandrine followed by an iambic trimeter) may be intended as an analogue to Buchanan's Horatian form, a heroic hexameter followed by an iambic trimeter, acatalectic. And so forth.

83  My attention was drawn to the passage by Anne Prescott, *French Poets and the English Renaissance*, New Haven, 1978, 17.

84  John Gouws in this volume, p. 67.

85  The tradition is established by elaborate quotation from patristic sources in the first part of an essay on Chaucer's pardoner, whose implied literal eunuchry is counterpointed ironically against the idea of the scriptural eunuch. See Robert P. Miller, 'Chaucer's Pardoner, The Scriptural Eunuch, and The Pardoner's Tale', *Speculum*, XXX (1955), 180-99.

86  It appears in a Dutch anthology of echo poems edited by Theodore Dousa.

87  Duncan-Jones, 'Philip Sidney's Toys', *Proceedings of the British Academy*, LXVI, 178.

88  J. C. A Rathmell ed., *The Psalms of Sir Philip Sidney and the Countess of Pembroke*, New York, 1963, ix-x; Donne, *Divine Poems*, ed. Helen Gardner, 2nd ed. Oxford 1978, 34-35.

JACKSON BOSWELL AND H. R. WOUDHUYSEN

## SOME UNFAMILIAR SIDNEY ALLUSIONS

The sheer quantity of references to Sir Philip Sidney in print testifies to the legend he had become, almost in his own lifetime: knight and lover, soldier and poet—the epitome of a Renaissance gentleman. The purpose of this essay is to collect some of the more unfamiliar and obscure allusions made in books printed in English in Britain and abroad within the first fifty or so years after his death.[1]

Serious consideration of Sidney's contemporary reputation must begin with W. H. Bond's unpublished dissertation,[2] and John Buxton's classic *Sir Philip Sidney and the English Renaissance* of 1954. We are deeply indebted to both works. In our selection we have in general ignored dedications,[3] funeral elegies, derivative works and references well-known to Sidney scholars, as well as mere echoes of and parallels to Sidney's works and material already easily accessible in the various collections of allusions which have been published relating to Chaucer, Spenser, Shakespeare and Jonson. Even within these narrow limits we have not been able to use fully all the allusions which we have collected—though it should go without saying that we are probably aware of only a fraction of the references to Sidney which appear in print before 1640.

A full-scale 'Sidney Allusion Book' would certainly require a great deal more research, but it would be the foundation of any reconsideration of his personal and literary reputation and influence.[4] Until such a work has been completed it is very difficult to draw any overall conclusions about Sidney's image in the period immediately after his death, beyond pointing to his familiar association with the perfect Renaissance figure. Yet it is still interesting to notice how powerful the legend was, by citing some of the contexts in which Sidney's name and works are mentioned. The allusions gathered here may add little or nothing to our knowledge of Sidney's life and they may not speak very highly of the state of late sixteenth and early seventeenth century critical judgement, but they do show the different uses to which the reputation of an internationally renowned Protestant writer and hero could be put.

For this reason our presentation of the allusions tends primarily towards the thematic, rather than the strictly chronological. This has some disadvantages for the user, but we hope will be more illuminating. We have tried to keep our commentary as brief as possible, so that as many allusions can be included here as space allows. All quotations have

been reproduced as accurately as possible, with the exception that allusions largely printed in italic have been reprinted here in roman type.

### i. *Life and Death*

So pervasive and strong was the Sidney legend that there is no shortage
of biographical and personal allusions relating to his exploits and death
in the Low Countries. He was still remembered in 1621 as the first
Governor of Flushing by Peter Heylyn in *Microcosmus, or a little description
of the great world*, Oxford (STC 13276; 137), and in the same year William
Slatyer in *The history of Great Britanie to this present raigne*, (STC 22634),
recalled in both English and Latin verses Sidney's part in the Earl of
Leicester's expedition to the Netherlands (pp. 278-81). Still there in
'When Collonell *Goring* Was beleev'd to be slaine, at the siege of
BREDA' included in Sir William Davenant's *Madagascar; with other
poems*, 1638 (STC 6304), Endimion asks Arigo to seek out 'Where
*Sidney's* ever-blooming-Throne is spred'. Sidney, he goes on to say, will
find room for the Colonel:

> Whom he must needs delight to celebrate,
> Because himselfe, in manners, and in Fate,
> Was his undoubted *Type*.

Endimion repeats the point 'Though *Sidney* was his Type … ' (p. 125).
  The exact date on which he received his death wound at Zutphen is
recorded in the context of religious and political controversy in G.D., *A
briefe discouerie of Doctor Allens seditious drifts*, 1588 (STC 6166; 47).
Christopher Ockland, *The fountaine and welspring of all variance, sedition, and
deadlie hate*, 1589 (STC 18778), records a few details about the 'very hot
and bloudy skirmish', and referring to the Cambridge University
memorial volume proudly writes:

> The noble king *Carolus Iacobus Sextus* king of *Scotland*, and diuers others of
> the Nobility of the same country, beside infinite numbers of euery degree
> in *England*, mooued with his vertues, valour and prowes, made Latine
> verses most learnedly lamenting his vnripe death happening in the flower
> of his age. (sig. F1)

Sidney and James are also linked in Francis Rous the elder's *Thule, or vertues historie*, 1598 (STC 21348; sig. A2ᵛ), and in William Vaughan's *The
golden-grove*, 1608 (STC 24610), where Sidney is said to have 'excelled all
our English Poets in rarenesse of stile and matter' and to have displayed
'the glorie of his golden eloquence' in his 'Apology of Poetrie'; James is
described as 'a notable Poet' who 'daily setteth out most learned Poems,
to the admiration of all his subiects' (sig. Y6).

'Our such new fantasied men of warre' are reproved by Sir John Smythe for imitating Sidney's not wearing his full armour (sig. B2ᵛ). His *Certain discourses ... concerning the formes and effects of diuers sorts of weapons*, 1590 (STC 22883), which was suppressed by Queen Elizabeth goes on to say that:

> in the opinion of diuers Gentlemen that sawe him hurt with a Mosquet shot, if he had that day worne his cuisses, the bullet had not broken his thigh bone, by reason that the chiefe force of the bullet (before the blowe) was in a manner past. (sig. B3)

His death is still extravagantly mourned on his sister's behalf by Thomas Heywood in *Troia Britanica: or Great Britaines Troy*, 1609 (STC 13366; 359), where the Countess of Pembroke is compared to Cassandra, Creusa and Polyxena. The same poem records that in 1586 'at *Zutphen* dide, / Noble Sir *Phillip Sidney* souldiers pride' and that 'His death a generall griefe mongst souldiers bred, / a Parlyment' (p. 465). He has his place in other more unashamedly doggerel histories of Queen Elizabeth's reign, such as Martin Parker's *An abstract of the historie of the renouned maiden queene Elizabeth*, 1631 (STC 19217.5; sigs E4-4ᵛ), and *The life and death of Queene Elizabeth in heroicall verse*, 1639 (STC 7587), where he is linked with thirty-four other 'brave Commanders in Queene Elizabeth's Raigne' (sig. B6ᵛ). Sidney's death is simply listed in Henry Isaacson's *Saturni ephemerides sive tabula historico-chronologica*, 1633 (STC 14269; sig. Kk4ᵛ).

His military achievements, such as they were, were also remembered. Sir Lewis Lewkenor in *A discourse of the vsage of the English fugitiues, by the Spaniard*, 1595 (STC 15662), illustrates Spanish jealousy and suspicion by describing Mondragon's bad behaviour 'vpon the taking of *Axhil* by that braue and worthie souldyer Sir *Philip Sidney*, of worthie memorie' (sig. D2). The same author in the enlarged edition of his *Discourse*, 1595 (STC 15564), refers to the Spanish attempt at Gravelines 'to haue intrapped noble sir *P. Sidney*' (sig. G2), and to Zutphen 'where the honour of the worlde and ornament of *England* sir *Phillip Sidney* by his aduenturous valour was slaine' (sig. Q4ᵛ). He also tells the following story which does not seem to be recorded elsewhere about a treacherous English deserter, who with a company of horsemen was

> vpon the plaines neere adioyning [Breda] encountered & defeated by sir *Phillip Sidneys* companie of English lances, & among the rest Captaine *Walsh* in two places grieuously wounded, and taken prisoner, & brought into *Holland*, where my L. of *Leicester* gaue commandement presently to hang .him. Sir *Phillip Sidney* (being full of true honor) earnestly intreated my Lord for his pardon, & obtayned it, in respect that he knew him to be valiant, and ... yet he had euer borne a dutifull regard towards her Maieiestie [sic]. (sig. C4ᵛ)

Spanish treachery at Doesburg and Zutphen 'where that most renowmed Knight *S. Philip Sidney* was slaine' is also referred to by Richard Cromp-ton, *The mansion of magnanimitie. wherein is shewed the acts of sundrie English kings, princes, etc.*, 1599 (STC 6054; sig. N2).[5] Even Roman Catholic writers felt they had to respect Sidney's conduct in the Netherlands. The author of *Observations concerning the present affaires of Holland*, [St. Omer] 1621 (STC 13576), mentions Leicester as an actor 'in this rebellious Tragedy' in whose 'broyles ... was slaine his sisters Sonne *Syr Philip Sidney*, a Knight worthy to haue deserued more Honour, if he had serued in an honourable cause' (p. 85).

Two additional references to Sidney's death and burial can be noted. On the verso of the title page of Henri Marc Gouffier's *A declaration made in the consistorie of Rochell*, 1616 (STC 12108), 'The French Printer to the Reader' reprints ('Because that otherwise this page had beene left emp-tie'), Du Bellay's epitaph on Bonivet, and adds 'The English whereof is the very same which wee finde to be the Epitaph made vpon the death of our Country-man the noble and thrice-worthy Knight Sir *Philip Sidney*', which he reprints '(*mutatis mutandis*) the names onely altered'.[6] In his *Miles Mediterraneus. The mid-land souldier. A sermon*, 1622 (STC 4023), the preacher Samuel Buggs makes a remark which could be taken as an implied criticism of the circumstances surrounding the return of Sidney's body to England and his interment:

> And surely, had the *funerall rites* of the famous, Sir *Philip Sidney* bin duly per-formed, *Mars* and *Mercury* should haue bin the *chiefe Mourners*, as one, in whose death, the glory of them both was much *eclipsed*. (p. 37)

Yet the general perception of Sidney's life and death was such that the movement into legend happened rapidly and almost imperceptibly. So that to Thomas Cutwoode in his *Caltha poetarum: or the bumble bee*, 1599 (STC 6151), Sidney was a contemporary, 'The flower of our age, sweete pleasing *Sidney*' (sig. A5). With the new century, but only a few years later, for Dudley Digges in *Foure paradoxes, or politique discourses. All newly published*, 1604 (STC 6872), 'though he liued an age before me, I yet honor, I loue his memorie' (p. 74).[7] In 1611 Anthony Stafford can com-plain in the second edition of his *Staffords Niobe: or his age of teares* (STC 23130), a work full of allusions to Sidney, that 'I want information of the circumstances of thy life' (part 2, p. 159). '*Diuine Sidney* ... deceas'd ere I begun' makes George Wither lament in *Abuses stript, and whipt*, 1613 (STC 25891; text taken from STC 25894): 'I haue oft sighed, and bewail'd my *Fate*, / That brought me foorth so many yeeres too late / To view that *worthy*' (sig. R2). Even so his fame is secure as Sir William Davenant announces in *Madagascar*:

... the God-like *Sidney* was a Type [of these lovers],
Whose fame still growes, and yet is ever ripe;
...
Our *Sidney's* full-growne Fame will still endure:
*Sidney*, like whom these Champions strive to grace,
The silenc'd remnant of poore *Orpheus* race. (pp. 8-9)

This sudden growth of the feeling that Sidney lived in a different age may be the cause of the scarcity of new biographical allusions. The only contemporary reference which we have found, that seems to have escaped Sidney scholars, is by Christopher Clifford, *The schoole of horsman-ship*, 1585 (STC 5415), who reveals that 'I was preferred to the seruice of the right noble Prince Duke *Cassemerus*, by the right Worshipfull Sir *Philip Sidney*, with which foresayd Duke I passed out of *England*' (sig. K2). Sidney had some contact with Casimir during his visit to England early in 1579. Against this slim fact one can place an early instance of the favoured legend that Sidney was offered the Polish crown. In *The guide of honour, or the ballance wherin she may weigh her actions*, 1634 (STC 23124), Anthony Stafford puts Sidney '(next her Kings)' as

> the first glory this Iland can boast of. A man deserving both the Lawrels, and the Crowne to boote, design'd him by the Votes of many [*in a side-note* The polish Crown] brave Spirits who discovered in him all the requisits of a King but the Title. (sigs. A6ᵛ-8)[8]

Sidney continued to be remembered, and in a sense live on, through his family and his friends. Nor was his own motto from Ovid ('vix ea nostra voco') forgotten in relation to this. The

> golden saying so much pleased that worthie and noble knight *Sir Philip Sidney, Learninges champion, Englands miracle, Europes fauorite*... that he vsed them for a mot: And I know not whether *Ouid* his inuention, or *Sir Phillippes* election be more to be commended: And nobilitie without vertue and merit was accompted as an image without life,

William Fulbecke notes in *The pandectes of the law of nations*, 1602 (STC 11414; sigs. R3-3ᵛ). William Vaughan records the same motto in *The spirit of detraction, conjured and convicted in seven circles. A worke both diuine and morall*, 1611 (STC 24622; sig. Vv 2ᵛ).

Family connexions were not forgotten even by his enemies. Robert Parsons under the name R. Doleman in *A conference about the next succession to the crowne of Ingland*, [Antwerp] 1594 (STC 19398), is quite clear about them in his discussion of the Earl of Huntingdon (part 2, pp. 254-55). The family connexion is often evoked in dedications, for example by Robert Barret in *The theorike and practike of moderne warres*, 1598 (STC 1500), where Sidney is mentioned as the uncle of the dedicatee, William Herbert (sig. § 3). In *Linsi-woolsie. Or two centuries of epigrammes*, Oxford

1613 (STC 11544), William Gamage, a cousin of Robert Sidney's wife, tells Sidney's niece Lady Katherine Manners:

> And the rather I builde on your all favourable patronage by reason of your Ladyships neere affinity with that worthy, and Tresnoble *Sir Phillip Sidney*, whose golden Pen vouchsafed to Apologize the renowned art of Poetry. (sig. A2)[9]

Most writers of course associate Sidney with his sister, as Henry Lok does in his version of Ecclesiastes, 1597 (STC 16696), in a sonnet to the Countess, which praises

> .... that pregnancie of spright,
> Whereby you equall honour do attaine,
> To that extinguisht Lampe of heauenly light,
> Who now no doubt doth shine midst Angels bright. (sig. Y1ᵛ)

After her death the association is still made: Thomas Heywood in Γυναιχέιον *or nine bookes of various history, concerninge women*, 1624 (STC 13326), while discussing female poets, notes that Sir John Harington in Book 37 of his *Orlando Furioso* commends an Italian lady called Vittoria:

> who writ largely and learnedly in the praise of her dead husband: with whom (though not in that Funerall Elegeick straine) I may ranke (if in the comparison I vnderprise not) the beautifull and learned Ladie *Mary*, Countesse of Penbrooke, the worthie sister to her vnmatchable brother Sir *Philip Sydney*. (p. 398)

Couplings of Sidney's name with other members of his family are fairly frequent. John Davies of Hereford's *Microcosmos. The discovery of the little world*, 1603 (STC 6333), has verses in 'A Preface' connecting Robert Sidney with his brother 'Our little *Worlds* great *Paragon* of fame' and in the same poem refers to Dyer as 'Great *Sidneies loue*' (p. 17). Later in the volume Davies offers another poem to Robert Sidney in whom 'divine Sʳ *Philip* liues' (sig. Mm4). The same author in his *The scourge of folly*, 1611 (STC 6341), includes a poem 'In praise of Sʳ. Henry and Sʳ. Phillip Sidney, Syre and Sonne deceased' (no. 79, p. 37), and includes Sir Philip among those he addresses in a poem 'To the deere & eternal memory of our renowned late English millitary-Knights and Chieftaines ... Englands nine Woorthies' (no. 185, p. 88). He similarly appears with five other soldiers ('whose Woorths these late times haue displaid ... had they liu'd in aged *Priams* dayes, / Had dim'd the *Greekes*, and matcht the *Troians* prayse'), in Thomas Heywood's *Troia Britanica* (p. 246); with three others, 'All vertuous Captaines, most praise-worthy all' in Richard Zouch, *The dove: or passages of cosmography*, 1613 (STC 26130; sig. D4);[10] with four others all involved in the Low Countries in Henry Hexham's *The principles of the art militarie*, 1637 (STC 13264; sig. π2), and with three other 'unimitable Presidents of Courage and Valour' in Henry Peacham (under the name Mis-Amaxius), *Coach and sedan, pleasantly disputing for place and precedence*, 1636 (STC 19501), all of whom, with several Earls, are cited as examples of foot rather than coach men (sig. C4).[11]

Two other sets of associations deserve mentioning. Firstly, the lesser known one between Sidney and Sir Henry Unton, whose Oxford memorial volume, *Funebria nobilissimi ac praestantissimi equitis, D. H. Untoni. à musis Oxoniensibus apparata*, Oxford 1596 (STC 24520), is peppered with references to Sidney and his works. The second association, with the Earl of Essex, is more familiar, not least because Sidney left him his best sword in his will. *Sir Thomas Smithes voiage and entertainment in Rushia*, 1605 (STC 22869), refers to

> that Noble but vnfortunate *E.* of *Essex*, of whom many through the world, do make in diuers kinds, but (as that learned and heroycall Poet *Sir Phil. Sidney* speaks of *Prince Plangus*) neuer any can make but honorable mention. (sigs D3ᵛ-D4)

In *The differences of the ages of mans life*, 1607, but written in 1600, (STC 6103), Essex's secretary Henry Cuffe cites Sidney as an authority: 'But Eternitie and Chance, being (as the learned *Sir Philip* obserued) things vnsufferable together; If Chanceable, then not Eternall' (p. 13). The line of descent could also be less obvious, as when John Davies writes of Sir Christopher Heydon in *The scourge of folly*:

> *Learning* and *Armes*, both being much distrest,
> For want of *harbour* (since our *Sidney* dyde,
> Sith they sought *harbour* in one single Brest)
> At last they entred thine. (p. 191)

## ii. *The Poet*

The temptation some writers felt simply to refer to Sidney and by association to appropriate his fame for their own ends was not always easily resisted. Thomas Powell in *The passionate poet. With a description of the Thracian Ismarus*, 1601 (STC 20167), exclaims 'Once was there such a *Sidney*. It sufficeth, / That from the graue his onely name reuiueth' (sig. F2ᵛ). But this sort of attitude did not escape without criticism.

> Not euery *brickel Poet*, that aspires,
> And faine would *flie* with *Sidneys* noble *fires*
> Into the *brest* of *greatnesse*, we insert
> Into the *laureat Chorus* of quick *art*

writes Robert Anton in *The philosophers satyrs*, (STC 686; 59). Sidney's own reputation as a poet was of course quite secure. Horace's line

'Dignum laude virum Musa vetat mori' is frequently associated with him. It is used as a tag in Francis Davison's *A poetical rapsody*, 1602 (STC 6373), among the poems mourning Sidney's death and had appeared on the title page of the New College memorial volume *Peplus*. William Fulbecke in *The pandectes of the law of nations* says that Horace's words 'may be verified, if euer they might be truely pronounced of any' (sig. R3), and Thomas Digges quotes them in *Foure paradoxes*, with an English version 'To labour that the memorie / Of worthy men may neuer die' (p.75).

One familar way of acting on this and so strengthening the Sidney legend was to enrol him among the English poets and writers. He is among the

> great Princes, Earls, Lords and Knights for the Ornament and honour of learning, who for generall and particular causes and benefits haue added their names to the society of writers, and divulged their workes in print,

whom Edward Topsell lists in the slightly unlikely context of the dedication to his *The historie of foure-footed beastes*, 1607 (STC 24123). These include the Earls of Surrey, Dorset, Northampton and Salisbury, Sir George More, Sir Francis Hastings and the obscure Sir Richard Bartlett (sig. A3ᵛ). Sidney is among 'The Pleiade of Poets', 'The seuen stars of Greece ... Which are easily put downe' by their English equivalents, Chaucer, Spenser, Daniel '& those others who haue made their *Diatribes* vpon *Tom Coryats Parua naturalia*' in *Coryats crudities: hastily gobled up in five moneths trauells*, 1611 (STC 5808; sig. h2).[12] In his device for the Lord Mayor's pageant, *Monuments of honor*, 1624 (STC 25175), John Webster places Sidney 'as worthy both Souldier and Scholler' with Chaucer, Gower, Lydgate and More in the Temple of Honour in St. Paul's Churchyard (sig. B1). Hugh Holland links Sidney as 'Astrophill' with Chaucer and Ben Jonson in his preliminary poem addressed to Sir Thomas Hawkins' translation of the *Odes of Horace*, 1625 (STC 13800; sig. A3ᵛ).[13] The Oxford volume celebrating King Charles's marriage to Henrietta Maria, *Epithalamia Oxoniensia. In ... Caroli, regis, &c. cum Henretta [sic] Maria, connubium*, Oxford 1625 (STC 19031), contains a poem by Richard James in which Sidney is mentioned with Chaucer, Hoccleve, Beaumont and Spenser (sig. L1).[14] Oxford's admiration for its former pupil also comes out in the dedication to the University of George Hakewill's *An apologie of the power and providence of God*, Oxford 1627 (STC 12611), where he asks 'How renowned in forraine parts are thy *Moore*, thy *Sidney*, thy *Cambden*? what rare Lights in the Church were *Humfreyes*, *Foxe*, *Bilson*, *Field*, *Abbott*?' (sig. b2ᵛ). Finally Sidney's apotheosis comes in *A pleasant and delightfull poeme of two louers, Philos and Licia*, 1624 (STC 19886), where the unknown author describes how

Next *Ioue, Apollo* came: him followed *Fame*
Bearing a lawrell, on which sweet *Sydneys* name
In golden letters, plainly to be read,
By the Nine Muses had beene charrectred:
On whose each side Eternitie and Praise
Enroll'd mens deeds, and gaue tham fame to raise. (sigs A4-4ᵛ)

When Samuel Austin advises 'honour'd Willy', who is evidently
William Browne, to 'bid the world farewell with *Sydney*', in his *Austins
Urania, or, the heavenly muse, in a poem*, 1629 (STC 971), he confidently
refers to Sidney as '(he / That was the Prince of English Poesie)' (sig.
A7).[15] The reverence due to him can easily be idolatrous, as when
Thomas Bancroft in *Two bookes of epigrammes and epitaphs*, 1639 (STC
1354), writes 'On Sir *Philip Sidney*': 'Idols I hate, yet would to *Sidneys*
wit / Offer *Castalian* healths, and kneele to it' (sig. C4). This sort of extravagant praise can equally become semi-humorous: Stafford in his
*Niobe* calls Sidney 'this Miracle of Nature ... the Oracle of wisdome' (sig.
§ 3), and goes on to address him as:

> Thou Atlas to all vertues, thou Hercules to the Muses, thou Patron to the
> poor, thou deseruest a Quire of ancient *Bardi* to sing thy praises; who, with
> their musickes melody, might expresse thy soules harmonie. (pp. 113-14)

When he turns to the devil he tells him:

> Had he beene with you, hee would haue turned Hel into an Academy, and
> taught your fiends the Art-military ... hee that beautified the earth, doth
> now adorne the heauens. And I am verily perswaded, that the *Nuntius
> Siderius* would, with his perspectiue glasse, sooner discouer *Sidus
> Sydneyanum*, than any planet aboue the number of seauen. (part 2 sigs
> H6ᵛ-8ᵛ)

In time this light-hearted tone becomes explicitly comic and the legend
acquires a new form. In 'The Authors Inuocation' to his *Wheresoeuer you
see mee, trust vnto your selfe. Or, the mysterie of lending and borrowing*, 1623
(STC 20171), Thomas Powell apostrophises

> Thou spirt of old *Gybbs*, a quondam Cooke,
> Thy hungry Poet doth thee now inuoke,
> T-infuse in him the iuyce of Rumpe or Kidney,
> And he shall sing as sweet as ere did *Sidney*
> ...
> I wish not for Castalian cups not I,
> But with the petty-Canons being dry,
> And but inspir'd with one bare Qu: let any
> Compare with vs for singing (O *Sydany*). (sig. A4)

James Hayward's address to the reader before his translation of G. F.
Biondi's *Donzella desterrada. Or, the banish'd virgin*, 1635 (STC 3074), is full

of admiration for Sidney but mocks among other things his fondness for compound epithets, calling him (sig. A3) 'our-as-yet-unparallel'd Sydney'. Sidney's own sense of irony and humour was equally apparent to some. Henry Peacham notes that 'The wisest Counsellers, and greatest Scholars have ever season'd, and sweetened their profoundest Studies, and greatest employments, with these and the like passages of inoffensive Mirth'. Justifying his own present work, *Coach and sedan*, he cites Erasmus's example in *The Praise of Folly* and Homer's in the *Batrachomyomachia* and adds 'Sir *Phillip Sydney* made good sport with *Rhombus* his Countrey Schoole-master' (sig. A2ᵛ). This is the only direct allusion to Sidney's famous comic character of which we know. Some found Sidney's ironic tone an influence for the bad, as Richard Young describes it in *The drunkard's character, or, a true drunkard*, 1638 (STC 26111):

> Allasse! if they have once read but the Fayry Queene, the *Arcadia*, and *Montaigne* his essayes, (I dare not say the booke of statutes, or the Chronicles) or can but breake a jeast, as many of them are like *Sarmantus*, a gentleman of *Rome*, who was famous only for his scoffing, then they conceit of themselves, as *Menecrates* the *Physitian* did, who (though not worthy to be *Æsculapius* his Apothecaries boy) would needs be *Iupiter*. (p. 121)

### iii. The *Arcadia*

'Sir *Phillip Sydneyes Arcadia*', George Hakewill says in his *An apologie*, 'is in my judgement nothing inferiour to the choisest peece among the Ancients' (p. 236). The work's popularity hardly needs to be demonstrated. It is both highly serious and entertaining as Sir William Cornwallis suggests in his *Essayes*, 1601 (STC 5775), where in number 47 he talks about disposing 'The instruments of a States-man':

> according to their nature ... as doth that Maister-peece of English, which in a light Historye meanes the most graue matter, I meane the *Arcadia*, where the besieged *Amphialus* teacheth the vse of seruants & inferiours most exactly: there shall you finde constitutions fitted with charges and imployments according to their nature, & the disability of one man for al places. (sig. l8ᵛ)[16]

Perhaps the most curious use of the *Arcadia* is made by the Scottish poet Alexander Craig in *The amorose songes, sonets, and elegies*, 1606 (STC 5956), in which he takes characters and incidents from the romance as *exempla* (sigs. C8, D2ᵛ, E1 and E2).[17] While Biondi has to admit in the dedication of his *Donzella desterrada* to Prince Thomas of Savoy that having promised to translate for him Books I and II of *Arcadia*, presumably into Italian, he found he could only paraphrase them, Sidney 'alone having the talent of both, conceiving and expressing himselfe' and so had abandoned the project (sigs A4-4ᵛ).

Among the numerous works derived from or influenced by the *Arcadia*, John Day's *The ile of Guls*, 1606 (STC 6412), is explicit about its debt, not just in the names of the play's characters, but also in its Prologue:

> and the argument beeing a little string or Riuolet, drawne from the full streine of the right worthy Gentleman, Sir *Phillip Sydneys* well knowne Archadea, confirmes it: onely a Duke to make tryall of certaine experiments, retyres with his retinue into a Namelesse desart ...(sig. A2v.)

The full title of Sidney's romance became popular as a model for similar and quite dissimilar works during the 1620s. Robert Newton's *The countesse of Mountgomeries Eusebeia: expressing briefly, the soules praying robes* (STC 18509) appeared in 1620 and was dedicated to the Countess of Pembroke. In the following year Lady Mary Wroth's *The countesse of Mountgomeries Urania* (STC 26051) was published, and in the year after that Elizabeth Clinton's *The countesse of Lincolnes nurserie* was printed at Oxford (STC 5432). Patrick Anderson, the editor of James Caldwell's *The countesse of Marres Arcadia, or sanctuarie. Containing morning, and evening meditations, for the whole weeke*, Edinburgh 1625 (STC 4366), makes the relation between the two works clear in his dedication to Mary Stewart (Erskine), Countess of Mar:

> *Sr Philip Sidneys Arcadia* hath manie faire and recreatiue discourses for Ladies; a faire Field in deede to feede on, for young and fond Lovers. The Countrie it selfe, is a fresh and pleasant Soile in the middle of *Peloponesus*, a ground that floweth of manie delicates, fyne pasturages for flockes, and pleasant Rivers ... The *Countesse* of *Pembrokes Arcadia* is for the bodie; but the *Countesse* of *Marre* her *Arcadia* is for the Soule. The author of the first, was a worthie and Noble Knight, the author of the other, was a sincere and devote Pastor ... (sigs *3-4)

There are surprisingly few specific allusions to the main characters in the *Arcadia* during the period we are concerned with. The example of Musidorus is used by Richard Nugent in *Rich: Nugents Cynthia. Containing direfull sonnets, madrigals, and passionate intercourses*, 1604 (STC 18745), to comfort himself when:

> ... my fierce faire, a stranger doth possesse,
> Yet *Sydneys* gentle sheepheard could deuise,
> In such a case, to find a remedie,
> who blear'd his iealous hosts mistrustfull eyes,
> By his kind hostesse handsome industrie. (sig. C2)

Arthur Johnston briefly mentions Pyrocles in his *Parerga Arturi Jonstoni Scoti, medici regii*, Aberdeen 1632 (STC 14714; p. 58). Stafford in his *Niobe* demands 'to associate this Pirocles, bring mee a Dametas, who hath of

late extracted gentility out of dung' (part 1, pp. 58-59). Dametas is frequently alluded to, but the characters that caught people's imagination
were Argalus and Parthenia.[18] Peter Heylyn quotes the first two lines of
their epitaph, with the sexes reversed, in his *Microcosmus*:

> as that which S$^r$ *Phillip Sidney* said of *Argalus* and *Parthenia*,
>    Her being was in him alone,
>    And she not being he was none.
> I may iustly say of these two *Gemini* Historie and Geographie. (p. 11)

William Heale in his *An apologie for women*, Oxford 1609 (STC 13014),
cites 'the Lady *Parthenia* of *Greece*' along with Penthesilea and the Empress
Livia as 'a stoute and valiant woman', whom 'if I shoulde chaunce to
marrie ... & after a while from *Cupids* warres fal vnto Martial armes, J
doubt my learning woulde not saue mee from some vnlearned blowes' (p.
15). Throughout Heale's interestingly titled work Sidney is a constant
source of reference and authority, suggesting contemporary admiration
for his understanding of the relations between men and women. 'And
howbeit al women are not beautiful, neither hath nature bestowed al
perfections on every wife: yet a true-louing husband must imagine the*m*
al in his truly beloued wife', he writes and goes on to cite a passage from
Book II of the *Arcadia*, 'For loue esteemes not a thing beloved, as in it
selfe it is; but as it appeares in the lovers eie' (p. 14). Book III is said
to be the source of his remark:

> *Neither is there any* sweeter taste of friendship, then the coupling of soules in
> this mutuallity either of condoling or comforting: where the oppressed
> minde findes it selfe not altogither miserable, since it is sure of one which
> is feelingly sorry for his misery. (p. 19)

And elsewhere he quotes the last two lines of OA 64 as 'Sure tis no
iealousie can that prevent, / Whereto two persons once be full content'
(p. 34). Christopher Newstead in his *An apology for women: or, womens
defense*, 1620 (STC 18508), quotes lines 102-08 of OA 67 as an authority
for his remark 'what more conuenient, then to haue, when wee returne
from our labours, then the comfort of our wiues, as that one eye of
*Minerua* testifieth of them?' (pp. 45-46). James Caldwell's description of
the *Arcadia's* appeal 'for Ladies' and 'for young and fond Lovers' has
already been quoted. When Changelove in Thomas Nabbes' *Totenham
court*, 1638 (STC 18344), discusses women he says:

> There's Magick in their company that charmes
> All masculine affections, but of pleasure
> In their enjoying. I'le spin or threed their needles;
> Read *Spenser* and th'*Arcadia* for their company. (p. 32)[19]

Musidorus and Pyrocles are 'noble paires of friends' (p. 71) for Joseph

Wybarne in his interesting collection of miscellaneous essays *The new age of old names*, 1609 (STC 26055), where he also paraphrases Pamphilus's specious argument about love in chapter 18 of *Arcadia* Book II:

> Another soyling of constancy, is an immoderate kind of selfe-loue, such as *Pamphilus* pretends in Arcadia, who though he loued many by a successiue mutabilitie, yet proued that he was constant, by this reason: The thing which I loued was my fancie affecting her, when that fleeted to an other, still I pursued the same fancie, and therefore cannot be accus'd of inconstancie, which is as much as if hee had made himselfe the Center, and had drawne all the lines of the Circle, from the circumference of his actions to that one vndiuided point. (p. 62)[20]

Anthony Stafford in *The guide of honour* defends Sidney against 'These severe Iudges' who

> lately have not spared even *Apollo's* first borne, incomparable, and inimitable Sir *Phillip Sydney*, whose *Arcadia* they confine onely to the reading of Chambermaids; a censure that can proceede from none but the sonnes of Kitchinmaids. Let me perish, if I thinke not his very Skull yet retaines more: witt then the passive braines of these wretched things, betweene whose Soules, and Knowledge, there is a Gulfe. (sigs A6ᵛ-7)[21]

## iv. *Style*

Sidney is invoked by William Covell in *A just and temperate defence of the five books of Ecclesiastical Policie: by R. Hooker*, 1603 (STC 5881), when discussing 'The stile and maner of writing':

> That honorable Knight S. *Philip Sidney*, gaue a taste in an argument of recreation, how well that stile would befit an argument of a grauer subiect; which it may be is more vnpleasing in the taste of some, because the maner is learned, & the subiect is not agreeing to their humour. (p. 148)

His 'historie, or rather Poeme' the *Arcadia* is recommended by James Cleland in 'Ηρωπαιδεία, *or the institution of a young noble man*, Oxford 1607 (STC 5393):

> both for the worth of the writer, and the eloquence of the English stile. His discourses & poesies are so iudicious, his passages so pleasant, and variety so delightsome, that I may with out reproach or offence applie *Homers* elogie vnto his praise; his wit is so excellent, his invention so rare, and elocution so rauishing. (p. 152)

Implicitly he is acknowledged as a suitable model for epistolary style in Thomas Gainsford's *The secretaries studie: directions for the inditing of letters*, 1616 (STC 11523). In a letter addressed 'To his much esteemed Friend, C. G.' and stating that 'A man out of good manners must answer letters howeuer they proue vnsauory in the acceptation', he writes:

> Fifthly, to make you beleeue, there is some good thing in me allowable and
> iustifiable, and therefore worthy of a small regard, as noble Sir *Philip Sydney*
> was wont to say, Let vs loue him for one good qualitie; for a great many
> haue none at all, and no man hath all. (p. 20)

As late as the 1630s his style was still admired. Before his translation of
Biondi's *Eromena, or, love and revenge*, 1632 (STC 3075), James Hayward
modestly disclaims 'If language thou expects, then pore not here, / But
*Sidney* read, whose Pen ne're yet found peere' (sig. b1)

Perhaps the only English poet who can be talked about in the same
breath as Sidney as a stylist is Samuel Daniel. Augustine Taylor does this
in his *Encomiasticke elogies*, 1614 (STC 23721), where he writes: 'Our
language giues, as best: 'tis *Sidneyes* friend, / And he its more: Sweets't
*Daniell* (as vnkend) / My better deere respect, respects' (sig. A3ᵛ). In his
translation of *The familiar epistles of M. T. Cicero*, [1620] (STC 5305),
Joseph Webbe associates Sidney as a prose writer with Bacon and '*Sandys*' (presumably Sir Edwin, not George), and cites him as a vernacular
writer comparable to Boccacio (sigs. A6 and 9). The idea of Sidney as
the English Cicero is taken up directly by Nathaniel Whiting in *Le hore
di recreatione: or, the pleasant historie of Albino and Bellama*, 1637 (STC 25436),
where he praises 'the *Sidney*-skill' (p. 10) and says

> I've heard a worthy man approv'd for learning,
> Say, that in Playes and Rithmes we may be earning
> Both wit and knowledge, and that *Sidney*-prose
> Out-musickes *Tully*, if it scape the nose. (sig. A6ᵛ)

As a stylist Sidney was often invoked in theological debate. The
English rector of the University of Rheims, Matthew Kellison, cites him
in *A reply to Sotcliffes answer to the survey of the new religion*, Rheims 1608
(STC 14909):

> Certes you are al *Sotte* to cauil thus. do not Philosophers call the world
> *vniuersum*, Alle? Read Sir *Philip Sidneyes Arcadia*, and you shall find that he
> (as good an Inglishman as you) vseth the same word in the same sense. (sig.
> Ggg2ᵛ)[22]

Edward Coffin scores another sort of debating point in *A refutation of M.
Joseph Hall his Apologeticall discourse*, [St. Omer] 1619 (STC 5475), over
the nature of Heliodorus' work, but in doing so reveals more about the
changing meanings of the word 'history' at this time:

> it cannot but moue laughter to see M. *Hall* tearme him [that is Bishop
> Heliodorus of Thesalia] in his margent, *Author of the Aethiopicke historyes*, as
> if *Heliodorus* had written some history of *Aethiopia*, whereas he only intituled
> his wanton work *Aethiopia*, and wrote no more history thereof, then *Syr
> Phillip Sidney* did of *Arcadia*, or *Apuletus* [sic] of the *Arcadian Nightingale*, that
> sings so sweetly to the Harp. (p. 150)[23]

The side note to this passage reads 'Heliodorus his wanton booke entituled Aethiopia'. Against this rather genial recusant use of Sidney should be placed Alexander Baillie's harsh attack in *A true information of the unhallowed ofspring of our Scottish Calvinian gospel*, Wirtsburgh 1628 (STC 1202), on the 'archheretiks' whose preaching is

> decored with faire words & plausible eloquence (as now doe our Ministers trimme & culoure their hereticall sermons with the termigant tearmes & affectate language of *Arcadia* or *Amadis de Gaul*). (p. 219)

And Anglican can mock Anglican in terms of Alethes' contre-blason of Mopsa in OA 3.11: 'But the *Doctour*'—who is Peter Heylyn the object of John Williams's polemic in *The holy table, name & thing, more anciently, properly, and literally used under the New Testament, then that of an altar*, 1637 (STC 25724)—'in this Conceipt, is (as S$^r$ *Philip Sidney* calls it) *Heavenly wide*, as wide from the true sense, as the North of the Heaven is from the South' (p. 208).

### v. *The Authority*

The references and allusions gathered here go some way to showing the transformations and adaptations through which Sidney's life and work went to establish and promote the legend. Yet perhaps the most remarkable manifestation of that legend is the way in which the ever youthful and ironically quick-witted Sidney comes to be seen both personally and in his writings as a source of practical and learned authority, of popular wisdom and sound judgement. Writers of very different outlooks quite happily make use of him. So that the nonconformist minister of Nantwich, John Paget in *A primer of christian religion*, 1601 (STC 19100), when arguing that 'The path to virginitie and chastitie is to keepe the house' can add in a side note: 'And yet too much restraint is to be taken heed of: for as a curre by tying waxeth fiercer, Phil. Syd. and as new wine breaketh weak vessels: so too much seuerity ouerthroweth and spilleth quite a tender mind' (sig. L7$^v$). At the same time the Jesuit Henry Fitz-Simon draws on an episode from *Arcadia* Book III, chapter 13 to make a point in *A catholike confutation of M. J. Riders clayme of antiquitie*, Rouen 1608 (STC 11025):

> Maister *Rider*, (as the hare is wonte, before he seate him selfe in his forme) had a great desyre to strayne him selfe to greater leaps, and girds, toward the ende. Yet all will not serue. As farr as my remembrance serueth me, I reade in S$^r$. Phillip Sidneis Arcadia, a pleasant fiction of one Dameta who had ernestly prouoked one Clinias to combat thinking that he would not accept the challenge. But Clinias being with much wooking animated to answer him; Dameta excepted against the promised performance of

Clinias that it was not in such tyme, place, and maner, as it deserued by
him now to be allowed. Let my Dameta, proue me a Clinias yf, and when
he can: For I am suer I can now discouer him a Dametas in relenting in
the mayne prouocation and excepting at trifles, most timorously; and im-
pertinently. (p. 282)

The irony of this deference to authority would not, perhaps, have
escaped Sidney himself. Nor did it completely pass his admirers by.
Again it is Dametas who supplies the material. His little poem OA 5
seems to have been found useful for comic purposes. Edmund Langston
uses its sixth line in commendatory verses to Edward Hoby's *A curry-
combe for a coxe-combe. By Nick-groome of the hobie-stable*, 1615 (STC 13540):

By my consent that noble *Sydneys* verse,
When thou art dead shall cleaue vnto thy herse.
If that the man such praise must haue,
Then what must he that keepes the knaue? (sig. A1ᵛ)

And John Cotta in *Cotta contra Antonium: manifesting Doctor Antony his
Apologie for Aurum potabile to be false*, Oxford 1623 (STC 5832), uses the
last two lines of the same poem to mock his opponent:

There is no doubt howsoeuer your mouth dissembleth it, that your vaine
heart doth foolishly glorie with the sot *Damæas* in the worthy Sidney,
    And if my man such praises haue.
    What then shall I that keepe the knaue?
Thus saith he, thus thinke you. (p. 103)

What above all persists in the legend, created so much by Sidney's death,
is an affectionate knowledge and gentle mockery of life; as the nonconformist divine Ezekias Woodward writes in the autobiographical Preface to
his *Vestibulum or, a manuduction towards a faire edifice*, 1640 (STC 25972),
to illustrate his own experience of education:

In all this time spent in Grammar (sixe yeers is a great length in our span)
I know not which lost me most time, *feare* or *Play*. I know I played away
much of the time (for all the sorrow) but, I know also, feare hindred me
most, and cast me farthest back. I remember the noble Knights words in
his feigned *Arcadia*, "His minde, saith he, was fixed upon another devotion,
so he minded the speech no more then a Boy doth his lesson, when he hath
leave to play".²⁴

NOTES

1  The majority of these Sidney allusions were noted by Jackson C. Boswell; they were
   collected and transcribed by H. R. Woudhuysen who is responsible for this article.
2  *The Reputation and Influence of Sir Philip Sidney*, Harvard PhD. 1941. There are
   microfilms of Bond's thesis in the Bodleian Library, Oxford, and in the Cambridge
   University Library.
3  James Maxwell in his translation of *Herodian of Alexandria his history*, 1629 (STC

13222), refers to Etienne's dedication of his edition of Herodian to Sidney and quotes three sentences in an English translation from it (sigs A3-3ᵛ).

4 Sidney allusions to 1700 are reportedly being collected for *A Reference Guide to Sir Philip Sidney*; its editors were announced in the *Sidney Newsletter*, II, No. 2 (1981), 3, as C. S. Hunter and Donald V. Stump.

5 On sig. H3 he borrows a few sentences relating to Sidney from sigs. G1v-G2 of the enlarged edition of Lewkenor's *Discourse*.

6 This supplements the account of early references to the epitaph's imitation of Du Bellay collected by W. H. Bond in 'The Epitaph of Sir Philip Sidney', *MLN*, LVIII (1943), 253-57.

7 Digges's allusions to Sidney in this work have been reprinted by Lily B. Campbell in 'Sidney as "The Learned Soldier"', *HLQ*, VII (1943-44), 175-78.

8 Mona Wilson in *Sir Philip Sidney*, London, 1931, 319-20, cites Robert Dowe's contribution to the Oxford memorial volume for Sidney as the source of this story. It is canonised by Naunton's use of it in his *Fragmenta Regalia*, compiled in the early 1630s but not printed until 1641.

9 In the first century of epigrams Gamage includes poems touching on 'noble Sydneys Line' in relation to Lady Katherine Mansell (no. 2, sig. A6), Zutphen (no. 49, sig. B6) and Robert Sidney (no. 60, sigs. B7ᵛ-B8). In the second century there is a distich 'On Sir Phill: Sidney's Arcadia' (no. 11, sig. D1).

10 Zouch's work also contains (sig. E5v.) what appears to be an allusion to John Hoskins' *Directions for Speech and Style* (see H. H. Hudson's edition, Princeton, 1935, xii, n. 6).

11 The worthies are respectively: Davies: Robert Earl of Essex, Sir John and Sir Edward Norris, Sir Francis Vere, the Earl of Devonshire, Sir Roger Williams, Sir Thomas Baskerville, Sir Edward Wingfield; Heywood: Grey, Norris, Essex, Vere; Zouch: Norris, Vere, Uvedale; Hexham: Norris, Willoughby, Vere, Morgan; Peacham: Drake, Frobisher, Baskerville.

12 The Chaucer and Spenser allusions are uncollected.

13 This 'Astrophil' rather than 'Astrophel' spelling is not noted by Ringler, *Poems*, 458. The Jonson allusion is uncollected.

14 The Chaucer and Spenser allusions are uncollected.

15 A side note '*vid. Sydneys* last Sonnet at the end of his Arcadia' shows that Austin is thinking of the penultimate line ('Then farewell world, thy uttermost I see'), of Sidney's *Certain Sonnets* 32, 'Leave me ô Love, which reachest but to dust'.

16 He is alluding to Book III, chapter 4, section 4 of the 'new' *Arcadia*, as D. C. Allen notes on p. 264 (referring to p. 215, 9-10) of his edition of Cornwallis's *Essays* (Baltimore, 1946). In his *Essayes of certaine paradoxes*, 1616 (STC 5779; sig. C1), Cornwallis cites Sidney's *A Defence of Poetry*.

17 Cf. Alastair Fowler, *Triumphal Forms*, Cambridge, 1970, 175-76.

18 Cf. *Poems*, 493.

19 The Spenser allusion is uncollected.

20 On p. 71 Wybarne mentions Pyrocles and Musidorus in a list of 'noble paires of friends'.

21 Stafford may here be answering Thomas Powell whose *Tom of all trades* had appeared three years earlier in 1631 and in which he had advised housewives against reading the *Arcadia*: the passage is quoted by John Buxton in *Sir Philip Sidney and the English Renaissance*, 182.

22 The earliest citation that the *OED* has for 'all' in the sense of the universe (*all* B. 3) is 1598; its earliest citation for 'universe' as being all things (*universe* 2) is from Puttenham in 1589.

23 That Sidney's *Arcadia* belonged to the same kind of literature as Heliodorus' *Aethiopica* is implicitly recognized by Joseph Wybarne in his *The new age of old names*, p. 112 and by James Hayward in his address to the reader before his translation of Biondi's *Donzella desterrada* where he writes of Sidney's '*Helidoran* straine' (sig. A3).

24 The marginal reference is to 'pag. 11.'.

# NOTE ON CONTRIBUTORS

*Dominic Baker-Smith* is Professor of English Literature at the University of Amsterdam. He was formerly University Lecturer in English, University of Cambridge, and Professor of English at University College, Cardiff.

*Sander Bos* is a student assistant in the Department of Art History at the University of Leiden.

*Jackson Boswell* is Professor of English Studies at the University of the District of Columbia in Washington, D.C., and the author of *Milton's Library*.

*John Buxton* is Reader Emeritus in English Literature, University of Oxford, and Emeritus Fellow of New College. Among his numerous publications are *Sir Philip Sidney and the English Renaissance*, 1954, and *Elizabethan Taste*, 1963.

*Jan van Dorsten* was Professor of English Literature and Director of the Sir Thomas Browne Institute at the University of Leiden. His publications include *Poets, Patrons and Professors*, 1962, *The Radical Arts*, 1970, and, with Katherine Duncan-Jones, *Miscellaneous Prose of Sir Philip Sidney*, 1973.

*Katherine Duncan-Jones* is a Fellow of Somerville College, Oxford. In addition to *Miscellaneous Prose* she has edited *Selected Poems of Sir Philip Sidney*, Oxford, 1973, as well as the *'old' Arcadia* in The World's Classics Series, 1985; in 1980 she delivered the British Academy Chatterton Lecture on 'Philip Sidney's Toys'.

*John Gouws*, educated in South Africa and England, is Associate Professor in the Department of English, Rhodes University, Grahamstown, S.A.; he has edited *The Prose Works of Fulke Greville, Lord Brooke*, Oxford, 1986.

*Arthur F. Kinney* is Professor of English, University of Massachussets, Amherst, U.S.A. He is founding editor of *English Literary Renaissance* and editor of *Essential Articles for the Study of Sir Philip Sidney*, 1986. Among his many books are *Humanists Poetics* and *Markets of Bawdrie: the Dramatic Criticism of Stephen Gosson*.

*Jan Karel Kouwenhoven* has studied and taught English in the Universities of Amsterdam and Edinburgh; he is the author of *Apparent Narrative as Thematic Metaphor: the Organization of* The Faerie Queene, Oxford, 1983.

*Marianne Lange-Meijers* is a student of English at the University of Leiden and teaches in a secondary school.

*Marjon Poort* graduated in English at the University of Leiden and is currently working as a research assistant at the Sir Thomas Browne Institute.

*William A. Ringler, Jr.*, currently Senior Research Associate at The Huntington Library, is Emeritus Professor of English at the University of Chicago. He is editor of *The Poems of Sir Philip Sidney*, Oxford, 1962.

*Jeanine Six* is a student of Art History at the University of Leiden.

*Victor Skretkowicz* is Lecturer in English at Dundee University; he is editor of the forthcoming edition of Sidney's *'new' Arcadia*.

*Seth Weiner* is Assistant Professor of English at the University of California, Los Angeles. His essay in this volume reflects some of his concerns in a booklength study he is preparing on the intersection of Renaissance musical theory, prosodic thought, and ideas about Hebrew poetics.

*R. W. Zandvoort*, C.B.E., is Professor Emeritus of English Language and Literature at the University of Groningen. His study, *Sidney's Arcadia*, was published at Amsterdam in 1929.

# INDEX

Agricola (Roman governor of Britain), 22
Alabaster, William, 96
Alasco, Albertus, 5, 89
Albemarle, Duke of, see Monck, George
Alençon, Francis Duke of, Duke of Anjou, 5, 7, 93, 130, 133, 134
Alex, Johne, 56
Alexander the Great, 22, 71
Angus, see Archibald Douglas, Earl of
Anjou, see Alençon
Anne, Queen of James I, 183, 189
Anton, Robert, 227
Antonio, Don (claimant of the throne of Portugal), 5
Aragon, see Ferdinand, King of
Archer, Henry, 14
Arckenwell, Mr, 56
Aristotle, 19, 127, 130-33, 135, 140, 147, 148
Arran, Earl of, see James Stewart
Ascham, Roger, 9, 95, 197
Ashley, Robert, 85
Ashton, Thomas, 127
Aubrey, John, 42, 59
Austin, Samuel, 229
Augustine, St, 201, 202

Bacheler, Danyell, 53, 54
Bacon, Antony, 185
Bacon, Mr, 56
Baïf, Jean Antoine de, 197-99
Baillie, Alexander, 235
Baldi, Bernardino, 218
Bancroft, Thomas, 228
Banks, Sir Joseph, 59
Barnes, Joseph, 85, 89
Barnfield, Richard, 184, 185
Barret, Robert, 225
Bartas, Guillaume du, 85, 93, 113
Bartlett, Sir Richard, 228
Baskerville, Sir Thomas, 237
Batchiler, see Bacheler
Baudartius, Wilhelmus, 32, 33, 46, 60
Baudoin, Jean, 108
Beaumont, Francis, 13, 228
Becon, Thomas, 63, 76, 81
Bede, 201, 202, 216
Bedford, see Francis Russell, 2nd Earl of
Bellay, Joachim du, 224, 237
Benedicti, Georgius, see Werteloo

Bertie, Peregrine, Lord Willoughby de Eresby, 55, 68
Beza, Theodore, 209, 219, 220
Biondi, G. F., 229, 230, 234, 237
Blount, Charles, 182, 183, 187, 192
Blunt, Mr, 56
Boccacio, 234
Bor, Pieter, 36
Boulstrod, William, (Boulstred), 53
Bowes, Roger, 53, 56
Bowser, Sir George, 53
Boyle, John, 14
Brahe, Tycho, 94
Brederode, Walraven van, 47
Breton, Nicholas, 14
Brij, Derick Theodoor de, 42, 58, 59
Brij, Johan Israel de, 59
Brij, Johan Theodoor de, 59
Britton, Mr, 56
Browne, Sir Thomas, 168
Browne, Sir Valentine, 53
Brysket, Lodowyck, 14, 88, 104, 105
Buchanan, George, 93-95, 102, 219, 220
Buggs, Samuel, 224
Burggrave, Daniel de, 43, 55, 60
Burghley, see William Cecil
Burton, Robert, 83, 84, 101

Cadnam, Thomas, 113
Caedmon, 216
Caesar, Julius, 22
Caldwell, James, 231, 232
Calvin, John, 164
Camden, William, 14, 102
Cammingha, Wytze van, (Caminga), 55
Campion, (Edmund), 101
Campion, Thomas, 170, 197
Carew, Sir Peter, 61
Carew, Richard, 12
Carleton, George, 14
Cary, Lucius, Viscount Falkland, 84
Case, John, 85
Casimir, Prince, 5, 140, 225
Castiglione, Baldassare, 10
Cato the Younger, 65, 71
Cecil, Robert, 1st Earl of Salisbury, 228
Cecil, Thomas, 1st Earl of Exeter, 2nd Lord Burghley, 89, 145
Cecil, William, 1st Lord Burghley, 5, 28,

30, 49, 84, 89, 90, 94, 103, 110, 139, 140, 182
Cevallerus, Antonius, see Antoine Chevalier
Chard, Thomas, 89, 102
Charles I, King, 59
Charles V, Emperor, 46, 60, 154
Chaucer, Geoffrey, 9, 12, 18, 83, 102, 122, 221, 228, 237
Cheke, John, 84, 95
Chester, Robert, 109
Chevalier, Antoine, 210, 211, 219
Churchyard, Thomas, 14, 88
Cicero, 3, 65, 88, 129
Cleland, James, 233
Clerk, Bartholomew, 102
Cleyton, Mr, 56
Clifford, Christopher, 225
Clinton, Elizabeth, 231
Coffin, Edward, 234
Constable, Henry, 96, 183, 192
Cook, Francis, 14
Cooke, Charles, 56
Cooke, Robert, 38, 54, 57
Cooper, John, 183, 186-188, 191
Coprario, Giovanni, see John Cooper
Cornwallis, Sir William, 230, 237
Cotta, John, 236
Courville, Joachim Thibault de, 197
Coverdale, Miles, 211, 219
Covell, William, 233
Covert, Mr, 56
Cox, Mr, 56
Craig, Alexander, 230
Cranmer, Thomas, Archbishop of Canterbury, 210
Crispe, Mr, see Edward Cryppe
Croche, Mr, 56
Crompton, Richard, 224
Cryppe, Edward, 53
Cuffe, Henry, 227
Cuffe, John, 52
Cutwoode, Thomas, 224

D., A., see Day, Angel
D., G., 222
Daniel, Samuel, 127, 183, 186, 187, 191, 216, 228, 234
Dante, 171, 182
Davenant, Sir William, 222, 224
Danveres, Henrye, see Henry Danvers
Danvers, Henry, 53, 109
Dareius, 71
Davers, Henry, see Henry Danvers
Davies, John, 52
Davies, John, of Hereford, 226, 227

Davison, Francis, 106, 228
Davison, William, 26, 29, 30, 146, 154
D(ay), A(ngel), 14
Day, John, 231
Demosthenes, 129
Denny, Edward, 186
Desecourte, Mr, 56
Dethicke, Nico: (alias Windsor), 58
Devereux, Dorothy, 182
Devereux, Penelope, Lady Rich, 80, 125, 151, 170-74, 181-89
Devereux, Robert, 2nd Earl of Essex, 38, 39, 43, 109, 173, 182-84, 227, 237
Devereux, Walter, 1st Earl of Essex, 66, 101, 182
Devereux, Walter (younger son of 1st Earl of Essex), 182
Devonshire, Earl of, see Blount, Charles
Digges, Dudley, 224
Digges, Thomas, 81, 228
Donne, John, 213, 220
Dorset, Earl of, see Thomas Sackville
Douglas, Archibald, 8th Earl of Angus, 94
Douglas, James, 4th Earl of Morton, 94
Douglas, Richard, 188
Dousa, Janus, 89, 95
Dousa, Theodorus, 220
Dowland, John, 85, 217
Drake, Sir Francis, 5, 13, 26, 28, 53, 101
Drant, Thomas, 214
Drayton, Michael, 12, 171
Dudley, Catherine, Countess of Huntingdon, 182
Dudley, Edmund, 168
Dudley, Guilford, 168
Dudley, John, Duke of Northumberland, 168
Dudley, Mary, see Sidney, Mary (I)
Dudley, Robert, Earl of Leicester, 5, 7, 13, 16, 17, 22, 23, 25, 26, 28-35, 38, 39, 43, 49, 50, 51, 60, 69, 84, 87, 88-91, 95, 98, 99, 101, 102, 107, 110, 136, 143, 145-47, 151-55, 157-59, 162-66, 168, 173, 182, 224
Dudley, Thomas, 43, 54
Du Plessis-Mornay, Philippe, 19, 81, 93, 102, 113, 136, 137, 140, 212
Dyer, Edward, 43, 54, 88, 104-06, 226
Dyckensone, Mr, 56

Elizabeth I, Queen, 5-7, 10, 11 16, 21, 22, 28-30, 35, 37, 49-51, 62, 84, 86, 90, 91, 93, 94, 96-98, 102, 125, 130, 133, 134, 138-40, 146, 151, 152, 154, 155, 158, 162, 163, 189, 223
Enerwitz, Gisbert, 172

Ennius, 83, 88
Erasmus, Desiderius, 230
Eresby, Lord Willoughby de, see Peregrine Bertie
Essex, Earl of, see Devereux
Estienne, Henri, 210
Estienne, Robert, 219
Evans, Johne, 56

Faice, Gorge, 56
Falkland, Viscount, see Lucius Cary
Farmer, Sr George, 53
Ferdinand, King of Aragon, 46, 60
Feryman, Peter, 13
Fitzgeffrey, Charles, 3
Fitz-Simon, Henry, 235
Fitzwyllmes, Mr, 56
Fitzwilliams, Sir William, 54
Fletcher, Giles (I), 13, 96, 97, 100, 102, 103
Fletcher, Giles (II), 96
Fletcher, Phineas, 96
Florio, John, 123, 170, 188
Ffloyd, Davye, 56
Ford, John, 183, 187, 191
Fowler, William, 93
Francis I, King, 87
Fraunce, Abraham, 96
Fraunce, Mr, 56
Fulbecke, William, 225, 228

Gager, William, 85, 89-91, 101, 106
Gainsford, Thomas, 233
Gamage, William, 226, 237
Gascoigne, George, 91-93, 102
Gelée, Jacques, 28
Gibbes, Mr, 56
Gifford, George, 18, 19, 24, 63, 64, 67, 76, 80, 88, 193, 214
Gifford, John, 95, 103
Glover, Robert (alias Somersett), 54
Golding(e), Arthur, 14, 113, 137
Goldwel, Henry, 11
Goltzius, Hubertus, 42, 46, 47, 60
Gomarus, Franciscus, 210
Goodyear, Sir Henry, 43, 54
Googe, Barbabe, 92, 206
Gouffier, Henri Marc, 224
Gower, John, 228
Gray, Patrick, 6th Baron Gray, 94, 102
Greene, Robert, 108, 127
Greville, Fulke, ix, 3, 6-9, 11, 18, 19, 24, 36, 43, 49, 54, 60, 62-64, 66-81, 90, 105, 111-13, 116, 118-21, 123, 127, 133, 143, 172, 173, 193, 194, 213
Grey, Lady Jane, 168

Grey, Arthur, 14th Baron Grey de Wilton, 157
Grifftyhe, Edw., 56
Grindal, Edmund, 92
Grimeston, Edward, 14
Gruithuissens, Mlle, 173
Guise, Charles, Duc de, 84
Gwinne, Dr Matthew, 11, 14, 85
Gwyne, Mr Rych., 53

Hakerton, see Halkerston
Hakewill, George, 228, 230
Hales, Humphrey (alias Blewmantle), 54
Halkerston, James, 94, 102
Hannibal, 88
Harbert, Sir William, 53
Hardwicke, Bess of, 96
Harington, Sir John, 170, 218, 226
Harrington, Sir Henry, 54
Harrington, Sir Thomas, 54
Harvey, Gabriel, 95, 96, 102, 152, 165, 197
Hastings, Sir Francis, 2nd Earl of Huntingdon, 38, 39, 43, 182, 225, 228
Hatton, Sir Christopher, 42
Hatton, Sir William, 53, 56
Hawkins, Sir John, 101
Hawkins, Sir Thomas, 228
Hayward, James, 229, 234, 237
Hazlitt, William, 171
Heale, William, 232
Heneage, Sir Thomas, 30
Henry IV, King of France, 84
Herbert, Henry, 2nd Earl of Pembroke, 38, 39, 43, 89, 90, 108
Herbert, William, 68, 78, 225
Hermogenes, see Tarsus
Hexham, Henry, 226
Heydon, Sir Christopher, 227
Heylyn, Peter, 222, 232, 235
Heywood, Thomas, 223, 226, 237
Hoby, Edward, 236
Hoccleve, Thomas, 228
Hohenlohe-Langenburg, Count Philipp of, 73-75, 77, 82
Hogenberg, Frans, 46
Holinshed, Raphael, 82
Holland, Hugh, 228
Hollock, Count, see Philipp Hohenlohe-Langenburg
Homer, 69, 70
Hooft, P. C., 87
Hopkins, John, 212, 219
Horace, 83, 218
Hoskyns, John, 89
Hotman, Jean, 192

Hout, Jan van, 22, 89
Howard, Henry, Earl of Northampton, 228
Howard, Henry, Earl of Surrey, 83, 228
Howard, Charles, Earl of Nottingham, Lord Admiral, 6
Hudson, Thomas, 93
Humphrey, Dr Lawrence, 91, 102
Hunget, Edw., 56
Huninges, Mr, 56
Huntingdon, Countess of, see Catherine Dudley
Huntingdon, 2nd Earl of, see Francis Hastings

Isaacson, Henry, 223

James, Dr, 53
James, John, 17
James I & VI, King of England and Scotland, 6, 92-97, 102, 122
James, Richard, 228
Jenkynson, Thomas, 53
Jerome, St, 205-07, 218
Joanes, Robt, 54
Joanes, Wyll., 54
Jobsone, Thomas, 56
Johnston, Arthur, 231
Jonson, Benjamin, 13, 183, 186, 221, 228, 237
Josephus, Flavius, 206
Junius, Franciscus, 203, 206-09, 212

K., F., see Francis Kinwelmarsh
Keats, John, 18
Kelley, Wyllm, 53
Kellison, Matthew, 234
King, Edward, 174
Kinwelmarsh, Francis, 66
Knight, Edm. (alias Chester), 58
Knollys, Sir Francis, 154
Knollys, Lettice, 95, 182
Knowles, Sir William, 53

L., T., 57
Langesford, Mr, 56
Langston, Edmund, 236
Languet, Hubert, 86, 120, 139, 140
Lant, Thomas, 14, 38-50, 52, 56, 58, 94, 173
Lasko, see Alasco
Latewar, Richard, 14
Lawes, Henry, 188
Lea, Richard, 38, 39, 50, 52, 54
Legge, Thomas, 96, 97, 103
Leicester, Earl of, see Robert Dudley

Levita, Elijah, 205, 211, 218
Lewis, Allin, 56
Lewkenor, Sir Lewis, 223, 237
Lily, William, 219
Lipsius, Justus, 22, 23, 96, 99
Livy, 92
Lloyd, John, 89, 95, 103, 106
Lodge, Thomas, 206
Lok, Henry, 226
Longfellow, Henry, 195
Lucan, 81
Lucretius, 1
Lullius, Antonius, 216, 217
Luther, Martin, 164
Lydgate, John, 228
Lyly, John, 9, 127
Lynley, Henry, 54

Mackered, Mr, 56
Madocke, Griffith, see Gryffin Maddox
Maddox, Gryffin, 53
Maitland, Sir John, 94, 102
Manners, Lady Katherine, 225
Mansell, Lady Katherine, 237
Mantell, Mr, 56
Mar, Countess of, see Mary Stewart
Markham, Gervase, 170
Marot, Clément, 209, 219
Marshe, Henrye, 56
Martin, St, 72
Mary, (Tudor) Queen of England, 84
Mary, (Stuart) Queen of Scots, 25, 39, 94, 155
Mauduit, Jacques, 198
Maxwell, James, 236
Medici, Lorenzo de, Grand Duke of Tuscany, 171, 174
Mendoza, Don Bernardino de, 49
Menin, Joost de, 34, 35, 55
Mercerus, Joannes, 209-11
Merian, Mattheas, 59
Mersenne, Marin, 198-203, 211, 215, 217
Mésières, François Perrot de, 209, 211
Meteren, Emanuel van, 14
Mildmay, Sir Walter, 154
Miltiades, 70
Milton, John, 174, 188, 202
Minturno, Antonio Sebastiano, 202
Moffett, Thomas, 6, 14, 18, 68, 78, 81, 193, 194, 214
Mollerus, Henricus, 219
Mollyners, Mr, 56
Molyneux, Edward, 75, 78
Molyneux, Mr, 6, 14
Monck, George, Duke of Albemarle, 46
Mondragon, Christoforo de, 223

Monmouth, Geoffrey of, 150
Montaigne, Michel de, 123
Montanus, Arnoldus, 60
Montemayor, Jorge, 189
Montgomerie, Alexander, 93
More, Thomas, 12, 128, 228
More, Sir George, 228
Morrell, Roger, 96
Morrysone, Mr, 56
Morton, Earl of, see James Douglas
Münster, Sebastian, 205, 211, 217, 219

Nash, Thomas, 96
Nassau, Count Maurice of, 28, 30-32
Naunton, Sir Robert, 237
Neuelt, 55
Neville, Alexander, 89, 91, 92, 94, 95, 98
Newman, Thomas, 12
Newstead, Christopher, 232
Newton, Robert, 231
Newton, Thomas, 92
Norris, Sir Edward, 237
Norris, Sir Henry of Rycotes, 35
Norris, Sir John, 237
North, Roger, 2nd Baron, 38, 39, 43, 55
Northampton, Earl of, see Henry Howard
Northumberland, Duke of, see John Dudley
Nugent, Richard, 231

Ockland, Christopher, 222
Olney, Henry, 12, 165, 167
Orange, Elisabeth of, 16
Ornithoparcus, 217
Ortel, Joachim, 55
Ovid, 108
Owen, John, 89
Oxford, Earl of, see Edward de Vere

Packenham, Edmund, 43, 54
Paddy, Nicholas (alias Rouge Dragon), 54
Paedts, J., 89
Page, Wyllm, 56
Pagenham, Mr, 54
Paget, John, 235
Pagninus, Sanctes, 211, 219
Palmer, John, 96-98
Parker, Matthew, Archbishop of Canterbury, 92, 211
Parker, Martin, 223
Parma, Duke of, 31
Parrot, Sr Th., 53
Parry, Mr, 56
Pavell, Thomas, 227
Payne, Mr, 53
Peacham, Henry, 227, 230

Pecoke, Tho., 52
Peele, George, 183
Pelham, Sir William, 3, 69
Pembroke, Countess of, see Mary Sidney (II)
Pembroke, Earl of, see Henry Herbert
Pérez, Antonio, 184, 185
Perrot, François, see Mésières, François Perrot de
Perrot, Sr Thomas, 56, 211
Petrarch, 3, 84, 88, 102, 171
Pettingall, Henrye, 56
Philip, John, 14
Philip II, King of Spain, 49, 50, 154, 155, 162, 163, 184
Philophilippos, 14
Pindar, 218
Plantin, Christopher, 22
Plato, 9, 65, 86, 126, 127, 135, 140
Plutarch, 62, 65, 69, 70, 81
Pompey, 22
Ponsonby, William, 11, 12, 113, 167
Poudrelles, Wyllm, 56
Powder, Hughe, 52
Powell, Thomas, 229, 237
Pratt, Mr, 56
Price, Henry, 95
Probye, Mr, 56
Purvey, Thomas, 52
Puttenham, George, 197, 216, 218, 237

Quintilian, 129, 200, 201, 206

Raleigh, Walter, 3, 5, 14, 42, 88, 103, 104, 106, 149-51, 171
Randolph, Thomas, 76, 93, 94, 102
Raphelengius, Franciscus, 22
Reuchlin, Johannes, 218
Reynolds, Henry, 14
Rich, Lady, see Penelope Devereux
Rich, Robert, 3rd Baron Rich, 125, 170, 174, 182, 183
Richardson, Samuel, 145
Rogers, Daniel, 154
Roper, Johne, 56
Rose, Francis, the Elder, 222
Roydon, Matthew, 14, 88, 103, 104, 106
Russell, Francis, 2nd Earl of Bedford, 154
Rycotes, see Henry Norris

Sackville, Thomas, Earl of Dorset, 228
Salisbury, Earl of, see Robert Cecil
Salisbury, Sir John, 109
Sandys, Sir Edwin, 234
Sanford, Hugh, 11, 111, 120
Saunders, Edward, 14

Scipio, 3, 83, 88
Seager, William (alias Portcullis), 54
Seton, Alexander, 1st Earl of Dunfermline, 94
Shakespeare, William, 5, 13, 14, 104, 107-09, 221
Shelley, Percy Bysshe, 4, 6
Shortholt, Mr, 52
Sidney, Henry, 43, 54, 78, 133, 138, 142
Sidney, Mary (I), 138
Sidney, Mary (II), Countess of Pembroke, 11, 88, 93, 104, 105, 120, 123, 133, 143, 145, 171, 193, 223, 231
Sidney, Robert, 25, 28, 35, 43, 54, 78, 131, 226, 237
Sidney, Thomas, 54
Sidney, William, 43, 54
Sille, Nicasius, 34, 55
Singleton, Mr, 42
Skydmore, James, 53
Slatyer, William, 222
Smyth, Tho., 56
Smythe, Sir John, 7, 8, 69, 81, 223
Snowe, Robert, 53
Socrates, 65
Solms, Johan Albrecht, Count of, 60
Sonibanke, Charles, 14
Southampton, Earl of, see Henry Wriothesley
Spenser, Edmund, 3, 6, 13, 14, 84, 88, 96, 104-08, 110, 127, 149-53, 155-57, 163-67, 169, 197, 221, 228
Stafford, Anthony, 224, 225, 229, 231, 233, 237
Stanyhurst, Richard, 197
Stapleton, Sr Rob., 53
Stephanus, Henricus, see Henri Estienne
Stephanus, Robert, see Robert Estienne
Sternhold, Thomas, 212, 219
Stewart, James, Earl of Arran, 94
Stewart, Mary, Countess of Mar, 23
Stow, John, 14, 21, 38, 39, 58, 82
Strange, Mr, 56
Stryll, Mr, 53
Surrey, Earl of, see Henry Howard
Sylla, Dr, see Nicasius Sille

Tacitus, 22
Tarsus, Hermogenes of, 216
Tasso, Bernardo, 105, 110
Taylor, Augustine, 234
Temple, Mr, 56
Temple, William, 14, 95-97, 103, 173
Tessier, Charles, 185, 186, 188
Themistocles, 68, 70
Thomas, John, 52

Thomson, J. Radford, 76, 82
Thucydides, 130
Topsell, Edward, 228
Tremellius, 203, 206-10, 212
Tryll, Tho:, 56
Turner, Mr, 56
Tyndall, Dr Humphrey, 95
Tyard, Pontus de, 197-99, 201

Udall, Nicholas, 78
Umpton, Sir Henry, 56
Unton, Sr Hen:, 53, 84, 85, 101, 227
Uvedall, Mr, 56

Val(c)ke, Jacob, 34, 55
Vata, Franciscus, 209-11, 219
Vaughan, William, 222, 225
Vere, Edward de, 17th Earl of Oxford, 62, 77
Vere, Sir Francis, 237
Virgil, 83, 128

Wakefield, Thomas, 210
Walpole, Horatio, 59, 60
Walsingham, Edmund, 43, 54
Walsingham, Sir Francis, 42, 43, 49, 50, 51, 58, 75, 90, 94, 101, 102, 113, 116, 123, 140, 143, 147, 154, 173
Walter, Joseph, 95
Waterhouse, Edmund, 66
Waterhouse, Sr Edw., 53
Watsone, Mr, 56
Webbe, William, 197
Webbe, Joseph, 234
Webster, John, 228
West, Benjamin, 76
West, Tho., 54
Werteloo, Georgius Benedicti, 89, 91
Whetstone, George, 49, 60, 73, 78, 81, 82, 105
White, Thomas, 42
Whitgift, John, Archbishop of Canterbury, 92
Whiting, Nathaniel, 234
Whitlock, William, 106
Whytt, Captayne, 54
Whytton, Mr, 56
Wilde, Oscar, 171
Willes, Richard, 203, 205, 206
William I (the Silent), Prince of Orange, 16, 46, 47, 60, 87, 99, 154, 161, 162
William III, Prince of Orange, 162
Williams, John, 235
Williams, Sir Roger, 237
Willney, Allexander, 53
Willoughby, see Peregrine Bertie

Wilson, Arthur, 154
Wilson, Thomas, 85
Wilton, see Arthur Grey
Windet, John, 89
Wingfield, Anthony, 96
Wingfield, Sir Edward, 237
Wingfield, Sr Tho:, 53
Wither, George, 224
Wood, Anthony, 49, 60, 106
Woodward, Ezekias, 236
Wordsworth, William, 90, 145
Wotton, (Wootto), Edw., 43, 54
Wright, Robert, 85
Wriothesley, Henry, 3rd Earl of Southampton, 108, 109
Wroth, Lady Mary, 231
Wrothe, Mr, 56

Wrought, James, 56
Wroughton, Mr, 56
Wyatt, Sir Thomas, 212
Wybarne, Joseph, 232, 233, 237
Wyer, Johan, 76, 78, 173
Wyllmes, Allexander, 56
Wynckfield, Jacques, 56
Wyngfeld, Sr John, 56

Xenophon, 128, 130

Yong, Bartholomew, 189
Young, Richard, 230

Zarlino, Gioseffo, 200, 203-06, 210, 211, 216-18